ROGER STEVENS
MARCH, 1994

Seasons of Life

*Our Dramatic Journey
from Birth to
Death*

Seasons of Life

JOHN KOTRE

AND

ELIZABETH HALL

Little, Brown and Company

Boston   Toronto   London

For Kathy and Scott

FIRST EDITION

Unless otherwise credited, all illustrations copyright © 1990 by QED Communications and the Regents of the University of Michigan.

LIBRARY OF CONGRESS CATALOGING-IN-PUBLICATION DATA
Kotre, John N.
    Seasons of life : our dramatic journey from birth to death / John Kotre and Elizabeth Hall. — 1st ed.
        p.   cm.
    Includes bibliographical references and index.
    ISBN 0-316-50252-9
    1. Developmental psychology — Case studies.   2. Socialization — Case studies.
    3. Aging — Psychological aspects — Case studies.   4. Life cycle, Human — Case studies.
    I. Hall, Elizabeth, 1929-   . II. Title.
BF713.K67 1990
155 — dc20   90-40376

10 9 8 7 6 5 4 3 2 1
MV-PA

Published simultaneously in Canada
by Little, Brown & Company (Canada) Limited
Printed in the United States of America

Contents

Acknowledgments

Seasons of Life took eight years to develop from a vague impulse to tell the story of human development to what it is today: a five-part public television series, a twenty-six-part public radio series, a university telecourse — and this book. The original impulse took focus in meetings between John Kotre and the Media Resources Center of the University of Michigan during the summer of 1982. WQED/Pittsburgh joined the enterprise in the fall of 1983; a year later, the Annenberg Project of the Corporation for Public Broadcasting announced it would provide underwriting; and in 1986, Little, Brown joined in with plans to publish a book.

There were times during those years when it looked as if the enterprise would fail. Contractual and financial difficulties — and the sheer complexity of the task — turned two years of scheduled production into five. It took time for producers in three cities to coordinate their efforts and to discover what each of the media involved — video, audio, and print — does best. It took time to cull insights from close to seventy-five scholars, to integrate research from four academic disciplines, and to record stories from the lives of perhaps a hundred people. Most of all, it took time to let these stories speak to us and find their place in the story of human development. Inevitably, the story you think a person will tell — the one that would be ideal for your script — is rarely the one the person actually does tell. Having to respect the integrity of the stories, we were constantly reworking our scripts.

There was a benefit, however, in developing slowly, though it would be hard to convince underwriters and publishers of that. Something as complex as *Seasons of Life* needed time to grow and find itself. When you want the finished product, in various configurations, to work *as* television, *as* radio, *as* a credit-bearing college course, and *as* a book for the lay reader, it takes a long while to hit upon those central images and metaphors that will make the overall story simple but not simplistic.

In that respect, *Seasons of Life* grew as human beings grow. Compared with other species, we humans are "held" in immaturity for an extraordinarily long time. In the fast-paced world we inhabit, it seems odd to say that part of our success as a species is that we develop so slowly, but that's what stands out about our schedule for biological maturation. It's also what stood out about the development of *Seasons of Life*. We only hope the result is as spectacular as a fully grown person.

Now that the book is done and the final piece of the puzzle is in place, we take great pleasure in retracing our steps and thanking all those who got us started and kept us going. We're grateful, first of all, to the University of Michigan and to Elaine Brock and George Williams in particular. They invested far more than their share in the creation of proposals and then — paradoxically — had to deal with the consequences of being successful in their efforts. With persistence, resilience, and salvific humor, Elaine and George have kept us afloat — and even on course.

Michigan was the site of audio production: twenty-six half-hour programs and twenty briefer feature modules. There, in the beginning, Alec Friedman lent his practical expertise to our planning process, and there Stacey Deanne Millett, Angela DiFrancesco, and Kathy Kotre produced a number of memorable programs. Josephine Wenk and Susan Bareis kept us up-to-date on the budget, and Lesley McCafferty did so with our files. Our administrative secretary, Violet Dalla Vecchia, saw to it that we were organized, happy, and well fed. We're grateful to Richard Straub, who wrote the study guide and instructors' manual for the telecourse, and to Jonathon Niemczak, an engineer with uncommon skill, sensitivity, and patience. His ability to work unobtrusively with people, his love of detail, and his technical expertise made him a rock of dependability. And we owe a great deal to Gregg Zajic, a man with an ear for the subtleties of the human voice and a passion to get things exactly right. As series producer, he brought his considerable talents to our audio recording, editing, and writing. Then, at the very end of the project, he brought them to capturing video frames for the book and to an intense review of the manuscript. He left his mark.

Because this is a companion volume to the television series produced by WQED and hosted by David Hartman, we are indebted to the producers and crews who were responsible for researching and recording nearly all the stories that appear in it. At the top of the list art Mort Silverstein, whose inner graciousness found its way onto the television screen, Linda Blythe, and Chris Fennimore. Each saw the material we were working with in a different light, but all agreed that the strength of the series lay in the stories that people entrusted to us. Todd Norbitz, Shirley Saldamarco, Sam Shirakawa, and Ray Weiss developed stories that are now a part of this volume. Marc Pollock organized WQED's contribution to our original proposal, and Jeanne Paynter helped secure additional funding. Scott Ferguson, Craig McTurk, Christine Ochtun, Larry Solomon, Nicholas Spies, and Jim Sweenie all had roles to play in video production that had an impact on this book.

David Hartman was a godsend. When he agreed to host the television series, we said it was the icing on the cake. But David turned out to be part of the cake itself — a communicator known to millions, a professional with unflagging energy (even when it rained and rained and rained), above all, a man who relished plain English. David Hartman became the vital link between our stories, our scholars, and our audience. We remain in his debt.

For managing the intricacies of contracts related to this book, we owe special thanks to our agent, Donald Cutler of Sterling Lord Literistic. For insisting from the beginning that the book deal with ideas as well as people, and for thoughtful reviews of the manuscript, we're grateful to Bill Phillips and Colleen Mohyde, our editors at Little, Brown. Diane Taraskiewicz did a superb job of copyediting, and Karen Dane helped with numerous details. My-Linh Kotre, Pamela Hartford, and Fred Zinn were responsible for creating or acquiring photographs and illustrations. We kept Little, Brown nervous about our ability to deliver a manuscript on time, but they never let it show. Saving their apprehension for Don Cutler, they allowed us to continue working in an atmosphere of unfailing, almost embarrassing support. Other authors should be as fortunate.

Many scholars contributed in a substantial way to *Seasons of Life* — through meetings, conversations, and recorded interviews. Many of them appear in the television and radio series and are quoted in this book. We would like to take this occasion to recognize our "core panel" in particular: Urie Bronfenbrenner of Cornell University, Janice Gibson of the

University of Pittsburgh, David Gutmann of Northwestern University, Bernice Neugarten of the University of Chicago, Anne Petersen of Pennsylvania State University, Alice Rossi of the University of Massachusetts – Amherst, and Sheldon White of Harvard University. Barry Bogin of the University of Michigan – Dearborn was an invaluable resource regarding the human biological clock. These scholars shared much more than findings from their research: they shared wisdom, and they encouraged us to tell the story of the seasons in our own way. That we did — the responsibility for particular lines of interpretation is our own.

We make a great deal in this book of the story that each of us creates over the course of a life. We believe that a baby is born not just into a family, but into a family's stories. We believe that these stories nourish — and sometimes cripple — the growing child, and we believe that when a person dies, the story of his or her life becomes part of a family's web of meaning. For these reasons, we reserve our deepest gratitude for those who told us, in whole or in part, the story of their lives, and who gave permission for a wider audience to come to know them.

Now that *Season of Life* is done, a very complex undertaking seems very simple. People in all the seasons of life telling their stories. Readers coming to know not only the lives of individuals, but the story of the seasons of life itself. Much of our work was done in the belief that voices of those who "go before" help those who "come after."

It's been our privilege to hear these voices, to come to know these lives, and to bring them to you as part of the dramatic story of our journey from birth to death.

May 1990

JOHN KOTRE
ELIZABETH HALL

Seasons of Life

A TIME FOR *Prologue*

STORIES

As the first thin light of an August morning touches the land, a long line of cows, their udders heavy with milk, ambles toward the barn. The sun still lies below a neighboring ridge, but work has already begun on the Kennedy dairy farm in Butler, Pennsylvania. These days, twenty-two-year-old Janice Kennedy isn't doing as much as she used to. She still feeds the calves and helps out around the house, but she no longer drives the tractor or pitches hay. She's allowed to help with the milking, but not to reach up and change the mechanical milkers. And she's not to carry things — unless she can put them in a wheelbarrow.

Janice is a sturdy, full-cheeked woman with auburn hair and a girlish smile. In the quiet of these gentle Pennsylvania hills, anticipation surrounds her, and a womb of protection envelops her. She's a week or two away from having her first baby.

"Right now, I'd like to do as much as I can and keep in touch with what's going on here," she says later in the morning, sitting in the shade of a walnut tree. "The due date is the twenty-third of August. I don't think it's going to come early, the way I'm feeling. Some days I don't even feel pregnant, and other days it's like, oh! I feel so bad. Some days the baby kicks a lot, and other days it's like, are you in there? I've gone in for two sonograms where you can see it moving. The first one, it was only about that big, and you could just see the little flick of the heartbeat. Jeff went with me for the

Janice Kennedy, twenty-two. "Some days the baby kicks a lot, and other days it's like, are you in there?"

Jeff, twenty-two. "I want to be right there the whole time."

second one, and he could see its arms and legs moving. And then they give you a picture to take home, so I have two pictures of him already. Or her — whatever it'll be."

Jeff is Janice's husband, a sinewy young man of twenty-two with close-cropped hair and stubble on his face. He doesn't say much about the baby, but he's gone to classes at the hospital so he can be there when Janice has it "natural." "I want to be right there the whole time," he says. "They even told us at the last class that we get to cut the baby's navel cord, and I'm looking forward to that one. A lot of people wouldn't do such a thing, but I guess, being farm-oriented, I'm used to that kind of stuff and I'm just excited to see. It's my first baby to see born. I've seen probably seventy calves a year being born, but it'll really be different."

Jeff is the oldest of five children born to Jim and Rita Kennedy. He was followed by Jill, Janelle, John, and Jason, the youngest at eleven. None of

Rita, forty-five. "Jeffrey keeps forgetting to do things, so I know he's worrying."

Jim, forty-five. "I said, 'Rita, did we bring you up here to sleep, or did we bring you up here to have a baby?'"

Jeff's brothers or sisters is sure what it's going to mean to be an aunt or uncle, but his mother has a good idea of what's coming. Rita is a talkative woman of forty-five, with clear blue eyes, a slender face, and short curly hair brushed back over her ears. Today, she's wearing a T-shirt that says, "Milk — America's Health Kick." Years ago, Rita was a Kennedy daughter-in-law expecting her first, and she was no different from Janice. "I never stopped. I always wanted to be with Jim, and do what he was doing. He didn't allow me to drive the tractors, and he didn't allow me to move milkers — same things we don't do with her. Now, you're probably used to your husbands going away to work and you go nuts if they're home all the time. I'm the opposite. If Jim is gone for a day — if he goes judging or something — I just tinker around, and it's like I'm a lost person. I enjoy my husband and my family around, all the time."

Jim and Rita have put together a farmstead of about 700 acres, some of it

Francis, sixty-nine. "He was comin' a-flyin'. I couldn't believe it!"

owned, some of it leased. Jeff and Janice live on a parcel near the main farm, and come there each day to work. Rita knows her family well, starting with her eldest son. "Jeffrey keeps forgetting to do things, so I know he's worrying. He came up here twice without the papers for the sheep and the hogs. He said, 'I forgot.' Jeff forgot to do three things yesterday, and Jim said, 'I know it's because the baby's coming.'"

At forty-five, Jim is an older, filled-out version of his son. His hair is darker and curlier, his eyebrows bushier, his smile quicker. Often, he has a day's growth of beard on his face and a red baseball cap on the back of his head — a cap that looks as if it's been around as long as Jim has. Jim anticipates the birth as keenly as his son, says Rita. "He said to me one day, 'You know, I think I'm the most excited person there is.' But he doesn't tell anyone else. He just doesn't. The only comment he'll say is, 'Oh, I have to sleep with a grandma now.'"

Jim has not forgotten when he was in Jeff's shoes, about to become a father in 1965. "I can remember that like it was yesterday. The day before, a tractor wouldn't start in the morning. So I had Rita come out there and pull that darn tractor for me. It was cold. That night she said, 'Hey, I think we better go to the hospital.' Well, at that time, they gave the ladies what they call a twilight medicine. Put you off to sleep. She went off and on, and finally I said, 'Rita, did we bring you up here to sleep, or did we bring you up here to have a baby?' So in the morning we finally got a baby. We had to get back home, you know, to get the milking done!"

Jim wasn't allowed in the delivery room when Jeffrey was born. "No way. You were sort of trapped on the lower floor there. They'd call you when it's over." Things are different today, but given the choice, Jim would stay on the lower floor. It's not the physical side of birth that bothers him — he's

Martha, seventy-two. "I still remember sitting partway up and seeing her pull that veil off his face."

seen thousands of calves being born — but the risk. "You gotta realize, we're dealing with animals down here in the barn. Birth of a human is a lot different. I guess watching babies be brought into this world isn't for me. I understand almost all the young couples today go along with it, and they enjoy it, and I think the world of these guys. But I don't think it's for me. I anticipate a lot of the good things, but I also anticipate the one in a million. And you know, I just couldn't handle it."

When Jim, the third of four children, was born back in 1943, his father, Francis, wasn't pacing the lower floor — he wasn't even in town. "It was on a Saturday morning," says Francis, a white-haired man of sixty-nine. "I had gone to market, the old farmer's market. And gosh, the first thing you knowed, Jim was on his way. No doctors all around. So somebody called me at the market and said, 'Hey, you got a new son.' He was comin' a-flyin'. I couldn't believe it! But I think that was one of the things that just . . . at that time, the ladies knowed how to handle it themselves."

The "ladies" were his wife, Martha, and his mother, Melverna. Now seventy-two, Martha speaks deliberately and serenely of a different era, quiet pride in her unwavering blue eyes. "Early in the morning, about four-thirty I guess it was, I felt like, oh boy! This is gonna be it. And Francis and his father went to market, so I didn't say nothing until after they left. And then I said to my mother-in-law, 'I'm afraid I'm going to have this baby, you better call the doctor.' But she said, 'First of all, I'll go down and fix the furnace,' because it was October and it was beginning to get cold. She went to shake the furnace — we had a coal furnace — and the pipe fell off. And the poor soul came up to the bedroom and she was all over soot. So, we had no heat. All we had was black smoke.

"She called the doctor, and here he was in Pittsburgh at the Allegheny

General, delivering another baby. He told her that he would try to get out as fast as he could. 'He will never make it,' I said to my mother-in-law, because I felt like I was going to have it. She said, 'Well, all we can do is pray.' That was her way in anything. We'd stop and we'd pray.

"And I said to her, 'We're going to have to deliver this baby by ourselves.' She was a very wonderful woman, and she guided me right through it. The doctor was phoning, and my mother-in-law was taking the message and running back and forth up the stairs. And I said to her when the baby was born, 'There's something wrong — see what's on his face?' He had a veil over his face. And she took that off. I still remember sitting partway up and seeing her pull that veil off his face. And he cried. It was a birth that no one helped with except my mother-in-law. The doctor came out later in the afternoon and said he couldn't have done any better himself."

Jim Kennedy had been born with a caul, which according to folk wisdom foretells a prosperous future. If riches are measured by health, that veil was indeed prophetic. Jim has lived long enough to stand on the threshold of being a grandfather. On this fine August day, his family goes about its business, sustained by the land they've lived on for generations, and sustained by something else, too: the family memories that speak of births and deaths, of comings and goings, of all the transitions of life. As the Kennedys look to the future, they're nourished by the past — by the stories that tell them who they are and where on earth they belong.

Soon, there will be another story to tell.

The Story of the Seasons

The story beginning on the Kennedy farm is the same simple yet wondrous story that's beginning wherever anyone awaits the birth of a child. It's the story of human development through the entire span of life, from the first day to the last.

People have been trying to fit that story into a familiar and sequential order for as long as they've thought about lives at all. Metaphors abound for the "journey" from birth to death — in the times of the day, the circling of the planets, the phases of the moon, the growth and harvesting of crops, and the seasons of the year. The ancient Greeks taught that childhood was warm and moist like an Aegean spring, youth hot and dry like summer, adulthood cold and dry like autumn, and old age cold and moist like winter. The metaphor of the seasons has always held a powerful attraction for the human imagination.

Very recently, we have begun to investigate the human life cycle in a scientific way. Biologists, anthropologists, psychologists, sociologists, and others are converging on a new "life-span" perspective, one that says that you can't understand the young without understanding the old, and that you can't understand young or old without understanding everyone else in between. This new perspective — an attempt to see all the seasons of life in a single glance — is the subject of this book. We're going to tell the stories and interpret the lives of people such as the Kennedys, people of many ages and from many walks of life. We'll introduce a number of studies of human development, some of which have followed the same individuals for more than half a century. And we'll trace the ticking of three developmental "clocks" that regulate the seasons of life: a Biological Clock that keeps time for the body, a Social Clock that keeps time for society, and a Psychological Clock that keeps time for the individual self. We will see how the self makes meaning in response to these clocks, and how it comes to fashion the story of a life.

Human lives have changed dramatically in this century. In 1900, the typical newborn in the United States could expect to live forty-seven years. The new Kennedy baby can expect to live seventy-five. That increase of more than twenty-five years in less than a century is unprecedented in human history. Barring some manipulation of our genetic code, nothing like it will ever happen again. The change has not come about because our genetic potential for long life has increased, but rather because improving health conditions have allowed more of us to reach the potential we've had all along. Infants and children have benefited more than other age groups, and females more than males, but people of all ages and both sexes can anticipate more years of life than their counterparts could in 1900. In this century newborns have gained twenty-eight years of life, twenty-two-year-olds like Jeffrey and Janice have gained thirteen years, forty-five-year-olds like Jim and Rita have gained nine, and seventy-year-olds like Francis and Martha have gained four. Nothing has changed *all* the seasons of life as profoundly as this increase in length of life.

The twentieth century is a landmark for another reason. By the year 2000, a way of life that prevailed for more than 95 percent of human history will have come to an end. Humans seem to have originated in Africa more than 100,000 years ago — perhaps as long as 200,000 years ago. Their numbers were small, and they lived a nomadic life in which men hunted and women gathered plant foods and cared for children. Today we call such people "hunter-gatherers." About 30,000 years ago, some of them migrated across the Bering Strait to America; a few came to roam the land the Kennedys now inhabit. But, as far as we know, it wasn't until about 10,000 years ago that humans began to give up hunting and gathering. This was a significant moment in human history, and it dramatically affected the seasons of life. Today we find ourselves living with a timetable in our bodies — a Biological Clock — that was calibrated to a life of hunting and gathering, and in many ways is out of sync with contemporary existence. By the end of this century, the few hunter-gatherers that remain in places such as Africa and Australia will have given up their way of life. Hunting and gathering will be extinct, and with it the context in which our Biological Clock evolved.

An estimated sixty billion people have preceded us in the journey through life.[1] More than five billion are alive today, a staggering number that our planet can barely accommodate. And increased longevity has created some of the oldest populations on record. In 1900, for example, less than 5 percent of men and women in the United States lived to reach the age of sixty-five. Today, more than 10 percent are that old, and in the year 2000, almost 15 percent will be. All of these changes make this — the end of the twentieth century — an ideal time to resurrect the ancient story of the seasons and tell it in an entirely new way.

The most mysterious part of any story of life is its beginning. If we search our individual lives for how we began, we reach back eventually to darkness: most of us remember nothing before the age of three or four. Our family stories may extend for generations or even centuries, but they, too, begin in oblivion. As for the story of the seasons of life, we will never know how, when, and where it began. The human life cycle took millions of years to evolve and left few clues as to what happened: some bones and stones, some species related to our own, a dwindling number of humans who still live the kind of life our distant ancestors did, and a genetic code whose history we're just beginning to probe. As individuals, as families, and as a species, we use whatever's at hand to probe the darkness surrounding our origins. We are the only creature on earth that tries to tell its own story.

The Kennedy Stories

"I think that a lot of our problems today are caused by cement," explains sixty-nine-year-old Francis Kennedy. "You take yourself. You go to town, and stand on cement all day — you're irritated. I don't care who you are, and whether you'll admit it or not, you're irritated, see? Because your feet are sore. I don't know when anybody's gonna recognize it — that in life you gotta get your feet comfortable first. And if you get out on the soil, your feet will be comfortable."

Francis sounds as if his feet have been comfortable for most of his life, even now that he's come to his final season. "We're not gettin' any older," he says, rubbing his square Irish jaw, "but the summers are gettin' closer, and as the summers get closer, maybe we find some joints that we didn't have before." Francis has had his share of ailments — a diabetic condition, hypertension, heart problems, eyes that required cataract surgery. Several years ago, his wife Martha had a mild heart attack. Their problems are under control, but they've made their wills and purchased cemetery lots. They've done what needs to be done, and they're not going to worry about what might happen. They don't have time for that, says Francis. "Why, you or I could sit down and, Man-o'-War, we could really cry the blues with each other. That wouldn't do any good. You gotta get goin'. Tomorrow's another day. Be ready for it. Meet it as a challenge."

Francis is the storyteller in the Kennedy clan, and he knows a few things about his family's roots. His first memory of life comes from the time his family moved to the eighty-acre farm in Butler County that's still part of the Kennedy holdings. The Kennedys drove there in a horse and buggy, only to find the house locked. Small enough to squeeze through a window, Francis climbed in and opened the house from the inside. "I can still see that window today," he says, "where I got in and unlocked the doors."

The young boy who wriggled through that window had no idea that the first Kennedys came to these shores looking for a better life in a new country that promised religious freedom to all. The Kennedys were from Northern Ireland, part of the great wave of sturdy Scotch-Irish Presbyterians that began to roll across the Atlantic during the eighteenth century, people who were fleeing absentee landlords, enforced tithes to the Church of England, and religious oppression. These self-reliant farmers settled the Pennsylvania frontier, where, as buffers between the settled farmland and the wilderness, they bore the brunt of Indian fighting. They became noted for their hospitality and cooperation. The sign of a Scotch-Irish household was a latchkey hanging beside the door to welcome any wanderer.[2] By the time of the American Revolution, one-seventh of the colonists would be Scotch-Irish.

The Kennedy clan arrived after the Revolution had been won, but Americans were getting ready to fight England once more. James Madison was president and the War of 1812 was brewing when Thomas Kennedy, born in Londonderry in 1788, fled Ireland's religious and political turmoil for the freedom of Philadelphia. He pushed on west to the wide-open country north of Pittsburgh, a settlement at the intersection of three great rivers that was already a smoky industrial town, full of foundries, sawmills, and glassworks that flourished on the seams of coal that lay beneath the ground.

The government was selling uninhabited land north of the Ohio River for $1.25 an acre, and Thomas, a carpenter by trade, took up 400 acres in the same area that figures in Francis's first memory. He built a log cabin beside a spring and began to clear the ground for crops. In 1824, he brought his bride, Anna Purvis, to this land, where they raised five sons and buried two infant daughters. Thomas and Anna prospered, adding hundreds of acres to their holdings. When Thomas died at the age of ninety, he divided the land among his sons.

Francis Kennedy is the fourth generation down from Thomas. His father, Harold, was born in 1898, the fourth of eleven children, and died sixty-nine years later — out in the fields, tending his crops. Plans had been under way to celebrate his and his wife Melverna's golden anniversary. Francis tells the story, with the hope that he will share his father's fate. "I seen his dog, laying up in the cornfield. Went up in there, and there he was laying. He had the corn husker in one hand, ear of corn in the other, and his dog sleeping right at his head. Must have had a heart attack and never knowed what hit him, 'cause he couldn't drop the ear of corn or the husker. Got to leave this world, it's a great way to go."

The Kennedy family stories focus on the land and the rhythms of the seasons. When members of the newest generation hear them, they will learn how their great-great-grandparents carried water, milked by the flicker of lantern light, and depended on horses and manpower to till the soil. They'll hear about threshing wheat and oats by hand and feeding fifteen men around the kitchen table. They'll hear about the farm's first dairy cows, acquired in great-great grandfather Harold's day, and how great-grandfather Francis began the prize-winning Brown Swiss dairy herd. Such stories will tell the youngest Kennedys that they're part of a family wedded to the land, people for whom the best way to leave this world is the way Harold did, with your feet firmly planted in your own soil.

The story of Francis's own generation begins in the simple world of horse-drawn plows and hand-milked cows, a kind of farming little changed since the first Kennedys came over from Ireland. Francis was born in 1918, shortly before the end of World War I. He grew up in a country connected by rail, and one of his favorite memories is the weekly train trip to

Farming as Francis knew it. "In life you gotta get your feet comfortable first. And if you get out on the soil, your feet will be comfortable."

Pittsburgh, about twenty-five miles away, to sell sweet corn and strawberries, chickens and sausage to the city folk. "My mother and father, and my grandfather before that, had a stand in the old Farmers' Market down in Diamond Street in Pittsburgh," he recalls. "They started taking me when I was only two or three years old. The old Harmony Short Line used to travel between Pittsburgh and Butler. They would always pick sweet corn, and we'd go by train into the old Allegheny Market, and they'd put me to sleep on the sacks of corn, and that's where I slept till daylight."

Francis was the oldest of four children. He grew up with his sister Ethel by his side, but two other children died in infancy. He was nine years old when his little brother died a few hours after birth, and Francis remembers the tiny body laid out on the back porch and the ride to the cemetery with the small casket in the back of the car.

The years of Francis's boyhood and adolescence were not good ones for farmers. The 1920s ushered in an acute economic recession, one from which farmers had not yet fully recovered when the Great Depression of the 1930s hit. For Francis, it was a time of scrimping and saving, of wearing patches on top of patches — but always feeling secure. "I was old enough in the depression years to know my dad and mother saved like the dickens to make a payment on the farm and taxes. So we didn't have much of anything. But, by golly, we always had plenty to eat, because my dad raised buckwheat and wheat. He'd have that buckwheat made into flour and the wheat cracked. Mother'd steam that wheat for two or three days, and you've never had a better meal than that cracked wheat. And buckwheat cakes. Always in the fall of the year, she'd start buckwheat batter, and every morning she'd take so many out. Man, there was nothing like that. Those are nice things you look back at, to think, here's somebody that knowed how to provide."

Francis married Martha in 1936, in the closing days of the Great Depression. He was eighteen and she was twenty-one. But, like Jim and Rita, and Jeffrey and Janice — who also married young — the two had known each other for most of their lives. Martha remembers their first meeting. She was five-and-a-half and recently orphaned by the loss of her mother. "I had just come to this vicinity to live with an aunt who lived across the creek from the Kennedys," she says. "Every Monday morning we had what they called 'the peddler' who came around and brought your groceries that you ordered the week before. My aunt and I used to go across the swinging bridge to the foot of Kennedy's lane and meet the grocer there. And Francis's mother would be carrying his sister and bringing Francis down with her by the hand. That was the first recollection I had of Francis. They were two real tow-headed kids. And I was shy."

At first Francis and Martha paid little attention to each other. They got better acquainted when they took the Harmony Line to their one-room schoolhouse, with Martha already settled in her seat when Francis climbed aboard at the next stop. Then Martha moved away, but just one township over; she still saw Francis at church, where his mother played the organ. They were only acquaintances, because Martha found him "too devilish," a boy who threw water-soaked snowballs at her — until he hit her one too many times, and she retaliated. Romance blossomed after they both joined the Grange, an association that promoted farmers' interests. They became leaders in the organization and traveled together to other towns, where they conducted initiation ceremonies for new members. The Great Depression had been hard for Francis, but even harder for Martha. "My uncle was blind, so it seems odd to say, but I have plowed a field," she says. "I have planted potatoes and picked them and graded them and done all tne garden work, because all my uncle could do was hold the plow in while I led the horse. He couldn't even make a living, but we would never accept any help. So that's where I learned how to do things. We wondered if the depression would ever end."

Even when the economic climate improved, the Kennedys faced the disasters that all farmers encounter from time to time. No sooner had Francis and his father built up a promising herd of purebred dairy cows than they lost it. A new heifer, bought to improve the stock, spread brucellosis through the herd, and the Kennedys had to destroy every one of their prized cows, wiping out years of work.

Twice, Francis narrowly escaped death in the sort of accidents that are all too familiar on a farm. Not long after he bought his first tractor, he tried pulling a load down a hill. In those days, tractors had neither cabs nor roll-bars. As he angled the tractor across the hill, it began to tip. In that long, sickening moment before it went over, Francis knew it was going to flip, perhaps crushing him. The tractor jumped a stream and overturned, but Francis escaped injury. He's sure it was because the Lord was riding with him.

His second brush with death came in 1954, in the days before anyone knew about the lethal nature of agricultural chemicals. Francis had used a highly toxic preservative on his silage. "I remember crawling up in that silo, trampling down the silage. Next thing I know, I found myself way up in the woods. I still don't know how I got out of the silo, how I climbed down, or how I got myself up there in the woods, where I passed out. It was a near thing. The preservative poisoned my liver — hepatitis. When I came out of the hospital, the doctors didn't know if I'd ever be able to farm again." Once more, the Lord was there.

Religion has always been an important thread in the lives of the Kennedys. The first American Kennedy, Thomas, made the family's dependence on God clear. Any of his sons who did not hold regular family worship services was to be disinherited. His oldest son, Samuel, donated land for a church, but he stipulated that unless the building was used by "Psalm singing congregations," the land would revert back to his heirs.

As farmers, the Kennedys see themselves and their families as part of the handiwork of creation. "It's God's earth, not ours," is the family motto. Working with the land, watching the crops grow, witnessing the birth of an animal, the Kennedys are continually made aware of their Creator's presence. One day, Francis will tell his great-grandchildren about the strict Sundays of his childhood, when his grandmother would not allow a Sunday newspaper in the house, and about the church elders with their big mustaches, who stretched the long-handled collection baskets clear across the rows. He'll also tell them how God helps him make important decisions. Whenever Francis has had problems to solve, he's always climbed to the highest hill on the farm — just about the highest ground in Butler County. There he sits, alone with God, and ponders his problem with the woods and streams, the pastures and fields, spread out before him.

Although Francis and Martha are primarily farmers, their lives have extended beyond the borders of their farm. A cluster of stories centers on the family tradition of politics, tales about persuading the unwilling to support a consolidated school, about buying a bus to gather the children each day. Kennedys take their civic responsibilities seriously. Like his father and grandfather, Francis was a roads supervisor, and, like his father before him and his son after him, he served as a member of the local school board. Once the children were grown, Francis spent twelve years as a member of the Pennsylvania State Legislature, and Martha served as his secretary. Francis remembers how he worked to pass laws requiring that mining companies restore the land after stripping it, and how he helped establish a state park in Butler County, with a man-made lake for boating and fishing.

"We had to make sure that all those oil wells were perfectly sealed, so they could never come back and pollute," he says. "Had to refill a lot of those strip mines so that we'd keep the acid out. I think we must have done a pretty good job of it, because today it's one of the best fishing lakes in Western Pennsylvania. I don't think you're gonna go to a place that's more beautiful in the fall of the year, when the leaves are turning. Everybody should go up and just sit there. It's a good place to go to dream."

All the Kennedys have a love of nature and relish the history it yields. Francis recalls how, after spring planting in his boyhood, the first rain always turned up arrowheads — once even a tomahawk. Jeffrey can tell about the hollow section of petrified wood he once found in a field, a piece from a long-extinct tree that had been lying in the earth since before the time of Jesus. And Jim talks about the sheer pleasure of taking a solitary walk across the pasture near the woods, looking for signs of deer, wild turkey, or foxes. Early in life, the newest Kennedy will hear about the family's attachment to their animals, about the old cow that Grandmother Rita and Grandfather Jim loved so much that they retired her to pasture when her calving days were done. Then she was buried up in the apple orchard so she'd always be with them.

These stories will nourish generations of Kennedys to come, giving them people to emulate and ancestors to be proud of. Out of this web of stories, Kennedy children will learn what it means to be a member of a family and

The Kennedy farm today.

the importance of belonging to one. They'll learn how the world works, by hearing how it has treated their relatives. They'll absorb a culture, one that's influenced by their family's ethnic background, its way of making a living, its religious and social values. Without being conscious of it, they'll pick up the guidelines the stories provide for what they might do with their lives, the instructions and warnings the stories carry. Francis seems to speak for the entire family when he says, "Things were tough, but we didn't know it. We just made up our mind: this is where we're at, but this is where we're gonna go. Many times we didn't know where the next dollar was gonna come from, or how. We had problems, but we didn't look at them that way. We looked at them as opportunities. I think that's 'cause you never, one thing I'll tell you, you never talk about the things that are wrong. You always figure out how to make them right. Then, talk about them. Brag about them!

"I always figured that I was just passing through this world, see. What you do for yourself really don't count. It's what you do to make life possible, and better, for these little kids."

A Memorable Day

While the newest Kennedy baby didn't "come a-flyin'" into the world as Grandfather Jim had, he did come more than a week early — on August 14, 1987. He was a seven-pound, seven-ounce boy, and in the tradition of the Kennedys, he was given a name beginning with J — Justin. The story of his birth reflects a very different era from when "the ladies knowed how to handle it themselves," but it will be told over and again in its time.

"The day before, I was up at the farm show," says Janice. "The Holstein

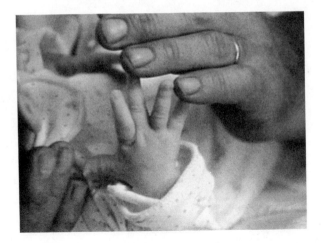

Justin meets Grandfather Jim. "You did a good job, we'll keep him."

show was that day, so I worked the booth most of the day and came home. That was — what? — eleven o'clock. We came home that night, and the next morning when I got up, I could tell my water had broke. So I came down and told Jeff that I thought today was the day. And he was like, no!

"He went to the barn. I called the doctor, and I packed, and we got to the hospital about ten-thirty. They hooked me up to the monitor to hear the baby's heart beating and find out how long the contractions were. They were about six minutes apart. They got me ready and told me I could walk around, so we walked around a little bit and then came back to the room and watched TV.

"I just kept working through the contractions till about four, and they were getting too much for me, so the doctor came in and said I could have a painkiller. So then I was more or less in and out of it. Then about six, I guess, it started getting too much for me again, and I asked for another painkiller. The nurse told me no. She came in one time and caught me pushing, and she said, 'Do you have to push?' I said yes, and she went and called the doctor. And they had everything ready to go, and when they told me I could push, it was maybe five or six contractions, and I had him. Then they cleaned him up and gave him to Jeff.

"My dad was outside, I guess, when Jeff called. My mum said my dad had a big grin on his face as soon as my little brother yelled, 'It's a boy, it's a boy!' The next day, Monday, Jeff's mum called, and they come up, and she couldn't wait to see him and hold him. His dad even held him. He's real stiff, you know. She sat him in his arms, and he kept telling me, 'You did a good job, you did a good job, we'll keep him.'"

A few days later, it was time to go home. Janice was driven past fields of

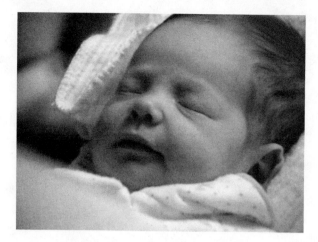

"He's definitely a Kennedy."

golden oats, green pastures, and tall stands of corn to be greeted by balloons dancing over the mailbox. "My mum and dad and all my sisters and brothers were here. They had a little sign: Welcome Home. My sister, she didn't get to come to the hospital, the first thing she said was, 'Let me hold him.' So she brought him in."

Within a week, remembers Janice, Grandmother Rita brought her some pictures. "She said, 'Your pictures from the hospital came already.' I opened the envelope and looked at it, and it looked exactly like Justin. But it was black and white, so I said this isn't. . . . She said it was Jeff's baby picture. And he looked exactly like Jeff. That's why nobody can say it's the milkman. He's definitely a Kennedy."

In the years to come Justin will become more of a Kennedy. His great-grandfather Francis intends to have a hand in making him one. "I'm just hoping that our health keeps good enough that when he's ready for 4-H we're able to give him a steer that he can raise to be a grand champion. It would be the greatest thing in the world to see him up at the Butler County Farm Show, selling the top steer. We're looking forward to that day."

I

Infancy

1

THE BIOLOGICAL STORY OF INFANCY *The Biological Clock*

Whatever Justin Kennedy may achieve in his life — even at the Butler County Farm Show — his story will never be more spectacular than it was in the nine months before he was born. During that period, he traveled the same path that all his human predecessors had traveled before him. The first leg of the journey through the seasons of life has remained unchanged since the dawn of our species.

What happened to Justin during those nine months is largely the work of the Biological Clock. The term "Biological Clock" is a metaphor for the timing mechanisms that guide the body's journey, not only through prenatal development but throughout all of life. The settings of this clock determine the length of our stay in the womb, the rate at which we grow, the timing of our passage from childhood to sexual maturity, the appearance of gray hair and wrinkles, and, ultimately, our death. The Biological Clock is no single organ, such as the heart or the brain. Its timing mechanisms are found throughout the body — in every cell, not just in one place.

The Biological Clock has its own kind of memory, one that stretches back millions of years. Like the stories told in families, this memory is transmitted from one generation to the next. Like family stories, it evolves and revises itself, albeit over vast stretches of time. But the memory in the Biological Clock is so powerful that it can enact what it has stored. When that memory summons up the enactment of a human body, it creates questions as well, questions about the biological origin of the seasons of life.

Why are humans so immature at birth? So slow to reach reproductive age, and so long to live once reproduction is over? It's difficult enough to piece together the history of our skulls and skeletons. Even more mysterious is the evolution of the Biological Clock.

The First Nine Months

Before the Biological Clock began to tick in Justin Kennedy's life, his father's sperm and his mother's egg had to meet within one of the passages leading from his mother's ovary to her womb. The timing of that meeting was critical. Unless a sperm reaches an egg within twenty-four hours of its release from the ovary, conception will not take place.

The drama leading to conception begins just after the act of intercourse, when several hundred million sperm begin to swim up the vagina toward the opening in the womb that will lead to the egg, each sperm struggling valiantly against a strong current of vaginal fluids. Only about fifty of the sperm ever reach the egg, completing a trip equivalent to a three-mile swim for a human being.[1] Most of the others die along the way — either destroyed by the acid secretions of the vagina, or unable to find their way through the oscillating threads of mucus at the opening to the uterus. About half of those that don't get lost in the womb travel up the wrong fallopian tube. Nearly all the rest go astray toward the end of their journey, wandering past the egg to die at the far end of the fallopian tube, lost in the convoluted folds that loom like mammoth caverns in their path.

The few sperm that finally reach the egg find new obstacles between themselves and their goal. A thick, gelatinous coat, called the "zona pellucida," surrounds the egg. When the sperm contact this coating, special receptor molecules bind to them, holding them fast. In response, the sperm release an enzyme that dissolves enough of the barrier for them to wriggle through. As soon as the first sperm works its way to the final membrane surrounding the egg, tiny projections on the egg's outer surface enfold the sperm with their interlacing fingers, drawing the head inside. Almost immediately, the zona pellucida is transformed. It hardens, becoming an unyielding wall that repels all other sperm.

In the meantime, the tail of the sperm drops off and a minor eruption occurs within the egg. Genetic material bursts from the head of the sperm — twenty-three gossamer chromosomes, many times thinner than a single strand of a spider's web. Each chromosome bears thousands of genes, those minuscule chains of the extraordinary chemical substance deoxyribonucleic acid, known as DNA. Quickly, the paternal chromosomes pair off with their maternal counterparts to form a package of forty-six. This package contains the total genetic inheritance. It's where our species' memory of how to build a body is stored.

Scientists are trying to estimate how much space exists in genetic memory. Because a good deal of the information stored there is redundant, their estimates depend on how they treat duplication. But if each of the billions of links in the DNA chain is like a letter of the alphabet, each chromosome would represent several dozen sets of encyclopedias. The total genetic package would be the equivalent of a small library — an impressive amount of memory space, but only a tiny fraction of the room that will later be available in the brain. This small genetic library contains instructions on how to build the huge cerebral one.

Most of the genes Justin inherited were structural genes; they told his body *what* to build — blood, bone, muscle, digestive organs, hormones, and the like. But scattered along the intricate chains of DNA were other genes that acted as on-off switches — timing genes that form the mainspring of the Biological Clock. These timing genes told Justin's body *when* to begin building and when to stop.

After Justin was conceived, the fertilized egg set about its task of producing his body. At first he was only a single cell, no bigger than a speck of pepper, a cell that divided again and again, each time making a copy of its genetic legacy. This cluster of identical cells grew and drifted down the fallopian tube, sped along by the waving, beckoning hairs that lined the tube wall. After several days it entered the womb, only to float aimlessly for another four or five days. Justin's body was still only a flat, two-layered disk, whose cells were just beginning to get their construction orders. These orders came in the form of special molecules on the surface of each new cell, which determined whether various cells would connect with or shun one another.[2] Soon the rapidly differentiating cluster burrowed its way into the wall of the womb, gaining access to the nourishing blood of Justin's mother. Once anchored, this two-week-old organism, no bigger than the head of a pin, began to develop in response to the Biological Clock.[3]

By four weeks or so, Justin had grown enormously. He was 10,000 times larger than the original fertilized cell, which made him about one-fifth of an inch long. Surrounded by a protective sac, he floated safely, connected to his mother by the placenta, a supple structure that furnished him with oxygen and nourishment and carried away his waste products. Young Justin was now an embryo, and his task for the next four weeks was to develop his major organ systems. His brain was beginning to form, and so was his heart, but part of that tiny organ still lay outside his tubelike body. He had a fore-head, eyes, and a mouth, but did not yet look human. Within the next four weeks, all his major organs would form, and Justin would graduate to the status of a fetus.

At eight weeks, Justin measured more than an inch from head to toe. His first bone cells had begun to form, and he could move his miniature mus-cles. His head was still enormous compared to his body, and his eyes were sightless and half-closed. By twelve weeks, he could kick, close his fingers, turn his head, and open and close his mouth. His three-inch body weighed about an ounce. In the next four weeks his weight quadrupled; at sixteen weeks, he no longer seemed all head. Six-inch Justin looked human in body as well as face. His basic systems were in place, although they could not sup-port him unaided.

At twenty-three weeks, Justin slept and stirred. When he wasn't sleep-ing, he moved about, as if exercising or seeking a more comfortable posi-tion. Had Justin been born at that point, he might have survived, but only after heroic efforts by dedicated medical teams. His brain was still too immature to take over the direction of his body systems. It was another fifteen weeks before Justin burst into the world with a lusty cry and the abil-ity to survive on his own.

The Evolution of Timing

It took millions of years and countless genetic experiments in nature to work out the schedule of events that guided Justin's prenatal develop-ment — and shapes that of all human babies. But once the work of evolu-tion was done, once events not only in the womb but throughout our entire life span were timed as they are now, we became us — Homo sapiens, the human family.

To understand how the Biological Clock of any species comes to be — how it evolves from that of antecedent species — we have to realize that genes don't sit still. Some of them shuffle and reshuffle their segments, or jump to other places on the chromosome, rearranging information in ways that can be passed along to the next generation. When one of these restless genes is a timing gene, there may be evolutionary consequences.

Without the precise placement of timing genes on Justin Kennedy's chromosomes, the cells that became him — a human baby — might have become another sort of primate. That's because 99 percent of our structural genes — the ones that determine *what* to build — are identical to those of a chimpanzee. These genes are building blocks that can be arranged to produce almost any primate, with timing the key to the final product. Evolution takes the same structural genes and, by shifting the timing genes, comes up with a new species. Within the womb, a limb bud's growth is cut short, and the resulting arm is human instead of apelike. Or timing genes that govern the brain allow tissue to keep growing at its fetal rate even after birth, while other timing genes postpone the date of skull closure. That may be all it takes to produce a human skull and brain from chimpanzee genes.[4]

The timing genes of each species not only build a particular kind of body, but also determine how long that body will live and what biological events will occupy its life span. At the moment Justin Kennedy was conceived, the timing of his seasons was established. The major events would be those of any species — birth, reproduction, and death — but the scheduling of events would be that of his fellow humans. No other species allots its time the way we do. No other creates our biological seasons of life.

Our seasons are unusual in their sheer length, and in the rate at which events in them unfold. "The Biological Clock in our lives is lengthened relative to what you'd expect by standard mammalian design for our body size," says Stephen Jay Gould of Harvard University, who studies the evolution of the Biological Clock. "Moreover, and more interesting, we develop so slowly. We mature sexually very much later than any other mammal with anything close to our body size. That's the most curious and characteristic aspect of our Biological Clocks."[5]

As they seek to understand this long, slow life of ours, geneticists look for clues that will enable them to reconstruct the history of the Biological Clock. Genes manufacture protein, the basic building blocks of brain cells, blood cells, bone cells, skin cells — every kind of cell. Our genes began yielding clues to the history of the Biological Clock just over two decades ago, when researchers at the Berkeley campus of the University of California found almost no difference between the blood protein of humans and that of chimpanzees. Other geneticists found support for this close relationship when they compared the entire DNA program of human beings, chimpanzees, and gorillas and found that gorillas were probably the first to evolve on a separate path. Somewhere between five and eight million years ago, chimpanzees and humans parted company. The settings on timing genes changed, and the ancestral hominid was born.[6]

Surviving bone fragments from pelvis, leg, and foot indicate that nearly four million years ago, short, apelike hominids with small brains were walking upright in Africa. They were not yet human, but they weren't apes either. Named *Australopithecus afarensis*, they trotted along on their hind feet, leaving their hands free to carry their young or to use a tool. Yet they made no stone tools that could be preserved over time. They don't seem to have done any hunting, but gathered their food using whatever was handy, then tossing it away — twigs to dig out termites, sticks to unearth edible roots, rocks to crack nuts and hard-shelled fruits.

Australopithecus had a life span far shorter than our own. Judging from his brain and body weight, scientists estimate that his maximum potential was about forty-seven years.[7] But rarely did *Australopithecus* avoid enough accidents to live that long. The famous "Lucy," whose skeleton is more complete than any *Australopithecus* yet discovered, was only about twenty when she died — which is the average age of the rest of the skeletons *Australopithecus* left behind. The best guess is that only about 15 percent of Lucy's people reached the age of thirty.[8] It took this first hominid at least two million years to evolve into the first members of the Homo family, and perhaps another two million years to become *Homo sapiens* — ourselves. If the broad scale of evolutionary time were reduced to a single year, we emerged on the planet less than a half hour before midnight on December 31 — sometime between 100,000 and 200,000 B.C. By that time we had developed the biological potential for a little over a hundred years of life, although we rarely lived that long.

Most creatures don't live out their natural life spans; predators, accidents, or disease cuts them down long before they have exhausted their biological potential. So estimates of the maximum life span of our prehuman ancestors are only guesses. We can be more certain, however, that the human maximum of just over a hundred years has remained constant throughout the thousand or so centuries of our existence. After all, if our Biological Clock changed in any major way, it would not produce us, but some other species. What has changed over the ages, and what has increased dramatically during the present century, is not the human potential for long life, but the number of people who actually come close to that potential.

Just as remarkable as our potential for longevity is the timing of our biological seasons. The unshaded areas in the illustration on page 29 are as distinctive to our species as the size of our skulls and the shape of our skeletons. These areas represent the years after infancy when humans are unable to reproduce. At birth, human males and females seem to be headed straight for sexual maturity. Both have high levels of sex hormones, principally testosterone in boys and estrogen in girls. But some unknown switch in the Biological Clock shuts those hormones down by the age of two and keeps them down for about eight years. The result is a period of childhood. As normal as human childhood seems to us, in comparison with the growth patterns of other species it is quite abnormal — a remarkable invention of the Biological Clock. Childhood is an extra "leg" of the journey from birth to reproductive maturity.[9]

Not only do humans live an inordinate number of years before reproduction begins, they are granted an absolutely outlandish stretch of time after reproduction ends. Male fertility diminishes in the second half of life, though

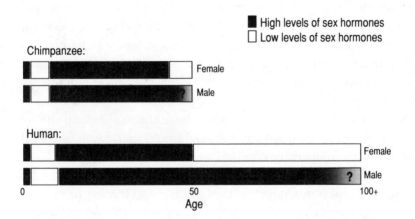

The biological seasons of life as reflected in sex hormones. Maximum potential life span is depicted.

it does not come to a clear-cut end. Female fertility does end abruptly. When women experience menopause at about fifty, their childbearing years are over. Even though evolution has apparently lost all interest in them, they may live another fifty years, half their potential life span.

Our closest living relatives are chimpanzees, yet their biological seasons differ sharply from ours. Our life-span potential is more than a hundred years; theirs is about fifty. Female chimpanzees are fully grown, physically mature, and ready to begin their own families by the age of ten or eleven, but in human girls that age falls between fourteen and eighteen. And female chimpanzees appear to be fertile almost to the end of life. Some who reach their forties experience the same hormonal changes as human women in the midst of menopause,[10] but this chimpanzee menopause comes at the equivalent of eighty or ninety human years.

Since the goal of the Biological Clock of any species is to construct an organism that will reproduce, it seems odd for humans to "waste" all those years on nonreproductive activities.

But then we are a singularly peculiar species. The way anthropologist Owen Lovejoy tells the story, the key to the evolution of our life cycle was social behavior.[11] In his view, our ancient forebears' care of their children, the cooperative bonds between parents, and the ability to walk upright — freeing their hands to carry infants and use tools — combined to enlarge their brains. Larger brains made our ancestors smarter. They provided progressively better care for their children and cooperated even more effectively, with the result that their brains grew larger still. As the brain kept getting bigger, the length of childhood increased, giving the young a greater chance to learn. Adulthood lengthened, too, giving elders time to teach where dependable fruit trees were located, where to find birds' nests and small game, where streams ran, how to respond to natural disasters that occurred once in a lifetime — all the things that made a difference between living and dying. However it happened, the Biological Clock seems to have discovered that when children have time to develop the intelligence implicit in their brains, and when there are grandparents around, the species gains a competitive edge.

It's much easier to figure out how evolution could have extended life before reproduction than how it could have extended life afterward. Favorable changes in genes that boost our ability to reproduce can be passed on to successors, but those that affect life after reproduction cannot, unless some hidden mechanism sets them in motion earlier in life. Currently we have little idea of how — or if — timing genes create the scenario of later life.

Yet enough is known to be confident that the Biological Clock is far more active in the first half of life than in the second. In the womb, biological events are precisely timed, but precision diminishes as the years wear on. In the later years, the effects of the physical and social environment seem to accumulate. The Biological Clock can be sped up or slowed down by the food we eat, by exercise, and even by companionship and love.

The Clock and the Sexes

Because the Biological Clock is concerned with successful reproduction, it plans from the very beginning for our sexual nature. Its basic blueprint appears to be female. Researchers are coming to realize that the biological development of females follows a more direct path than that of males. The difference is evident in survival rates (see figure below). About 120 boys are conceived for every 100 girls, but more males die before birth. As a result, the ratio at birth is 106 males for every 100 females. By the age of eighty, it's down to 50 males per 100 females. In terms of survival, females are clearly the superior sex. Their advantage is commonly found throughout the animal kingdom.

From conception, Justin was destined to become male, his fate foretold by the chromosomes in his father's sperm. One of the original twenty-three

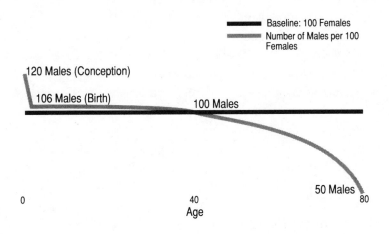

Sex ratio across the life span. Values represent the number of males per hundred females.

chromosomes is called the sex chromosome. From his mother, Justin inherited a large female sex chromosome, known as the "X" chromosome. From his father he inherited the smaller male, or "Y" chromosome. Only half of his father's sperm carried the Y chromosome; the rest carried a female X, and had one of those sperm penetrated the egg, Justin would be a girl.

For the first six weeks of his growth, the only way to discover whether Justin was male or female was to examine his chromosomes under a microscope. Until then, there is no difference between the sex organs — the "gonads" — in male and female embryos. But about the beginning of the seventh week, the Biological Clock sent out a signal, and Justin's neutral gonads started developing into testes and were soon secreting male hormones. One of the substances secreted by Justin's tiny testes was testosterone. This major male hormone first guided the development of primitive ducts designed to become his internal sexual organs; later it directed cells destined for external genitals along the male route of development. Another substance secreted by the testes went to work on the internal structures that were meant to become the inner reproductive organs of a female, causing them to disintegrate.

Had Justin been a girl, the gonads would have continued on their neutral path for several more weeks. Not until after the twelfth week would the Biological Clock have moved them along the female path to become ovaries. This delay means that female internal reproductive organs begin developing in the absence of any sex hormones — or any special signal at all. Without the stimulation of testosterone, the structures that would become male internal organs shrivel and disappear. About the time that the male fetus develops a penis and scrotum, the female is developing a clitoris, labia, and vagina. Once the gonads have developed into ovaries, they go about their business of secreting hormones — principally estrogen — and begin to manufacture eggs. Before the end of the prenatal period, they must produce a lifetime supply.

By eight weeks, Justin's testes were producing high levels of testosterone, which flowed through his miniature blood vessels. Throughout the last six months of his stay in the womb, this testosterone bathed his small brain, altering the hypothalamus and the pituitary gland, the master endocrine gland that nestles at the base of the brain. This bath fixed a setting on another timepiece, one that won't start ticking until Justin reaches puberty. At that time, his brain will order the release of sex hormones in the male pattern, with its daily rise and fall of testosterone. Without this prenatal exposure to testosterone, girls' brains are set to follow the female pattern, in which the proportion and kind of hormones in the blood will vary in a monthly cycle that controls ovulation and menstruation.

Some researchers are convinced that the prenatal bath of male hormones changes the brain in other ways. We know that this happens in rats, because researchers can control rats' exposure to hormones and then examine the brain. Male hormones seem to be responsible for a host of brain differences in rats: metabolism, protein content, distribution of chemicals that carry signals through the nervous system, the size of brain cells, and the connections between them. These brain differences are linked to the rats' activity level, combativeness, sleep patterns, and the way they play, groom themselves, and threaten one another.[12]

No one has demonstrated such effects in our own species, although some researchers believe that similar sex differences exist in our brain tissue.

They have found a few differences — such as the size of the band of connecting fibers that carries information back and forth between the brain's two hemispheres. But their primary evidence comes from "experiments of nature," cases in which development has taken an unusual course because of some genetic aberration, or cases in which children have been accidentally overexposed to sex hormones before birth. Cases such as these hint that other differences in the brain's organization may exist and may provide a small push on behavior. But even where the evidence is strong, it is indirect.

No one knows for sure why the path of male development is so hazardous. Perhaps more males die because their development is full of extra complications — something must be added to the basic mix. Perhaps the mother's body is stimulated to produce a kind of antibody against a male fetus, but not against a female fetus that is genetically more similar to her.[13] Or perhaps males lack the protection of estrogen, which some researchers believe gives the developing immune system a life-preserving boost. For whatever reason, girls and women are biologically sturdier than boys and men.

At Johns Hopkins University, geneticist Kirby Smith thinks that genes on the Y (male) chromosome may be responsible for the difference in death rates between men and women. He has been studying Amish families and has found one family in which the men are all missing the same part of the Y chromosome. Men in this family outlive their female relatives by about five years; in other Amish families, it's the women who have a five or six year advantage. He sums up his study by saying, "Too much Y and you die."[14]

One day, scientists may conclude that the basic stuff of which we're made is female. But however we end up thinking about the matter, it's clear that the embryological story of creation is very different from the one told in the Bible. If one sex is really "made" from the other, it is male that is made from female. It is Adam who is made from Eve, not the other way around.

The Clock and the Brain

With all its complexities, sexual development seems simple compared to the intricacies of the unfolding human brain. This is the organ that commands the attention of the Biological Clock and whose schedule other systems in the body must accommodate. Researchers estimate that about 30 percent of our genes are expressed only in the brain — and that figure does not include the genes that turn on for only brief periods.[15]

The brain's game plan is surprising. Once it has created a lifetime supply of nerve cells, it grows not by adding new cells, but by allowing existing ones to die. And once it has forged billions of connections between the cells, it begins to destroy many of them. The brain sculpts itself once, then does it again and again, as if gray matter were a clay that hardens very slowly over the course of a life and is still malleable at the end.

Four weeks after Justin Kennedy was conceived, even before his sexual development began, the flat plate of cells destined to be his nervous system rolled into a tube and sealed itself off from other embryonic cells. Inside the tube, cells divided at a dizzying rate, producing 250,000 new offspring each minute. One end of the tube swelled and bent over; within a week it became a two-lobed brain. While this was going on, the rest of the tube transformed itself into a spinal cord, sprouting nerves that would extend throughout Justin's body. Eighteen weeks after conception, Justin's brain had the shape and structure of an adult brain. In fact, every nerve cell of his adult brain had already formed.[16]

Only primates complete their production of nerve cells, or "neurons," so early. Whether monkey, ape, or human, the fetus finishes this task during the first half of the prenatal period. In other species neurons are still forming at birth, and in a few species they continue to appear during the newborn period. But in humans, a lifetime supply is present three to four months after conception.

An extra cell division scheduled by the Biological Clock produces twice as many neurons as the brain will need — and for good reason. Once a neuron is formed, it faces a long, perilous journey to the cortex, the heavy, convoluted mantle of neurons that cover the brain. The cortex is where Justin's thinking, planning, and learning will take place, where two-thirds of his brain's neuronal mass and three-quarters of its connections will eventually be found. The challenge of reaching the cortex, settling in, and making the proper connections is so great that half the nerve cells die in the attempt.

The newborn neuron migrates along a tortuous pathway from the center of the brain to the cortex. On the way, it passes through a cellular lattice and across rapidly expanding brain areas, often making temporary connections with cells from other areas of the brain. Before it enters the cortex, the neuron locates a glial cell, which will guide it to its appointed place. Glial cells, which outnumber neurons by about ten to one, are the hard-working servants of the nervous system, feeding the neurons, escorting them, and coating them with insulation.

Each neuron follows its guide's long fiber to its destination. Like pioneers in a new land, the first neurons to make the journey take up the closest positions, building the brain from the inside out. The later a neuron begins its journey, the farther it must travel, past earlier arrivals who are already settling in. Once the neuron reaches its ordained place, it sends out fibers of its own, trying to link up with other neurons of its type, some nearby, others in more distant parts of the brain. The searching fingers of the neuron's fiber can recognize "kin" by a distinctive molecule shared only by neurons of its own class.

Those who fail to connect with other neurons will not live, and as many die as succeed. In its search for the "right" neuron, the fiber must travel through dense undergrowth made up of the questing fibers from other neurons. A neuron may perish because its extending fiber becomes lost and wanders to the wrong area of the brain. Or it may err in recognizing "kin." Or it may die of malnutrition, beaten out by other fibers in the struggle to get a share of the growth-promoting factor produced by glial cells. Even after losing half his neurons, Justin will still have a hundred billion — far more than he needs to handle the most intricate intellectual tasks. Neurons are so underworked that they have no trouble picking up the duties of those that die.

As neurons reach the cortex, the glial cells begin sheathing them with myelin, a fatty substance that insulates the fibers and keeps neural impulses traveling along the right path. Myelination is a prodigious task, one that had barely begun when Justin was born.

At birth, the cortex is far from ready to deal with complex information. Neurons are still immature and have not yet arranged themselves in neat, layered columns. Many of Justin's nerve cells are still unable to generate nerve impulses or manufacture the chemicals that carry those impulses from one neuron to the next.[17] As a result, connections between neurons are sparse.

Throughout infancy, the cortex gets heavier and thicker. Within it, new glial cells, the neurons' helpers, are being born, and those that are already present are becoming larger and changing their shapes. During the early months, some neurons are still finding their final positions in the layered columns of cells. Myelin sheaths form around the long fibers of neurons, insulating them and enabling them to pass signals quickly and efficiently. Across the brain, these fibers stretch, grow, and sprout new branches that will connect with other neurons in other parts of the brain.

When Justin is eight months old, the cortex of his brain will start to wrinkle and bunch up, so that it looks more like an adult's. The connections between his neurons, known as synapses, will reach "critical mass." He will then have more connections than he'll ever need. Yet the dense

Born "too soon," Justin needs close contact with his mother.

thicket of connections will continue to grow, only to undergo its own stringent pruning, beginning in the preschool years. Afterward, his brain will do what it's biologically designed to do: revise itself over and over again. It's all part of the surprising strategy of the Biological Clock.

Born "Too Soon"

For a creature that grows so slowly and lives so long, it's astonishing that we're born so early in the game. When Justin Kennedy entered the world after thirty-eight weeks in the womb, the size of his brain was only about 25 percent of what it will be when he's an adult. In contrast, the brains of chimpanzees, who spend thirty-four weeks in the womb, have reached 40 percent of their adult size at birth. Those of macaque monkeys, after only twenty-four weeks of gestation, have reached 65 percent.[18]

Justin's immaturity and helplessness were immediately apparent. He could breathe on his own, but do little else. His mother's nipple had to be placed near his mouth before he could eat. He could not turn over, sit up, crawl, or stand. About the time he does sit up, his chimpanzee cousins will be scampering about on the ground. It's no wonder that some researchers regard the human baby as a fetus shoved out of the womb by evolution some six to twelve months sooner than it "ought" to be born. But if our babies stayed in the womb as long as they "should" — up to twenty-one months, according to one estimate — they would have such enormous heads that they'd never make it through the birth canal.[19]

Being thrust into the world "too soon" makes babies extremely vulnerable. Why should evolution, whose interest is survival, put young humans at such risk? The most popular explanation is that the Biological Clock set the time of our birth as a compromise between two conflicting evolutionary trends. One trend fought to keep human hips small so that we could move about efficiently on two legs. The other struggled to enlarge the hips so that the big-brained human fetus could pass through. Neither was completely victorious — our hips got just large enough to let a fetus emerge and still allow us to walk. But that compromise produced a fetus that had to be born prematurely.

To reduce the risk to our premature babies — especially the danger to their brains — the Biological Clock endowed them with a reserve of fat. The babies of chimpanzees and other nonhuman primates are quite skinny compared to our own. The fat on our babies represents stored energy. To grow rapidly for most of their first year, they require a tremendous amount of energy, most of it for the brain. Human fetuses begin to store fat during the last months of pregnancy, when they gain about half a pound each week. This fat is a kind of insurance policy in case the mother's milk becomes insufficient to supply their needs.[20]

But insurance for the baby and its immature brain is even more extensive. To make sure the human fetus receives what it needs outside the womb, the Biological Clock also stores fat in the mother. Nature places such a priority on preparing the mother to nourish her baby that, whenever food becomes scarce, it directs fat to her body rather than to her fetus's. The mother gets the major share, because she will be producing milk for several years. Fat deposited on her body can later transform itself into milk for her baby.

And milk is not just milk. It's the milk of a cow, a rabbit, or a human — designed to meet the needs of newborns of its species. Cow's milk has twice the protein of human milk; rabbit's milk has six or seven times as much. These milks are designed to grow muscle mass. But human milk is high in sugar, because it's designed to feed the enormous appetite of the brain. Human breast milk is so ideally suited to a baby's needs that it seems to override other shortcomings in the environment. During the first six months, there's almost no difference in growth among adequately fed babies in developed and developing nations, despite the environmental advantages bestowed on babies in developed countries.[21]

Because breast milk is low in protein and high in sugar, it doesn't stave off hunger for long. Among our forebears, babies probably nursed two or three times an hour, sucking vigorously for a few minutes. Half an hour later, they were ready to eat again — that's the primate eating pattern.

Among contemporary humans who live the hunting-gathering existence that may be closest to that of the first *Homo sapiens*, it's still the prevailing pattern. Those repeated short bursts of feeding seem suited to bring the brain on line quickly. By the time a child is four, about the age when hunter-gatherers wean their infants, the brain is nearing the end of its growth, but the slower-growing bones and muscles have only reached the halfway point.

The composition of human milk tells us that the first order of biological business for Justin Kennedy is his developing brain. His birth was timed to occur when his cranium was still small enough to fit through the narrow passage of his mother's birth canal. Now his brain will far outpace the rest of his body in reaching adult size. In the Biological Clock's schedule, we find a parallel between Justin's story and that of the entire human species. In both, it's the brain that dominates the plot.

Indeed, much of the story of our species is hidden away in the intricate timetable of the Biological Clock — in the oldest form of memory we have. The Kennedy family stories go back hundreds of years, but the biological events that build our bodies go back millions. The Biological Clock's memory goes back farther than home videos or photo albums, farther than the invention of writing, farther even than the beginning of speech. In evolutionary time, it's only yesterday that we, as a human family, began to open this clock and explore our most ancient recollections of life. As we probe their complexity, as we compare our clock to that of other species, we will discover ever more about the origin of the biological seasons of life.

2

THE SOCIAL   *The Social*

STORY OF INFANCY   *Clock*

At birth, Justin Kennedy's path began to diverge from that of other newborns. He entered a specific time — not 100,000 B.C., but 1987 — and a particular place — not a rolling plain in Africa, but one in Pennsylvania. He was born into a family with two parents, not one, a family that is thriving, not struggling. He became a member of a clan with its own history, its own stories and traditions, its own place on earth.

Justin's journey along the life course will follow the road laid out by the culture of his time and place, for each society has its own definition of the life span and its own placement of milestones along the way. Laid over the biological timetable that measures Justin's life is a social timetable, which we call the Social Clock. In each life, it begins to be heard at birth.

The Biological Clock builds a body, but the Social Clock shapes a person for society. It represents a culture's way of saying "when" — when to go to school, when to leave home, when to marry, when to have children, when the nest should empty, when to retire. These "whens" are age norms, the equivalent of timing genes in the Biological Clock. The norms exert their power every day, in gossip, films, and well-meant advice: "she's too young to have a baby"; "he's too old to be living at home"; "why don't you act your age?" We measure our lives against these norms, deciding whether our progress through the seasons is "on time" or not.

In the distant history of our species, the Social Clock must have evolved alongside the Biological Clock, the product of the various cultures our ancestors created as they formed cooperative groups. But unlike the settings of the Biological Clock, those of the Social Clock were more easily changed. Humans fashioned them; humans could therefore refashion them. And so we find that the social seasons of life have differed dramatically from time to time and place to place, while the biological game plan has remained essentially the same.

Bernice Neugarten, a specialist in human development at the University of Chicago and originator of the term "Social Clock," believes that its impact is stronger in the first half of life than in the second. Young children may have no idea what an "age norm" or a "Social Clock" is, but they do know they're supposed to act their age. "Mothers and fathers and siblings say, 'You're not a baby anymore, you shouldn't need a bottle. You should learn to drink from a cup.' Most infants don't understand those words, but they get the notion. These are the ways you begin, in the first years of life, to communicate with a child that there are patterns of behavior appropriate to one's age. As one grows, those expectations change," says Neugarten.

"In the school years the Social Clock is very strict. Children come into school at a given age. They're expected to progress through a school system on the basis of age. And everybody knows that first grade leads to second grade, and you better make it into second grade or you'll be a failure." The Social Clock ticks just as loudly as the school years come to an end. "The whole notion of being on time comes down very hard on people as they make the transition from adolescence into adulthood. There's a time to finish school, and that's compelling. There's a time to get settled in a job. And there's a time — particularly, I think, for women, although it's broader than it used to be — to marry and have a child."[1] But, says Neugarten, once the reproductive years are over, the Social Clock follows the lead of the Biological Clock and quiets down.

The Social Clock sets the rhythm of life in a particular time and place. Sometimes it ticks in synchrony with the Biological Clock; sometimes it doesn't. But when the Social Clock is out of sync with the Biological, it's always possible for a society to reset it. In the United States, one generation's views of the "right" time for life's events were set by the Great Depression, another generation's by the booming economy after World War II, and a third's by the social upheavals centering around the war in Vietnam and the civil rights movement. The picture shared by a generation affects our personal lives as strongly as our genes do. As an Arab proverb puts it, "A man is more like his times than like his father."

The Womb of the Family

As two-month-old Justin gazes up at his mother, he is unaware that he's a human baby — let alone that he is a boy, born into an American farm family toward the close of the twentieth century. He doesn't know anything about his family's history or the history of his community, much less the history of his species. He doesn't know about the world of computers and space satellites and nuclear weapons that he will enter. He doesn't know about the cows and the corn that provide his family's livelihood. He can tell his father from his mother, but he probably doesn't remember the difference until the next time he sees them together.

Justin certainly can't hear the ticking of the Social Clock, although it's already beginning to influence him through his family's actions and expectations. His mother and father have decided whether he'll be fed on a rigid schedule or whenever he demands to eat, when he'll be weaned and how soon he'll eat solid food. If Justin's parents had been hunter-gatherers, he would have been in almost constant contact with his mother, carried in a sling at her side or on her back during the day and nestling close to her at night. But Justin is a child of the twentieth century and has his own bed and his own room. From the first few hours in the hospital nursery, he began to discover that his wants weren't always immediately met, and that he must spend long stretches of time without the comfort of another heart beating close to his.

Justin left the warm, watery world of the womb for a cold, gaseous environment, and adjusting to that new atmosphere and the sharp drop in temperature were the first tasks he had to solve by himself. When he arrived, all his senses were working — though he was probably much better at detecting changes in touch, taste, smell, and hearing than he was at perceiving differences in things he saw. For the first few weeks, everything in his world was blurred.

As a human baby, Justin left his mother's womb "too soon." His well-being, therefore, depends on people around him, on the social womb of his family. It will take months for Justin to begin holding up his end of social activities, but his parents, Janice and Jeffrey, don't mind. From the very beginning, parents in our culture treat babies as if they are intelligent people who understand the world and have intentions. It's fortunate for infants that parents are so easily fooled, because unless babies are treated as if they're already social creatures who share their parents' goals, they might never become people in their own right.[2]

Justin's earliest lessons in social graces come at feeding time. When nursing, he eats in bursts and pauses, sucking for about ten seconds, resting about the same length of time, then sucking again. This feeding pattern is universal among members of our species and exclusive to us — researchers have found it in no other animal. Whenever Justin stops sucking, his mother jiggles the nipple in his mouth, as all human mothers do. But, like all babies, Justin won't begin to suck until his mother stops jiggling the nipple. It's a seemingly inborn routine that researchers have been unable to explain as any aspect of feeding. Babies don't use the pauses to breathe, swallow, or rest. Mothers don't need them to let milk down. The pause/jiggle/suck sequence may provide a way of laying the first bricks in the foundation of language, a lesson in turn-taking that is essential to communication. The sequence may also be a lesson for the mother, because it teaches her to adapt her own behavior to the natural rhythms of her child.

The fascinating feature at the heart of this interaction, says developmental psychologist Kenneth Kaye, is the mother's misunderstanding of the pause.[3] She assumes that her baby has stopped sucking because of drowsiness or wandering attention. So she jiggles the nipple to get the sucking started. In truth, if she didn't jiggle, the baby would begin sucking a little sooner. But her misunderstanding — a misunderstanding shared by all human mothers — is essential if the social lesson is to be learned on schedule.

Because Justin's mother feeds him, provides most of his care, and is with him continually in these early months, a special closeness is developing between them. When Justin was only a week old, Janice spoke of the hours she spent in fascinated observation. "I just like watching him. He'll go from one laugh to a wrinkly forehead and pucker his lips. I like watching that. And then he's got a swirl in the back of his head, just one big swirl of hair. I play with that a lot. Now his fingers are getting fat. It's hard to think he can change that much, but he does."

Psychoanalyst Margaret Mahler saw the relationship between mother and infant as a unique form of symbiosis. She would say that Justin's dependence on his mother and his inability to satisfy his own needs are so strong that, throughout much of the first half-year, he feels that he is literally a part of her. It's not just Justin and Janice, but Justin/Janice, a symbiotic state in which Justin has no sense of self or identity apart from his mother. Justin's hatching into a person in his own right will be a slow process, governed by another timepiece that counts off the days in our lives — the Psychological Clock.

It will also be guided by Justin's family. Whenever young Justin looks at his mother or father, they feel impelled to respond. Even if they're told to remain impassive, it's almost impossible for them to avoid greeting their baby's gaze with raised eyebrows, widened eyes, a slightly open mouth, and, often, a big smile. The greeting usually merges into the social lessons of playtime. From Justin's very first day, his parents have treated him as if he understood what they said to him, and they interpret his facial expressions, small noises, and shifts of gaze as thoughtful replies. Justin's smiles seem to say that he understands their words. His frowns, cries, and fretting seem to say that he's puzzled by their words or actions.[4]

Play between a parent and a child takes the form of a *pas de deux*, as if two expert dancers were going through the practiced steps of an intricate ballet. The parent reacts so quickly to the baby's moves that it seems impossible for the movements to be the result of studied, rational decisions. Psychologists who have spent thousands of hours watching parents play with their tiny babies have been struck by the seemingly automatic adjustments made by both parents, even during their first meeting with their firstborn child.[5] The parental role consists of lengthy gazes into the baby's eyes, exaggerated facial expressions, and similarly exaggerated vocalizations — spoken in a high-pitched voice when the baby seems to enjoy the interchange, but in a slowly falling, soothing pitch when the baby begins to fuss.

Many of these expressions and sounds are imitations of the baby. Kaye says that nature has made it easy for babies to learn the rules of the social game by providing them with a biological mirror and echo, one that is especially easy to see and hear. If the baby's eyes widen, the parent's eyes bulge; if the baby smiles, the parent grins; if the baby frowns slightly, the parent scowls. And if the baby coos or gurgles, the parent responds with speech.

During games, the parents' movements and words take the form of simple, repetitive patterns that are easy for the baby to classify and predict. The baby has some control over this dance. When the game gets too exciting, the overstimulated baby looks away and stops responding. The pause and the escape from eye contact gives the baby a chance to calm down and figure out what's been going on. Most parents respond immediately to the baby's signal. If they insist on continuing the game, the baby will frown, and then cry.

Over his first year, as Justin learns to be social, playtime will change. Slowly, he'll begin to take an active role in the game, and eventually he'll initiate the game himself. He'll learn to share, whether by rolling the ball back to Daddy or pulling a diaper over his face to start a game of peek-a-boo. This will be a sign that he understands that you wait for your turn — as long as you don't have to wait too long.

To absorb the settings of the Social Clock, Justin must first become a social being. If his mother fosters this development in the intimate world of nursing, his father does so in the extended world of the farm. Jeffrey has already introduced his son to some animals. "We take his hand and wipe it on the cow so he can feel the softness of the cow," he said when Justin was five months old. "The other day when we had him at the barn, it looked like he was petting the cow. But he grabbed hold of her ear. The cow just turned and looked at him. I think at first he was maybe a little frightened. But I just hope he's starting to feel at ease with them."

Justin is being nourished in the social womb of his family. In years to come, he will learn a lot more about being a Kennedy in Butler, Pennsylvania, at the end of the twentieth century. He will absorb the customs, values, and age norms of a rural American culture. He will come to hear for himself the steady ticking of its Social Clock.

Social Seasons of Life

The "stages" of life that the Social Clock lays out for Justin will appear quite natural to him, as if they always were and always will be. But in reality these stages are human constructions, the products of one culture's history and the economic and social forces of its present. And they change as the culture in question changes.

All cultures seem to recognize infancy, and most see a difference between adulthood and old age. Certainly, in every society, people are aware that infants cannot care for themselves, that children cannot reproduce, and that adults in their later decades are growing old. But society does not always institutionalize its awareness that people's needs and capabilities differ from one stage to the next. When society takes official notice of a life stage, it sets the stage apart with laws, institutions, ceremonies, or customs.

Among some traditional Eskimo societies, once a child survives infancy, there are simply boys and men, girls and women. The notion of "adolescence" or "middle age" doesn't exist. "Old age" is not a matter of chronology, law, or ritual; it stands for "too frail or sickly to keep on working." That means that men usually reach old age before women, because of the physical stamina needed for hunting and fishing in the Arctic.

The life course also differs for the sexes in Kenya, where the Gusii divide a woman's life into five stages, but a man's into only four.[6] Both go through infancy, but once they are no longer babies, each gender has its own terms for life's stages. From the time she can talk until about age seven, a Gusii female is known as an "uncircumcised girl." After the circumcision ceremony, in which the clitoris is removed, she's known as a "circumcised girl," a stage that lasts until she marries, usually at fifteen. The next stage, that of "married woman," endures until her first child is married. She then becomes a "female elder," with much wider social privileges, even though she may be giving birth for another decade.

For a Gusii man, the life course has no "marriage" stage. He moves from infant to "uncircumcised boy"; at about age ten, he is circumcised and becomes a "circumcised boy warrior." The boy warrior marries at twenty, but remains a boy warrior until his first child is married. Then he's promoted directly to "male elder."

Among the Gusii, the settings of the Social Clock have shifted in a dramatic fashion. The circumcision ceremony, which occurs today around seven for girls and ten for boys, used to be a puberty rite that took place only after sexual maturity — during the early to mid-teens for girls and during the late teens for boys. But that was during the precolonial era, a time when the main duty of the circumcised male was to take up his spear and fight. As Gusii society changed when it encountered Western cultures, the ceremony was pushed to a younger and younger age.

Among the Masai, who are neighbors of the Gusii, a different device keeps track of social time. Each Masai is a member of an "age set" that moves through the life course in lockstep.[7] Initiations into an age set are held only about once every five years, so a boy might be anywhere from fourteen to eighteen when he joins his cohort. Before that time, he is "uninitiated." During the induction ceremony, a boy is circumcised, his head is shaved, and he gets a shield, a spear, and a sword. Officially, he becomes a "man" and a "warrior," but actually his manhood is in some ways a protracted adolescence. For the next fifteen years, he is considered old enough to fight and have sexual relations, but not old enough to marry, to own cattle, or to escape the supervision of older tribe members.

When the young man's age set is about thirty, the members are initiated as "junior elders." After this promotion, the men turn to domestic concerns: marrying, raising children, and accumulating a cattle herd. This makes thirty (give or take a few years) the threshold of full adulthood. After another fifteen years, the age set goes through another series of rituals and is promoted to the rank of "senior elders," the group that runs society and controls the entire system of age ranks. The age set's final move comes about fifteen years later, when the few surviving members hand over the reins to the next age set and retire from public life. Among Masai men, old age, when men are considered authorities in matters of tradition but have no power, comes some time between fifty-nine and sixty-four.

Masai women's social roles are limited to wife and mother. In a curious arrangement, they become full adults much earlier than their male counterparts. Within a few years of their puberty rituals, they marry junior elders and assume their full social roles. But they do not become senior elders the way men do.

This view of life is linear. Other societies picture life as a circle that returns in some ways to its point of origin, like the hands on a clock face. Among the Akwe-Shavante of Brazil, who have age sets like the Masai, men's lives take such a course. When they relinquish social control to the next age set, they don't move along life's path into a respected old age. Instead, they re-enter the adult cycle and assume many of the duties of their youth, such as helping junior-grade men build their huts.

All over the world, in the rituals and institutions of various societies, we see different pictures of life — as a line or a circle or a square or spiral, as going up or down or straight ahead. Societies also differ in their definitions of when "human" life begins — and when it ends. Some claim life begins at the moment of biological conception, but others believe that children aren't even worth naming until they have survived smallpox. Australian aborigines think of the unborn as the spirits of departed ancestors who have entered the wombs of women. Hindus regard them as the spirits of persons or animals who have lived in former incarnations. The Hidasta Indians of western North Dakota believe that the spirits of babies live in the nearby hills, and when a baby decides it is time to be born, its spirit comes down from the mountain and enters a woman.

Among some peoples, the dead are believed merely to have entered a new season, to have surrendered one set of rights and duties for another. Anthropologist Ralph Linton wrote of the Tanala of Madagascar that the dead remain an integral part of the clan. "They must be informed of all important events, invited to all clan ceremonies, and remembered at every meal. In return they allow themselves to be consulted, take an active and helpful interest in the affairs of the community, and act as highly efficient guardians of the group's mores."[8] In other societies, no distinction at all is drawn between dead ancestors and living elders; both must be honored and obeyed.[9] The last setting on the Social Clock has proven to be as varied as the first.

The number of "stages" on the clock's face has been equally varied, as we clearly see in art, literature, philosophy, and religion. Confucius listed six milestones along the path of life; the Talmud recognized fourteen. In the sixth century B.C., Solon, the Athenian statesman and lawgiver, saw the life course in terms of ten stages, each seven years in length. During the Middle Ages, philosophers linked the stages of life to the seven known planets, the twelve signs of the zodiac, or the four humours of the body: blood, phlegm, black bile, and yellow bile. Ever since humans began to wonder about their journey through life, they have been trying to find a sequence in it. It matters little how many "stages" or "seasons" they find, or what names they give to the settings of the Social Clock. What matters is the fact that the numbering and the naming go on.

The Seasons in the West

How the Social Clock is set depends in large measure on how long people live in a particular time and place. And while the biological potential for longevity hasn't changed in the eons of our existence, the number of people who achieve it has.

Two thousand years ago, a Roman baby could expect to live between twenty and twenty-five years.[10] That doesn't mean that all Romans lived until their early twenties and died suddenly at twenty-five. The early demise of the typical Roman was predicted primarily by the enormous death rate among babies and children. Once a Roman made it to the age of twenty-five, life expectancy increased enormously. Nor should we suppose that life expectancy in ancient Rome, which wasn't much greater than that of little *Australopithecus* millions of years ago, represented an historical high for its time. In fact, one estimate leaves Roman life expectancy precisely where it stood for our hunter-gatherer ancestors 100,000 years ago.[11]

Records that exist today document a steady rise in life expectancy in the Western world over the last several centuries. In the eighteenth century, English babies could expect to make it to their thirty-fifth birthday, although babies in the American colonies faced a grimmer future: they could expect to live no longer than twenty-eight years. By 1900, when Justin Kennedy's great-great-grandfather Harold was a two-year-old, life expectancy in America had reached forty-seven years. And Americans born when Justin was can expect to blow out seventy-five candles on their birthday cakes.[12]

Most of these gains in longevity have resulted from the survival of more infants and children into adulthood. The striking effect of death at an early age becomes apparent when we look at those New England colonists of the early 1700s who had a life expectancy of twenty-eight years. Massachusetts colonists who reached the age of fifty could expect to live until seventy-one, and those who were still alive at sixty could expect to reach seventy-five. But very few of them made it to the end of their fifth or sixth decade.

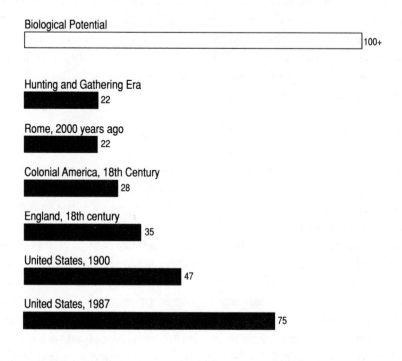

Life expectancy at selected times and places. Ages before 1900 are approximate.

Our own century's record jump in life expectancy has affected females more than males. Fewer women are dying in childbirth today than in 1900, and it seems that improved health conditions have allowed the biological superiority of women to show itself. At the turn of the century, a baby girl could expect to live only two or three years longer than a baby boy. Today, her counterpart has an advantage of more than seven years. Had Justin been a girl, she could have expected seventy-nine years of life. As a boy, he can look forward to only seventy-two.

Life expectancy statistics provide a striking demonstration of the way the time and place of our birth affect our individual lives. They also point to a powerful reason for changes in the settings of the Social Clock. "I think one could make the case that people born in the 1990s will go through more seasons of life than their great-grandparents," says Bernice Neugarten.[13] History tends to support her view. Though scholars don't always agree on how people of a particular era thought about the stages of life, it's clear that the number of stages has increased.

During the Middle Ages in Europe, infancy was a clearly recognized stage, but it went on for an astoundingly long time. People made little distinction among infants, toddlers, and young children, perhaps because their existence was so tentative. One out of every three babies died before its first birthday.[14] Once they were out of swaddling clothes, youngsters were allowed to play undisturbed with their toys, primarily in the care and company of women. Until the first stage of life came to a close at the age of six or seven, children were generally ignored by men, the church, the state, and the world.[15]

Those who survived infancy were thrown into adult life. Children and adults wore the same clothes, ate the same food, played the same games, shared the same jokes, and worked at the same tasks. Some scholars argue that a stage of childhood hardly existed. As education claimed more of children's time, they were increasingly separated from adults, but not until the nineteenth century did parents begin to center family life around their offspring and regard them as people with a special status of their own. It's probably more than coincidence that during this period of increased interest in children, infant and child mortality began to drop. During the eighteenth and nineteenth centuries, food production increased throughout the Western world, and more food meant better nutrition and higher resistance to disease. Life became even brighter for urban children when cities began purifying water, constructing sewers, and pasteurizing milk. As more children survived, the emerging middle class started consciously limiting the size of its families. Their new prosperity meant that fewer of their children had to work. But the joy of a stage of childhood was primarily a middle-class joy. Not until the twentieth century did child-labor laws free working- and lower-class children from the mills and the mines.

It took Western societies much longer to recognize adolescence, despite its demarcation by medieval philosophers. Rousseau saw life after puberty as a special period, but the modern concept of adolescence did not begin to develop until children were taken from the labor market and segregated in schools. Once schooling began to extend past the age of puberty, at least for the middle class, the need arose for a special stage in which young people

Tree of the Twelve Ages of Life by Ulrich of Lilienfeld, Concordantia Caritatis, 1351. For most people in medieval society, there were fewer stages of life. The Pierpont Morgan Library, New York

The Life and Age of Woman. Currier and Ives lithograph, 1848.
Museum of the City of New York

were past childhood, but not yet adults. Soon, an affluent society was requiring youngsters to stay in school until they were fifteen or sixteen and passing laws that prohibited their employment in most jobs. The stage of adolescence was now official.

Adults, of course, have always been with us. The word comes from the Latin for "grown" and seems to have entered English before the middle of the sixteenth century, but the *Oxford English Dictionary* can find no use of the word "adulthood" until 1870. Like the Gusii of Kenya, the people of the Western world spoke of "manhood" and "womanhood," as if referring to two different species.

As life expectancy increased in the twentieth century, so did the number of adult seasons of life. First, we reset the Social Clock to toll the passage into "old age." During the nineteenth century, no arbitrary marker set this stage apart from the rest of the life course. People usually worked as long as they were able, because pensions were virtually nonexistent. Those who could not work were either supported by the family or had to depend on the kindness of strangers.[16] Most went to the poor house — the county or state home for the aged. In 1935, we institutionalized old age by setting age sixty-five as a marker of eligibility for the new Social Security pension. Society had become wealthy enough to allow older workers the resources that would permit a period of protected leisure. Compulsory retirement ushered them into a new season of life: "old age."

With old age established, middle age followed close behind. Families got smaller, children were born closer together, and we suddenly realized that a new stage of life had developed. At the turn of the century, the average couple had less than two years together after the last child left home. By 1970, the average couple spent thirteen years in their empty nest. We began to call this period "middle age" and distinguished it from the first part of adulthood, which we christened "young adulthood."

In the past few decades, two more adult stages have begun to take shape. One is a period of "youth" that spans the years between high-school gradu-ation and the assumption of full adult responsibilities. The length of this stage is dictated by the demands of schooling, so for some it ends at twenty or twenty-two, but for others it may last until twenty-seven or twenty-eight. Today, youth is primarily a stage of middle-class life, but that's the path by which childhood and adolescence gained recognition. Its spread and ultimate recognition depend on the prosperity and educational demands of society.

The other new stage is emerging at the other end of the life span. Large numbers of people are retiring before the age of sixty-five, and they're stay-ing in such good health that it's hard to tell them from the middle-aged. They're independent, active in political and community life, and most have enough money to live comfortably. The period of old age has been transformed so radically that researchers, starting with Neugarten, have begun to partition it into two separate segments. They suggest that we call all those past retirement age who are healthy and vigorous "young-old," and those who are frail and sickly "old-old." Some of these researchers place the dividing line at eighty-five, but in practice, the distinction has become disconnected from chronological age. A person who is playing golf at eighty-five is still young-old, but a sixty-five-year-old who needs assistance to handle the chores of daily life is old-old.

Perhaps there will be eight recognized stages of life as the United States enters the twenty-first century. Perhaps we will talk about infants, children, adolescents, youth, young adults, the middle-aged, the young-old, and the old-old the way we talk about spring, summer, winter, and fall. But don't bet on it. The social seasons of life are constantly changing, and in a society as large and complex as ours, there are always many clocks sounding varia-tions on life's Big Ben. There is one clock for men and another for women, one for the city and another for the country, one for each of the social classes. But no matter how age norms vary, it's clear that the Social Clock is ticking longer than it did at the beginning of the century, and announcing the arrival of more seasons of life.

Infants Past and Present

Justin Kennedy is an "infant," and he couldn't have picked a better time or place to be one. Biologically, babies are what they've always been; but, socially, they've changed. Their very helplessness seems to invite extremes of definition. When there are too many of them, and when it's uncertain whether they'll live very long, they may be ignored or even destroyed. When fewer are born and more survive, their status tends to improve. Like the very old, the very young are powerless to resist whatever value society places on them.

All cultures recognize a season of infancy, but they mark off the boundaries of that season in different ways. On a distant Pacific atoll, babies of the Ifaluk people are neither named nor referred to until they're about a week old. Once it is clear that they will survive, they get a name and a social identity — and infancy begins. The period lasts until the age of two, and only after that time — when they are weaned, walking, and talking — do the Ifaluk say that youngsters can learn. The Northern Cheyenne also see infancy as precarious and infants as "empty of mind," but they don't give children names or identities until they learn to talk, usually at about two.[17] Among the Kipsigis of Kenya, infancy lasts until a younger sibling comes along to push a child out of the favored position. This usually happens at about two, but it may be earlier or later.[18] In a majority of societies, infancy lasts about two years, with speech or sometimes mobility setting the time of graduation.

Yet in medieval Europe, infancy lasted six or seven years — until the child began to get permanent teeth. As thirteenth-century authorities described the period, "In this age that which is born is called an infant, which is as good as saying not talking, because in this age it cannot talk well or form its words perfectly, for its teeth are not yet well arranged or firmly implanted."[19] This definition comes from a time when many babies died in infancy, when children were snatched away by typhoid, dysentery, plague, tuberculosis, influenza, or smallpox. The very precariousness of early life may explain why the world paid little attention to the very young, except to baptize them as soon as possible in the hope of saving their souls.

Today, we would describe such children as "neglected." But throughout history babies have suffered a worse fate. Letters, literature, documents, records of every kind indicate that for thousands of years infanticide was widely practiced. Unwanted children — whether illegitimate, deformed, or "merely" female — were simply disposed of. Until the fourth century A.D., there was little opposition to the custom of abandoning babies or deliberately destroying them.[20] Even the moral theologians of the early Christian church were willing to tolerate the practice. They seemed to regard it as inevitable, given the circumstances that surrounded birth in the West for nearly two thousand years.[21]

Historian Lawrence Stone of Princeton University believes that when we consider those circumstances, the seemingly casual disposal of infants becomes more understandable. "It has to be remembered that these abandonments occurred in a society where poverty was so extreme that many families were incapable of feeding and clothing all their children; where contraception was virtually unknown, and if known, was regarded as morally sinful to employ; where abortifacients were not only banned by the Church, but also often mixed with mercury and other heavy metals, with disastrous and often fatal results for the mothers. By and large, there were no known means, except sexual abstention, for the prevention of impregnation and childbirth. There were always more children born to the poor than their parents could or would support. The only solutions available were deliberate infanticide, including exposure or willful malnutrition, or abandonment in some public place on the off-chance that someone with large resources or some material use for the infant would pick it up and feed it."[22]

What we also forget when reading accounts of infanticide is the low value that ancient cultures placed on individual life — any life. In societies with an average life expectancy of less than twenty-five years, death is a constant companion, and the chances of an infant surviving the first year are no better than even. In ages past, it was important that the family survive, but not that a particular child live to carry on the line.

Yet when parents in these cultures kept their babies, they lavished love upon them. Infanticide was common in ancient Greece, but throughout the pages of Greek literature, small children are fondled, kissed, hugged, and embraced. When the young daughter of Plutarch, the Greek biographer, died, he wrote his wife a moving letter. "Our affection for children so young has a poignancy all its own; the delight that it gives is quite pure and free from all anger or reproach. . . . Just as she was herself the most delightful thing in the world to embrace, to see, to hear, so too must the thought of her live with us and be our companion, bringing with it joy in greater measure than it brings sorrow."[23]

Today we regard infants much as Plutarch did. Their existence is less precarious than it was in the past; we need give birth to fewer to insure that some will survive. The practices of contraception and abortion have radically reduced the proportion of newborns in the population, and our affluence allows us to indulge those we have. We're horrified by child abuse, and we find infanticide incomprehensible.

As the ranks of infants have shrunk, our views of their abilities have expanded. Despite the helplessness and immaturity of our babies at birth, we have come to see them as extraordinarily competent. Fifty years ago, our views of what infants were capable of were closer to those of the Cheyenne and the Ifaluk. We believed that infants were unresponsive, that they entered the world as blind as newborn kittens — at the mercy of the meaningless stimuli that assailed them. Now we believe that even in early infancy babies are curious and actively seek out stimulation.

Psychologists have had much to do with this revolution in our thinking. They've discovered that babies can tell you a lot — if you know how to ask. These days researchers are "asking" with television cameras and computers that monitor a baby's eye movements, and with pacifiers connected to polygraphs that record when babies start to suck and when they stop. Experiments, some of them controversial, suggest that at three days infants may be able to identify the sound of their mother's voice;[24] that at one week breast-fed babies can recognize their mother's smell;[25] and that at six weeks babies can learn to suck in a pattern that will clear up a movie screen so they can watch the picture.[26]

Experiments have even been designed for fetuses. At the University of North Carolina, psychologists Anthony DeCasper and Melanie Spence arranged for mothers to read aloud twice each day during the last six weeks of pregnancy.[27] The story was always the same — a three-minute excerpt from Dr. Seuss's tale, *The Cat in the Hat*. When the babies were three days old, a pacifier connected to a tape recorder was placed in their mouth. Vigorous sucking kept a tape of the familiar story playing, but weak sucking brought on a tape of a story they'd never heard before. Babies seemed to remember the sound patterns of the familiar story. At least, they adjusted their sucking to keep it playing — something that newborns never exposed to the prenatal story failed to do.

In just a few decades, the "helpless" infant has become the "competent" infant. Zealous experimenters are now calling young babies "information-gathering machines." As the twentieth century comes to a close, a creature that is born "too soon" is seen by some as an alert perceiver of the world, with sensitive social and emotional qualities and considerable intellectual abilities.[28] Infants haven't changed, but the social definition of the season of infancy has.

Bonding and Attachment

At nine months, Justin couldn't care less about the social construction of the life course, about changes in the setting of the Social Clock, or about revolutions in our definition of infancy. His social concerns are far more immediate and intimate. They have a lot to do with his mother.

Janice has noticed a change in him. "If I turn to walk out of the room and don't take him with me, he gets upset," she says. It's getting a little harder to leave him with a grandmother or a baby-sitter, and when Janice has been away and returns, she's greeted as she never was before. "When I come home and he sees me, that's when it hits him that mum's been gone so long. He gets all smiles and he's real excited to see me."

Out of the *pas de deux* that Justin has been dancing with his mother has come a strong emotional tie that psychologists call "attachment." This tie develops to specific individuals that Justin now recognizes as his principal caregivers. Although the tie is critical to a species that's born so early in its development, it is not present at birth. The attachment has to be formed, and because of regularities in the Biological Clock, it's formed on the same schedule around the world.

Social relationships run two ways. While babies become "attached" to those who care for them, caregivers "bond" to babies. The distinction is important, because the two sides of the relationship develop on different timetables. On both sides, the formation of the emotional tie is a lengthy process, but the parents' bonds are firmly in place long before the baby seems to find the parents much more than enjoyable playmates.

Psychologist Michael Lamb, chief of the section on social and emotional development at the National Institute of Child Health and Development, has been studying the mother-child relationship for more than two decades.[29] He reminds us that parents probably begin bonding to their child long before birth. They think and dream about the growing baby, and feel it kick against the wall of the mother's womb. When at last the child is born, fantasy becomes reality and the process accelerates.

In the 1970s, Marshall Klaus and John Kennell, a pair of Chicago physicians, presented evidence suggesting that close contact in the first hour or so after birth fostered a mother's emotional bond with her baby.[30] Early contact seemed to make better, more affectionate mothers out of poor, inner-city women. Klaus and Kennell concluded that improved mothering came about because of a "critical period" just after birth, when a mother was primed with hormones to respond to the sight, feel, and smell of her baby. Separating mother and child during this period fostered child abuse and neglect, they warned — or at least set the stage for mediocre mothering.

Does it? Such critical periods clearly exist in cows, sheep, and other herd animals. If separated from their offspring for the first few hours after birth, mothers cannot recognize their babies and invariably reject them. Unless rescued by a friendly farmer, the rejected calf or lamb dies, because neither the parent nor any other cow will allow it to eat. For herd animals, the quick bonding process is essential to survival. Calves and lambs can walk within an hour of birth and often stray from their mothers' side, mixing with other newborns in the herd. One calf looks like another to the mothers, so the bond — which depends on smell and taste — evolved.

But such a critical period serves no obvious, and perhaps no useful purpose in human beings. Among our ancestors, mother and baby were never apart. The human baby cannot stray, and should a separation occur, the human mother could recognize her baby by sight. Perhaps that's why later research failed to support the early, enthusiastic claims about bonding; study after study either showed no change in a mother's behavior or found trifling changes, unrelated to mothering or to the findings of other studies. Today most researchers have concluded that, although socializing with newborns has helped to turn a cold, forbidding medical ordeal into a welcome human experience, early contact has little or no effect on the behavior of either parent.[31]

Justin's side of the connection to his mother — his attachment to her — took six or seven months to form. In the first few weeks of life, he showed no particular preference for either of his parents and was as content being held by a stranger as by his mother. From about the second month, he preferred his parents, but was not unhappy when they left. Their existence quickly slipped from his fleeting memory. If he cried when put down, he wasn't fussing because he missed his parents, but because he wanted the social contact to continue. Early in his second month he began to smile; it was a way of saying, "Stay with me. This is fun." But at two or three months Justin was still content to stay with anyone who was reasonably adept at caring for him and willing to socialize.

At nine months, peek-a-
boo with Dad.

Over the months Justin learned that he could count on his mother to be
there when he needed her. She responded to his cries of distress and his
social overtures. Often, she met his needs before he was certain just what it
was he wanted. While all that social growth was going on, Justin was gradually learning that people and objects still exist when they're out of sight.
Once he understood that his mother would come back after she disappeared, his attachment to her solidified. Normally, this happens at about
eight months.

The signs of attachment were clear. Justin began to crawl after Janice
when she left the room. If kept from following her, he sometimes cried — or
at least became visibly upset. Researchers call this anguish "separation distress." Before long, Justin started to become uneasy around strangers, looking anxiously at his mother to see whether the enormous giant looming
over him was "okay" or dangerous. Researchers call this uncertainty
"stranger wariness." It may be no coincidence that these feelings of discomfort appear at about the time when most babies begin creeping. Such built-
in distress may have helped our ancestors survive, because it helps babies
avoid situations and predators that might endanger their lives. It keeps
them from straying too far from their mother on forays to explore the world
around them.

Indeed, evolution has done all it can to foster a closeness between parent
and child. Few people can look at babies — even kittens or pup-
pies — without wanting to cuddle them. The combination of a large forehead and foreshortened facial features seems to evoke this response. It's so
automatic that ethologists call the appearance of a young baby a "releasing

"It's nice to know he misses me."

stimulus," because it "releases" the adult's tendency to care for the helpless infant.

The timing of attachment suggests something about the best time to place a baby with adoptive parents. For the easiest, smoothest transition to a new mother and father, babies should probably move in before they're six months old. As Lamb points out, "If the baby is forming its first attachment by six, seven, eight months of age, then a move before that point allows the baby to establish its first relationship with the person it's going to be with permanently. If the placement comes after that point, the baby may have to go through a process of grieving over the loss of the first attachment figure before it's possible to invest emotionally in a new one."[32]

But babies are resilient. Though it may take time, they can recover from the breaking of one attachment or from a delay in forming their first attachment. Babies who are adopted by the time they are ten months old become toddlers who cannot be distinguished from youngsters who have always lived with their biological parents.[33] Lamb reports many instances of successful adoptions among youngsters who spent their first year in an institution or were passed from one foster home to another. Once they found themselves in a loving atmosphere, they rapidly established strong, secure attachments to their new parents.

Like Justin, two-thirds of all babies become securely attached to their mothers. When they seek her out, they know they'll get a warm reception. And so they pay special attention to her comings and goings. If she leaves for any reason, they make a point of greeting her on her return, starting some kind of social interaction. And when they're upset, they want her. No other comfort is so consoling, no other snuggle so soothing to a tired or frightened baby.

There are evolutionary reasons why attachment occurs when it does and why the schedule allows for variation, but they matter little to Janice Kennedy. "I must be doing something right," she says. "I mean, I'd hate to come home and have him think, oh, it's just mum. It's nice to know he misses me."

3

THE PSYCHOLOGICAL   *The Psychological*

STORY OF INFANCY   *Clock*

On a hot afternoon in August, the strains of "Happy Birthday" echo through the farmhouse where the Kennedy clan has gathered to celebrate Justin's first year of life. As tow-headed young Justin stares wide-eyed from his highchair, his father Jeff approaches with a yellow and blue frosted cake, walking carefully to protect the single flickering flame. Once the cake is in front of him and the candle's blown out, Justin dives in — scooping up great handfuls, squishing the frosting between his chubby fingers, and smearing it across his face.

Later, all washed and his presents inspected, Justin toddles outside, his bare feet carrying him across the sunny lawn to where great-grandfather Francis waits in the cool shade of a maple tree. Beside him is a plastic horse, large enough for Justin to ride. "Look what we got!" says Francis, swinging his great-grandson onto the blue saddle. "Who's gonna have more fun, me or you?" It's a hard question to answer, but a good one to ask, because Justin is now a *person* whose reactions make playtime fun for young and old alike.

The realization that he is a being in his own right has come slowly to Justin. The process has been called the "psychological birth" of the infant by Margaret Mahler.[1] What is born is a self — a self that will construct its own world, become the keeper of its own time, and eventually write its own story. We cannot pinpoint the day, the week, or even the month when the self appears, but when it does, the Psychological Clock begins to tick.

The term "Psychological Clock" is another metaphor to describe the timing of the journey through life. It refers to our own inner schedule for growth and development. While the Biological Clock is the body's way of keeping time, and the Social Clock society's way, the Psychological Clock is the individual's way. Justin will walk and talk and eventually pass all of life's milestones not only when his body is prepared, and not only when his society thinks he should, but when *he* is good and ready. He will hear the Psychological Clock.

If the Biological Clock builds a body and the Social Clock shapes a person for society, the Psychological Clock drives us to become ourselves, determining when we embark on the major passages of life. This clock expresses our personal sense of the seasons, how old we feel rather than how old we are, psychological age rather than biological age. The Psychological Clock is an expression of the self, and it reveals the self. It starts ticking when the self is born, sometime before the first birthday.

The Birth of the Self

When Justin came into the world, he had no notion of himself as an individual. He was aware of internal sensations — feelings of hunger, discomfort, warmth, and the like — and he was aware of sounds and smells, tastes and touches. He could see, but his world was a blur of lights and shadows, as if he wore glasses smeared with Vaseline. His actions were reflexes given him by evolution. He sucked, he cried, and he clung to whatever touched his palm, as if it were the fur of a mother's moving body. Justin was a creature with no idea of where his body ended and where the world began.

But in the second half of his first year, something happened. About the time Justin "should" have been born, were it not for the size of his head and the narrowness of his mother's birth canal — and about the time he was becoming attached to his mother — a self began to emerge. This self was not conceived at any particular moment, nor was it born on any special day. It appeared one week and disappeared the next, but gradually it established itself. An "I" came into being that knew it wasn't "you." That "I" is what we call the self.

The self does not emerge fully formed. It develops, in the root meaning of that term, which is to "un-envelop" — to come out of a wrapper, or an "envelope." That is what Justin's self will do throughout his life. To paraphrase Harvard psychologist Robert Kegan, the self comes out of a succession of envelopes, one inside the other. And it never discovers the envelope it's been in until it has outgrown it.[2]

The self's first envelope is its symbiotic union with the mother. In that oneness there is no distinction between "I" and "you." But gradually Justin learned about the regularities of the world, about the connection between his actions "in here" and what happened "out there." He moved his muscles "in here" and discovered something "out there" — a touch, a voice, a mouthful of warm milk. But sensations also appeared "out there" on their own, with no corresponding movement on his part. Slowly, Justin separated the internal from the external. As he drew a line between inside and outside, and connected the two, he took the first step toward a notion of the self.

At first, Justin's memories were so fleeting that from one occasion to the next he probably forgot about the connections he experienced. Memories of what very young babies have seen or sensed begin to slip away in about ten seconds. Yet they may recognize something that repeats on a regular basis, just as the newborns who spent their last weeks in the womb hearing mothers read the same story again and again seemed to recognize the tale after they entered the world.

Justin remembered some things better than others, especially actions of his that had some effect on his surroundings. The drive to control events in the world around you appears early. When one end of a ribbon is tied to a tiny ankle and the other end to a mobile hanging above the crib, two-month-olds quickly learn to make the mobile bounce by kicking that foot vigorously.[3] Having discovered the connection between their kicks and the mobile's dance, they begin to smile and make delighted noises. As little as eighteen minutes of practice, spread over three sessions, fixes the memory of their triumph in their young minds. Even after a lapse of two weeks, they still recognize the mobile and begin jouncing it as soon as they feel the ribbon around their ankle. Such memories of something "in here" affecting something "out there" strengthened Justin's distinction between himself and the world.

At about three months, babies become fascinated by their hands, holding them up and watching intently as they move their fingers.[4] They turn their heads to keep their fingers in view, or bring their hands into their field of vision. These actions provide them with more information about control over events "in here" and their connection with effects "out there." The actions lay the foundation for a notion of the self as having a specific location in space. But actions in themselves are not enough to create a sense of self. Something else has to happen.

In the words of Swiss psychologist Jean Piaget, babies at three months lack the concept of "object permanence."[5] They don't know that people and objects continue to exist when they disappear from sight. As far as Justin was concerned, when his mother left to go to the barn, she ceased to exist; when she came back, she was recreated. Piaget demonstrated this curious belief by hiding an object and watching babies respond to its sudden departure. Until babies are about four months old, they are neither surprised nor especially interested when a toy disappears. No matter how fascinated they are by the toy, they do not react to its loss. As Janice said of Justin at this age, "We tried to play hide-the-toy with him, but it was a flop. When you hide the toy, he couldn't care less. He never looks for it." Out of sight was more than out of mind; for Justin, it was out of existence.

The signs of object permanence appear at about eight months, when babies begin to search for objects they've watched others hide. Their search testifies to this new knowledge that their rattle, favorite blanket, or teddy bear have an existence of their own, an existence that has nothing to do with them. At the Yale University School of Medicine, brain researcher Patricia Goldman-Rakic has discovered that this giant step occurs just about when the synapses in the frontal cortex of the brain reach critical mass. At this time the brain's pattern of activity starts to resemble an adult's.[6]

All of our primate cousins travel the same road to object permanence that our own babies do, but they make the trip faster. A rhesus monkey begins to search for hidden objects at about three months, and by five months it has reached the level that Justin has attained as he celebrates his first birthday.[7] But that's where rhesus monkeys — and most other primates — stop. At the University of Virginia, psychologist Sandra Scarr has concluded that human babies and infant apes share the same kind of nonverbal intelligence described by Piaget, and that there is little difference between them until human babies are about eighteen months old and begin to speak in two-word sentences.[8]

Before Justin began searching for hidden toys, he could only *recognize* events, objects, and people he had seen before. But once he began to look under the pillow for a vanished toy, it was evident that his memory had developed new capabilities — such as relating the present to the past. He could remember that his mother was here, but now she's gone; that his favorite toy had rolled under the sofa; that the cookie jar stands on the

Justin at one. He is now a person.

counter next to the icebox. And yet these memories — along with memories of the time the calf sucked his whole fist, the first time he rode on the tractor with Daddy, and the time great-grandfather Francis bounced him and sang to him — will not become part of his life story. The incidents of the first three years will slowly slip away, lost in the reorganization of memory that comes in early childhood.

Many psychologists have placed the emergence of the self at about nine months. At that age, Justin's knowledge that objects had an existence apart from him testified to his division of the world into "I" and "not-I," and indicated that the self had awakened. Justin had become a person. For the first time, he saw himself as an active agent, separate from his mother and all the other people in his world. This sense of self, combined with his new powers of memory, added a new joy to games. Now he could anticipate the moves in familiar play routines. Instead of laughing at the end of a game, he chortled or squealed *before* his mother said "peek-a-boo" or his father nuzzled his stomach. His power to anticipate made a new emotion possible in Justin's life; for the first time, he could be surprised.[9]

As Justin blows out the candle on his first birthday cake, his selfhood is not yet complete. He is missing the other major aspect of the self — the self as object. He still has no sense of "me." This "unwrapping" takes longer, in part because Justin cannot visualize how he looks to other people. When he looks into a mirror, he doesn't recognize the baby who looks out at him. As far as Justin is concerned, it's another child.

The traditional test of a baby's awareness of "me" is an experiment with mirrors that was devised by Gordon Gallup, a psychologist who worked with chimpanzees.[10] Gallup anesthetized chimpanzees and, while they were unconscious, put a smear of odorless red dye on their foreheads. When they awoke and looked at themselves in the mirror that hung in their cage, the chimpanzees immediately fingered the red spot, indicating that they knew they were looking at their own reflection. (Monkeys were utter failures at this task, indicating that chimpanzees have a self-concept but monkeys do not.)

Psychologists Michael Lewis and Jeanne Brooks-Gunn have adapted this experiment with babies and toddlers.[11] They hand each youngster's mother a cloth with rouge on it and have her wipe her baby's nose, leaving a red smudge behind. The mother then places her child in front of a large mirror that rests on the floor. Before they are a year old, babies seem incapable of connecting the smudge on the reflection's nose with themselves. By the time they are eighteen months old, about a quarter of the babies realize that their noses are dirty, and by their second birthdays, about three-quarters do.

Babies who reach for their noses after looking into the mirror have developed a sense of "me." They are beginning to realize how they differ from other people in appearance. It's a step in the development of self that children with secure attachments are slow to make. Insecure babies with "avoidant" attachments (after a brief separation, they tend to ignore their mothers) pass the mirror test of self-concept early. At sixteen months, when less than 13 percent of securely attached babies recognize a reflection of themselves, 40 percent of avoidant babies do.[12] The spur to an early sense of "me" may be the forced independence of these babies, who usually rely less on their mothers than securely attached babies do.

Infants who can recognize "me" in a mirror also apply labels to what they see there. They can name their reflection, and they can compare pictures of themselves and another baby and identify themselves. It seems more than coincidence that the self as object emerges just as children's grasp of language is growing. Before Justin can decide that he's a baby and not an adult, a boy and not a girl, lives on a farm and not in the city, he will need a way to label these characteristics. The growth of a "me" that Justin can grasp, evaluate, and tell stories about will never be complete. His self-image will change over the course of his life. Every time a new "I" comes out of an envelope, there will be a new "me" for it to discover.

Theorists are not of one mind in assigning dates to the first emergence of the self. Part of the problem is definitional: what exactly is a "self"? Your answer will affect your reckoning of when it comes into being. Part of the problem is that no one can communicate from the perspective of the infant. Babies have the perspective, but they don't have the words to describe it. Children and adults have the words, but they can't recapture the perspective. Despite the problem of assigning dates, however, this much is clear: a newborn does not recognize that it is separate from its mother — or from anything else "out there." By its first birthday, it has made that distinction. The self has started to "un-envelop."

Psychological Seasons of Life

As Justin Kennedy's self develops, he will become a maker of meaning and a keeper of his own time. He will create a unique sense of the seasons of life. But not unique in all respects: Justin cannot escape the biological time kept by his body nor the social time kept by his generation, so his Psychological Clock will share some of the settings of others. This is especially true in the first half of life, when the Biological and Social Clocks are most insistent.

The common elements in our Psychological Clocks have provided the building blocks for grand visions of the life course, for theories about the development of the self. Some theories are "pessimistic," portraying life as growth, plateau, and decline. Others lack connotation, depicting growth followed by a flat landscape that runs on, past the horizon, to the end of life. And some theorists are "optimists," painting a portrait of life as a steady ascent.

Only a few psychologists have looked at the entire span of life. One of the first was Charlotte Bühler, a German psychologist who, just after World War I, established an institute in Vienna to study human development. Bühler and her students spent years analyzing biographies and autobiographies. They found enough commonalities to convince them that the life course followed a steep climb up, a short plateau, and then a slow descent toward death. In this picture, life was a process of growth, stability, and decline. Childhood and early adolescence formed the first stage of "entrance into life." The second stage, late adolescence and young adulthood, provided an exciting period of expansion and self-determination. The middle years of life were the plateau, a time when we modified our lives, making any necessary corrections in its course, and reaped the fruits of our endeavors. In late middle age and early old age, we entered the fourth stage of life and began the downward slide. It was, said Bühler, the period of life when we "retreated behind our achievements." Yet it wasn't all downhill. In the midst of our physical retreat, we remained highly productive and took new interest in life's accomplishments. During the final stage of life, old age, we were focused on ourselves, intensely preoccupied with our past and concerned about our immediate future.[13]

More than thirty years before Bühler set up her Viennese institute, a young physician named Sigmund Freud established a medical practice treating nervous diseases in the same city. Combining his training in neurology with observations of his patients, he fashioned not only a psychoanalytic therapy, but a vision of development as well. In his psychosexual theory, the stages of childhood were clearly marked, with each step taking the child farther up from the pool of impulses that makes up the newborn. Unlike many theorists, Freud limited infancy to the first year of life — the oral stage, in which babies' pleasures centered on the lips and mouth. Toddlers were in the anal stage, when pleasure was in the rectum and battles over toilet-training often erupted. During the phallic stage, which occupied the preschool years, the source of pleasure moved to the genitals; it was a time when youngsters fell in love with the parent of the other sex. From the age of six until puberty, children were in the latency period, when a diminished interest in sexuality interrupted the course of psychosexual development. With puberty, the genital stage was under way and sexuality blossomed.

At this point — the entry to adulthood — Freud lost interest in charting development. Though he worked with adults, Freud focused on childhood; he strongly believed that how we ended up in life was determined by how we began, by what happened to us in infancy and early childhood. At the time of his death in 1939, many of Freud's followers in the psychoanalytic movement believed that the course of an individual's life was fixed by the age of six.

One who took a different path was Erik Erikson, who had met Freud in the Austrian Alps in 1927 and received psychoanalytic training from Freud's daughter, Anna. In 1933, when Adolf Hitler became chancellor of Germany and Freud's writings were burned in Berlin, Erikson came to the United States. Here he studied the Sioux and other Native American tribes and became involved in one of the first long-range studies of human development. In 1950, he proposed a theory of human development that went far beyond Freud's. Not only were infancy and childhood important; so were adolescence, adulthood, and old age. For Erikson, our social nature and the influence of our culture were much more important than our sexuality — and also more interesting. He saw life as an upward staircase, with each of its eight steps taking us to greater maturity and wisdom. At each of life's stages, we resolved a new, more sophisticated conflict.

Life's first conflict was between trust and mistrust. In their first year, infants learned whether they could rely on others for care — whether they could have faith in life itself. In toddlers, a sense of willfulness created the next struggle, between autonomy and shame or doubt. The challenge was to develop an independent sense of self without jeopardizing a basic trust in life. During what Erikson called the "play age" of the preschooler, the crisis was between initiative and guilt. If they successfully resolved this conflict, youngsters knew that they were basically good and were filled with a sense of purpose. In the school years, the task was to develop a sense of industry in the face of feelings of inferiority. Children had to feel confident in their skills, take pleasure in completing difficult tasks, and know that they were useful.

Puberty brought with it the challenge of Erikson's fifth stage. This was the time for adolescents to begin establishing an identity, discovering who they were and what they wanted to be, and avoiding what Erikson called "role confusion." The move into young adulthood was accompanied by a conflict between intimacy and isolation; the task was to learn to love another person without sacrificing the recently won sense of identity. Middle age brought a struggle between generativity and stagnation: mature adults either turned their thoughts to shepherding the next generation, or they became absorbed in themselves. Life's final conflict, said Erikson, was between integrity and despair. As older people reviewed their life, they either accepted or rejected what had happened, finding meaning in the outcome of events or being filled with regret. What they chose had a bearing on generations to come. In Erikson's view, healthy children would not fear life if their elders had integrity enough not to fear death.

The successful resolution of each conflict did not banish the defeated quality from our lives; instead it shifted the balance so that a "positive" quality predominated. Erikson was quick to point out that there were situations in which a healthy dose of mistrust, doubt, or any of the other "negative" qualities in his theory was a valuable resource. How could any old person, he asked, have integrity and not also despair about certain things in his own life, and about the human condition?[14]

About twenty-five years after Erikson presented his theory, Daniel Levinson returned to the ancient metaphor of the seasons as a way of depicting the life course. A psychologist in the Department of Psychiatry at Yale University, Levinson had been struck by the dearth of theory and research on middle age. He and his colleagues conducted intensive biographical interviews with forty middle-aged men and, later, with forty-five middle-aged women.[15] This research led him to describe four major periods of life, one overlapping the other, each lasting about twenty-five years: childhood and adolescence, early adulthood, middle adulthood, and late adulthood. Each season represented a period of calm in which the self and the world fit together in a satisfactory "life structure." But, said Levinson, the fit inevitably breaks down and the calm gives way to crisis, once in the middle of each season and once in the transition between seasons. When a transition is successful, self and world fit together in a new, more satisfying way. A period of stability returns. "Everyone goes through the same basic sequence," Levinson wrote, and each "developmental period begins and ends at a well-defined [average] age, with a range of about two years above and below this average."[16] Stability and crisis continue to alternate throughout life, creating stages closely linked with ages.

By the time Levinson completed his theory, the life-span balance had been tipped from childhood to adulthood. With his emphasis on the early years, Freud had put his weight with the former. But Levinson put all his effort into the latter. And something else had happened to theoretical pictures of development. No longer was middle age portrayed as the peak to which we rise and from which we begin to decline. Now the life course was drawn, as Erikson had portrayed it, with a steady ascent to old age. The shift in balance occurred just as the proportion of middle-aged and older people in our society began to rise. This demographic change, even more than the theorists, ultimately made the difference. Our visions of the psychological seasons of life have proven to be as varied and imaginative, and as strongly shaped by culture, as our portraits of its social seasons.

The Story of a Life

Today's psychologists do not agree on the major "stages," "passages," or "seasons" of life, and for good reason. When you study an individual life, you become aware of everything that makes it unpredictable: historical events such as war and economic depression, people one happens to meet, whatever comes "out of the blue." Accidents, chance encounters, good fortune and bad — life events that psychologists now call "non-normative" — prevent any of our lives from precisely matching a particular theory of development. It's especially difficult to create an overarching scheme of "ages and stages" for the second half of life. Then, the Biological and Social Clocks are quieter, their programs less determinative. The effects of random, non-normative events begin to accumulate, making each of our paths unique. The Psychological Clock becomes the dominant regulator.

The shocks and surprises of life are the bane of theories, but there's nothing better for a story. Perhaps that's why Bühler, Freud, Erikson, and Levinson all used biographies in their studies of development. Freud's early case histories, in fact, were criticized for reading like novels, and the finest applications of Erikson's theory were his interpretations of the lives of Martin Luther and Mohandas Gandhi. In the end, it may be truer to the complexity of a life to see it as a story — as a good, page-turning mystery that's full of suspense. You never know how it's going to come out.

As Justin Kennedy grows to adulthood, the mystery of his life will begin to unfold. Part of his story will be like *all* other stories, an archetypal tale of birth, growth, reproduction, and death. These universal parts will be the work of the Biological Clock — the body's timeline. Although this clock has unique things in store for each of us (it brings some of us to puberty sooner than others, for example), its overwhelming impact is to make the seasons of our lives alike.

Part of Justin's story will be like *some* other stories — like those of his generation, but not of others. That will be due to the Social Clock. Not only are people who live at the same time and place affected by similar age norms, but they also experience the same historical events. They march together in cohorts through World War I or the Great Depression or the civil rights movement. Their shared experience unites their lives in distinctive ways.[17]

But much of Justin's story will be like *no* other story. Events will come when he is totally unprepared for them, and he will develop his own sense of surprise and readiness for change. When the last page of his story is written, it will be the Psychological Clock that makes it his — and no one else's.

Early in childhood, Justin will acquire what researchers call "autobiographical memory." He will learn what a story is and begin to cast his experiences into narrative. In adolescence, he will gain a time perspective that enables him to integrate past, present, and future, to weave stories *from* his life into the story *of* his life. In adulthood, his "I" will continue to unwrap itself, and Justin will reflect on the many forms of "me" he has left behind. Throughout life, his story will change as he changes, and when he dies, certain episodes will be remembered by others. His narrative will become part of the web of meaning on which future generations of Kennedys live their lives.

How the Story Begins

How will Justin's story end? No one can tell, of course, but his parents want to get it off to a good start. And, like most parents, Jeff and Janice wonder how the first year of life will affect all that come after.

Sigmund Freud thought the beginning of a life had a strong effect on its end. Though his position has been overstated, he believed that babies could get "fixated" — stuck in the orientations of infancy and early childhood. In a similar vein, Erik Erikson believed that babies who did not learn to trust others could not begin to deal adequately with subsequent tasks. Unable to handle frustration, the mistrustful toddler would find the prospects of autonomy and self-control too much to handle. For Erikson, the unmastered tasks of one stage cast a shadow over life's next stage, and the effects reverberated up the staircase of development.

Today, we know that a third of all babies are not as lucky as Justin Kennedy. Although they love their mother, their behavior shows their attachment to her to be insecure. Some of them are "avoidant" babies; they seem to have learned that when they seek their mother out, they will be rebuffed. Instead of a warm welcome, they get cold comfort, so they ignore her comings and goings. Other babies are even less secure. If their mother leaves, they become distressed, perhaps even inconsolable. But as soon as their mother returns and her arms enfold them, they angrily push her away and squirm to get down. These "resistant" babies may be angry and confused because they cannot predict what their mother will do.[18] Some researchers studying attachment believe as Erikson did that infants who do not trust their mother will find it hard to trust in life itself.

Early research on attachment seemed to support Erikson's position. John Bowlby studied British babies who were separated from their families during World War II, when children were taken from the cities and placed in the country to escape Nazi bombs.[19] These babies, who were already attached to their mothers, became withdrawn and inactive, increasingly sad and hopeless. Later, their relationships with others tended to be pleasant, but shallow. Bowlby concluded that unless children formed — and maintained — an attachment during the first two or three years, they would never be able to develop warm, loving relationships in later life.

Over the past decade, it has become clear that attachment is linked in predictable ways to a baby's future. Most babies who are securely attached to their mothers become preschoolers who are cooperative, sociable, independent, and self-confident. When they encounter challenging situations, they usually persist until they solve the problem. If they fail, they bounce back. But the benefits of a secure attachment come only if a child remains in the same good rearing circumstances that produced the attachment in the first place. As a result, we can't be certain whether the connection between the first year and the fourth and fifth years lies in the person of the child or the consistency of the parents. More likely, the latter is true: that the social environment, more than the child, is the source of continuity.

The implication of this view is that a bad start in life can be overcome if the environment changes. Some years ago, psychologist Jerome Kagan of Harvard University studied infants in the Guatemalan countryside.[20] Until they were able to walk, these babies lived in dark, windowless huts, under conditions that would be appalling to middle-class Americans. The babies had no toys, no one played with them, and hardly anyone talked to them. They were undernourished and apathetic. As we might expect, they developed slowly — physically, emotionally, and mentally — compared with American infants. But develop they did. Once they emerged from their huts, they made rapid strides, and by the time they were ten years old, they were vibrant, alert children.

Or consider the case of homeless European children who were adopted by middle-class Americans after World War II. They were as young as five months and as old as ten years. Some of the older children had been living on their own, surviving by scavenging in garbage cans. Plunged into a new culture, hearing only a strange language, these youngsters were troubled at first. Some were anxious, had trouble sleeping, and were frightened by nightmares. Slowly, the children mended, and when researchers examined them six years later, they found a group of healthy, socially competent children with above-average IQs who had warm emotional ties to their new parents.[21] The story of bereft orphans recovering from violence and wartime horrors repeated itself after the Korean War, and again after the war in Vietnam. When placed in good environments and given loving care, children who are malnourished, seriously ill, or emotionally traumatized respond.[22]

The key to these stories of resilience is a change in environment. The darkness of a hut becomes the light of day. The alleys of devastated cities give way to warm, loving homes. It's not surprising that an animal so immature at birth, so slow to grow up, and so malleable throughout the course of its life can recover from damaging experiences. For humans, the die is not cast at one — or even at five or ten. Changing the story becomes more difficult as we get older, but it still remains possible.

Researchers also have discovered that some motifs present at the beginning of a life may continue to the end. Certain aspects of character — what is now called "temperament" — appear to be genetically determined and capable of lasting a lifetime. Twenty-five years ago, researchers would have scoffed at the idea that any part of our personality is present at birth, but many psychologists now hold that we are already different when we enter the world — a discovery that parents of more than one child have already made for themselves.

Some babies are highly responsive to the sights and sounds of the world; others pay little attention unless the lights are bright and the sounds loud. Some are restless and move about vigorously; others are placid and move slowly. Some cry and fret most of the time; others seem sunny and content, crying only when they are hungry or uncomfortable.

A baby's temperament consists of this broad emotional reactivity, which provides the foundation for later personality.[23] In the 1950s, Alexander Thomas and Stella Chess began an important study at New York Medical Center, hoping to discover the sources of personality.[24] They found clear differences in the temperament of the babies they studied. Many babies showed a cluster of tendencies that could make their path through life smooth or rough. Like Justin, some of the babies were "easy." They were friendly and pleasant, welcomed new situations, and adapted easily to new routines. They got sleepy, hungry, and playful on a regular basis. Others were "slow to warm up" — generally inactive babies whose reactions to the world were never intense. They were hesitant about new people or objects, and slow to adapt to new routines. About 10 percent of the babies were "difficult." Their sleep, meal, and play times were erratic; their mood was generally sour. They reacted intensely when they liked or disliked something, avoided new situations, and had trouble adapting to new routines.

Personality is more than temperament, of course. It encompasses self-concept, attitudes, expectations, motivations, values, standards, and probably much more. But the newborn baby is all temperament, because none of the other aspects of personality has had a chance to develop. As Chess and Thomas followed their babies through the years, some differences persisted. Donald, a highly active baby who wriggled about even in his sleep, squirmed incessantly as a toddler when his mother tried to dress him. At the age of three, he climbed "like a monkey" and ran like "an unleashed puppy." According to his kindergarten teacher, he would "hang from the wall and climb on the ceiling." Later in school, his restlessness gave him trouble; he couldn't stay in his seat long enough to learn much, and his rambling about the room disturbed his classmates.

Donald's hyperactivity is an extreme example, but Jerome Kagan has found clear evidence of a personality trait that is linked to biological differences.[25] From the time babies are a year old, about one in ten are shy, restrained, and subdued when they meet new people or find themselves in new situations. They seem to be perpetually wary. At the age of eight, about three-quarters of these children are still shy and inhibited; they are extremely quiet in the company of others and cautious in new situations. Their bodies also react differently when exposed to mild stress, such as answering a question. Compared with other children, their heart rates are higher but steadier, their pupils larger, and their throat muscles more tense. Apparently, their "stress threshold" is abnormally low, and situations that other children take in stride trigger in them a response of alarm. Their hearts pound, their muscles tense, and hormonal changes get them ready to cope with the "threatening" situation.

Shyness appears to have a stronger genetic push than other aspects of personality — or at least researchers have found the strongest evidence for it. At Pennsylvania State University, behavior geneticist Robert Plomin believes that a thousand or more different genes influence the tendency to be shy.[26] He watched the way two-year-old twins reacted to strangers and found that identical twins (who share all their genes) reacted much more similarly toward a stranger than did fraternal twins (who share only some of their genes). If one identical twin was shy, so was the other. When Plomin looked at three-year-olds who had been adopted at birth, he found that when the youngster was shy, the chances were high that the child's biological mother was shy as well.

Plomin's team of researchers has discovered that genetic influence on temperament is still apparent in middle-aged and older adults.[27] In Sweden, where a registry keeps information on twins born between 1886 and 1958, the team enlisted 700 pairs of twins, most between the ages of fifty and eighty, for a study of temperament. More than 300 of the pairs had been separated in infancy or early childhood and reared apart. The researchers found that identical twins, whether or not they had grown up together, were most alike on measures of fear and shyness. Genetic influence also surfaced in other aspects of temperament, but in general the strength of inherited factors seemed to dwindle somewhat in the second half of life.

Inherited temperamental tendencies are modified by experience, and long before midlife some may have faded until they are difficult to discern.

At twenty-two months, playing the kazoo.

"Pap-pap tractor."

Most tendencies, say Chess and Thomas, shine through only when a person is suddenly cast into a new situation that makes the customary ways of handling problems ineffective.[28] And Kagan found that a quarter of his extremely shy children had lost their inhibiting fears by the time they were eight years old.

Can we tell how a life story will end by knowing how it began? Developmental psychologist Sheldon White of Harvard University likens the beginning of a life to the beginning of a symphony. "The best we can do at the moment is strongly suspect that a few of the melodies and the leitmotifs that we recognize at the beginning are probably going to be there at the end, played in another key, played more rapidly, played more slowly, played with different harmonies. To that extent, probably, one can tell. I don't

Justin's infancy is coming to a close.

know that one can tell much more."[29] One of the melodies that seems to endure is temperament.

As he nears his second birthday, Justin Kennedy has been given the run of the barn. He's showing all the autonomy of a two-year-old, pedaling his Big Wheel down a concrete walkway next to the animals and climbing a pen to get closer to the calves. When his grandmother picks him up and asks, "Where's Pap-pap?" he responds, "Pap-pap tractor." Back at home, he can play a kazoo or construct mighty towers with colorful plastic blocks — and take just an instant to destroy what he's made. He can look in a mirror and realize that the toddler with curly blond hair is himself. When Justin was five months old, his father predicted, "He'll be easy-going, but he'll be a real windjammer. He likes to talk." Justin has changed a lot since then. In fact, his infancy is coming to a close. But some things about him are already staying the same.

II

Childhood

4

THE BIOLOGICAL *No Longer*

STORY OF CHILDHOOD *"In-fans"*

As Justin Kennedy's infancy comes to a close, a little girl in pink corduroy pants scampers into childhood. Meredith Wilson is barely two years old, but today, on a trip to the shopping mall, she's all brave explorer. "Ready to get some shoes?" her mother Patti asks.

"Shoes? Um-hmm, okay!" A bright, energetic response.

And Meredith is off, riding wide-eyed up an escalator, then racing toward a beckoning display of dolls, her mother in hot pursuit. Meredith's temperament is different from Justin's — something like a hurricane, Patti says. In the shoe store, Meredith reaches for some dark blue sneakers but is told that girls wear pink. She settles down on the floor with some musical toys, but the sight of a baby sucking lustily on a bottle changes her mood once again. Meredith tearfully demands a bottle of her own. "You're getting too big for a bottle," says Patti. "How about if we ask the nice lady for a pretzel?"

Moments later, Meredith is sprinting out of the store and into the mall, flinging a hasty "bye-bye" over her shoulder. When Patti quickly corrals her, Meredith protests angrily, throwing back her head, screaming, kicking, and pushing herself away from her mother's enveloping arms. But the tumultuous struggle is as brief as her freedom; after a lullaby and a few minutes of rocking, she's content to cuddle on her mother's lap.

This whirlwind of a child roared rather unexpectedly into her parents' lives. Through eight years of marriage, Patti and Philip had not planned on

Two-year-old Meredith Wilson. "Shoes? Um-hmm, okay!"

children, but they hadn't ruled out the possibility. "I found out we were going to have a family on the Ides of March, March 15," Patti recalls. The date, and the whole idea, seemed ominous. "It was a very unnerving experience. I was much more sure that I would never have children than I was that I'd never get married. And I was positive I'd never get married!"

Now thirty-one, Patti has red hair and fair skin, and is herself a crackling bundle of energy. She wasn't sure how her husband would react to her pregnancy, but Philip embraced fatherhood. It has changed him "pretty much completely," he says. Growing bald at thirty-two, Philip has a dark mustache that flows into a neatly trimmed beard. He jokes with a slow, wide smile about how Meredith was as a baby. "She was only two months old, and she could throw me down on the ground and get me in a hammerlock. Anything to keep from getting a diaper change. If you could get her diaper and suit changed within, say, four minutes, you were okay. Then she started to grab the bars on the crib. These days even the dogs can't keep up with her. Sometimes they go and hide."

No question about it, Meredith is "very demanding," says Patti. "Very active. Constantly moving. She wants to be up and dancing and reaching and pulling. It wears you down after a while."

Patti has changed a great deal since those Ides of March. "How can a nonparent understand what a parent goes through?" she asks. "When the baby cries and cries and cries, and you don't know why, and you can't get her to stop? You hold her and coo to her and talk sweetly and . . . just pace. You cry with her. I couldn't imagine what that was like until I had to go through that when Meredith had colic. And the feelings when she learned

Patti, thirty-one. "How can a nonparent understand what a parent goes through?"

Parenthood has changed Philip, thirty-two, "pretty much completely."

how to give hugs! I'll tell you, one of the sweetest moments was my first hug from my baby. I'll always remember that.

"To be a mother to my daughter, it's an incredible trip. Because she's just an overwhelming kid. She's smart and she has a brilliant smile. And to think that I had some part in creating that smile. Well, it's just like gold to me." This woman who never thought she'd be a mother now believes that motherhood was always in her. "Before, I didn't want to hold kids. I always wanted to give them back to their mothers. Now, I'm just so anxious to get her and hold her. I feel like I found something that I already had, but I had no way to get to. Like a new room, a new room in your house. You pass the door so many times, but you never bother to open it. Well, I opened it. And it's the best room in the house!"

Two years of motherhood have changed Patti profoundly. Now she senses that something else will be required of her, another transition. Meredith is growing up. "I know she's going to be an independent person and I bless her for it. But it's tough on me already. It's going to be hard to let go. She's already showing me when to let go — when she's ready to try something new."

Meredith *is* ready for something new. She walks and runs energetically, she recognizes herself in a mirror, and she's fighting harder than ever for her autonomy. On the brink of a new season of life, she is no longer an infant. The word *infant* comes from the Latin, where *in-* means "not," and *fans* means "speaking." A sign of the end of infancy is children's newfound facility with language. Though they use single words long before this time, they do not yet do what humans alone can do: use rules to combine words into sentences. Between eighteen months and two years, however, children begin to make primitive sentences. At that moment, they begin to speak like humans. They are no longer "not-speaking," no longer "in-fans."

When the Sex Hormones Vanish

Biologically, another sign marks the end of infancy. It occurs silently, deep within the toddler's body. Meredith is unaware of this change, and her mother sees nothing in her daughter's body or behavior to reveal it. Yet the change is one of the keys to being human. While Meredith was growing inside her mother's womb, she was exposed to lots of the female hormone estrogen. And once she was born, estrogen coursed through her body in concentrations close to those of an adult woman — just as the male hormone testosterone streamed through Justin Kennedy's body at levels rivaling those of a grown man. By the age of two, however, levels of sex hormones in the bloodstreams of little girls and boys drop dramatically. Some unknown mechanism in the Biological Clock shuts them down until puberty.

Sex hormones act as potent stimulants to growth. Researchers aren't certain whether they work primarily on muscles, bones, or brain, but it's no accident that the time when an infant's hormone levels are so high is also a period of rapid physical growth, brain development, the establishment of control over joints and muscles, and the awakening of the mind. Some endocrinologists suspect that the hormones may be doing even more than spurring growth; they may be sensitizing tissue and setting the stage for the explosion of growth during puberty. Perhaps they are continuing to set the brain in male or female patterns. But hormones work in such mysterious ways, and their signaling system is so complicated, that no one knows for sure.

If sex hormones continued at full production, humans would have no childhood. We would continue at a pace of all-out growth and enter puberty at about the age of three. Spurred by pubertal processes, our bones would grow excessively for a few years, then seal themselves off from future growth. At the tender age of six or seven, we'd be physically mature adult midgets.

But humans do have a childhood — an excessively long one. Childhood is so long, in fact, that it gives the appearance of being an extra stage in the life span. How that stage developed may never be known, but hints and conjectures abound. Some of the clues are ancient jawbones, which tell us how rapidly teeth were formed and how soon they erupted. Such clues have led anthropologist Barry Bogin of the Dearborn campus of the University of Michigan to suspect that the lengthening of childhood may have begun as a feeding adaptation. When early hominids began eating seeds and other tough, hard-to-chew foods, those whose permanent molars erupted late and lasted longer had an advantage. They were more likely to survive. But hominids whose teeth were slow to erupt would develop more slowly in other ways, too. Their entire bodies probably took longer to grow and mature.[1]

We'll never know if that's how our long childhood began, but, looking back, we can find a flock of advantages in the outcome. If children stayed small for a longer period of time, they would eat less and food supplies could be stretched out. Small creatures tend to bow to the wishes of large ones, so life probably ran more smoothly within families and social groups. And an extended childhood might have reduced hostility on another front: postponing sexual maturation "protected" young boys by keeping them out of competition with adult males for mates.

Studies of hunter-gatherers suggest another benefit: older children could care for younger ones. Among such people today, children are left at the base camp as soon as they're weaned. All the children play together in a large group, with older children responsible for younger ones. One adult usually stays behind to supervise, but spends the time on other activities, such as preparing food or making tools. The assistance of older children not only frees adults to gather food, but also makes it possible for parents to have more children, because having to care for a child limits a woman's ability to reproduce.

Child-tending seems to be a universal chore for human children. When anthropologists Beatrice and John Whiting studied youngsters in a variety of cultures, they found them caring for younger siblings in every society examined.[2] In settled societies, even the very young had child-care duties. In Taira, on the island of Okinawa, five-year-olds strapped a baby brother or sister to their backs and marched off to kindergarten. Among the Nyansongo, a farming society in Kenya, six- or seven-year-olds generally took over the care of babies as young as two months, freeing their mothers to work in the fields. In no other species do we find this pattern of "babysitting." It suggests another evolutionary pressure to keep children children as long as possible — another force behind the biological lengthening of childhood.

Towering over all these advantages of an extended childhood is an increase in the time the young could spend learning. Young chimpanzees learn by imitation and so do young humans, but in the case of many essential survival skills, young humans also have to be taught. Among our early ancestors, children had to learn to find, gather, and process foods that were hidden away in shells, in husks, or under the earth. They had to learn about the sort of processing that made poisonous food palatable. They had to learn to locate the raw materials and then fashion the tools that enabled them to retrieve and prepare foods. This gave them a tremendous advantage, because we know that tool-using human gatherers produce twice as much nutrition from a savanna-woodland terrain as primates who don't use tools.[3]

For mammals other than humans, the return of sex hormones at puberty means that the time for learning is over. "Juvenile mammals play; adult mammals don't," says Stephen Jay Gould. "Sexual maturity in most creatures — not so much in humans — is essentially the end of any flexibility in behavior."[4] Humans can still learn in adolescence and throughout adulthood — it's part of the "plasticity," the malleability of our life course. But certain kinds of learning do become more difficult as we grow older. Even among humans, it's children who are biologically primed to soak up knowledge.

Though there were evolutionary advantages in children gaining time to learn, there were also serious drawbacks. Chief among these was the increased number of vulnerable years before reproduction. Fewer infants would grow to adulthood and be able to propagate the species. The only way to compensate would be for parents to lavish a great deal of care on their children, to invest in them for a long period of time.

Some researchers believe that our Biological Clock has evolved to insure that investment. Human growth is distinguished by "neoteny": our children retain baby-like features — large head, big round eyes, small nose, receding chin — longer than any other mammalian species. Barry Bogin argues that a "baby face" elicits care and concern from parents, and that the longer the young retain such a face, the longer the parents will invest in them. In the same way, small body size secures the investment of grown teachers by making clear the distinction between the role of student and that of instructor. "During at least the past two million years since the appearance of Homo," says Bogin, "natural selection would have favored biological traits that facilitated parental care, teaching, and the learning of cultural behavior."[5] Neoteny is a remarkable case, but not the only one, of social advantages coming to shape the way our bodies grow.

When we try to reconstruct the origins of the Biological Clock, we cannot help but inject meaning after the fact. We make the outcome of genetic play and random events seem almost inevitable — just as we do with the story of our lives. So be it: one might even speak of a "wisdom" in our schedule for growth — something that keeps children looking like babies to prolong the investment of parents. "How can a nonparent understand what a parent goes through?" asks Patti Wilson. "Before, I didn't want to hold kids. I always wanted to give them back to their mothers. Now, I'm just so anxious to get her and hold her."

As we compare ourselves with other species, we realize the intensity of our investment in children. We're the only mammal, for example, that regularly feeds its young after weaning them. This practice is so basic to our ability to survive and flourish that it's been called "the hominid adaptation."[6] Among today's hunter-gatherers, babies stay close to their mothers and are breast-fed for the first four years. For another ten or more years, when they are unable to compete with adults, their parents continue to provide them with food.

Anthropologist Jane Lancaster of the University of New Mexico believes that this pattern helps explain why humans have spread across the planet while the number of chimpanzees have been diminishing for millennia. Chimpanzee babies are weaned at about the same age as babies among hunter-gatherers, but young chimpanzees are then expected to find all their own food. The demand that they feed themselves throws chimpanzees into what Lancaster calls a "selection funnel." Many young chimpanzees enter it, but few emerge alive at the other end. Whenever food gets scarce, the chimpanzee children go without — pushed aside by larger, stronger, older animals. Food in the wild is so undependable that only one chimpanzee out of three survives childhood.[7] Protected from starvation as well as from danger, one out of two hunter-gatherer babies reaches adulthood. The reproductive schedules of chimpanzees and hunter-gatherers are fairly similar, but the outcome is drastically different. The average chimpanzee mother adds 1.5 adults to the next generation — not enough to keep the population steady — but the average hunter-gatherer mother adds 2.5 adults. That difference can spell success or failure for a species.

The biological "invention" of childhood was risky, and riskier still was adding year after year to its length. Throughout the ages, parents have borne the cost of that risk by investing a large part of their lives in the care and protection of children. The investment of Patti and Philip Wilson is just beginning, yet already there are times when they feel worn down just trying to keep up with their daughter. Our biological and social evolution has created a distinctly human profile. We stand out not only because we stand up, not only because we have such a large and complex brain, but also because we take such a long, long time to grow up.

The Language Switch

As one switch in the Biological Clock brings on childhood by shutting down the sex hormones, another triggers the learning that childhood is for. Somewhere in Meredith Wilson's brain, a biological program for language acquisition, a program that's written into her genes, has begun to run. Linguists can describe with precision each step Meredith will take along the path to fluency, but even after decades of intensive study, they're still not certain what will drive her progress.

At the Massachusetts Institute of Technology, linguist Noam Chomsky has argued that the development of language is primarily a matter of physical maturation. He proposes the existence of a language acquisition device, or LAD, which refers to whatever collection of genes is responsible for determining the common principles, rules, and structures that underlie all human language. Because of LAD, the human mind always develops languages that include the familiar grammatical categories of subject, predicate, verbs, and objects. In Chomsky's view, babies are born to talk, and need only to interact with people using language. With the aid of LAD, they pick up the fragments of language they hear, analyze them, and fit them into the universal grammar. Language becomes as inevitable as walking or sexual maturation; it is not learned, but acquired.[8]

All over the world, no matter what their native language, children go through essentially the same steps in acquiring speech. They are sensitive to the human voice at birth, and tiny babies will work diligently for the reward of hearing someone talk. Cooing, the joyful sounds babies make when someone talks or sings to them, appears at about two months. Between four and six months, infants begin to babble, playing with sound possibilities: squeals, growls, yells, whispers, "raspberries," and what sound like single syllables. At about seven months, they start spouting the same syllable in a continuous string — "babababababa." At one year, give or take a few months, they speak their first word, and at about eighteen months, their first sentence. Though this sentence consists of only two words, it's the beginning of rule-governed speech, of language as humans know it.

Even deaf babies follow the same basic schedule. They babble at the same age that hearing children do, though many never get past the stage of the single syllable.[9] Deaf babies also learn sign language at the same rate that hearing children learn spoken language, or perhaps a little faster. The regularities in the timing of language acquisition point to the existence of consistent settings in the Biological Clock. As infancy comes to a close, a "language on" setting is tripped and a period of simple, almost effortless language acquisition begins.

This period lasts until puberty. Some psycholinguists believe that it's a "critical" period during which language must be acquired if it's to be acquired at all. According to this view, a "language off" switch trips at puberty, making it no longer possible to learn a first language — or even a new language with the fluency of a native speaker. This controversial position is extremely difficult to prove; almost no child lives until puberty without being exposed to language, and no psychologist is cruel enough to bring up a baby in an environment deprived of language.

Supporters of the idea that a critical period for language is built into the Biological Clock point to several kinds of evidence. They note that most severely retarded children steadily improve their language skills until puberty, when all progress abruptly stops. They point to the aftermath of brain damage — young children often regain language function, whereas adults rarely do. This suggests that the adult brain is no longer flexible enough to make the sort of adjustments required in language acquisition.[10]

A spectacular case has shed light on whether the Biological Clock has such rigid settings. In 1970, a girl was discovered locked away in a house in Los Angeles.[11] Genie, who was almost fourteen, had lived in an upstairs bedroom since she was twenty months old. She spent her days strapped to a crib or tied to a potty chair. Her only society was that of her nearly blind mother, who fed her but never talked to her. When Genie made any noise, her father beat her. At the time of her rescue, Genie could not stand erect, chew solid food, or talk. She weighed only sixty pounds. That she was emotionally disturbed seemed inevitable.

Genie was placed with a caring foster family and studied by a team of psycholinguists. Over the next seven years, she slowly acquired language. She learned to understand what others said to her, and then she began to speak. But at the age of twenty, Genie's speech had progressed no farther than the typical three-year-old's. She used no passive sentences, no auxiliary verbs, and no pronouns or other words that change in meaning depending on who is using them. The notion that "me" meant Genie when she used the word, but someone else when spoken by that person, was beyond her grasp.

Genie's language never became normal, which supports the notion of a critical period. But she did crack a good portion of the language code. She spoke in rule-governed sentences and understood what others said to her. So the settings on the Biological Clock cannot be as remorseless as early theorists believed. Indeed, it may have been Genie's twelve-year ordeal — she was malnourished, abused, and deprived of any meaningful social contact — that was responsible for her inability to grasp some aspects of language.

Today, the existence of Chomsky's LAD is in dispute, at least as an inborn, unlearned grammar that young children recognize in whatever speech they encounter. Yet no one doubts that the brain's maturation is essential to speech. Many brain areas probably are involved, principally a region in the left hemisphere. A number of cognitive psychologists are currently convinced that language acquisition is not the result of a specific device that is suddenly activated, but rather of a maturation of the same mental processes that we use in other aspects of daily life.[12]

Other psychologists are willing to accept LAD, but find it far too weak to handle language acquisition by itself. Psychologist Jerome Bruner of the New School for Social Research maintains that LAD requires a LASS to function properly.[13] LASS — language acquisition support system — refers to common experiences and familiar formats, especially routines with reversible roles, that adults provide to help the child master the uses of language. According to Bruner, simply exposing children to language is not enough; the language must be directed to them and "fine-tuned" to their level of understanding. A child who watched television all day, but never engaged in any joint activity, might not learn to speak.

Determining how much of language acquisition depends on LAD and how much on LASS is as difficult as specifying how much of the area of a field depends on its length and how much on its width.

No matter what the process, by the time they are two, children are skilled at combining words in sentences that vary little from one culture to the next. Youngsters in China and Czechoslovakia, Senegal and the Soviet Union, Uruguay and the United States all talk about similar things — what something is ("That cow"), where it is located ("Car road"), what it's like ("Big dog"), who owns it ("Ivan ball"), who's doing what ("Mommy put") and to whom ("Daddy shoe"), when something should recur ("More milk") and when it no longer exists ("Allgone milk").[14] The content of their sentences shows how children understand the world and what concerns them. They spend a good deal of their time trying to figure out what they are allowed to handle and explore and what is forbidden, which may explain why they're so fascinated by who owns what.

Until they are about two-and-a-half, most children are limited to two-word sentences, because their memory is so immature that it takes all their mental powers to connect two words and speak them. If they try to use three words in a sentence, they usually forget the first before they can string them all together. That limitation strips their conversation to the essentials. They sound so much like someone sending a telegram that psychologists call these two-word sentences "telegraphic speech."

Toddlers get along just fine with two-word telegrams because they rely on intonation and context. By stressing one word or the other, they can make their meaning clear. "Mommy book" usually means, "This is Mommy's book," but "Mommy book" tells Mommy to do something with the book — pick it up, give it to the child, or read it aloud. Mommy usually knows which meaning her child is trying to convey by the situation. Without context, it would be impossible to know what a toddler was talking about.

A few months after children reach the two-word stage, their memory stretches and they can handle three or four words at a time. Now they're off to the races — ready to learn all sorts of intricate language rules. When Meredith figures out the rule that allows her to indicate the past tense, she will sound for a time as if she's forgotten some things she already knew. Three-year-olds who say, "We went to town," "Mommy made chocolate cookies," and "Rover ate my cupcake" often turn into four-year-olds who say, "We goed to town," "Mommy maked chocolate cookies," and "Rover eated my cupcake." It's a leap forward that looks like a slide backward.

The leap reveals children's discovery that adding "-ed" indicates the past.

It also reveals that children apply the "-ed" rule with unyielding rigidity. The youngster who stops talking about "mice" and "feet" and starts saying "mouses" or "foots" is going through the same process with the rule for forming plurals. Children may even go through a period when they make doubly sure they get a rule right, saying, "We wented to town," "Rover ated my cupcake," or "The mices ran under the sofa." It takes them a long time to understand that every rule has exceptions. By the time they are seven, most children have worked it all out. They know when to apply the rule and when to use the exception.

They also have made amazing progress with vocabulary. Between the ages of two and six, a child's vocabulary expands from about 200 words to between 8,000 and 14,000 words. That means children are learning six to ten new words a day — sometimes after hearing the word only once. As adults, we may not learn that many words in a month, or even a year. But then, we're not in the season of life that's biologically primed for learning.

The Brain Leads the Way

One of the reasons early childhood is especially suited to the acquisition of language is that it's a period of rapid brain growth. Ever since Meredith was conceived, the Biological Clock has been concentrating on her brain, as one can see from the sheer size of her head in relation to the rest of her body. Two months after conception, about half of Meredith's overall length was from the neck up — she was half "head" and half "body." At birth, her head represented only a quarter of her length; at her current age of two, only about a fifth. By the time she's six, she'll be approaching adult proportions, in which only one-eighth of her height will be attributable to her head. In the years before we go to school, the brain dominates the story of physical development.

Meredith is at an interesting point in that story. At the age of two, the outer layer of her brain, known as the cortex, has perhaps twice the number of connections (or synapses) it will have when she's an adult. In the years ahead, many of the connections that have been fashioned for her will be pruned away.

Many researchers have been baffled by the purpose of this overproduction and cutback of synapses, particularly when new production will occur later on. But at the University of Illinois, William Greenough and his colleagues have begun putting pieces of the puzzle together. They believe we have to look at the relationship between brain development and experience.[15]

Greenough suggests that the Biological Clock calls for a rampant overgrowth of synapses during infancy to make certain we're prepared to deal with the essential information that every member of our species has used throughout history. We all see lines, corners, movement, contrast, depth, and patterns; we all hear human voices; we all become attached to a caregiver. As Greenough sees it, genes rough in the overlapping, multiple connections needed to deal with such information, making sure they're in

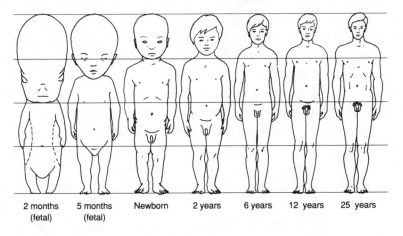

| 2 months (fetal) | 5 months (fetal) | Newborn | 2 years | 6 years | 12 years | 25 years |

Head size in relation to body size. Adapted from W. J. Robbins et al., Growth, *Yale University Press, 1929*

place by the time we encounter the necessary experience. Then, the circuits we actually use when moving, seeing, hearing, speaking, and the like are organized into networks of synapses. Connections that go unused at the anticipated time simply die.

If this is the way our brain grows, we can no longer picture it as a blank slate, ready to receive whatever's written on it. A better picture would be a chalkboard covered with connections — "expectant" circuits, each waiting for the right stimulation. If that stimulation fails to occur at the proper time, a circuit's connections are erased.

Researchers have found evidence of this process in monkeys. If a monkey's eye is sutured shut during a short period after birth, most of its connections to the visual cortex are lost.[16] Neurons from the free eye usurp connections that would normally have routed themselves to the shuttered eye; when the sutures are removed, the monkey's sight in that eye is seriously impaired. Apparently, there is a critical period in a monkey's life when these cells are establishing their permanent circuits. If this period passes without the appropriate stimulation, the ability to see is severely restricted.

Even so, says Greenough, brain development must be more complex. It must require chalk as well as eraser — the creation of new connections as well as the survival of old ones. If we had only expectant circuits, we would be inflexible creatures, unable to deal with unique aspects of our environment. That's why a second process generates new synapses whenever we have to learn something that's not part of the universal human experience. These new synapses, which depend on our own unique experiences, make us "learning animals," able to take advantage of changes in the world. The second process may even compensate for failures of the first. In the case of the monkey with impaired vision, if the good eye is sutured shut and the bad eye left open, neurons from the bad eye begin seeking new connections and vision greatly improves.

Greenough believes that these two processes can explain some of the staggered growth that researchers have found in the young brain. Synapses in the visual cortex, where we perceive pattern, color, contrast, and form, are fairly stable by the time we're two years old, while patterns in the frontal cortex, which does the thinking and planning, are not stable until adolescence. The existence of two processes may also explain why critical periods — sharply restricted spans of time when particular developmental events must occur — are not so critical in human beings. If we miss out on an experience that is bound to an expectant circuit and the vital connections are erased, we may be able to make up for it by rebuilding circuits using the second process.[17] Although Greenough has looked primarily at sensory systems, his dual-process theory may explain why children can recover from devastating early experiences. Having two ways of forming circuits gives the brain the power to revise itself.

Erasing some synapses and creating others may be enough to bring some new skills on line, but neural connections are only part of the biological story of learning.[18] Before an area of the brain can be fully functional, other things must happen. The production of chemicals that transmit nerve impulses must be underway. The synapses that are already formed must become adept at sending signals from one neuron to the next. And nerve fibers must be sheathed with the insulation known as myelin. Many new functions seem to coincide with the myelination of neurons, a process that is largely finished by the age of four. But myelination continues in some areas of the brain until adolescence — and perhaps far beyond.

Some areas of the brain take up their intended duties early. The portions of the cortex that have primary responsibility for vision, hearing, touch, and movement assume their jobs as soon as they become functional, with the primary motor and sensory areas leading the way. That's when brain circuits are reorganized and the primitive areas beneath the cortex give up their control over our actions.

But the rest of the cortex seems to run on a split schedule. In human babies, the left side of the brain develops faster than the right. Perhaps that's because the left hemisphere is slated to process that essential human skill, language. The slower developing right hemisphere seems best at processing spatial relations and patterns. This division of labor is known as lateralization, and it may reflect a basic difference in the way information is dealt with. The left hemisphere seems designed to handle information that comes in separate pieces, one after another, and the right hemisphere is built to blend many pieces of information into a simultaneous pattern.

Twenty years ago, neuroscientists were convinced that a newborn's cerebral cortex was more or less unspecialized. Very slowly, as the hemispheres matured, each took over its prescribed tasks. Some researchers said that this division of labor was not apparent until children began to talk, and not complete until they reached puberty. That view is rapidly falling out of fashion. At Canada's McMaster University, neuroscientist Sandra Witelson believes that the hemispheres already are specialized for their basic functions at birth.[19] Even within the womb, a portion of the left hemisphere associated with language function is noticeably larger than the similar area on the right. From the moment of birth, the left hemisphere dominates in processing the sounds of human speech. At the tender age of two years — the youngest age tested — children are using the right hemisphere to process spatial relationships. What appears to be a gradual assumption of tasks by each hemisphere, says Witelson, is actually the development of new skills. As soon as a skill appears, it gets handled by the appropriate side of the brain.

But not inflexibly: if one hemisphere is damaged — or even removed, as it sometimes is in a child with severe localized epilepsy — the other hemisphere can take over most of the damaged hemisphere's work. Yet the transfer is not perfect; those with only a right hemisphere never develop some aspects of language, and those with only a left hemisphere always show some defects in spatial skills.

Each hemisphere has its own assignments, but information flows freely between the two halves of the brain. They are linked by a broad band of neural fibers known as the corpus callosum. This band of fibers develops slowly and is not completely myelinated until children are nine or ten years old. In fact, until children are about five years old, the fibers may have such a sparse myelin coating that a good deal of information never gets passed across the bridge.

Lateralization is linked to handedness, because each side of the brain gets sensations from and controls the voluntary muscles on the opposite side of the body. The left side of the brain controls the right hand, and vice versa. Handedness emerges gradually during infancy. Most newborns use their right hands when reaching out, but this preference drops off sharply during the early months. Even so, a four-month-old will hold a toy with the right hand longer than with the left. Some children have a strong hand preference by the age of two, but other children may not settle on a single hand until they are five. Among little girls, those who have developed a consistent hand preference by eighteen months generally score much higher on tests of cognitive development throughout their preschool years than girls who haven't decided which hand works best. With little boys, hand preference has other effects. Those who reach their fourth birthday without a hand preference tend to be awkward and poorly coordinated, while those with a strong preference — whether left or right — tend to be well coordinated.[20]

At the University of Maryland, neuroscientists have traced brain waves that signal an upsurge in the left hemisphere's power between the ages of four and six, and a similar surge in power in the right hemisphere between the ages of eight and ten.[21] Weaker surges appear in both hemispheres as children enter puberty, and again in the mid-teens. These neuroscientists are convinced that tracing children's brain waves gives us an indirect look at leaps in cognitive development. It's apparently no accident that the power surge in the left hemisphere comes just before children all over the world begin to take on more responsibility within their families and just before they get down to the serious business of going to school.

By the time Meredith Wilson sets off for school, her brain will have done most of its growing. More of the glial cells that support and nourish its neurons will have been born, and existing ones will have grown larger. Blood vessels will have developed, and her total brain mass will be more than 90 percent of its eventual adult size. At the same time, Meredith's body will be only 40 percent of its eventual size, and her reproductive maturation will be only 10 percent complete. If she were to put on her mother's hat as she goes off to school, she would look cute. But if she were to put on her mother's coat, she'd look ridiculous.

As Meredith's body grows during the preschool years, it will follow the same "down-and-out" principle of development that has governed it since conception. In infants and young children, control of the muscles works its way down from the head and out to the extremities. Babies lift their head

"These days even the dogs can't keep up with her." Meredith's father, Philip, wants her to take a lot of time growing up.

before they sit, and sit before they stand. Today, when Meredith throws a ball, she uses only her arm, but in a few years she'll be able to coordinate her use of wrist, hand, and fingers.

Our ability to use our hands skillfully is so important to our species that Jerome Bruner considers it a window on the nature of problem solving.[22] He describes our use of the hands as "manual intelligence" and notes its relationship to making and using tools. Because the joints and tendons up and down our arms, hands, and fingers can operate independently, part of older children's control consists in knowing which muscle groups to combine for each task. The combination that works for hammering a nail differs from the combination used to open a jar, and both differ from the combination needed to write a letter.

Gradual growth of control over the entire body depends in part on the maturation of the cortex, but being able to send commands from the brain is only part of the story. Muscles, tendons, and joints also grow, with the watery, weak muscles of infancy becoming the sturdy muscles of childhood. A baby's leg muscles simply won't support its body, and the baby's body proportions — large head, short legs, and high center of gravity — are not designed to keep it upright. Now that she's two, Meredith has enough control over her muscles and joints to explore the world, and she has a brain that's mature enough to allow a surprising amount of learning. Yet there's still a long way to go.

And there's plenty of time to get there. Meredith's father Philip seems to have a sense of what the Biological Clock is about during childhood. He doesn't know that the sex hormones nearly vanish at the end of infancy, but he does have a feel for the overall strategy of slowing development down. "I don't want her to be in a hurry," he says. "When I was a kid, I was in a big hurry. I felt time pressing on my back. I thought I had to be going somewhere, I had to be doing something." But he wants Meredith to take her time, have fun, and not grow up too fast. Biologically, our species has flourished by doing just that.

5

THE SOCIAL STORY *The First*
OF CHILDHOOD *Day*

Hand in hand with her grandmother, six-year-old Jamillah Johnson walks down the sidewalk on her way to a great adventure. A pink bookbag bounces on her back, and with her free hand she swings a lunchbox. It's a sunny September morning in Roxbury, Massachusetts, and this is Jamillah's first day of school. Her new clothes — bright blue dress, white kneesocks, saddle shoes, and sparkling white ribbons on her pigtails — testify to the importance of the occasion.

Jamillah and her grandmother, Harriet Lyons, have been living together for several years now, ever since Jamillah's mother was no longer able to care for her. For Harriet, this walk is like the ones she took years ago with her own children. "When you get to school," she asks, "do you know what you have to do? What's the first thing you have to do?"

"Listen."

"And what do you say to the teacher?"

"Hi!"

"Good morning, teacher. She'll say, 'Good morning, class.'"

"And I'll say, 'Good morning, teacher.'"

"Um-hmm. Then she'll introduce herself. That means she'll tell you what her name is."

"I know what 'introduce' means."

"Then she'll ask everybody to say their name. And you'll say, 'My name is . . .'"

"Jamillah."

Jamillah Johnson, six.
"No, I'm not nervous."

"Jamillah has two names. What's your last name?"

"Johnson. Jamillah Johnson."

They continue their walk, crossing a busy street. "You stop and you look both ways," says Harriet, "and then you cross the street. Okay? Would you remember that for me? Please?"

A block later, they see an orange brick building with a concrete face and a long flagpole angling from the front wall into the sky. The building is surrounded by a picket fence of iron. Children approach in twos and threes, some of them black like Jamillah, but most of them white — and almost all of them bigger. "See that big building?" says Harriet. "That's your school. That's where you're going to the first grade. Grandma's gonna give you a big kiss good-bye, and you're gonna be on your own. You think you're ready? You kinda nervous?"

"No, I'm not nervous." The words barely come out.

"Okay, you give me a big hug. You're gonna learn everything for Grandma, right?"

"Right." Jamillah hugs her grandmother, and then lets go of her hand.

The Five-to-Seven Shift

Today, Jamillah Johnson is entering a whole new world. She has much to gain there: in the years ahead, she will benefit from everything that formal education has to offer, and she will form friendships that may last a lifetime. But on this day she's losing much as well: the familiarity of her home and the ongoing presence of her grandmother. The transition may seem frightening to her, and so will others in her life. Passages to come will involve a

"And I'll say, 'Good morning, teacher.'"

similar mix of loss and gain, and the same feeling of being little in the face of something big.

Jamillah has come a long way in her first six years. She has a firm grasp of language and can understand rules — linguistic rules, mathematics rules, rules that govern games, rules of all kinds. Developmental psychologist Sheldon White sees more. "She has some kind of ability to stand clear of the family and to do business with the world by herself that she didn't have a few years before. She has an ability to be away from the folks for long periods of time during the day. She has abilities to form alliances with peers. She has abilities to 'get along' with other children. That will be very important because a large part of school, maybe to her the most important part, will be her engagements with her peer groups and her formation of social groupings with other children.

"She has begun to know that there are different groups of people in this world. And she has begun to understand where she fits, that she's female as opposed to male, that she's black as opposed to white. She's quite interested in these things because they identify her as a certain kind, but she doesn't know yet how tough things get between her kind and another kind."[1]

In no time at all, Jamillah will learn a new set of age norms. She will be told that she must be quiet and listen, that she must follow the school's regulations, that she's not a baby anymore. She will be measured by her teachers in terms of how much academic knowledge she can absorb, and by her peers in terms of how well she gets along with them. For the next twelve years, she will be expected to be in a certain grade at a certain age. And everyone will know whether her progress is on schedule or off, whether she's a success or a failure. The Social Clock will be ticking very loudly.

What's interesting about Jamillah's entry into this new world of school and friends is its timing in the life cycle. Most societies recognize that children change in important ways between the ages of five and seven, and build that recognition into their Social Clocks. White sees one example of this "five-to-seven-shift" in the "vision quest" of Native American children, which occurs at about age five. "They go out into the woods and they're supposed to meet an animal. And the animal speaks to them and, having spoken to them, becomes connected with them. It becomes their totemic animal and remains with them for the rest of their lives. So the child becomes in league with an owl or a badger or a chipmunk, whatever the animal is. The child has been connected with the world via its parents. Now the child makes its own connection to nature, makes its own connection to the world."[2]

Across many cultures — perhaps across all — there is a consistent pattern of children taking on adult-like responsibilities between the ages of five and seven. Among the Kipsigis of Kenya, this is the time when children begin shouldering their share of the family economy. Their mothers begin to expect more of them, trusting them to take a message across the hilly fields to another homestead or to run by themselves to the shop for a small purchase.[3] Among the neighboring Nyansongo, it's the time when children begin preparing meals — boiling maize and beans or roasting potatoes — and when they assume the major care of very young siblings, feeding, bathing, and caring for the babies while their mothers work in the gardens or go to market. In Khalapur, a village on India's fertile Ganges plain, it's the time when children take over the care of cattle, driving them long distances, supervising their grazing, and keeping them out of the crops.[4] And on the Kennedy farm in Butler, Pennsylvania, it's the time when children take up the job of seeing that the calves are fed.

This change in status has been institutionalized in legal codes. English Common Law assumes that, at the age of seven, children have a working knowledge of right and wrong and may be tried for a crime. Catholic Canon Law makes the same assumption: seven is the beginning of the "age of reason," when children become capable of sin and confession.

Some historians have argued that in the Middle Ages the five-to-seven shift ushered youngsters into something very much like adulthood. Among the upper classes, they were sent to another castle or fine home, where the boys became pages and the girls, "bower maids." Farther down the social scale, youngsters were apprenticed to a trade and moved into the home of their master. Peasant children toiled in the fields alongside their parents.[5]

The child as adult. Five-year-old Infanta Margherita d'Austria, portrayed by Diego Velasquez (1599–1660). Scala/Art Resource, New York

Not even school distinguished child from adult. In medieval schools, which existed primarily to fill the ranks of the clergy and court, ten-year-olds sat on the hay-strewn floor beside twenty-five-year-olds, all working diligently on Latin grammar or rhetoric, geometry or astronomy, music or logic, and, certainly, theology. It was a Latin school — all lessons were given in that tongue — and it did not teach reading, writing, or the use of the local language. That was the job of the home or the apprentice's master tradesman.[6] Although parents, priests, and masters knew that children were not yet mature, the young were treated as miniature — if inadequate — adults. The notion that children might have unique needs was nowhere to be found.

In our country, the system of apprenticing children was still thriving in the last quarter of the eighteenth century. Just four years before the American Revolution, in the New York countryside about fifty miles north of Manhattan, Ezra and Mary Smith apprenticed their nine-year-old daughter Mary to work for a couple in another colony until her eighteenth birthday. In return for her labor and her promise not to play, gamble, marry, fornicate, or embezzle from her master, Mary would be fed, clothed, and housed, and taught to read, spin linen and wool, knit, and sew. At the end of the apprenticeship, she was to receive a feather bed, two dresses, a cloak and bonnet, two pairs of stockings, and a Bible.[7]

America's first attempt to regulate the labor of children came in 1836, when the state of Massachusetts forbade the employment in manufacturing of youngsters under fifteen unless they got at least three months' schooling each year. Before long, most New England states ruled that children could work no longer than ten hours each day. But as we entered the twentieth century, most other states still allowed seven-year-olds to work unlimited hours in coal mines, factories, textile mills, and fields. In 1916, Congress passed a law forbidding the products of child labor in interstate commerce, but it was struck down by the Supreme Court. By that time, thirty-three states required children to attend school until they reached the age of sixteen. In 1924, an attempt was made to protect children through a Constitutional amendment, but the Child Labor Amendment failed to be ratified by enough states before the allotted time elapsed.[8] At last, in 1938, the Fair Labor Standards Act forbade industrial labor by children younger than sixteen and prohibited those younger than eighteen from working in hazardous occupations.[9] Children were finally freed from a premature adulthood and allowed to go to school.

The social boundaries of childhood have varied a great deal from time to time and place to place. On many occasions, the Social Clock has deprived

Before child-labor laws. A group of young cotton pickers, photographed around 1910 by Lewis Hines. The Granger Collection, New York

the young of the very years the Biological Clock thought it "wise" to give them. But children have never been pushed into the adult world before the five-to-seven shift. Something must happen during those years — some biological event whose effects society recognizes when it directs children to school, an apprenticeship, or a factory. Perhaps children become ready for responsibility because the brain has done most of its growing and is approaching adult size. Perhaps it's a maturing of the hippocampus, an area deep within the brain that is crucial to memory. Or perhaps it's the power surge in the left hemisphere that some neuroscientists relate to new cognitive capacities.[10] Something we presently know little about has enabled Jamillah Johnson and children her age throughout history to leave the womb of the family and set forth on their own kind of "first day."

The Changing Nature of the Child

The children filing into Jamillah's school are blissfully unaware that, 350 years ago, children living on the same Massachusetts soil were regarded quite differently by adults. That's because adults of a given time and place not only set the Social Clock for childhood, they also define the nature of the child. And throughout history there have been astonishing changes in the way adults have viewed the young.

Today we see six-year-olds as competent individuals, full of energy and imagination, with a potential that needs encouragement to flower. But in the days of the Puritan colonists, we would have seen them as prideful, potentially evil souls who needed to learn obedience.

The Puritans, who left England to found the Massachusetts Bay Colony, believed that children were born ignorant and sinful, in danger of eternal damnation. And so they expressed their love for children in ways that seem harsh to us. Their worry over their children's souls led them to dwell on the terrors of hell and to insist on absolute obedience as a way of forcing their evil-natured, obstinate offspring to act according to reason and the will of God. As Martin Luther put it, "Children should be educated not only to fear their parents, but to feel that God will be angry with them if they do *not* fear their parents."[11] Until Puritan children were six or seven, their minds were considered too shallow for anything but rote learning, but after that time, they spent their hours in work and study, so that they were never idle and open to the devil's wiles. The aim was to strengthen the will, so that by the time children reached their teens, when they were capable of rational thought and behavior, they could combat their evil inclinations.

The Puritan view of the child was challenged by the Enlightenment of the eighteenth century. The rise of science fostered a less dogmatic, more liberal view of the world as an orderly universe, in which God was good, wise, and more remote. Notions of individualism and political freedom were in the air. As they took hold, they even affected the way parents named their children. Since the Middle Ages, children had been inter-changeable, seen only as members of the family. A newborn often received the first name of an older child who had died. But as the Enlightenment spread, children became unique individuals. The practice of reusing names, as if the same child had been reborn, died out.[12]

The most influential exponent of the Enlightenment was philosopher John Locke, who gave us the reasonable child. Locke maintained that chil-dren were not evil by nature, but essentially neutral; evil came from the environment. Although children came into the world with their own unique characteristics, their minds were blank slates. Because their minds were formed by their experiences, it was the parents' duty to mold character by instruction and by example. Almost as soon as they could talk, children were capable of reason, but only in regard to things they could see and touch. Until children could reason in the abstract, they needed a firm but kind hand. Overindulgence and physical punishment were equally destruc-tive, because both kept the child from exercising reason and controlling impulse. In Locke's words, the indulged child lacks "the true principle of virtue and industry and is [in] danger never to be good for anything," while corporal punishment "strengthens that in us which is the root from whence spring all vicious actions and the irregularities of life."[13] Locke's views crossed the sea to the mid-Atlantic colonies, where children were seen as trusting and vulnerable, in need of love, education, and a firm but understanding discipline.

Seventy-five years after Locke, just before the American Revolution, Jean-Jacques Rousseau popularized the romantic view of the good child. Rousseau believed that children are innocent at birth and then corrupted by an evil society. Rousseau's child was not the reasonable being of the Enlightenment but essentially a creature of feelings and sensations. Because they lack common sense, he said, children should spend the years between two and twelve exercising their bodies and storing up sensations and experiences. Protected throughout childhood from rote learning, religious doctrine, and attempts to stir the intellect, children could indulge their natural impulses. It was the adult's duty to arrange children's experiences so that they matched the maturing of various abilities. Corruption came when adults allowed youngsters to have experiences for which they were not ready or tried to teach them things their minds were not prepared to learn. "Nature wants children to be children before they are men," Rousseau wrote. "If we deliberately pervert this order, we shall get premature fruits which are neither ripe nor well-flavored, and which soon decay. . . . Childhood has ways of seeing, thinking, and feeling peculiar to itself; nothing can be more foolish than to substitute our ways for them."[14]

Rousseau's ideas were not quickly adopted by American parents, or even matched by his own deeds. He deposited his own five children at a foundling hospital, leaving them for others to rear. Still, he formed our conviction that children have special needs and that they should be allowed to grow at their own pace. Following "nature" meant following the child's biological program of growth.

Between 1825 and 1875, major changes in American society made Rousseau's ideas more acceptable. From a nation of farmers, artisans, and professionals who worked at home, we became a nation in which work was done in specialized places by specialized people. Perhaps spurred by this separation of work and home, the sexes came to live in different worlds. The world of men was increasingly secularized; it was seen as ugly, aggressive, corrupting, chaotic, sinful, and irreligious. At the same time, women became bearers of religion and caretakers of the culture; their world was sweet, chaste, calm, cultured, loving, protective, and godly. Since children

The pure and innocent child. "The Old Farm Gate," steel engraving after a painting by William Collins (1788–1847). The Granger Collection, New York

were cared for at home by women, they became increasingly sentimental-ized.[15] The Puritan's evil child in danger of damnation and the Enlightenment's reasonable child who was learning rational self-control became the pure and innocent child who would redeem society. As the century drew to a close, the ideal parent had become a tolerant, gentle nur-turer who provided authority without anger, focused on the child's natural virtues, and led by example rather than instruction or prohibition.[16]

Early in the twentieth century, Freud introduced the idea of the sensual child, motivated by unconscious forces and filled with sexual and aggressive needs. The job of the parents became one of seeing that the child gave up the "pleasure principle" for the "reality principle," but without frustrating the child's expression of these instinctual impulses. As parents refrained from imposing their authority, permissiveness became the rule and children were allowed to express their aggressive impulses freely. The warning that personality problems could be traced to unresolved internal conflicts exalt-ed the task of child-rearing, but also made it risky .

Over the past quarter century, a quiet social revolution in this country has altered our view of children once again. Women's roles have changed, and they have returned to the work force in ever-increasing numbers. Divorce rates have climbed, sexual standards have shifted, and adults have claimed the right to pursue their own lives. To do that, claims David Elkind of Tufts University,[17] we've had to see children as adaptable, thriving in day-care, and able to deal with many aspects of life that were once thought beyond them. So parents have come to believe in the competent child. Surveys support Elkind's contention. Over the last half century, parents in the United States and other developed countries have changed their minds about what they value most in children. Before, it was obedience; now, it's self-reliance.[18]

In the future, our views of children may be shaped by their declining numbers in our population. In 1960, one-third of all Americans were younger than eighteen; currently, one-fourth are; and by 2030, this age group will make up only about one-fifth of our population. Will children be treasured as a scarce resource, or will their interests be obscured by the growing number of older Americans?[19] Though the answer is not yet clear, children are already the poorest group in the country. In 1987, 21 percent of them were living below the poverty line, compared with only 12 percent of the elderly and 14 percent of the population at large.[20]

The history of childhood demonstrates that our views of the young — and the way we treat them — are fashioned out of adult fears, hopes, beliefs, and interests. Changing with the flow of time and imposing their will on biologically vulnerable creatures, these views tell us far more about the nature of the adult than they do about the nature of the child.

The School

In her classroom Jamillah Johnson sits quietly, staring at a huge, red, crepe-paper apple on the front wall. Beside it is a sign that reads, "Welcome back to school." Miss Hynes, a veteran of many first days, is calling her students' attention to the American flag next to the window in the front corner. "Everybody turn this way and put this hand out," she intones. "Put it over on your heart. Eyes on the flag. And we will say, 'I pledge allegiance to the flag of the United States of America, and to the republic for which it stands, one nation under God, indivisible, with liberty and justice for all.'" The words are new to Jamillah, and she has trouble reciting them, but already she's learned about a powerful symbol in her social world.

There's more to learn on this first day. When you're in class, says Miss Hynes, you raise your hand if you wish to speak, and you wait for the teacher to recognize you. When you form a line, you stand still and close to the person in front of you. You don't move from side to side, "so when you're standing in front, it looks like there's only one person."

Jamillah will spend the next nine months with Miss Hynes, a far greater amount of time than children spent with their teachers in the past. One hundred years ago, American children attended school eighty days each year, and only 5 percent of them went on to high school. Jamillah will spend 180 days a year under the direct influence of the school, and she will attend high school, if not college. Through homework, clubs, and social activities, through the way it brings children together and structures their social world, the school will extend its socializing influence into every corner of her life.

Pressures at school are steady and unyielding, and six-year-olds find that the nature of the socialization process changes dramatically. Parents are personal, but the school is impersonal. Parents offer stable relationships; schools offer a series of overlapping, brief relationships. Parents provide consistent views over the years; schools provide views that may conflict not only with those of the parents, but with one another. And whereas parents rate their children privately, sporadically, and in terms of the child's past performance, schools tend to rate children publicly, regularly, and in terms of the way their performance compares with that of others.[21]

Jamillah's experiences in school will prepare her to live in an industrialized society, one that is largely bureaucratic and impersonal. She will learn to act by herself and to accept responsibility for her own behavior. She will find that success depends on her making deliberate, perhaps painful efforts to master whatever tasks the teacher assigns. She will discover that all too often schoolwork consists of manipulating facts taken out of context and presented without any regard for their practical use. And she will learn to interact with others in a different way. At home, she sees her grandmother as a person with a variety of interests and moods, whose actions depend in good part on the circumstances of the moment. At school, she will see people in limited terms — as teacher, nurse, cafeteria worker, custodian, principal — and learn to interact with them in terms of their social roles.[22] Some of the attitudes and values she brought with her from home will be strengthened, but others will be changed. Schools have powerful effects on children's aspirations, moral values, political views, achievement, and the way they think about the world.

According to Sheldon White, it will take Jamillah and her school several years to get to know each other. "In the first two or three years of schooling the teacher, the parent, and the child are trying to make up their minds about how well the child will do. About the fourth grade, there's a kind of hardening — maybe a premature hardening but a hardening nevertheless — in which everybody decides what the child is or is not capable of. One of the visible signs is achievement tests, which make the declaration that one child is able and another child is less able. But in the first grade it's all negotiable. It's hard to find a first-grade child that isn't excited about going to school."[23]

Today, some educators and parents are calling for children to begin school earlier than they do now. They want to advance the Social Clock by about a year. That would mean compulsory schooling for four-year-olds and all-day kindergartens for five-year-olds. The arguments behind the proposal are many. American children are apparently falling behind in the world educational race, and starting them on the serious business of study a year early may be a way to narrow the gap. The success of enrichment programs for economically disadvantaged preschoolers has convinced some educators that incorporating such programs into the public schools would benefit all children. The discovery by psychologists that even babies have a remarkable ability to learn has persuaded many parents that letting youngsters spend their early years in play is a waste of time. Better to give them an early start in the competitive race they'll soon be running. Other parents simply want public schooling expanded to fill part of the gap left by inadequate day-care.

Our children clearly are capable of learning more than we ask of them. Preschoolers already know as much math as their parents did when they began the first grade. Many of today's preschoolers can already solve simple addition problems.[24] And a hefty proportion of them, veterans of day-care or nursery school, have mastered their parents' kindergarten curriculum: they know how to sit still and listen to instructions or stories, they can follow routines, and they are old hands at the business of group activities. Across the Pacific, Japanese preschoolers are hard at work; more than 90 percent of them go to private schools, where they learn language skills, a respect for education, and how to interact in groups.[25]

Yale psychologist Edward Zigler, a founder of the Head Start program for disadvantaged youngsters, agrees that learning comes as naturally to children as flying does to birds.[26] He says that children are programmed to learn and don't need to be pushed. In fact, you can't stop them from learning. But he's opposed to formal education for four-year-olds. Zigler cites a large body of evidence showing that the extra boost which has helped disadvantaged children would be wasted on middle-class children.[27] Studies suggest that by the time middle-class children are ten years old, it would be impossible to tell the difference between them and other ten-year-olds who had not had early education.

What worries Zigler most is the pressure that formal schooling would place on many children. He foresees a generation of children beset by achievement anxiety and turned off by school. Zigler's fears are echoed by Harvard psychologist Jerome Kagan, who stresses that just because a four-year-old *can* learn something doesn't mean that he or she *ought* to be given formal instruction. Both experts believe that the move toward early education ignores the wide span of individual differences. Some four-year-olds may thrive under educational pressure, but others will be crushed. Another worry gnaws at some psychologists; they fret that pushing formal study on four-year-olds will take them away from the real business of early childhood — exploring the world around them. The worldwide consensus that children are not ready for responsibility until they're at least five may indicate that the worries of developmental psychologists are well placed. Perhaps most children need an extra year or so of maturation before they can cope with the demands of academic work.

And perhaps, as Zigler suspects, what parents are really calling for is quality day-care. He suggests that instead of pushing four-year-olds into formal study, we open our schools earlier in the morning, keep them open later in the evening, and run them during the summer. With a staff trained to work with children, we could provide all-day care for three- and four-year-olds and keep older children occupied with supervised recreational activities. Then parents could go about the business of making a living without worrying about their children.

The Schoolyard

In Lunch Room Number Two, Jamillah and her new classmates chew slowly on sandwiches and sip quietly on straws from cartons of milk. They're huddled into their seats, staring blankly ahead, in awe of what's happening. The school principal moves among them with a microphone. "We eat quietly and we eat in our seats. No one gets up." On this day, no one seems inclined to test him. Boys and girls look timidly at the strange faces across the table from them, looking for someone who might play with them in the schoolyard, someone who might become a friend.

For these children, what happens in the schoolyard will be just as important as what happens in the school. And when they're out on the playground, there will be no one to protect them. No child will hold back to keep from beating them at a game, humiliating them in a test of skill, or harming them in a fight. No one will run interference or guarantee membership in a group. Out on the playground, it's sink or swim. No one automatically becomes your friend.

A few children, about one in ten, won't make friends. Some of them are overly aggressive and others are withdrawn, but these qualities in and of themselves are not the problem. Being rejected, rather, is due to the absence of positive social skills, according to Steven Asher, an educational psychologist at the University of Illinois. "There are many children in school who get into fights with other kids, but if these children can also be resourceful play partners — fun to be with, cooperative, and helpful — they tend not to be rejected." The same is true of shy children: if they have positive social skills, they make friends. "There are many, many shy kids in school, and their social adjustment, by and large, is quite good. They have friends; they're well liked; they're very thoughtful in their relationships with other people; but they may be a bit slow to warm up. Shyness per se doesn't seem to be a major risk indicator for kids in terms of the ability to form friendships."[28]

Researchers have discovered that the quality of the attachment that children form with parents often predicts the kind of relationships they develop later on with peers. Children who make friends easily and whose friendships are warm and satisfying are often children with secure attachments. Their parents tend to be responsive and attentive to their child's needs. The trust that these youngsters develop at home seems to carry over into their relationships with other people.

Parents of unpopular children are much more likely to be harsh and punitive in their discipline practices. Their children learn at home that the world is harsh and punitive, and they seem to carry this belief over into school, where they interpret the neutral actions of others as unfriendly. "Some children are quite good at discriminating teasing that is playful from teasing that is hostile," says Asher, "and other children have difficulties with these discriminations. Quite often they'll get into fights because they're more likely to think that another person is really trying to hurt them."[29]

Children who are rejected by their peers run a greater risk of having problems later on. A disproportionate number of school dropouts, children with emotional problems, and juvenile delinquents come from the ranks of rejected children. Children who find a friend early in the school year not only do better in their social adjustment to kindergarten or first grade; they do better academically as well. And children who have friends in the early school years graduate from high school at higher rates than children who are unpopular.

By the time they go off to school, children have already had considerable experience making friends. If you ask preschoolers to describe a friend, they will talk about painting pictures in the basement, about playing store, about things they *do* together. They are not yet able to put into words how important their friendship is. But, says Asher, if you take a closer look by audiotaping and videotaping children at play, you'll see much more going on. "Children will express all kinds of fears. Fears of inadequacy, fears that people will think they're stupid, fears that their parents are going to abandon them. And in their relationships with their peers they gain reassurance from a best friend who says, 'No, no, you're not stupid. You're really a good guy.' But of course if you ask five-year-olds what they get from a friend, they would never be able to articulate this quality of their friendships."[30] The companionship of a friend enables young children to learn new skills, gives them courage to take risks, and imparts the confidence they need to enter new situations. Researchers have discovered that, with a friend at their side, children are just as comfortable as if their mother were there. That's why children entering kindergarten adapt more smoothly when a friend is making the same transition.

These youngest friendships may shatter easily, because preschoolers often choose their friends on a single basis. Either they like their looks or the children share a common, perhaps transitory, interest. Young children have not yet learned that common beliefs and a wide similarity of interests underlie friendships that endure. As children get older, their view of friendship changes. Someone you've had fun with for the "whole day" is no longer a friend. The label is reserved for relationships that have a history of trust and confidentiality. And children now realize the qualities of friendship that went unrecognized in their earlier relationships. They treasure the emotional support they get from friends and the importance of having someone to confide in.

Someone in the schoolyard might become such a friend to Jamillah Johnson. Right now she's standing in the shadow of the school building, quietly surveying the scene. Children are running about, free from the rules inside, meeting friends they haven't seen all summer. The boys shadow box, the girls talk, and the entire playground hums with energy.

An older, taller girl stands next to Jamillah, leaning against the brick wall of the school. She seems to know the playground scene all too well. "Why are you leaning here?" Jamillah asks.

"'Cause I don't got no friend to play with," she answers matter-of-factly.

Jamillah thinks about her answer for a long time. Then she skips out into the swirl of children, singing to herself, laughing and smiling. It's her last big step on this, her first day.

6

THE PSYCHOLOGICAL STORY OF CHILDHOOD "How To" Time

Nine-year-old Karl Haglund is perched in his eagle's nest, a treehouse built high in the willow that grows in his backyard. Sometimes he sits there alone among the tree's spreading branches, his face turned toward the sky, a boy clearly enjoying his solitude. Sometimes he's with his friends, engrossed in the kind of talk that boys find fascinating.

This morning Karl is busy sawing and hammering. "It's fun to build," he says. "I started the house when I was four years old. Then when I was about seven, my dad built me this platform. 'Cause all my places were falling apart and they were crawling with carpenter ants. So we destroyed them and then built me a deck. And I built on top of it. It's stronger now. You can have privacy here, but it's a bad place to go when it's windy 'cause you almost get blown off."

This Huck Finn of a lad with light brown hair, a clear complexion, and cheeks the color of a ripe apple is the youngest of three boys in the Haglund family. The oldest brother, Jon, is fifteen; the middle brother, Jerry, is twelve. It's difficult for Karl to keep up with Jon, who is gifted, but he has to remember to slow down for Jerry, who's retarded. It's not always easy. "When Jerry's tired, he gets on my nerves. When me and my friends play, he always wants to play with us, and we don't want him to bug us. And he steals my tapes and drawings and hides them. And I have to leave my chemistry set under the bed because Jerry will, like, take the chemicals out.

Karl Haglund, nine. "I have a reading problem. I can do math fine, and spelling's easy."

Might eat them." Sometimes Karl bugs his brother back. "I make him play games with me. Each time he tries to grab the ball, I kick it away from him." But for all the teasing, Karl helps Jerry and often shows patience beyond his years.

Karl has his own difficulties — a serious learning problem that was discovered when he was in his last year of nursery school. "He just didn't seem to be getting his alphabet and his numbers," recalls Jenny Haglund, his mother. "Everyone told me not to worry, that it would all just come. About two months into kindergarten, his teacher contacted me and said she wanted to talk. I kind of thought , 'Oh, no.' When we went in for the meeting, she told us that Karl seemed to be putting all kinds of effort into trying to learn, and it just wasn't coming. She was concerned that there might be a learning problem. I thought deep down, 'I just had the sense that this might be.' We went through the testing, and the psychologist was very helpful. We did not want this to be a negative thing for Karl, and she helped us explain that we were going to learn how he learned best. His problem was with auditory sequential learning, and that meant he really wouldn't process any classroom teaching that was taught verbally. But his visual skills were very strong. We felt it necessary to put him into a special classroom for the learning disabled, but we really had to fight. We almost had to threaten a due process hearing to get him in.

"It was the best thing for him. He had a wonderful teacher who was able to develop his ego again. We're just so pleased with the school. He's being mainstreamed into a number of his courses now. He's been honored as student of the month and gets citizenship awards. I think it's just the best of both worlds right now. And he's learning. He's learning other ways to read.

Karl's a very hard worker, and I think that's the other reason why he has such success. He's really put his mind to wanting to do it, to accomplish this."

The disability doesn't seem to bother Karl. When asked why he's in the special class, his reply is matter-of-fact. "I have a reading problem. I can do math fine, and spelling's easy. I'm really the only kid in third year that's, like, doing this by myself in mainstream." Besides, Karl knows some mainstream kids who'd rather be in a special class like he is " 'cause they don't like the mainstream teachers."

Karl's teacher gives him stars on a bulletin board for reading pages from the *Weekly Reader*. But recently she assigned him something harder. He had to make up a book. "So I thought of my dog. She said that would be a good story so I wrote about that. It took pretty many days." Karl wrote about an important episode in his young life. "Well, all the kids wanted a dog, and my Mom and Dad were sick of us badgering them for a dog. So we were looking for one. And then my Dad's friend called and we went to their house to go swimming. They had this cute dog, and my parents asked them where they got the dog, and they said from their sister-in-law. The older son has a whole bunch of dogs, little ones. And so we said, 'Well, we'll see what Jon and Jerry say.' And when they came back from camp we told them about the dog and they said, 'Fine.' So we called the people back up and said, like, 'We want the dog.' And then they brought the dog."

So far Karl is getting along fine in school. "Some classes are fun," he says, "and some classes are boring." Walter Haglund, his father, explains how Karl has learned to compensate for his disability. "A true learning-disabled child is very difficult to pick up, because they use other faculties. Karl will memorize passages, so that people don't realize that he's not reading them. He's very artistic, and he uses those abilities. He has developed his mechanical abilities to a higher degree than a lot of children his age. And he uses his personality and beguiling nature to help compensate."

Much of Karl's compensation happens outside the classroom. "I like to draw. I like to play soccer. The favorite position I have is goalie. I like to collect shells when I go to the beach. I like to build clubhouses. I like to play with my chemistry set. And I like to ride skateboards and bikes and stuff." This list of what he likes to do is what Karl offers when asked to describe himself. It takes some coaxing to get him to acknowledge that he's good at carpentry, soccer, and video games, that he has a talent for drawing, and that he's a member of the safety patrol. If he's unaware of what he's doing, he will come up with a brief self-description. "Sometimes," he says,

"I'm a couch potato. When I'm home alone, we just watch movies the whole time."

Karl likes to work with his dad. Recently the two of them built a small wooden car for the Cub Scouts' annual Pinewood Derby. Karl did the designing. "First you frame the car from this big block of wood. After you do that, you cut it out and you put the wheels on. You paint it. I put on five coats of red paint. And then you put weights in the car. The night before the race, I put the decals on it and painted the nine on it. Half the cars in the race weren't even painted." Karl's proud racer didn't win the derby, as his brother Jon's had six years before, but he was a good sport about it. "I didn't care that much if I won or lost. It's just fun to make it."

Sitting in his treehouse, Karl thinks that someday it might be nice to have a job building things, like his dad does. "Dad's an architect and that means, like, he does buildings for the city and for other people on his own. We know this one person, Dad designed his house in Washington. He designed some of my friends' houses. Mom's a social worker, and she talks to the parents and she goes to meetings. But I don't want to be a social worker. 'Cause I would have to be in important meetings. It's a pretty hard job. But I might be an architect, probably. Or maybe a carpenter."

A Sense of Industry

Karl Haglund is responding to the biological and social imperatives of childhood. Despite a learning disability, he is acquiring knowledge and developing the sense of personal competence that Erik Erikson has called "industry." Karl loves to tell you about technique, about "how to": how to play soccer and video games; how to make a treehouse, a book, and a Pinewood Derby car; how to do all the things, both inside and outside the classroom, that are required in his culture. Karl is learning that he can do things and do them well, that he can be a productive and useful young man.

Children Karl's age have a self-imposed set of standards concerning mastery of various skills. These standards first develop during the preschool period, when youngsters discover they can't immediately do everything they'd like to, whether it's building a tower that's ten blocks high, winding up a mechanical toy, or pouring a glass of milk without spilling it. The obligation to do something well is so deeply felt that when they cannot meet a standard, children are visibly distressed, but when they master it, they smile with delighted satisfaction.

At school, Karl learns the academic skills he will need to assume the role of an adult in a technological culture. At home, he learns about carpentry and the skills involved in being a successful worker, husband, and father. In these important matters, adults bring children along, helping them to do things that youngsters could never hope to manage by themselves.

In hunter-gatherer societies, as well as in the agricultural and pastoral societies that supplanted them, children were always taught "on the spot." They could see the usefulness of the task they were learning. Most children in modern societies must learn in structured school situations that have little or nothing to do with the tasks of adult life. Karl is good at math, in part because he can see how it relates to success in carpentry, model building, and other "real life" situations. But filling out the blanks in a language workbook may seem neither important nor relevant to him.

Around the world, children seem to have little trouble learning things that make sense to them. When psychologists studied street children in Brazilian cities, they discovered an even narrower split between academic and "real" learning. The children, whose ages ranged from nine to fifteen, spent their days on the city streets selling popcorn, fruit, and corn on the cob. When asked how much a banana and an ear of corn cost, virtually every child could answer correctly: 148 cruzieros. But if asked to add 85 and 63 (the cost of the banana and the ear of corn), only 37 percent came up with the right answer.[1] Children learn what society requires them to learn for survival.

Sometimes, said Erikson, it takes mild but firm coercion to show children that they can accomplish tasks they would never have thought of trying on their own. This is how Karl's father taught him to use carpenter's tools, and how his mother taught him to heat a pizza in the microwave. The attractiveness of the enterprise comes from the reality and practicality of the task, and the fact that it gives children a token sense of participating in the adult world.

But much of the "how to" of childhood takes the form of play. Through play, children learn about adult culture, experimenting with various roles. It begins, of course, during the preschool years, when children play house or doctor or going off to work, but it continues in more sophisticated versions later on. Whether children are playing with combat figures, peering through a microscope, or sitting in front of a computer that's running a flight-simulator program, they're testing possibilities as well as having fun. Adult roles have physical, emotional, and economic consequences, but in play, children can learn without exposing themselves to the risks.

Play prepares children for the adult world in other ways. It's difficult to play games without learning something about the intentions and skills of others. So children playing rummy or Monopoly, marbles or checkers, are honing their ability to deal with people. They also learn important skills on the softball diamond and the soccer field. The Duke of Wellington once said that the Battle of Waterloo was won on the playing fields of Eton, and modern psychologists have concluded that sports do teach valuable lessons about life. Wellington was probably referring to the role of sports in building teamwork and encouraging persistence in the face of formidable odds. But sports also teach children to deal with competition, build self-confidence, and develop the ability to lead others. Losing in a soccer game or a Pinewood Derby helps children learn how to handle the inevitable disasters of life — whether it's being passed over for a promotion, losing a friend, or any of the other occupational or social adversities they may suffer.

Play also gives children a chance to experiment with unfamiliar activities. They can manipulate reality, try out new concepts, and think about the world in new and perhaps daring ways. Psychologist Jerome Bruner believes that our early ancestors might never have developed tools unless they had long periods of free time without pressure, which allowed them to play with various objects and experiment with new combinations.[2] Free investigation of the world, along with occasional coercion, helps children develop a sense of industry, a sense of competence at "how to."

Piaget and the Five-to-Seven Shift

The importance of children's free investigation was long championed by Jean Piaget, who cast new light on the process of children's intellectual growth. In 1929, Piaget began his attempts to trace the origin of thought by carefully observing the development of his own three children. The insights he gained from studying his children led to extensive experiments in which he presented specific problems to children of all ages. He was less interested in the correctness of their answers than in their explanations, which he regarded as clues to the nature of their thought. Piaget's work so dominated the study of intellectual development that for several decades most research in the field was aimed either at extending his theories or refuting them.

Piaget believed that a fundamental change in thinking takes place at the time of the five-to-seven shift. Only after the change, he said, could children think reasonably and logically about concrete objects — things they can see, touch, and hear. He called their new way of thinking "concrete operations." Gone is the charming child who, when asked how the sun began, replies that "God put a real lot of light bulbs in it."[3] Or the youngster who stoutly maintains that putting a dog mask over a cat's head transforms the cat into a dog — with dog's bones and a dog's stomach under its skin.[4] Children in the stage of concrete operations do not make such claims. They are not fooled by irrelevant changes in the appearance of things. They know that when you smash a ball of clay flat, you haven't changed the amount of clay, only its shape. Preschoolers are so overwhelmed by the appearance of things that such changes easily mislead them.

Psychologists are fond of demonstrating the irrationality of preschoolers' thought by pouring colored water into glasses of different shapes. If you pour water from a standard glass into a short squat glass, the preschooler believes that the amount of water has suddenly shrunk; but if you pour the same water into a tall, narrow glass, the preschooler believes that the water has expanded. Preschoolers are convinced of this even if they watch you do the pouring. They can think about only one aspect of a situation at a time, and their attention becomes so fixed on the dominant feature of the new arrangement (the height of the glass) that their minds do not register the fact that the breadth of the glass has also changed. They're also unable to reverse your actions mentally; they can deal only with what they see in front of them. They cannot think about how the water looked before, or what it might look like if you poured it back into the first glass.

Karl Haglund would not be fooled by someone who told him that his tall, narrow glass held more soft drink than his brother's regular glass. He can figure out when a change in an object's appearance is important and when it is irrelevant. He can think about several aspects of a situation at once — both the height and the width of a glass, for example — and mentally compare what an object looks like now with the way it looked before. He has grasped the principle of "conservation," one of Piaget's concrete operations.

This ability to grasp two aspects of a situation at the same time affects all aspects of a child's life. In their relations with others, for example, it means that children can keep two perspectives — their own and another person's — in mind at the same time. When Karl was three years old, he understood that other people couldn't always see what he saw. Someone in the next room couldn't see the television program he was watching. Now he understands that even when two people look at the same object, it looks different to them if they're viewing it from different positions. Karl also knows that other people's thoughts, motives, and intentions may not be the same as his own and that, placed in the same situation, they may react differently. He has learned to go beyond surface impressions and see people in terms of traits and abilities.

Karl is just beginning to see himself in that way. He is discovering whether he's shy or friendly, lazy or a hard worker, good or inept at carpentry, a "couch potato" or not. At about age nine, children's self-concept begins to depend on how they stack up against the real world. Until then, they're so delighted when they complete some task, whether it's hitting a baseball or solving a puzzle, that they don't pay much attention to how well others do. They check out other children only to make certain that no one is taking advantage of them — and so they count presents at Christmastime or inspect the size of cake servings. Nine-year-olds are beginning to compare themselves in a different way. They notice whether they read better than their classmates, hit balls farther, run faster, solve problems more quickly, or build better cars for the Pinewood Derby.

To psychologist Susan Harter at the University of Denver, these changes affect the relationship between the self-as-subject ("I") and the self-as-object ("me"). Six-year-olds can criticize others, but are not aware of their own faults. "I" cannot yet pass judgment on "me." Eight-year-olds begin to observe themselves ("I" can watch "me"), but children do not judge themselves until they are about nine. Nine-year-olds often get so caught up in self-criticism that they are extremely harsh on themselves. They try hard to please, but are so afraid of falling short that they rush to judgment, tossing off remarks such as, "Am I ever stupid!"[5]

Along with this complex view of themselves comes a deepened understanding of emotion. A year or two ago, Karl used to talk about emotion in terms of facial expressions ("It made me cry") or specific actions ("I shouted"). Now he talks about the way he feels inside, and he understands that his emotions are often mixed. He can be sad and angry at the same time. Like other children in the stage of concrete operations, Karl has picked up another sophisticated human skill: he can now hide his emotions.[6] When someone makes him angry, he can smother his urge to strike out.

Being able to think reasonably about the world allows Karl to think reasonably about people and the things they do. He can now understand that his mother can be *both* a mother and a social worker. A few years ago, this concept was beyond him, and he was unable to see people as filling more than one role.

Despite Karl's enormous mental advances, one area remains stubbornly beyond his grasp — he cannot understand the relationship between the individual and society. He thinks about social institutions only in personal terms. He knows about police officers and judges, but cannot grasp the concept of law; he knows about teachers, but not about education; about the president, but not about government. Such abstract understandings will not develop until he's an adolescent, like his brother Jon; but that's another story.

The Self as Male or Female

This evening, there's a Halloween party at Karl Haglund's house. As the children arrive, it becomes apparent that the boys and the girls have different ideas about costumes. Each boy tries to look uglier and scarier than the last — they are werewolves, vampires, Frankenstein monsters, Freddys from the *Nightmare on Elm Street* movies, and aliens from other planets. For the girls, costumes are an opportunity to be beautiful. One is a fairy princess, another a ballerina. There's a Princess Leia from the *Star Wars* films, but not an ugly witch in the bunch. As striking as the differences in their costumes is the disparity in their behavior. The boys chase around the house, wrestling on the furniture and trying to frighten one another. The girls are primly decorous; scorning the male roughhousing, they help Mrs. Haglund arrange cupcakes and candies. These nine-year-olds have thoroughly absorbed the gender roles prescribed by American society. If they learned their schoolwork as well, they would all be "A" students.

Children master their gender roles so thoroughly because they get continual lessons from every socialization source in their lives. Parents, peers, older siblings, teachers, the media, and the community collaborate in a relentless continuing-education program with an almost inevitable outcome. The lessons are so subtle that those doing the teaching are often unaware of what they're doing.

Children absorb what they're taught. As early as eighteen months, according to psychoendocrinologist John Money of Johns Hopkins University, they have a tenuous sense of whether they're male or female — what psychologists call "gender identity" — even though they can't put it into words.[7] By their second birthday, most can tell a man from a woman, and although they can't tell you which toys are for girls and which are for boys, girls already prefer dolls and dress-up, while boys prefer trucks and guns and hammers.

By the time children are three, they have a clearer sense of gender identity. Youngsters know their own sex, that there are two sexes, and that everyone is either male or female. They're also creating their own theories of gender, spun out of a web of associations they have noticed and expectations they have developed.[8] They discover that the distinction between male and female is a nice, clean way to organize the world, and for a while they examine everything they encounter in terms of gender. They classify every toy and game, every article of clothing, every occupation, telling you whether it's for boys or girls or mommies or daddies.

Some children pick up this skill earlier than others. The speed with which notions of gender are acquired seems to depend on the emotional reactions of parents.[9] Toddlers who are sensitive to gender at an early age usually have highly traditional parents whose responses leave no doubt that children should play with toys appropriate for their own sex. By twenty-seven months, these youngsters have decided that gender is important and, like three-year-olds, have homed in on the "right" toys and activities.

When given the opportunity, three-year-olds also use gender to sort themselves into play groups, a tendency that keeps getting stronger until puberty. The self-imposed separation of the sexes is not just a human trait; young monkeys also seek companions among those of their own sex. Psychologists have been puzzling over this tendency for some years. At Stanford University, psychologist Eleanor Maccoby believes that as children divide the world into male and female, their identity becomes bound up in their group membership. And so they are attracted to and play with "kids like me." They are also attracted to differences in styles of play.[10] Most boys love the rough-and-tumble play that throws them into body contact, while girls — even those who are extremely active — avoid pushing and shoving. So boys look for playmates who enjoy their rowdy overtures — other boys. Most boys also get their way by making direct demands, sometimes shouldering others aside to get their turn, but girls rely on polite suggestion. Since boys remain deaf to gentle requests, most girls look for playmates who respond to their mild attempts at influence — other girls.

Biology may be involved in these different play styles, which are as apparent in other primates as they are in human children. Young male primates return rough overtures with great interest and embark on a tumbling round of play, but young females shrink away from them. Maccoby believes that such responses can be traced to one of those tiny biological differences between the sexes, caused by the bath of prenatal sex hormones in males. Among babies and toddlers she has studied, boys quickly shift into a happy excited state that takes a long time to come down from, while girls' moods are less volatile and tend toward calmness and quiet. That may be why, she says, most little girls find rough, jostling boys' play unpleasant.

When psychologist Janice Gibson of the University of Pittsburgh studied play in twenty-two countries around the world, ranging from the People's Republic of China to Saudi Arabia, she discovered that in every country games were divided by gender, with the boys playing aggressive games and the girls playing games associated with domesticity. The boys in Saudi Arabia play games of hunting and attacking that are far more like those of Chinese boys than the games of Saudi girls. Even when children play with the same toys, they use them in a different manner. A little girl sweeps the floor with a broom; a little boy pretends it's a gun.[11] In every culture that's been studied, with every device that's been used to measure it, boys show more aggression than girls. Aggression seems to be an inborn difference that gets magnified by cultures everywhere, no doubt because it's associated with traditional male roles.

Most three-year-olds still have a long way to go before they complete their understanding of gender. Even many four-year-olds are slightly confused. First, children learn that people don't get to choose their gender; motives and wishes have nothing to do with it. The next step is the realization that little boys always grow up to be men and little girls always grow up to be women — that gender is permanent. Until they grasp this notion, children may believe that a girl can change her gender by cutting her hair short and joining the boys in playing war, and that a boy who lets his hair grow and plays house can become a girl. In studies of what psychologists call "gender constancy," six out of every ten preschoolers are fooled by changes in clothes or hairstyle.

One reason they are fooled is the way they think. The same preschooler who believes that a cat wearing a dog mask is a dog throughout is likely to believe that a boy wearing a dress is a girl throughout. But knowledge of anatomy makes as much difference as possessing the concrete operations described by Paiget. Cornell University psychologist Sandra Bem has discovered that a majority of three-year-olds who know their sexual anatomy also know that gender is permanent.[12] These clever three-year-olds are usually girls; in fact, three-year-old girls generally know as much about anatomical sex as five-year-old boys do.

The confusion that reigns among young boys produced a muddled conversation between two four-year-old boys within Bem's hearing. The first little boy came to school with a barrette in his hair, and the second boy accused him of being a girl, "because only girls wear barrettes." The first boy became indignant and pulled down his pants to display his penis and thus refute the charge. The accuser was not impressed. "Everyone has a penis," he said, "only girls wear barrettes."[13]

Once youngsters understand that their actions will not change their gender, they relax their vigilance and espouse positions they would have vigorously denied just a year or so before. After the age of seven or eight, girls and boys alike take a less stereotyped view of male and female behavior. They say that it's okay for boys to bake cakes or for girls to build model planes, and it's fine if men sew a seam or women fix the plumbing. They agree that society, not biology, determines most of what men and women do.

But for boys at least, these relaxed standards do not affect day-to-day behavior. Most continue to dislike girls' pastimes and avoid any involvement in them.[14] Karl Haglund isn't very subtle about the matter, especially when he's speaking for the record. "I don't like any girls in my class," he says. "They're weird. They're stupid. They're disgusting. They do temper tantrums. Some stick up their nose. And some always like to get you in trouble and stuff like that." No one can tell Karl that boys and girls like the same things. "Boys like to watch violence and girls like to watch plain TV. We like to watch Ninja movies and Rambo and movies that are rated 'R' just because they have violence in them. Some girls are afraid of them." At Karl's age, children know they will be teased unmercifully for having a girlfriend or boyfriend — or, worse, being "in love" — if they're seen with someone of the opposite sex. And so long-standing "brother-sister" friendships often go underground, out of the public eye.

All these generalizations about the differences between girls and boys obscure the greater similarities between them. The interests, actions, personality, and intellectual capabilities of girls and boys largely overlap. Some girls are more aggressive than most boys, and some boys are less aggressive than most girls. In the interests of intellectual economy, we tend to forget that point, and so most people operate on stereotypical assumptions most of the time. It's true that boys will be boys and girls will be girls, but the deeper reality is that children will be children. It's the similarites between the sexes that make Karl's Halloween party a success.

The Self as a Maker of Meaning

As Karl Haglund learns about being a male, he is becoming a maker of meaning. He's starting to interpret the "me" — the self-as-object — that he now can see and judge. Karl makes one kind of meaning when he describes how to do things, and another when he recounts episodes from his life. He loves to tell the story of his tree house and the time his family got a dog. Much of his storytelling is prompted by his parents, and much of the glue in his accounts is their doing. They make his stories adult-like. But every now and then we get a glimpse of Karl's stories as he tells them to himself.

In some aspects of his psychological growth, Karl may have been slower than his brother Jon and faster than his brother Jerry. "Late" with his ability to read, he was probably "early" with his use of tools. But the difference between himself and others his age is not as great as it will be later in life. In childhood, the Psychological Clock still falls under the homogenizing influence of the Biological and Social Clocks. As a result, the ability to shape stories from their experiences emerges at roughly the same age in all children.

When babies come into the world, their memory has no provision for sharing its contents with others. For several years, they store events in a very direct way — in terms of a physical sensation such as sight, sound, smell, or taste, or in terms of an emotion such as fear, excitement, or joy. When Marcel Proust wrote of early memories aroused by the taste of a tea-soaked morsel of cake, his description seemed an accurate rendering of the way a toddler might store an event in memory: "No sooner had the warm liquid, and the crumbs with it, touched my palate than a shudder ran through my whole body, and I stopped, intent upon the extraordinary changes that were taking place. An exquisite pleasure had invaded my senses, but individual, detached, with no suggestion of its origin."[15] Proust's character later traces the memory of pleasure to a boyhood treat connected with visits to his aunt: when he went in to say good morning, she gave him bites of madeleine dipped in tea.

Starting at about age three, most children can do more than remember smells, tastes, and feelings of warmth and pleasure. They can tell you about events in their lives. Three is the age when researcher Katherine Nelson of the City University of New York believes that "autobiographical memory" comes on line.[16] Before that age, she says, children lack the language with which to encode their experiences. Unless the language switch is on, they can't review an episode in their thoughts or tell it to others, so it never gets filed in the stacks of their memory. Children under three also lack "scripts" on which to hang their experiences. Scripts are routine descriptions of familiar events that are rather like the script for a play.[17] From about our first birthday, we begin piling up experiences that happen again and again — meals, bedtime, baths, trips to the day-care center or the doctor's — in Proust's case, visits to his aunt's. Scripts focus on actions, and without them, we'd be lost. By telling us what to expect, scripts help us understand the world.

The uncanny experience known as déjà vu is probably an outgrowth of our adult store of scripts.[18] While talking to a stranger at a party, you suddenly have the feeling that you've had this conversation before. The room, which you've never been in before, seems to be the same room where the earlier conversation took place. Yet you know the experience is new. What you have done is recognize elements of the present situation that are part of your standard script.

By the age of three or four, children are using scripts to tell what happens, say, at McDonald's (you order a Big Mac, pay for it, and eat it) or at a birthday party (you give presents, sing "Happy Birthday," have cake and ice cream, and play games). By the age of five, scripts are more elaborate, such as this one for going to the supermarket: "We get a cart, and we look for some onions and plums and cookies and tomato sauce, onions, and all that kind of stuff, and when we're finished we go to the paying booth, and then we . . . , then the lady puts all our food in a bag, then we put it in the cart, walk out to our car, put the bags in our trunk, then leave."[19]

Scripts do a curious thing to memory — they help determine what will be remembered. As memories are hung on the hooks in scripts, specific experiences tend to run together. Instead of remembering what happened at last year's birthday party, children remember what generally happens at birthday parties. When they retrieve their memory of a particular party, they may add some things that didn't happen (the birthday cake that was thrown at another party) and omit some things that did (the game of ring toss). Because of scripts, most recollections of events are in some ways inaccurate. Yet without scripts, remembering any event for long is probably impossible. Nelson believes that scripts precede our memory of specific events, and that they take several years to build up. That's why the autobiographical memory system is not operational before the age of three.

As autobiographical memory develops, children become more adept at narrative. Even preschoolers seem to understand what a story is, says Charlotte Doyle of Sarah Lawrence College. In weekly visits to a laboratory school, Doyle would ask children between the ages of three and six if any of them wanted to write a book. She would take a volunteer aside, fold a piece of construction paper into the shape of a book, and write in it whatever the child told her. Doyle found that children could combine sources in their narrative — Hansel and Gretel and Martians, for example — use props to keep a story going, and devise expressions, such as "kissing the nice trash," to amuse their peers. They even experimented with form: one little girl began her book with, "Mommy went into the store. Then Mommy came out of the store." She giggled as she realized that she could keep the story going indefinitely by repeating those two sentences. By the time children are in kindergarten, Doyle concluded, they understand storytelling as "a bounded, self-enclosed activity" with a sense of completeness.[20]

During the school years, children become more skillful and more confident storytellers. Before, they assumed that everyone knew what was in their mind and that their perspective was the same as everyone else's. Now they realize that's not so; with an ability to monitor two perspectives at once — their audience's and their own — they start to socialize their stories. Even the pictures they paint, says Boston-based art educator Nancy Smith, are "driven" by narrative in a way they weren't before and won't be again.[21] And children absorb stories as eagerly as they tell them. They hear about their family, their country, the religious and social groups that they're part of. They develop the ability to repeat the stories of their "people" in greater detail. Through such stories, they learn rules, values, and guidelines for living.

They also begin to store memories in a new way, paying attention to the markers used by their culture to share thoughts. Their memories become marked with notions of time ("yesterday," "last Christmas"), location ("Grammy's house," "at kindergarten"), people and their roles ("Daddy," "the policeman"), and causation ("the cat scratched me because I pulled its tail"). Using these social conventions, children connect their own stories to those of their family and their culture.

But their stories still differ from those of adults. When developmentalist Susan Engel of the Simon's Rock campus of Bard College asked seven-year-olds to write autobiographies, she was impressed with the idiosyncratic, personal nature of what they wrote, and with the immediacy and vividness of their expression. Most of this was achieved by what the children *didn't* do. They didn't reflect on or interpret events; they simply depicted them with words such as "I did" or "I saw." They used little of the conventional information that stories are supposed to have. And, as one story illustrates, they weren't concerned with chronology: "My dad got stuck in a storm and I was nervous. He came back the other day. I was walking my dog and my dog pulled me. I broke my arm. I go sailing lots of times. I was skipping and I tripped on a big rock and I got rocks in my knee. I visited my friend Janine in New Mexico." These autobiographies were collections of scenes; any chronological order was confined to a particular scene: "When I was three, I tried to save my friend and I fell in the pool and almost drowned. Then my brother tried to save me, then my other brother tried to save him. Then my mother cannon-balled in and saved us all. She made a tidal wave, man." These seven-year-olds were telling stories *from* their life but not yet a story *of* their life, and they were doing it with a freshness that would be hard to recapture as adults.[22]

Karl Haglund is growing in his ability to remember and narrate his experiences. As his memories become socialized, they become part of his family's and his culture's web of meaning. Right now, his autobiography is simply a collection of scenes strung together with the help of adults. But in adolescence, new cognitive powers will enable him to integrate past, present, and future — to introduce an overarching chronological sequence to his story. He will be able to reflect on his experience from a new point of view. He will see a different "me," and he'll make a different kind of meaning as a result.

As We Look Back

By the time we're adults, we'll be making sense of our experience with a story that's more or less integrated. The opening scene of that story will take us back to our childhood, to our very first memory of life.

Some adults claim to have a first memory that goes back even beyond childhood to infancy. They remember playing in the sand by a lake, or the taste and texture of their first birthday cake. Others can remember nothing before their first day of school. Most people, however, say that their earliest memory comes from the age of three or four, the point at which autobiographical memory begins . Women, on the average, assign their first memory an earlier date — by a few months — than do men.[23] But the age of the rememberer makes little difference in how far back a memory goes: twenty-year-olds remember no more about their preschool years than do forty-year-olds or seventy-year-olds.[24]

But are the ages associated with these memories — and are the memories themselves — accurate? Jean Piaget grew up with a vivid memory of nearly being kidnapped at the age of two. He could picture his nurse wheeling him down the streets of Paris, an assault by several men, and a scuffle in which the face of his nurse was scratched. The memory stayed with him all through childhood and into his adolescence. Then his nurse wrote to his parents, confessing that she had made up the whole story. The clarity with which Piaget had seen the event in his memory, and the personal conviction he had about its truth, was no proof that it had ever happened.

Psychologists are not surprised to find that our early memories sometimes have no basis in actual events. No matter what we try to remember, whether it's the office Christmas party or our first day of kindergarten, we go about it the same way. We weave together bits of information, guesses, faded snapshots we've seen in an album, stories we've heard others tell. And when we're finished, we are certain that our reconstruction of that old event is exactly the way it happened.

Some of the earliest memories of our life may indeed be picture-perfect, remembered vividly and accurately. But others may be fabrications, and still others a blend of fact and fantasy. In early memories we often see ourselves from the outside, watching, as it were, an actor on a stage. One woman who recalls peering down a laundry chute says, "I don't see the chute. I see *me*." Such a memory cannot be accurate — as a child, she wasn't watching herself from outside her body. Several studies have found that the older a memory is, the more likely it is to be reconstructed in this fashion.[25]

But that reconstruction does not mean that early memories aren't "true." It means, rather, that their truth lies elsewhere. Early memories often do for individuals what myths of the world's creation do for groups. They explain and legitimate the present by relating it to founding events that took place "in the beginning." In the words of psychoanalyst Alfred Adler, a person's earliest recollection is "his subjective starting point, the beginning of the autobiography he has made for himself." If the autobiography changes, so will its opening scene. "The person will remember different incidents, or he will put a different interpretation on the incidents he remembers."[26] Though early memories depict childhood events, they are better understood as intuitions of major life motifs — as single, clear recollections seized by the imagination because they say who I am today, and how I got to be the way I am.

A forty-two-year-old man, for example, whose life story revolves around the hurt of abandonment by his father, has a first memory of being a little boy, sick in bed. "And I was anxious because I know my dad was gonna come and I was gonna get a chance to ride in this big, black, shiny Plymouth, right? And he walked in, you know, this big, sort of lanky fellow, and I think he even picked me up and took me to the car."[27] His father drove him to the hospital — rescued him — but that was the closest the man ever got to his dad and the only time he ever rode in the big, black, shiny Plymouth. In his adult years, he has become the kind of parent his own father never was — the hero of the origin myth contained in his earliest memory of life.

A woman of forty-four who has had a lifelong fear of displeasing other people began her story like this. "My earliest memory is of being a little toddler, standing at my front door. It was a French door with little panes all down, even at my level. And mother was very, very mad at me — really cross with me. And she threatened to go off and leave me, which she did. She opened the front door and closed it behind her, and left me standing behind those little panes of glass, looking out, just crying. My heart was broken because my mother was leaving me. And she walked down the sidewalk and out of sight. I can still see the cracks in the sidewalk. That had a lasting effect on me. It was like, 'You do what I say or I'll leave you.'"[28]

Not all first memories are so poignant. Some are just fleeting images of pails of sand and birthday candles, of baby sisters and chicken pox, of backyards and little red cars. But now and then, as we look back on our life from the vantage point of adulthood, we find an early memory that says, "This is who I am because this is how I began." We find a memory that is "first."

Becoming a Kennedy Man

Francis Kennedy's founding memory goes back sixty-five years, to the time his family drove in a horse and buggy to a new farm, the one he grew up on. On the day of their arrival, no one could get in the house — no one except a four-year-old who was small enough to be pushed through a window, run to the front door, and open it from the inside. That four-year-old was Francis, and in his memory he is the key to the Kennedy farmstead. He is the competent child who could get something done when adults were stymied.

That sense of competence has run through Francis's life and is now being passed on to his grandchildren. The main reason is his son, Jim. "I'm raising my kids the same way my dad raised me," says Jim. "You have the responsibility, you can do the job. If you don't do the job, you'll do it right the next time. I expect my kids to take care of things like it was their own. If they're runnin' machinery, I expect them to be safe. I expect them to realize that tomorrow is still gonna come whether they hurry through the job and do it half right or do the job properly. They do a great job. Every one of them."

One of those children is his youngest son, Jason, the uncle of baby Justin. At eleven, Jason is nearing the end of his childhood. He still looks like a

Jason Kennedy, eleven. "I usually get first place, but sometimes I get beat."

boy, his brown hair cut short in the style favored by his peers. Today he's showing animals at a livestock competition, so he's wearing the white pants, white shirt, and white hat of 4-H club members.

Jason knows all the tricks of the experienced showman. He knows how to set the lamb's legs while never releasing his grip on its neck. He knows how to steady the animal when the judge comes around, how to hold the skin on its jaw to make it look long and lean. As he shares some of his secrets, his eyes strike a sudden spark. "If she walks too fast and her steps are too big, you slow her down some. Like if her back slouches down, you can tickle her belly and she pulls it up." He pauses, then says, "I usually get first place, but sometimes I get beat." By now Jason can stand up to the most experienced stockman. Competing against grown men, he has placed among the top three in national cattle shows.

Most eleven-year-olds are somewhat subdued, if not anxious, when they encounter a cow, but Jason was toddling around the local show ring, leading a 1,500-pound cow, at the age of two. His parents started him with an older cow, one that was calm and steady, and used to being trotted out for the judges. About the time he started school, Jason joined 4-H and began showing lambs and cattle. His mother Rita recalls his progress. "About three years ago, he wanted to show them and sell them at the end of the show string. He really enjoyed doing that. This year we had one lamb that was extremely large. He was afraid of it at first, because lambs can jump and get away. But he was very good at holding on to it. He's showing his cattle a lot better because he's a little taller and able to hold on to them. And he has the confidence that he can do it. He knows how to do it and he can do it right."

"I've gotta say that I've probably got some of the best showmen in the state of Pennsylvania," says his dad. "Jason's not to be taken slight when he gets out there with a bunch of adults to show cattle." Jim gives Jason a look of obvious pride, and his son looks down modestly, smiling with pleasure. It's clear that Jim's opinion is important to Jason, who identifies strongly with his father and strives to be like him.

There's a lot more to dairy farming than showing animals. It's Jason's job to feed the calves. That means carrying heavy pails of grain to the older calves and fixing bottles of warm milk for the younger ones. But that's not all that Jason does, says Rita. "He's always helped hay the cows, but feeding the calves is more responsible because he has to know to make the milk warm. And make sure the calf eats okay and isn't sick. He helps me milk sometimes. He has to wash the udders and prepare the cows. Put the milkers on them. He's quite good at that. He knows which cows will kick. He always sticks right there with me — the whole two and a half, three hours, whatever it takes."

Jason is learning farming the same way generations of Kennedys did before him. He accompanies his parents or an older sibling as they go through their day's work, handling the actual tools, helping with the real work of grown-ups. His schedule leaves little time for schoolwork. Every afternoon at 4:30, rain or shine, he reports to the barn. By the time milking and the evening chores are done, it's time for supper. By then it's eight o'clock, and it becomes hard to resist watching a little television. Then it's time for bed.

Jason's mother is concerned about his academic skills. "He's very good in math because of his work at the farmer's market — he changes a lot of money. But reading is a real struggle. The ability is there, but he just doesn't push himself. When he does have the time, he'd rather be hunting, playing down in the pond, walking through the woods, looking for deer, or almost anything but doing homework."

It may not occur to Rita that Jason's feelings about school are no different than her husband's were. "When I was his age," says Jim, "I disliked school tremendous. I mean, if I could get out of it, I did. I learned one thing, though, you didn't get out of it by stayin' home, because if you stayed home, you learned twice as hard as if you went to school. So I went to school, put my time in, and made passing grades. Finally in tenth grade I was gettin' my head together more often than not."

Nor was Jason's grandfather much of a scholar, but in his era there was built-in help for the child who was falling behind. "We had a one-room school with eight grades in it and an old pot-bellied stove sitting in the middle," recalls Francis. "In the wintertime the teacher would get there first and start the fire and have the school warm by the time you got there. On the real cold days she would make hot soup for us. And I think that was probably one of the best things that ever happened in my education. Because if you were in second grade and you missed something in first grade, well, there was a kid in first grade and the teacher was teaching him. So you had a chance to pick it up."

Both Jim and Francis gleaned from school whatever they needed to succeed as farmers. As adults, both took agriculture courses, and both served on their local school boards. Though they value formal education, they know there are things you learn on a farm that you could never learn from a book. As Francis says, "If every kid there in town had a rabbit, see, or something — a dog or a cat — and he was totally responsible for that animal, I think he would learn to appreciate life a little better. I feel that an animal teaches kids more than any man could, because they have to think like that animal does and be able to do the things it likes, so it will respond to their commands."

Few children know about the process of birth, but Jason has helped deliver calves. He has also learned, says Francis, about the end of life. "Jason's got a heart of gold. He raises lambs in his 4-H project, and you can just see he loves them the whole way through. And you can see the night they sell them lambs, and he knows they're going to be slaughtered, poor Jason's heart just breaks. But that's part of life, I guess."

As Jason's childhood comes to a close, Rita is beginning to see him change. "He's still in that little-boy stage, where he wants to play with his toys. But he's in the manhood stage, too, where he wants to drive tractors. He's sort of torn between the two. I still like to see him play. Even now he'll get his toy tractors and his disk, his plow, and his little wagon. Matter of fact, I just picked them up on the patio today. And he had his little racetrack and cars down here last night."

But it won't be long before the toys are gathering dust. Last summer, Jason learned to drive a tractor so that he can be more helpful in the fields. That's the big job, and it carries the recognition that you're ready to shoulder your share of the farming. Jason knows that, and he takes the responsibility seriously. As his mother says, "He drives very slow. Very careful. When the kids were complaining he was raking the hay too slow, he was learning. He said he wanted to be careful. He'll learn to drive faster later on. He thinks he's a big boy now that he can drive a tractor."

"He's still in that little-boy stage, where he wants to play with his toys. But he's in the manhood stage, too, where he wants to drive tractors." — Jason's mother, Rita.

Jason Kennedy has absorbed his family's tradition of industry. He is about to become a man, as his father and grandfather did before him — a Kennedy man. Deep within his body, invisible to others and unknown to himself, the change is already beginning.

III

Adolescence

7

THE BIOLOGICAL *Changing*

STORY OF *Bodies*

ADOLESCENCE

Candy Reed lives in Harmarville, Pennsylvania, about an hour south of the Kennedy farmstead. At twelve, she's just a few months older than Jason, but her body is already showing signs of adulthood. She has attractive features — sandy blond hair that she often ties behind her head, clear skin, and a sensitive, almost delicate, voice. She likes to wear makeup and earrings, curl her hair, and dress "preppy." Candy began attending a combined junior-senior high school just a few months ago, and she's still getting used to the change. Though she was one of the big kids in sixth grade, she has a different status in her new environment. On her first day of school, she recalls, "A few seniors called us names. 'Oh, look at the little seventh-graders, those little twerps walking down the hall.' It was hard, being called a little seventh-grader."

Much of Candy's adjustment to the changes in her life gets worked out over the phone. Because the house is empty when she comes home after school, her first call is to her mother, a physical therapist's aide at a local hospital, to see if there's anything special she should do. Maybe company is coming, and the living room needs cleaning. Or perhaps Candy should start preparing dinner. The next calls are the daily check-in with friends from whom Candy has been separated for at least an hour. One of those calls is always the same. "I really don't have a best friend, but there is one that I hang around with a lot. She's pretty special. She sleeps over and stuff. And we go places. I sit behind her in almost every class. We write notes and

Candy Reed, twelve (right), and friend. "I know that when I tell her a secret she won't spill the beans."

tell each other, 'This class is so boring!' We talk about our social lives and boys. And we share a lot of secrets. She tells me about the fights she has with her brothers or her mother or father. And I tell her my personal problems and stuff. And she tries to understand me and I do the same for her. She's nice and I know that when I tell her a secret she won't spill the beans. And she trusts me, too."

Though Candy doesn't talk much about the physical changes of adolescence, she is intensely aware of what's going on and how she compares with others. "The girls my age are not really mature physically. Probably around seventh or eighth grade you start to become aware of problems, and around ninth or tenth grade you start to have those problems and understand them better. Sometimes my friends discuss their periods. I mean we don't get into heavy conversation about it. We just talk about it."

Another thing Candy and her friends talk about is how they look. "My friends tell me my hair can never look bad, because my mom was a beautician, and she'll tell me what looks right and what doesn't. My clothes aren't the best or anything, but I try to put my own outfits together, and I think the way I look is okay. Big sweaters, jeans, and stretch pants are 'in' at school — and I guess curly hair. Some people like the prep look. Sometimes people get the impression that preppy is, like, prissy. I don't mind looking like a prep, but I try not to be prissy."

The changes in Candy's appearance and interests worry her mother. Bronwyn Reed, a solid woman with a quick smile, strawberry-blond hair, and glasses, has confidence in her daughter's good sense, but she remembers her own adolescence. Bronwyn became an unwed mother at nineteen. She raised her daughter alone, and the experience of being a single parent is one

"There have to be limits — and she expects limits." — Candy's mother, Bronwyn.

she doesn't want her daughter to have. "Candy's as impressionable as any teenager. I worry about peer pressure to be involved in some things that might just be beyond her understanding. I worry about drugs. I'm afraid of alienating her, yet I know there are lines you cannot cross. You can't be too permissive, you can't be too much of a teenager's friend. There have to be limits — and she expects limits."

Candy knows about her mother's misgivings. "She worries about the regular things that people worry about with their kids. I think she trusts me, but it's just the natural thing to worry about the big world that's out there, things like drugs and alcohol and sex. And I'm starting to date, and she's kind of worried about what he's like — if he's cruel, if he's nice, if he's too old for me."

Candy and her friends go to parties, dances, and movies in groups, then pair off with boys after they get there. For most of them, sexual activity lies some years down the road. Candy is firm about that. "Girls my age are starting to think about what the eleventh-graders do. But they're not sexually active. They're pretty young for that sort of thing. All I can say is that they're just getting to know about it themselves. They're curious, but I don't think anybody's real brave about it and ready to jump into it with their eyes closed. Kids are usually around tenth or eleventh grade before they start experimenting. And some people are just, like, real secretive about it. I don't know of any girls in my school that are pregnant. There might have been some a couple of years ago, but I really don't know of any right now.

"The guy I started going out with is in the ninth grade. It's not that much of an age difference. He's a really nice person. I like him a lot. And we talk

"Girls my age are starting to think about what the eleventh-graders do."

on the phone every night. I trust him and I think my mom does, too, even though she hasn't met him or anything. He's a real kind person, and he wouldn't do anything to hurt anybody."

Even though she likes her boyfriend, Candy is not beyond having a crush on someone even older. "My boyfriend's probably gonna get real mad if he hears this, but there's a senior. He's captain of the football team and he's real tall. He's real cute. He has sandy brown hair and the nicest eyes. And he's, like, real polite. He says, 'Hi, ladies,' in the hall. He's real nice to everybody, and he doesn't make fun of people. He's going with a cheerleader."

There are a lot of "nice" kids at Candy's school, and that's how she describes herself. "I think Candy is a person with feelings — a nice person when she wants to be. She can also be a stubborn, mean person. I don't know whether I would judge myself as pretty or not. My friends say that I'm pretty good-looking. And I try to be an all-around nice person."

But neither Candy nor her mother know if adolescence will be "nice" for her. The two of them sense something promising ahead, but also something threatening. Her mother may be worried, but so far Candy is taking it all in stride. "Some people say being a teenager is a whole bunch of trouble and everything. But I really don't think it could be that bad, if you try real hard. So far people say that I'm, like, kind of mature for my age."

The Hormones Return

Though she's nearly the same age as Jason Kennedy, Candy Reed has crossed a threshold and has entered a new season of life. She goes to a different kind of school than he does, has different interests, and has created a different pattern of social relationships. Most important, her body is becoming that of an adult, while his is still a child's. For most of human history, the physical changes Candy is undergoing introduced girls, in a social sense, to womanhood. But now the changes bring them to a new season, a period between childhood and adulthood that we call adolescence.

The physical changes of adolescence are known collectively as puberty. We tend to think of puberty as a sudden biological event that ushers in sexual maturation, but there's nothing abrupt about it, nor is it a single event. Puberty is a series of lengthy biological processes that begin in a child's body long before they produce any visible signs. Candy Reed has just turned twelve, but she's probably been in puberty for about three years. And though Jason Kennedy is still a boy, a period of "invisible" puberty has begun for him as well.

Puberty is the body's way of preparing for reproduction. It's what the Biological Clock has been pointing toward from the very beginning of life. When girls are about nine, and boys about ten, timing mechanisms in the Biological Clock signal a part of the brain known as the hypothalamus to end the "extra" season of life called childhood and bring on sexual maturation. Each night thereafter, as soon as the child falls asleep, the hypothalamus starts secreting a hormone known as gonadotropin-releasing hormone (GnRH) and sends it in pulses to the nearby pituitary gland.[1] The pituitary, in turn, releases hormones that activate the gonads — the ovaries in girls and the testes in boys. The gonads produce the sex hormones that flowed freely during infancy, virtually disappeared in childhood, and now resume their activity in adolescence. All of the triggering hormones are released in pulses, because neither the pituitary gland nor the gonads can handle a continuous flow of traffic. Unless GnRH arrives in pulses, the pituitary becomes overloaded with stimulation and shuts down, and unless pituitary hormones arrive in pulses, the ovaries and testes refuse to secrete sex hormones.

At the University of Michigan, pediatric endocrinologist Inese Beitens has been studying patterns of hormone release by taking small blood samples from children every twenty minutes, day and night. Simply by looking at the recordings of hormone levels, she can tell when a child has fallen asleep. She says it's as if the child's system bides its time, then as soon as it gets some signal that is associated with sleep, the glands start secreting hormones. At first, nightly hormone levels are about four to five times as high as daytime levels. Then, at about mid-adolescence, when the body changes have become apparent to all, high levels of hormones continue to circulate during the day as well — but still in pulses.[2]

The pulsating hormones set off a string of biological changes that produce a sexually mature adult. For most girls, the first visible signs come at ten or eleven, with budding breasts and pubic hair. Each of these developments is controlled by a different hormone, so they don't always follow the same timetable. In most girls, breast development happens first, but in a sizable minority the order is reversed.[3] While this is going on, the girl grows taller, and fat collects on her breasts, hips, and buttocks. Just after the peak

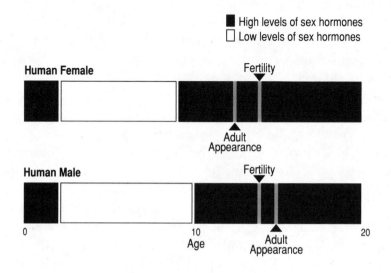

Timing of events at puberty. Ages represent contemporary averages in the United States.

of her growth spurt — at about twelve or thirteen — she has her first menstrual period. This event, which most parents and adolescents use as the marker of puberty, actually appears late in a girl's sexual maturation. Even so, she is not yet fertile, and probably won't be for some time.

Early menstrual cycles are merely dress rehearsals for the real drama of conception. Although the uterus goes through the monthly procedure of preparing a hospitable haven, then clearing it out, no egg is released by the ovaries. Ovulation does not begin until a year or so after a girl begins to have periods. That's fortunate, because the girl's pelvis and vagina take no part in the adolescent growth spurt. They grow at their own slow pace, so that a girl who begins menstruating at twelve does not have a fully developed birth canal until she's about seventeen.

In boys, it takes a bit longer for the sex hormones to produce an outward sign of maturity. Most boys are about twelve years old when their sex organs begin growing and pubic hair appears. About a year and a half later, they begin to ejaculate semen and presumably become fertile, though it's not known for sure if the first sperm are mature enough to fertilize an egg. After the first ejaculation, the visible signs of manhood arrive — the peak of the growth spurt, the lowering of the voice, and the appearance of facial hair. Unlike girls, who look like women *before* they're fertile, boys don't look like men until *after* they're able to conceive a child.

Though the sequence of pubertal events is a biological constant, individual children vary as to when the process begins, just as they vary in eye or hair color. The first signs of physical change can appear any time from eight to thirteen in girls, and from nine-and-a-half to thirteen-and-a-half in boys. Some children zip through puberty; girls may reach sexual maturity in as short a time as eighteen months, and boys may complete the sequence in as little as two years. Other children progress at a slower pace, with girls taking six years and boys taking five.

When breasts begin budding before girls are eight years old, or boys' sexual organs begin to grow before they're nine, physicians describe the condition as "precocious puberty" — a reminder of the prehuman era when childhood was shorter. An extreme case of precocious puberty involved Lina Medina, a Peruvian girl who began menstruating at the age of three and gave birth in 1939 when she was only five years and seven months old. Her birth canal was still so immature that her baby had to be delivered by cesarean section.[4]

Precocious puberty is far more common in girls than in boys, and for both, the process is relatively rapid: it takes only about two years for them to go through the entire pubertal sequence. The condition is usually not a threat to health in girls. About 80 percent show no physical cause; the Biological Clock has simply tripped the switch early, perhaps because of a genetic predisposition, and the girls can look forward to a normal adulthood. But about 20 percent need expert medical attention, because they may have a tumor on an ovary or on the hypothalamus itself. Among boys, the condition is always worrisome, because at least 70 percent have a tumor of some sort that has instigated their development.

Throughout history, the average age at which girls experience their first menstrual period — an event called menarche — has fluctuated within a range of about six years, from twelve-and-a-half to eighteen-and-a-half.[5] Two thousand years ago, girls in Greece and Rome experienced menarche at thirteen or fourteen, an age that's also found in medieval medical books. But with the coming of the Industrial Revolution, living conditions deteriorated. Diets worsened, crowding combined with poor sanitation let disease run rampant, and social stress accelerated. Children labored long hours under oppressive conditions. By the nineteenth century, girls in England reached menarche at fifteen-and-a-half; in Norway, at sixteen-and-a-half.[6] As living conditions improved again, the trend reversed. In 1900, girls in the United States were having their first period at about fourteen; today, Candy Reed's generation is menstruating at twelve-and-a-half. Few experts believe that the average age of menarche will drop any further; indeed, it has held constant in developed countries over the past two decades. The lower end of the range set by the Biological Clock appears to have been reached.

Comparable figures for boys are nearly impossible to get, because there are no records of first ejaculation. But eighteenth-century documents on voice changes indicate that boys have shared in the recent trend toward an earlier puberty. Johann Sebastian Bach kept records on the members of the Leipzig church choir, whose singing careers ended when their voices deepened. That happened to most boys shortly after their seventeenth birthday — at least three years later than a boy's voice changes today. The disparity may have been smaller on this side of the Atlantic, for American children have tended to enter puberty earlier than their European counterparts.

A critical factor in the fluctuations in the age of menarche may well have been the amount of fat girls were able to store on their bodies. In a hunting-and-gathering environment, it's extremely important that women carry energy reserves in the form of fat, reserves that can be transformed into milk for their babies. Through the course of evolution, the bodies of women became efficient at converting into storage the few fats and sugars that were available in their diet. Because fat reserves were critical for successful pregnancies, some researchers today believe that fat controls fertility: adolescent girls begin to ovulate as soon as a critical amount of "reproductive" fat has been deposited on their bodies.

Reproductive fat goes to special places, mostly to the hips, thighs, and buttocks. Until it reaches at least 22 percent of total body weight, a girl will not ovulate regularly.[7] This kind of fat is extremely hard to lose through dieting, says anthropologist Jane Lancaster. "It's heavily defended, so that behavioral changes will occur before it's lost. As food intake drops, women become sluggish, their appetites increase, and they change their activity patterns to keep from losing fat."[8]

In this century, the proportion of fat in our diet has increased by 25 percent.[9] Candy bars, milkshakes, hamburgers, and pizzas — combined with a more sedentary style of life — have turned girls into "hothouse tomatoes," says Lancaster, and tricked their bodies into menstruating and ovulating at the earliest age possible. The connection between fat and fertility may explain why ballet dancers, who have no desire to lose their slim, breastless look, manage to postpone puberty with a rigorous program of dance and diet.[10] It may also explain why girls who mature early tend to become women who are shorter and heavier than girls who mature late. This difference appears whether women were born in 1890 or 1940, so the relationship holds even as the average age of menarche changes.[11]

The environmental influence on the Biological Clock has not changed the basic settings in its genes. But it has affected the age range within which these genes express themselves. In this century, good nutrition and a healthy childhood have allowed children to devote the nutrients in their food to growth and maturation instead of to fighting disease. The irony is that fat and sugar, which are now available in abundance, are conspiring to circumvent a certain "wisdom" in the clock's program for growth, a wisdom that throughout human history has held off sexual maturation and allowed children to be children as long as possible.

An Evolutionary Puzzle

Those who study the history of the Biological Clock wonder about another kind of wisdom in the way it times the events of puberty. They're puzzled by a curious difference — the fact that, in girls, fertility comes at the end of the sequence of physical changes, but in boys, it comes in the middle. Human females look like adult women when they become fertile, but human males still look like boys. What's behind this peculiar arrangement?

One way of approaching the puzzle is to look at the way the settings of the Biological Clock relate to social needs. Lancaster, for example, wonders why breast development is one of the first signs of change in girls. "When we look at nonhuman primates," she says, "breasts don't develop until the last part of pregnancy, and they are strictly glandular. That is, they don't represent fat deposits as they do in humans; they are simply glands that are used for milk production. When a female primate is not nursing, those breasts disappear and she has just little nipples."[12] Among humans, breasts develop not only before a girl is pregnant, but even before she is capable of pregnancy. This has led Lancaster to speculate that, for humans, the enlargement of breasts is a social signal, a way of saying "I am a woman" long before a girl can bear children.

Anthropologist Barry Bogin carries the argument a step further. Among our ancestors, he says, those females whose appearance raced ahead of their internal organs had an evolutionary advantage. Once they had attained the outward appearance of adulthood, they were treated differently by those around them. Their new look enabled them to participate in adult social life, gathering and preparing food and practicing the sexual life of women. "Girls that possessed this sort of growth pattern — looking like women before they were fertile — were better spouses, better lovers, better mothers, better at doing all the things adult women do," says Bogin. "And so they would end up having more babies and rearing more of those babies to adulthood."[13] They would also pass more of their genes to subsequent generations, gradually encoding their schedule for growth into the Biological Clock.

If the Biological Clock seems anxious to advertise the fact that girls are becoming women, it seems intent on hiding the fact that boys are becoming men. Sex hormones run quietly in the bloodstream of boys for perhaps two years before they produce a change — longer than they do in girls. And although boys have their first ejaculation at about the same age as girls first ovulate, the signs of their manhood — increased height and weight, deep voice, and beard — are delayed. For a period during puberty, in the words of one pair of researchers, they are "fertile eunuchs."[14]

Bogin believes that hiding the signs of manhood was the safest way boys could learn to be men. "The sex hormones that are released by the brain pique the psychological interest of boys in observing and imitating adult social behavior — in terms of courtship and sexual life, in terms of providing for a spouse and children," he says.[15] But if boys started to look like men at this time, they would have been perceived by fathers, older brothers, and other males in their group as competitors for women. And so, as if for protection, their bodies wore the disguise of childhood as they went through their first sexual infatuations and learned the business of hunting, courting, and establishing a family. By the time boys had grown into their adult bodies, they would have picked up the social skills needed to function as men. Thus, the boy whose appearance lagged behind his fertility had the evolutionary edge.

If we could give the Biological Clock a voice and let it speak for girls during puberty, it would say, "I'm beginning to be a woman. Spread the word." If it could speak for boys, the message would be, "I'm beginning to be a man.

Keep it a secret." It's the best way each sex can learn that there's more to parenthood than conceiving and bearing children.

For both girls and boys, the arrival of sexual maturity and the promise of fertility sound an alarm. In the words of one researcher, a "chronic emergency" will soon enter the life cycle.[16] Bronwyn Reed has seen her daughter change and has already heard the alarm. Candy and her friends are no different. They are now aware of the powerful signals their bodies are giving off.

Early and Late

If you think about teenagers today, you get the sense that the Biological Clock is out of its evolutionary context. Today, early-maturing girls and late-maturing boys have difficulty during puberty — just the opposite of what seems to have been true in the past.

Unlike youngsters throughout most of human history, contemporary teenagers are surrounded by a large number of peers with whom they constantly compare themselves. The early-maturing girl is no longer welcomed into a society of adults; rather, she stands out as the tallest in her class, agonizing over prominent breasts and worried about being fat. Research is finding that during the sixth and seventh grades, early-maturing girls tend to do poorly in school. They're likely to be withdrawn and submissive, to lack self-assurance, to be uncommunicative with their parents and critical of their families.[17] Because they look older than their peers, they may be drawn into an older social group, where they may become involved in drinking, drugs, or early sexual activity. During these same years, late-maturing girls tend to be carefree and sociable, and to emerge as leaders.

Studies in Sweden have found that girls who reach puberty early are less likely to go on to college. Seeking their friends among older teenagers, they regard themselves as "more mature" than their peers. Their feelings of maturity seem to turn their thoughts away from school and toward marriage and children, so that the early-maturing Swedish girl is somewhat more likely to marry and start a family and less likely to prepare for a profession than other girls.[18]

For boys, the situation is reversed. The ones who look like adults "too soon" need not fear a society of men, because socially, they're far removed from it. So they can be men among boys and receive a boost to their self-esteem and confidence. Research shows that, among boys, early maturers are usually the ones who become leaders. Their greater strength and endurance often make them superior athletes, and in the world of adolescents, prestige belongs to the athletic. Late-maturing boys, on the other hand, stand out in all the wrong ways. They're smaller, weaker, and have less endurance than other boys, and they're not likely to do well on the sports field. They're the last to catch up with the girls in their class, who spend junior high towering over them. Boys who are slow to mature tend to make up for their appearance by being impulsive and assertive, but they rarely become leaders and are usually not popular.[19]

But the disadvantages of being an early-maturing girl or a late-maturing boy don't last forever. Eventually, everyone catches up with everyone else. Later on in high school, the early-maturing girl no longer stands out from the crowd; when all the girls are wearing bras, her breasts are not unusual. Studies show that early-maturing girls become more popular and autonomous at this time, turning some of their painful experiences into strengths. On the other side of the coin, late-maturing girls find that their status has evaporated. Their prestige is gone and the once unchallenged leaders fall behind early maturers not only in autonomy and self-assurance, but also in skill at handling personal problems.[20]

In adulthood, the balance that developed in high school remains. The initial disadvantage of early-maturing girls seems to push them into developing flexibility and coping skills. Their self-possession and autonomy remain strong, and they generally seem more competent intellectually, socially, and emotionally.[21]

As late-maturing boys go through adulthood, something similar seems to happen. By middle age, they may remain somewhat impulsive and assertive, but they usually become insightful, inventive, and creative. "Although they may have suffered during their high-school years," says Temple University psychologist Laurence Steinberg, "late maturers developed coping skills and psychological skills that were healthy and adaptive later on. Humor is a good example. Remember from your own adolescence the small class clown who had to be witty and quick on his feet in order to defend himself against the bigger, more muscular boys. During adulthood, humor and wit turn out to be more important than size and strength." [22] Unable to gain recognition simply by being "mature," these boys learn to take risks and to devise innovative solutions to their problems. In addition, late maturers may profit from their extra years of childhood, when they are free to experiment, invent, and learn without pressure. Boys who mature first in junior high, on the other hand, have no reason to look for creative ways to solve life's problems. As adults, many of them may retain their social ease and self-confidence, but they tend to be conventional and to lack the insight and playfulness of late maturers.[23]

The Ideal Body

No matter when they mature, teenagers are concerned with how their bodies look and whether they measure up to the ideal. The problem is greater for girls than for boys. All those tall, small-breasted, lean and leggy models on television and in magazines make the "perfect" body almost unattainable. When psychiatrist Daniel Offer and his associates at the Michael Reese Hospital in Chicago surveyed adolescents, they found that 77 percent of the boys, but only 57 percent of the girls, were proud of their bodies.[24] The rest said that they often felt ugly and unattractive.

The male ideal is to grow tall and develop muscles and strength. This matches the historical intent of the Biological Clock. Though late-maturing boys are slow to reach the ideal, their body image improves when they finally do. It's not uncommon for a late-maturing boy to enter high school as the shortest boy in his class and to graduate as one of the tallest. Eventually, nearly all boys can expect to measure up to the male standard.

The prospect for girls is different. The female ideal has changed radically in the last century, as becomes apparent if we put Miss America beside the women in Reubens' paintings or a photograph of a nineteenth-century beauty like Lillian Russell. Today's female ideal is thinner than the natural female figure — so thin that only a minority of girls can hope to emulate it. Uncertainty hangs over the process, because a girl has no way of knowing, as she enters puberty, the sort of body she will emerge with.

Most adolescent girls, even those who are not overweight, think they are far too heavy, and a good many become preoccupied with efforts to lose weight. At a time when the Biological Clock is trying to deposit the fat that underlies fertility, these girls are trying to shed it — and feeling helpless and frustrated when their attempts fail. Today's idealization of the unnaturally thin female body may be at least partly responsible for the wave of eating disorders that seems to be sweeping through developed countries. Anorexics, who are virtually always girls, diet so fanatically that they are in danger of starvation. Bulimics, again almost exclusively girls, engage in repeated binges in which they devour vast quantities of food in a short period of time. Most of them then either vomit or take a heavy dose of laxative to escape the effects of the excess calories. Both disorders are found primarily among affluent, well-educated girls, and both pit the girls in a fierce battle against nature.

How teenagers react to their changing bodies depends in part on the reactions of family and friends, in part on their own personalities, and in part on whether their bodies meet cultural standards of attractiveness.[25] If youngsters know what to expect, if their parents have made them feel comfortable about changes in the way they look and feel, they will probably take puberty in stride. If they enter puberty with high self-esteem, they're more likely to wind up pleased than embarrassed when their growing is done.

Puberty, says Steinberg, is a "crap shoot," especially for girls: you just don't know how your body is going to turn out. That's why it's important to keep physical appearance in perspective. Says Steinberg, "One of the most important things that teenagers can do for each other, and that parents and educators can do for teenagers, is to diminish the importance of the body as the source of self-esteem. That's the fundamental problem, really: that we pay too much attention to people's physical appearance and not enough attention to other skills and talents that young people have."[26]

A Perfectly Normal Body

When a young woman we'll call Beth Curtis was Candy Reed's age, she had no idea how the "crap shoot" of puberty would come out for her. Now nineteen, she is a poised young woman with a ready smile, blue eyes, and short, sandy hair. She wears the young American uniform — jeans, sneakers, and a T-shirt. A year ago, Beth would have been wearing a bulky sweatshirt or a shapeless sweater. But four months ago, she had breast-reduction surgery, and it has made a huge difference in her life. What she experienced in her teen years is unusual, but the feelings behind it are not.

Beth did not mature any earlier than her friends — in fact, she was a little late. "I remember when I was in junior high, kind of waiting for it to happen, wanting to get my period, wanting to be developing like other people were. I remember wearing a bra before I needed one." Until Beth was nearly sixteen, her breast development was not excessive. But unlike most girls, she kept growing, and by the time she was a junior, she began to have problems. Not being able to fit into pretty clothes was one thing, but being ridiculed by her peers was difficult to handle. "There was a guy a class above me, he was a graduating senior, and they had left senior wills. Every senior got a copy, and they posted one for the rest of the school to see. And he left me a periscope so I could see my feet. I knew the guy — I didn't mind what he did so much as the fact that afterwards people I didn't even know came up and commented on my needing a periscope. And to know that your breasts were the joke of the school wasn't easy.

"When I was a senior, I had a friend who was a sophomore, so I'd walk down sophomore hall all the time, and everytime I walked by this group of guys, one of them would say in a voice just loud enough that I heard — and he knew I heard, and all the people around him heard — 'There's the girl with big tits!' I remember feeling at the time like I wanted to yell, or scream, or say something back, and I never did. Because a little bit more than that, I just wanted to be swallowed up. I just wanted it to end.

"That Christmas, the student government sold candy canes and little cards. And I sent one to him. I put 'To,' on the card and wrote his name. I just wrote, 'Gentlemen hold their tongues.' And I signed it with my full name and sent it to him. And he never said anything about it, but he stopped making comments. And I don't think at the time he realized what he was doing in terms of hurting me. That was a way to be cool and get attention from the guys.

"Flat-chested friends sometimes said, 'Oh, you're lucky.' And I'd say, 'No, I'm not lucky.' There were times I couldn't explain what was happening to me without getting very emotional. In college, I remember explaining it to my roommate and starting to cry. Just thinking, you know, 'What makes people do this? Why do people feel like there's something funny?'"

Beth's parents had told her that things would get better in college, and in some respects she did. Physically, though, she became more and more uncomfortable. "I went swimming, but I had a really hard time buying swimsuits. I wound up doing aerobics, but I wore two bras and a leotard and still hurt. I got a lot of back pain, a lot of jarring." Emotionally, she held back. "I would have maybe gotten a little bit more physically involved with some boys, men, whatever, than I did because I was concerned about, you know, what's someone gonna think of my body? And I think everyone has that to an extent. For me it was very focused. I knew I was not in the normal scheme of things. But I began to realize as I was getting older, 'Hey, I'm running from relationships with men.' You know, consciously or unconsciously, I realized I had a problem with trust."

After Beth completed her freshman year at college, she decided that she wanted to have breast-reduction surgery. But not right away. "My older brother couldn't understand this. I told him, 'Well, I'm thinking about waiting on the surgery.' And he said, 'Why? You said it was a problem when I talked to you last. Just get it done. You're gonna feel better.'"

But Beth had a good reason for waiting. "I wanted to heal my mind before I started changing my body. One of the big things I had to go through was coming to grips with the fact that what happened wasn't nice, and it wasn't fun. And I wanted to deal with that first and then feel complete after the surgery, rather than have the surgery and still have to go through the mental stuff."

Beth found much of the mental stuff difficult to resolve. "The feminist in me had a hard time with the surgery. You know, why should I be changing my body to suit the world's image? There's nothing wrong with the way I look. And why should we have to conform to this set image? But then I said, well, first of all, dammit, I've got to live in this world. I'm not in an ivory tower. There are people out there who will look at me and meet me 'chest first.' There's nothing like having a conversation and realizing someone's talking to you about a foot below your face."

It took nearly a year for Beth to sort things out. By then, she knew that she wanted the surgery — and she knew why. "I did not have this done for cosmetic reasons. It was . . . I just wanted to be comfortable. I wanted to feel normal. I wanted to be able to do things that I couldn't do. And there's a big difference."

Beth had her surgery four months ago, and today she's happy with the results. But she doesn't see the surgery as a cure-all. It did not erase the memory of humiliating high-school experiences. And the surgery itself left scars. "It's my choice — a conscious choice. I have scars, they'll always be there. But it's the best thing, physically, I've ever done for myself. It's always better when you have control, and I didn't have control over that before.

"I don't have the perfect body," she says. "I didn't have a perfect body before, and I don't have one after. I have a perfectly normal body."

8

THE SOCIAL STORY
OF ADOLESCENCE

A Ten-Year Lag

"I had skipped two periods. And I go and tell my mom, 'Mom, I might be pregnant.' 'What? I'm gonna kill you! If you're pregnant, I'm gonna kill you.' That's the first words out of my mom's mouth."

Kim Henderson is a brash, tough-talking fifteen-year-old with blue eyes and bushy red hair. What happened to her during eighth and ninth grade changed her relationship with her mother and her friends, changed her plans for the future, changed her view of herself, changed every aspect of her life. Within the span of a few weeks, she made decisions that few teenagers are equipped to handle, but that more and more of them are now having to face.

Kim was only thirteen when she discovered she was pregnant. It happened, she says, because her boyfriend had doped her up with pills and alcohol. When Kim broke the news, Mrs. Henderson was angry because she felt her daughter was making the same mistake that she had. She, too, had been an unwed teenage mother, and she wanted Kim's life to be different — better than her own. And yet, as soon as the pregnancy was confirmed, Mrs. Henderson's attitude softened. "I supported Kim one hundred percent," she says. "It wasn't all her fault. It was the boy's fault, too, but they never seem to blame the boy."

Kim had to make some quick decisions. "After I found out I was pregnant, I went and told my boyfriend's parents. First thing they said, 'Get an

*Kim Henderson, fifteen.
"I was called a slut and
every other name they
could think of."*

abortion.' My mom and his parents got into a big fight because that was against our religion. We don't believe in abortion. So they said, 'Fine, have the baby and give it up for adoption.'"

Kim rejected both options, along with the possibility of marrying her fifteen-year-old boyfriend. Something in her knew he was just like her father. "When we were little, my mom was always sad. I think the best thing that ever happened to her was when my dad kicked us out. He was drunk that day and he told her, 'Get the hell out.' He threatened to burn down the house and everything that was in it. He threatened to kill me and my sisters and my mom. When we went back with our preacher the next day to get some of our stuff, my dad said he didn't do nothing. The only reason he doesn't remember anything is 'cause he was so drunk it wasn't funny. He couldn't remember any of it."

With the help of her mother, Kim decided to keep the baby, stay single, and stay in school. The hardest part of the decision was staying in school. Although several of Kim's girlfriends thought she was doing the right thing by having the baby and keeping it, they were in the minority. "I was called a slut and every other name they could think of. They called me 'Preggo.' They kept doing it, and I was in a lot of fights. People didn't think it was right for me to be pregnant. Most of all they didn't think it was right for me to keep the baby and raise her.

"Some of my teachers helped me out with the kids that were harassing me. My guidance counselor helped me a lot, and so did the vice principal and my attendance officer. But my history teacher didn't feel it was right for me to have a baby at that young age. We'd be going over something in history and he'd say, 'These people didn't have babies at fourteen years old.'

And he'd hold me after class, tell me that my grades were low, and that I needed to concentrate more on my grades than I did on having the kid. It made me mad. We got into a real battle, and I told the principal about what he was doing to me, and they found out it was true, because they recorded one of his lessons without him knowing it. They made him apologize to me in front of the class."

Kim was pregnant through most of the eighth grade. Her baby was born one night in May — six hours after Kim was admitted to the hospital. Surprisingly, her pelvis was mature enough that she could have a normal delivery. Kim's mother stayed right beside her — she was there when Kim asked for her teddy bear, and there to tell her boyfriend that he was the father of a five-pound, twelve-ounce girl named Angela.

The baby's father had treated Kim well during the pregnancy, but when he found out the baby was a girl, his whole attitude changed. "He told himself that it was going to be a boy, and when it turned out to be a girl, he got real mean. It was like he didn't care about the baby anymore. He was jealous of Angie because I wanted to spend time with her and not as much time with him. One night he came down to my house with a friend and told me he was going to take Angie 'cause I wouldn't let him see her. I said, 'Fine, you can see her for ten minutes, then you leave.' And he wired out on me. He hit me, and I know if his friend wasn't there he woulda hit me more and ended me up in the hospital. His friend got him away from me, and I went in the house and locked him out. And he started head-butting the wall. He tried to break down our door."

That was the end of Kim's relationship with her boyfriend. Today, Angie is just over a year old, and Kim is finishing the ninth grade. Mrs. Henderson cares for Angie while Kim is in class. "It wasn't the baby's fault that she was conceived," says Mrs. Henderson. "So I didn't think the baby should have to suffer for something they had done. It's been a new beginning, because I had mine so close that I never got to enjoy the age Angie is now. I'm enjoying through her what I missed with my own three. My oldest one was only eighteen months when Kim came. And Kim was only seventeen months when Cindy came. So I was trying to raise all three of them at once."

Angie has brought the Henderson women closer together. Kim gets along much better with her mother and sisters than she used to. "My mom knows that Angie's my baby, that I have to raise her in my own way. I also need my mom's help, 'cause I don't know how to do some of the stuff. But my mom's right there for me. She makes sure everything's going fine. She's even working now to get us off of welfare so that Angie can live a normal life.

"I don't want her to have a baby the same time I did. It could ruin her life."

"I've changed a lot. I never talked as much as I do now. A lot of people say I'm nicer now than before. I think Angie's changed me, because I've calmed down. I'm not as nervous. Before, whenever my mom would say something I didn't like, I would contradict her. I had a real bad mouth towards my mom. And I've calmed it down some, but sometimes it just bursts out. But I never get into those real long fights with my mom now."

Kim is fiercely protective of Angie and willing to fight for her if it comes to that. "I didn't have to learn to be tough, 'cause I was already tough. I had been ridiculed all my life because of my father's drinking, but I was always strong enough to take it and forget about it. But they're not gonna get away with ridiculing me, my family, or Angie. Especially not Angie."

The boys at school have not made things easy for Kim, but a few of them have been "pretty nice," she says. "They don't hold Angie against me. Some of them say that they think of me as a good mother because, when it came to having a baby, I had my mind straight. I knew what I was gonna do. I didn't get an abortion, and I didn't put the baby up for adoption. They think it's all right for me to have a kid, and they'll date me. But some of them don't like it that I have Angie. And I told 'em if they don't like it, they can kiss my rosy red ass."

Though Kim doesn't know how normal her life is going to be, she has charted a course for the future. Next fall, when she enters tenth grade, she plans to enter the program in cosmetology at her high school. It will take three years to complete; then, after she passes a state certification test, she'll be able to get a job as a beautician. "No, I'm not gonna drop out," she says. "I'm not allowed to. My mom told me that she wouldn't sign the papers for me to drop out. She said that I need a high-school education to get a good life for me and Angie so I won't end up on welfare like she had to, because my father wouldn't let her finish school. My father wouldn't let her work or nothing."

Next year, Angie will enter day-care. Mrs. Henderson is taking college courses so that she'll be able to get a good job. Kim is optimistic about her family's future. "Now that we're living on our own and my mom's back in school, everything's gonna turn out pretty good for us. I have a feeling it will."

Among Kim's hopes is one for her daughter. "I hope she doesn't turn out to be like me, rebellious at the age of thirteen. I don't think I could handle that. As soon as she starts her menstrual cycle, I'll put her on birth control. 'Cause I don't want her to have a baby the same time I did. It could ruin her life."

The Critical Years of Early Adolescence

When Kim Henderson announced that she was pregnant, just about everybody told her that she was "too young" to have a baby. It was a powerful message from the Social Clock, but it was inconsistent with the reality of her physical development. Physically, she was neither too young to conceive a child nor to have a normal delivery — although most girls her age are. Kim's situation is not typical in a statistical sense, but it illustrates the timing discrepancy that has brought about the typical season of adolescence.

Had Kim been alive during the hunter-gatherer era of human history, she would have married around the time of her first menstrual period. Her first child would have been born a few years after that. For most of the time humans have lived on earth, the Biological and Social Clocks set the same time for the beginning of adulthood. But in the teen years today, the Biological Clock is running early and the Social Clock is running late. Youngsters are reaching puberty earlier and earlier, even as it takes them longer and longer to achieve the social status of an adult. The difference between the clocks varies among social classes and individuals, but if we consider menarche a sign of biological adulthood and graduation from college a sign of social adulthood, the gap would be about ten years. If we take marriage to be a sign of social adulthood, it would be even longer for the average person. A lag of at least a decade has become a separate stage of life, a season that we call adolescence.

Today, many psychologists set the starting point of adolescence at the age of ten, which is when the hormonal changes of puberty are already under way for the average girl and just beginning for the average boy. These psychologists are coming to believe that the discrepancy between the two clocks hits hardest in early adolescence, the years between ten and fourteen, when youngsters must negotiate two transitions at once — the physical changes of puberty and the social changes mandated by a new kind of school.

In early adolescence, most young people in our country move from a neighborhood elementary school, in which most subjects are taught in the same room by the same teacher, to a school in which each subject is taught in a different room by a different teacher. Some make the change to a middle school, which usually incorporates grades six to eight, but most move a year later to a junior high school, made up of grades seven to nine.

No matter when the switch occurs, the school experience changes radically. Not only do students spend their days moving around from one room and one teacher to another, but most also find themselves in a tracking system, where the college-bound and academically talented are separated from the rest. Since students in schools that practice academic tracking tend to spend their leisure time with peers from the same track, the social costs of the practice may be high. The social gulf can produce emotional consequences: those in the college track may look down on the other students, while the students in noncollege tracks may resent their lower status — especially if they are placed in remedial classes.

Transitions between schools are tough, and the move to a middle school, junior high, or high school is usually followed by a slump in grades. The problem is that those who make two moves — to a junior high and, later, to a senior high — suffer twice. The junior-high experience has another down side: adolescents who enter high school via junior high go out for fewer extracurricular activities — in both junior high and senior high — than those who enter high school directly from an elementary school.[1]

At Pennsylvania State University, developmental psychologist Anne Petersen has discovered that young people who continue in elementary schools through the eighth grade do better in their early teens than youngsters who change to junior high school in the seventh grade. That's especially true for girls, because they generally go through the biological changes of puberty at the same time that they're changing schools. Petersen has found that youngsters who transfer from one school to another at the time of peak pubertal change tend to be anxious and depressed.[2] If they also begin dating when they enter junior high, they do even worse. Their grades tumble farther and their self-esteem suffers. Changes that an adolescent can handle when they come one at a time can seem overwhelming when they must be faced all at once.[3]

When elementary schools include all eight grades, the seventh- and eighth-graders have the opportunity to be big shots in their schools. In a combined junior-senior high school, they're at the bottom of the social heap and thrown into contact with older adolescents who may be experimenting with sex and drugs. Those who go to a separate junior high may escape that hazard, but just as they get settled into a routine, they change schools for a second time. Whichever route they take, the changes are so stressful that some developmentalists now question the wisdom of junior high schools. It seems that early adolescence went more smoothly when ninth grade marked the only transition between schools.

The stress induced by combined physical and social changes hits adolescents at the very time when they believe most strongly in their own invulnerability. As one mother plaintively wrote of her son, "As far as he is concerned, he can guzzle two six packs without getting drunk, he can drive a car without a lesson or license, he can fly without wings. He probably feels that he could smoke, snort, sniff, inhale, swallow, or inject any substance at all without overdosing, becoming an addict, or losing his grip. His response to everything is, 'I know. I *know!*'"[4]

This sense of personal invulnerability peaks in the years of early adolescence.[5] Before it wanes, many young people have made decisions that affect the rest of their lives. They do so without much experience of the world, using immature cognitive powers, and without understanding the consequences of their decisions. Most young adolescents who become sexually active, for example, do not appreciate the fact that one of the consequences of becoming a teenage parent is to shut off the world of opportunities that is opened by education. "If you think of growing up as being on a track that's moving into the future and moving across a series of transitions," says Richard Jessor, director of the University of Colorado's Institute for Behavioral Science, "you can do something early that gets you off track and makes it very hard to get back on track. Getting pregnant and bearing a child is one of those things. Dropping out of school is another. Getting a criminal record is another."[6]

A sense of invulnerability — the feeling that "it won't happen to me" — may be one reason girls who become sexually active early in adolescence are much less likely to use contraceptives than are older teens. Among girls who are not yet fifteen, the rate of giving birth has increased dramatically in recent years.[7] Although the pregnant teenager almost always does best when she stays with her parents and finishes school, most never complete high school. Without a high-school diploma, they become trapped below the poverty line, with no work skills, no education, and no time to work. They become dependent on welfare. Often, they soon find themselves right back in their original dilemma: 65 percent of pregnant teenagers who drop out of school get pregnant again within two years.

Marriage might seem the obvious answer, and those who marry are better off economically — but only at first. The problem is that teenage marriages are highly unstable. Fifty percent break up within four years; 60 percent within six years. Since the pregnant teenager who marries almost always drops out of school, too often she discovers that her life of poverty has only been postponed.[8]

Kim Henderson's story illustrates another aspect of teenage pregnancy. The adolescent daughters of teenage mothers tend to become pregnant themselves, as if the pair shared a clock that others in this country do not. Perhaps the mother's early pregnancy changes her children's expectations of what growing up is about, so that these teenagers simply assume that they will be parents before they leave adolescence — although few expect it to happen when they are as young as fourteen. As Kim's experience reminds us, the settings of the Social Clock are not uniform across society. In some groups, adolescents are expected to postpone pregnancy until their mid- or late twenties; in others, girls are expected to get pregnant almost as soon as they're fertile.

Most teenagers who give birth were themselves born into poverty. In some cities, early pregnancy is still the norm in African-American groups. On the south side of Chicago, where few young people go on to college and unemployment is widespread, teenagers who become pregnant are congratulated instead of condemned. In this environment, adolescents think there's something wrong with a sixteen-year-old girl who hasn't had a baby yet. Boys establish their masculinity by fathering a child. Peer pressure keeps the pregnancy rate high among black teenagers, who see nothing in their future that would give them a reason to delay parenthood.[9] When a teenager's social environment offers only bleak prospects, and when there's no stigma attached to being a young, unwed mother, the time for motherhood comes especially early.

Leaving school is another decision that teens often make without considering the consequences. Few teenage dropouts say that they quit school because their grades were low, but low grades are one of the best predictors that an adolescent will not graduate. Today, one out of four adolescents fails to complete high school, a rate that has not changed since 1965. Adolescents who drop out of school set the stage for a dismal future consisting of low-paying jobs, periodic unemployment, dependency on public assistance, and involvement in delinquency and crime.

Sometimes young lives get off track because of an entanglement with drugs or alcohol. All adolescents have easy access to these substances and many experiment with them, but only a small proportion abuse them. Most youngsters who use drugs say that they want to "get high," "feel better," or "get into music" they are listening to. But about a third say they are taking drugs simply because their friends do.[10] For some teenagers, drugs and alcohol provide a way to relax, a strengthening of social bonds, and an initiation into the rituals of high school. But when drug use becomes heavy, the users have moved into dangerous territory. Weekly drug use is associated with failing grades in school, academic suspension, conflicts with teachers, fights with parents, family crises, and crime.[11]

Involvement with crime is another experience from which it is difficult to recover. The interaction of a number of factors push youngsters into juvenile crime, but even among middle-class families, the single-parent household makes the development more probable. At the Stanford Center for the Study of Youth Development, Sanford Dornbusch and his colleagues have found that when a mother rears her children by herself, the likelihood that adolescents will run away from home rises, as does their chances of getting into trouble with the law and with school authorities. This is true whether the family is white or black, middle-class or below the poverty line.[12] It's also true whether the children are girls or boys, but the effect on boys is much more powerful.

Dornbusch believes that this higher rate of delinquency is connected to the tendency of single mothers to give their young adolescents too much control over their own actions. His studies show that even thirteen-year-olds in these families often make decisions with no input from their parents. Adolescents decide not only what clothes to buy and how to spend their money, but how late to stay out and which friends to go out with. When there's a second adult in the family, more of the control passes to adults and the rate of adolescent delinquency drops decisively — unless the extra adult is a stepfather. Conflict with stepfathers is so great that boys get into just as much trouble as when mothers alone shoulder the responsibility for child-rearing.

It would be a mistake to think that turmoil is inevitable during adolescence. Quite the contrary: every large study of teenagers, from the first national survey in 1966 to studies of Chicago high-school students in the mid-1980s, has found that 80 percent of all teenagers are doing just fine. They have realistic views of themselves and their future, and their goals and values are similar to those of their parents. About 20 percent of adolescents are troubled, but that level of emotional distress is no higher than the level of disturbance found among adults.[13] Still, when trouble does come during these years, it usually begins early, between the ages of ten and fourteen. As Kim Henderson well knows, what happens during that time has a profound effect on the rest of one's life.

An In-Between Season

Every society has recognized that a special period of life begins with the biological changes of puberty. Often this period was nothing more than a way station on the road to adulthood, a brief respite during which society redefined the person's status and formed new expectations for behavior and capabilities. In traditional societies, the official rite of passage was brief, although it often followed intensive training that lasted several weeks or months. For girls, the ceremony generally took place at menarche, and for many it included marriage. For boys, the physical changes of puberty often — but not always — marked the time of their formal passage into adulthood.

Some kind of visible markings made the child's new status plain. In one culture, it might be the assumption of adult garments; in another, it might involve ritual tattooing or scarification, in which rows of scars were carved into the youngster's back or face. Sometimes the nose was pierced. In other societies, the ceremony involved an operation on the sexual organs. A boy's foreskin was removed (circumcision) or the length of his penis slit (subincision). A girl might have her hymen cut or her clitoris removed. Once the wounds had healed, the passage into adulthood was complete.

In American society today, there's no single, clear-cut ceremony that marks the transition from childhood to adulthood. Instead, numerous small markers indicate that society has pushed a girl or boy another step along the path toward being a woman or man.[14] Some markers are unofficial, such as promotion to the "adult" table at the family Thanksgiving celebration. Some are religious, such as a bar mitzvah or confirmation. Some are written into the law: the minimum legal age for a driver's license, paid employment, attending an "R-rated" movie, voting, or buying a six-pack of beer.

Some, such as graduating from school, depend on your own efforts. But these markers are inconsistent in their definition of adulthood. Society says that a sixteen-year-old may drive, but that a young person must be eighteen to vote or marry without parental consent, twenty-one to drink alcoholic beverages, and twenty-five to become a member of Congress.

The adolescence of today is not a period of transition between seasons, but a season unto itself. It appears to have come into being during the last half of the nineteenth century, as more and more jobs began to require education beyond elementary school, and more and more parents were able to keep their youngsters off the labor market long enough to attend high school. Affluence and education, which hastened the recognition of childhood, played a similar role for adolescence — once again, beginning with the middle class. In society at large, only 5 percent of youths younger than eighteen were attending the high schools of 1871, but this figure would increase sixfold — to 33 percent — by 1929.[15]

Just after the turn of the century, G. Stanley Hall, who in 1878 received the first American Ph.D. in the field of psychology, christened this postpubertal stage as "adolescence." He saw it as a special time, because it opened the individual to instruction and training. In his estimation, curbing the unruliness of children was useless because each child had to retravel the path of human social evolution. Children, he said, were incapable of reason, morality, religious feelings, love, or sympathy. And so parents had no practical choice but to allow "the fundamental traits of savagery their fling till twelve."[16] Hall's view of childhood has been discarded, but society adopted his belief that adolescents had special needs and capabilities. In response, it passed laws compelling school attendance and extending childlabor laws to protect teenagers from adult responsibilities. Soon there were vocational schools to fill the duty-free time of those who could not expect to go to college — and juvenile reformatories for those who could not adapt.

Despite the current length of adolescence, a young person's actual transition into adult life is often abrupt and disconcerting. Adolescents today get little specific preparation for being a worker or a parent. When teenagers were engaged in adult work as apprentices, domestics, or unskilled laborers, they generally learned a trade or profession. Those whose families farmed were introduced to agriculture at an early age, just as children on the Kennedy farm are today. In 1990, most adolescents have a job, but parttime work behind a fast-food counter or at a gas pump provides almost no training for future trades and professions in a society that has little room for unskilled workers. As a result, most young people emerge from high school with only a hazy idea of what their future occupation might entail.

The same can be said of their preparation to be parents. When families were large and women spread childbearing over their entire fertile period, older children watched parents and other relatives care for younger children and got "hands-on" training themselves. Today, few adolescents have such experience, and so they embark on their reproductive roles with little knowledge and unrealistic expectations.

Adolescence is an "in between" season when a person is part child and part adult. Today, it represents the widest gap between biological and social maturation that has ever existed in the history of our species. Its climate has been captured by Anne Petersen. "I think this age period is like the seasonal changes in Minnesota, where I grew up. You have a period of time when, from one day to the next, you might go from winter to summer, back to winter, and then back again to summer. Kids this age are also changing from day to day. One day they're grown up, but the next day they revert. This can be confusing to parents, who sometimes throw up their hands and say, 'I can't deal with my child at this age.' But such changes are very typical."[17]

Puberty and Parents

At fifteen, Kim Henderson is far less rebellious than she was two years ago. Part of the change stems from the support her mother has given her and her baby, but part of it reflects the normal transitions of adolescence. Roles within the family change dramatically from the first half of the season to the second. In early adolescence, young people try to disengage from parents and establish their autonomy. Even in the closest of families, this is the age at which friction between parents and children often comes to a head.

Most of the battles arise over issues of personal taste and family duties — taking out the garbage, messy rooms, curfew, cars, clothes, how to spend spare time, the merits of MTV. The conflict is rarely about important issues, because adolescents and their parents generally share basic values and attitudes. Still, most young teenagers argue angrily with parents at least twice each week — about twice as often as married couples bicker.[18]

Laurence Steinberg has gathered evidence that the onset of fighting is not related to the age of a family's youngsters, but rather to their state of physical development.[19] No matter when puberty begins for an individual child, conflicts become most intense when physical changes are most rapid. One reason may be an increase in sex hormones that are associated with aggression — in girls as well as boys. Another may be the realization on the part of adolescents that they are starting to look like adults, a realization that prompts them to demand adult-like treatment. Their new, mature appearance also changes their social status, as peers involve them in "grown-up" activities. Why, the youngster asks, can't I be treated the same way at home?

Steinberg believes that minor conflict with parents is as natural to early adolescence as it is to the "terrible twos," another point in the life cycle when the establishment of autonomy is imperative. In fact, conflict at puberty may well be a vestige of our evolutionary past. "In virtually all other primate species, juveniles leave home at puberty," says Steinberg. "Typically, they leave on their own, but if they don't leave, they're kicked out of the nest by adults."[20] The smaller the primate band, the more rigidly this rule is enforced. Chimpanzees, who live in fairly large groups, send out only their adolescent females; gibbons, who live in smaller families, send out both sexes.

This pattern of behavior is probably adaptive. For nonhuman primates — as well as for our ancestors — having sexually mature young within the family group might lead to inbreeding that threatens the species' gene pool. Maintaining a healthy genetic diversity means having offspring seek out mates who are not close relatives. And so, says Steinberg, "Adolescent strife may be a headache for everyone concerned, but it may also serve an important role. It begets just enough distance between parent and child; without threatening the relationship, it forces adolescents to look outside the family for intimates and potential mates."[21]

In many past eras, that's exactly what happened. Children frequently left home before or during puberty. Many were indentured, apprenticed, or sent out for educational training. But today, physically mature teenagers may spend as many as seven or eight years living with their parents. Instead of leaving home, they stay to struggle for autonomy within redefined family roles.

Through all the strife of early adolescence, most young teenagers say that their parents are fair in matters of discipline, and believe that their parents are usually satisfied with them and will be proud of the way their lives turn out.[22] By the time the wrangling slackens — at about age sixteen — relationships within the family have shifted. Boys emerge with more influence over family decisions, second only to their fathers in power within the family.[23] In fact, at about this time many mothers begin deferring to their sons. By middle adolescence, both boys and girls have more control over their own lives. The new harmony may grow out of the parents' acceptance of their children's growing autonomy. As teenagers move through this period, most become more independent, both emotionally and financially. More than two-thirds have part-time jobs. Their earnings free them from the subservience of asking their parents for money and allow them to indulge their tastes.

Having their own spending money helps many teenagers achieve additional autonomy within the home, but in Kim Henderson's case, it's her baby that gives her adult-like status. "I never get into those real long fights with my mom now," she said. "My mom knows that Angie's my baby, that I have to raise her in my own way." Already an adult physically, Kim is trying to become one socially and psychologically.

Puberty and Peers

As young teens give up their emotional dependence on their parents, they begin to see them as ordinary people with strengths and weaknesses instead of the all-wise, all-powerful figures they had always seemed. As the power of parents wanes, that of peers usually grows. When we consider how much time adolescents spend with peers, the shift is not surprising. In one study, teenagers were given electronic pagers and asked to report whatever they were doing when the pager beeped. The records showed that these high-school students spent 52 percent of their waking hours in the company of peers, either inside or outside the classroom. Only 15 percent of their time was spent with their parents.[24]

The experience of Candy Reed during the first few months of junior high school is typical of many young teenagers. So is her love of the telephone. Among a sample of eighth-graders in one study, half of the boys and four-fifths of the girls phoned their friends every day, and once they reached them, the girls talked twice as long — at least an hour, compared with the boys' thirty minutes.[25]

When intimacy involves the disclosure of your innermost feelings, as it does in adolescence, parents no longer seem appropriate confidants.[26] And so it's not surprising that more than four-fifths of these eighth-graders said they had a best friend, and more than half said the friendship had lasted at least a year. Girls' friendships seemed more intimate and intense than those of boys — twice as many girls shared their personal problems with their friends.[27] The less intimate nature of boys' friendships may explain why so many eighth-grade boys say that when they need to share their secrets and private feelings, they turn to the girls they know.[28]

Junior high is also the time when cliques begin to form, as young people sort themselves out on the basis of their shared interests. Within a clique, adolescents tend to have similar attitudes toward school, perhaps because schoolwork often impinges on social activities. Unless members have similar values, conflicts may arise over whether to study or party. Clique members also tend to like the same kind of music, dress similarly, enjoy the same kind of social events, and have similar attitudes toward drugs.[29]

Whether their clique is made up of jocks, brains, nerds, burn-outs, or social butterflies, both boys and girls get deeply involved in their groups during adolescence. But by the time they're about seventeen, membership in the clique has lost some importance, and teenagers may find more satisfaction from individual relationships with friends of either sex.[30] At first, cliques tend to be segregated by sex. Then, as youngsters pass into middle adolescence and dating becomes important, a particular group of girls may begin to "hang out" with a particular group of boys, and a mixed group forms. Each member establishes a close relationship with a member of the other sex, allowing group members to learn about heterosexual relationships within the protection of the clique.[31]

The age at which dating begins varies from one school to the next. Most eighth-grade girls do not go out on "real" dates, but instead go to dances and parties in groups. Only after they reach the party or the dance do they pair off with boys. But no matter when traditional dating starts, boys are more interested than girls in the physical expression of sexuality. In a national sample, 86 percent of young adolescent boys, compared with 60 percent of the girls, agreed that "sexual experiences give me pleasure."[32] And though adolescent boys still believe that sexual intimacy should go "faster and farther" than girls do, the percentage of teenage boys who have actually engaged in intercourse appears to have changed little since about 1950. Like girls, they probably have their first experience of intercourse at a younger age, but the proportion of sexually experienced boys is about what it was a generation or two ago. The proportion of sexually experienced girls, however, has increased substantially during the same time.[33]

The peer pressure that friends and groups exert on an individual mounts steadily through junior high school and doesn't begin to ease until near the end of senior high. But the individual's susceptibility to this influence follows a different pattern, peaking around the eighth or ninth grade and declining gradually after that. In the peak years, teenagers develop a new kind of self-consciousness that creates what one psychologist has called the "imaginary audience." "Everyone," they think, "is looking at me!"[34]

Often the young adolescent is so susceptible to influence that he or she misreads what "other kids" are doing. When it comes to sexual activity, smoking, drugs, or alcohol, most adolescents overestimate the number of their peers who are "doing it." In one study, youngsters estimated that two-thirds of their peers were smoking, although only one-tenth were actually involved. When teenagers believe that some risky behavior is typical of a majority of their peers, it seems "normal" — and so the strictures against it are apt to lose their force.[35]

When parents see their children making new friends, becoming part of cliques, and beginning to date, they often worry about the negative aspects of peer pressure, fretting that the peer group will persuade their youngster to experiment with drugs, alcohol, sex, or crime. Sometimes this happens, but more often, peers persuade youngsters *not* to venture into forbidden waters. When queried by researchers at the University of Wisconsin, teenagers described peer pressure as mostly positive.[36] Peers tended to push adolescents into socializing, studying, and going out for extracurricular activities, but urged them *away* from involvement in drugs, alcohol, sexual activity, and delinquency. Those who did feel antisocial pressure said that it was easier to resist than pressure to become involved in school and social activities. Antisocial pressure tended to increase as youngsters moved into middle adolescence, but by then their ability to resist was beginning to improve.

The growing influence of peers on the lives of young adolescents is best seen in light of their quest for personal autonomy. Feeling unsure of themselves and not wanting to stand out in any way, eighth- and ninth-graders find refuge in a group. As they develop their autonomy, they come to feel more self-reliant, and the influence of peers starts to decline.[37] By the end of adolescence, the social context of their lives is very different from what it was at the beginning.

Despite their changed position in the family, most older teens still live at home with their parents, rely on them, and have to answer to them. Another transition will change that as well.

The Last Summer

It's summer in Myrtle Beach, South Carolina. On the teen scene, that means surf and sand, cars and dates. When slim, tanned Michael Shelton, who has just turned eighteen, strolls along the shore, he knows he's in his element. "It's no secret I'm carefree. My senior year, I didn't care if I was described as a bum 'cause basically I sort of was. I did homework five minutes before class started. I didn't want to take on any responsibility. I didn't have any goals but to get that diploma — and do as little as I could to get it."

Michael got his diploma, but now he's getting a little concerned about what comes next. "Graduation didn't become a reality until about three hours before I graduated. When my parents were saying, 'You better start thinking about the responsibilities ahead of you,' I didn't. Because it was like years away — why do I have to start thinking about that now? Believe it or not, that time crept up very fast. I had all these things to face, all these answers I should have been working on. I had to say, 'What do I do about this and this and this?' And my parents told me, 'You should have thought about all that before.'"

Michael has started to think about "all that," but a part of him would rather go on just as he is. Michael looks good on the beach, and he would like to make the summer last. A first-degree black belt in karate, he's well muscled and has a quick smile. A cap of brown hair dips to his neck in the back. Girls find him attractive, and he knows what he's looking for in them.

"No guy in his right mind is going to go out with a girl just for her mind or her personality. He's gonna go for her looks. I suppose when you get older, you start caring if they have a brain cell in their head, but at this age, you can afford to go just with their looks. My friends go after the clothes, see who can dance, who's got the nicest car, and stuff like that." Michael claims to be different, but not much. "I'm probably looking for a girl a little bit smarter. I'm not looking to settle down or anything, but just someone I can talk to, so it's not gonna be like talking to a wall. There's a lot of that around here.

"Before my time, I guess, it was like seventeen or eighteen when people started to get involved in sex, but nowadays we're talking ninth grade, tenth grade. Some of my friends, I suppose, they go out looking for it. There's not really a lot of pressure. We don't go out and say, you know, 'Tonight this is what we're going out to do.' We keep it our own personal business, and we don't broadcast it. My parents feel that if you think you're mature enough to handle it, you'd better make sure that the inevitable doesn't happen. People think about getting pregnant, but it's not a determining factor. AIDS isn't either, within this community. But the threat of AIDS has steered us away from going out with girls who come down here

Michael Shelton, eighteen. "I think my next investment might be a radar detector."

for vacation. Not just from having sex, you know, but even from kissing them. I don't know if that's a way to contract the disease, but when you're seventeen or eighteen, it's scary enough."

Besides karate, girls, and friends, Michael has wheels. "Getting a car of my own was really a big thing. I wanted the RX7s and the TransAms and the Corvettes, but my parents were talking something I could afford. Something under ten thousand, and I was looking over twenty-five thousand. My car's not a big car, but it's perfect for what I need, and it gets good gas mileage. I pay for it myself. I think you appreciate it a lot more when you pay for it yourself.

"I get lectures on speeding all the time. They say I rip out of the driveway too fast. I do admit that I speed. Not a lot of people obey the speed limit — why should I? It's funny, 'cause in the twelve weeks I took driver's education, not once was I penalized for speeding. Then I get in the real world and pow, pow, pow. Speeding ticket is usually a sixty-five in a fifty-five — I got an eighty-five in a fifty-five. I suppose I'd lose my license pretty quick if I had a Porsche. My dad's friends said I passed them on the freeway, and I was going so fast I about ripped the glass out of their cars. I passed a cop in an unmarked car, and it took him six miles to catch up to me. Then I got in a wreck, so my insurance keeps on going up the ladder. I've had two tickets, and a warning. I get one more ticket and I lose my license. I think my next investment might be a radar detector."

Michael pays for his car with money from a job and from a hobby that he has turned into a small business. He's a skilled airbrush artist, and there's a brisk market for his T-shirts among tourists and teenagers. In his room at home, he spreads out a gaudy shirt on which a knight in armor rides his

"I'm like a butterfly leaving its cocoon. I'm ready to fly."

steed. "That took me around three hours to paint, 'cause I used it as a display downtown. That's the type that stops people. When they're walking by, a beach scene is not gonna catch their eye. You have to have these extravagant displays so they'll stop and look at the rest of the stuff."

Michael wants to turn his talent into a career in commercial art. "I didn't know what commercial art was until eleventh grade, but I've always drawn. I started off with dinosaurs and army scenes. Then last year I got a job painting movie sets. I liked what I was doing, being able to work with artists. It's not like they shove you back in this little room and you have to sit and draw all the time. You actually get to go out and work in different environments.

"I go more towards the fantasy-type thing, the whole dungeons and dragons type. I like that kind of art — the women in skimpy bikini-type armor and the big masculine heroes. Hopefully, one day I'll be able to do my own cartoon with that. My imagination is endless in that field, but if someone said, 'Do a pretty landscape,' I'd have to sit there and think for a while. I think I'd despise having to sit there and draw peaches and apples and flowers in a bowl. I know I'll have to do that in college, but that's just to help me better my skills."

This fall Michael will travel to Fort Lauderdale in southern Florida, where he has enrolled in a two-year art school. "I wanted to stay on the coast because I like the beachy-type thing, where it's nice and warm in summertime and it gets cool in the winter. When I went down there and saw the building, it was impressive. Right when I walked in that front door, it was like, this is it."

Not everyone in Michael's family thinks he's ready to go away to school.

His stepfather, Gary Cale, grew up in a military family and is a master sergeant in the air force. He is skeptical about Michael's commitment to art — or to anything — and thinks the air force could do him some good. "The biggest problem I have is his refusal to think beyond the next five minutes. His only concerns are with what's gonna happen right now. He wants to go to college because he thinks that's where you have a lot of fun at this time in your life. He's going to an art school, where he doesn't have to concern himself with math, English, and the other things you typically have to handle in school. I think that Michael is maybe just a little bit too young for college, but I'm not gonna force anyone into changing their lifestyle based on what I think.

"The last few weeks of high school, my perception was that he was doing his best *not* to graduate, just so he wouldn't have to leave. He wouldn't admit it, but he never said I was one-hundred-percent wrong. I'm reading the same kind of signs this summer about going to college. Enlisted folks in the military aren't the greatest paid people in the world, and he knows that. He knows he has to earn some money to help with tuition costs, but he's more concerned with partying. I told him that the signs tell me you don't really want to go, that you'd rather stay home. And I still feel that way. I think he's real nervous about going, even though art is what he wants to do. But I think that it's all gonna change once he gets down there."

Kadriye Cale, Michael's mother, shares that perception. "Michael likes to do as little as possible because he knows he can do just about anything he sets his mind to. His point is, 'I know I can do it, who do I have to prove it to?' So he figures if he can get a C, that's just fine, because if he spoils the teachers by getting good grades, they'd expect that from him all the time.

"Our last argument came when Michael thought he'd postpone art school for another six months and get himself a full-time job. That's when I came unglued. His excuse was that maybe he could work, make some money and be less of a burden. Reading between the lines, that's not what it came down to. I know he's scared to be facing a world he has absolutely no knowledge of. He's gonna be doing a lot of growing up and a lot of falling down in the next six months. But then we all did. I hope we did some good while we were raising him so he won't take too many bad falls."

Michael is aware that life on the beach is coming to an end — probably more aware than his parents realize. "Since my parents haven't been around me a lot this summer, they haven't quite seen the new side of me. It's like I gotta put the brakes on. I don't go out and party as much. I try to get in as early as possible, so I can get enough sleep so it won't affect my work. Before, if I was tired, hey, I'd call in sick. And I watch my pennies. I don't blow my money on everything I see.

"Money's gonna be tight, and I can't leave that whole burden on my parents. It's just not fair. 'Cause my father put himself through college with no help at all from his parents. That's what I want to try to show them — that I can handle responsibility. I want to show them that I'll help.

"The hardest part about going to school will be leaving my family. Leaving this protectiveness. Like, if I don't hear my alarm clock go off, I'm not gonna have mom to come in and wake me up and say, 'You gotta go to school.' But that's part of growing up. I can't stay here forever. It's exciting because I'll be on my own, but it's kind of scary. I'm gonna get a taste of adult life. I'm like a butterfly leaving its cocoon. I'm ready to fly."

9

THE PSYCHOLOGICAL STORY OF ADOLESCENCE

The Story Is the Self

The first thing you notice about seventeen-year-old Nuket Curran is her hair. Her light brown locks are trimmed close on the back and sides — like those of a typical male in the 1950s. The entire top is roached, standing straight up for about an inch and a half. From the right side, just above and behind her ear, hangs a long, very thin braid.

"I started out looking like everyone else," she says. "In ninth grade I was more, like, preppy. Had the bob, it was down to here — just standard-looking. And then I got an undercut; it was called a wedge. Then I cut one side off and then I shaved it off and then I just had long, long bangs and black in my hair. It was, like, striped black and my natural color. Then it was red — cherry cola red — and black. Then it was orange and black. I looked like Halloween. Then it was blond and black. I just felt like doing it, you know, and I can't do that when I'm thirty-five. I can't get a job looking like that. So why not just do it now?

"People said, 'Well, she's dyeing her hair to be different.' In a way that's true. I mean, it's just a different way of expressing myself. I don't like to call it punk or new wave or any other terminology. It's a way of showing that I'm just another human being that's different from every other human being. I'm so bored with how everyone dresses the same. They have plain hair and plain everything. It's just monotonous. They're afraid to, like, stand out, to

178

Nuket Curran, seventeen.
"I'm not gonna find out
who I am in one day."

be themselves. And I just felt like I was being myself. I'm a human being and this is what I look like inside."

Green-eyed Nuket is anything but plain and monotonous. Along with her original hairstyle, she wears several earrings in each double-pierced ear, heavy silver rings on every finger, and pointy shoes. Perhaps because her hair is meant to be the center of attention, she wears very little makeup and favors mostly black clothes.

Nuket's singular name means "mountain flower" in Turkish. The name entered the Curran family when Nuket's father, a professor at the University of Pittsburgh, spent three years living in Turkey. Nuket is named after the niece of Professor Curran's best friend in that country. The unusual name pleases her. "Having the name has been a big plus all my life. People remember who I am because it's such a weird name."

People who see Nuket's room remember it, too. They are struck by the unusual drawings that line its walls. Colors and shapes are important to her, but not too long ago, words were more important. "I used to write a lot of poetry. That was a way of connecting myself with my unconscious thoughts. A lot of things that actually mean a lot to you come out in symbols when you write. But I stopped doing that because I can't write anymore. I have a little block."

Drawing came to the fore two years ago, when Nuket was "busy rebelling." At fifteen, she was prolonging the conflicts of early adolescence with some drastic testing that, on more than one occasion, left her confined to her home for "screw-ups" she'd rather not talk about. "I started drawing when I was grounded and really bored and depressed because I had nothing to do," she recalls. "My art's changed since then. Then I was more pointy and things had more definition. Now I'm kind of sixtiesish in a way: psychedelic, dripping stuff, round and curly. You can see the mood swings in that picture. I've got my sad psyche in the middle, and I've got my burning flame and my own birth sign, Aries. It was two years ago when I started that piece, and it's not really done. But now I'm continuing it on a new page. New page, new age.

Nuket's art has become a record of herself, a kind of pictorial diary. Although she cannot yet say who she is, her symbols spell out a history of her attempts at identity. One prominent symbol is an eye from which a large teardrop escapes. "That I've put in most of my drawings. It's kind of like that phase I was going through. 'Cause an eye is a representative of the psyche, which is the very soul of a person. And it was sad. My soul was sad. I think everyone is kind of sad in a way. It's just a universal symbol. It was my signature for a long time, because that's just how I was feeling. I was sad because I felt like I was going nowhere, that there was no point to everything that was going on."

Another symbol that appears in Nuket's art is the peace sign. "It's a dream, but it's also a symbol of unity. It's the idea of having peace of mind and not being, like, constantly a nervous wreck, wondering if you're doing the right thing. And the ankh, the Egyptian cross, which I wear all the time, it's a symbol of eternal life, because when you die you're gonna live eternally in everyone you know who loved you. And the candle with a flame — it represents a living person, like a living soul. You're burning either with energy or life. I like candles. I have them all over my room. I like watching them flicker, because they're so lively."

The flickering candles, tearful eye, black clothes, and gloomy music Nuket favors creates a melancholy mood. But she denies that it all adds up to a mournful message. Black has a special meaning for her, she says, one that has little to do with gloom or woe. "Black is all colors combined. So, symbolically, it's just like you've got all your colors together. You're not really wearing one specific color; you're wearing every single one — which nobody realizes because they can't see it. That's kind of like a person, too. You're kind of all inside and no one can see everything. And the music . . . music helps me deal with things. Just listening to it calms me or makes me happy or whatever. I couldn't really live without music. I relate to the music because I'm learning to play the bass right now. When you play it, you can feel it vibrating through your bones. I just love the feeling of it; it's like soul-touching music.

"Most of the music I listen to is dark. A lot of people call it gloom. And it is in a way, because this is not the greatest time in my life. I wouldn't want to be this age again ever, because it's just such a hard time. There's so much happening right now, as far as changing, and you really feel unsettled. So things are kind of inflated — the small things are inflated until they seem horrible. You know, you break up with your boyfriend, or you and your best friend have a fight. And you just feel so alone. That's the whole scare of being a teenager, because so many people think they're entirely alone.

"I've known of people who've committed suicide, and I remember once when I thought about it. Just because things seemed so horrible — like everything was huge and like I had this huge weight on my back, like 'Oh, my God, why am I here?' You know, wouldn't it be better if I just died and no one gave a damn about me? I mean, everyone's got to think it."

The thoughts of suicide came during Nuket's "rebellious" period. But she soon discovered she had a lot to live for, starting with her family. "They love me. They'll support me through anything. They have. I really have pulled a lot of crap on them — like seeing how far I can go before my parents get ticked off at me. 'Cause you're kind of insecure at this stage and you need to know that you've got someone to back you up. You're trying to find out how much they love you. And they've stuck by me.

"My parents don't give negative rays about how I look or how I dress or anything. In fact, they laugh at it. They just think, 'Well, fine. Do whatever you like.' I don't feel like I'm really rebelling 'cause they kinda defeated the purpose of it if they're gonna laugh at it, you know, and not really care. But now I just kind of enjoy it. It's independence. I guess I feel like I'm being more independent because I feel like I'm just being myself."

If her family means a lot to Nuket, her friends mean even more. "Right now we're all in the same state of mind, kind of confused. And all just fumbling around in the dark, trying to find the light switch. I have some really close friends that I confide almost everything to. If I didn't have them, I probably would be dead. They're kind of like a separate family, you know. I love them and they love me. They're kind of like my life support. My life source. They just keep me sane.

"I've tried just about everything that a normal teenager would try. And learned the better parts of it and the down parts of it. Having all these other people around you and watching them screw up, you kind of compare notes, and you keep the things that they've said in the back of your mind as sort of a little file cabinet. I've seen lots of kids who have gone to drugs — a lot of my really good friends who aren't doing very well now, who've become so closed off. Just seeing how they are right now, makes me think of how lucky I am, just being logical about it and not having picked that road.

"I want to know as many different people as I can, to take in all the experience I can, and see what good I can get from all these people and all these experiences. I'm taking any good part I see, anything I admire. Just using the experiences I get to help me decide where I want to go with things, what kind of person I want to be.

"The future's kind of foggy still. I have another year of high school. And I'm just gonna take it slow. I'm not in any rush. I mean, sure, I'd love to get out, get to college, and be independent. But the fact remains that I'm scared to death. What if I don't do well in college? What if I don't go? What if this? What if that? It's kind of hard to keep it all in perspective sometimes. Right now I'm neither an adult nor a child. I'm just sort of at an in-between point. And I'm not really sure if I want to be an adult quite yet, because there's just so many things that I know I'll have to deal with when I grow up.

"I'm not gonna find out who I am in one day. I'd like to be someone that people can trust, someone who's got their act together, who's not going to totally screw up all the time. I want to be someone you can depend on — and I can depend on. I'd like to be successful, too. Get a good job and, like, graduate valedictorian. The goal is to try and get it all together. Like, I'll be one human being with all these aspects rolled into one."

A World of Possibility

When Nuket Curran talks about herself, she sounds nothing at all like Karl Haglund or Jason Kennedy, children in an earlier season of life. Nuket thinks differently from them, and as a result she makes a different kind of meaning. Like other teenagers, she has moved beyond the concrete world of the here-and-now into the abstract world of possibility. Not only can she think about herself, she can think about herself thinking about herself. She moves easily in a world of symbols. A child simply would not — could not — think and talk the way she does.

David Elkind, a specialist in child development, has studied the mental changes of adolescence. "The new kind of thinking that comes in adolescence is much deeper and richer, involving the ability to think of many things at the same time, to consider possibilities. Teenagers can think in terms of metaphors and similes. Children may use metaphors, but they don't understand them very well. When the poet says, 'My love is like a red, red rose,' the adolescent knows what the poet means, but the child has difficulty grasping it."[1]

Psychologists Daniel Osherson and Ellen Markman have caught glimpses of the intellectual transformation of adolescence with a simple experiment using poker chips of different colors. The experiment begins when the psychologist tells the young person seated across from her that she is going to say several things about the poker chips and that the youngster is to decide whether the statements are true, false, or whether there's no way to tell. Then the psychologist picks up one of the chips without revealing its color, hides it in her hand, and says, "Either the chip in my hand is red *or* it is not red." Ten-year-olds, whose minds are mired in the mud of reality, are likely to say, "I can't tell." If the psychologist makes the same statement while holding the chip so the child can see it, ten-year-olds will say "true" if the chip is red or "false" if the chip is blue. In the same situation, adolescents know that the question has nothing to do with the color of the chips but everything to do with the logic of the words, and so they respond with "true" whether the chip is visible or invisible, red or blue. If the psychologist now conceals another chip and says, "The chip in my hand is red *and* it is not red," ten-year-olds again remain attached to the concrete, to what they read as a demand for the color of the chip within the closed fist, and say, "I can't tell." Again, adolescents respond to the logic of the statement and say, "False."[2]

Ten-year-olds are not stupid. If the last logical statement is dramatized, they can evaluate it properly. That became apparent when psychologists Martin Braine and Barbara Rumain of New York University placed a closed box in front of children and positioned a puppet on each side of the box.[3] One puppet said, "There's a dog in the box," and the other puppet said, "There's no dog in the box." Without missing a beat, children objected, insisting that one of the puppets had to be wrong. Even most five-year-olds were certain of it. These children were not responding to an exercise in logic, but to a familiar and meaningful situation. The child stands on the solid ground of reality, focusing on what *is*. The adolescent soars into the realm of the possible, considering what *could be*.

Piaget called this ability to deal with possibilities "formal operations." By that, he meant that while children can perform "operations" on concrete objects (manipulate them mentally), adolescents can perform "operations on operations" (mentally manipulate abstract processes and propositions). Equipped with formal thought, adolescents can think about the hypothetical and about the future. They can think about things that don't exist and things that are contrary to fact. They can even think about thinking — their own and other people's. And they can reason scientifically.

Faced with a problem, they first consider all possible solutions and then systematically test each possibility, eliminating those that are wrong. Only a few years ago, these same teenagers would have assumed that the answer lay in whatever obvious evidence lay before them — even if the solution it provided was clearly illogical.

Scientific reasoning seemed the essence of formal thought to Piaget, who described it in terms of logical principles. But this kind of abstract, logical reasoning is closely tied to academic settings. Adolescents who do well on Piaget's tests also achieve high scores on IQ tests, so it's not surprising that Piaget's tests of formal thought are regularly failed by a large number of adolescents and adults. Many people never develop the ability to solve problems in physics or chemistry, or to reason about statements that have been stripped of all connection with reality. But their ability with formal operations shows in other areas — in woodworking, for example, or in computer games. By late adolescence, most teenagers show some degree of formal thought. They can think about abstractions, understand historical time, recognize future consequences of contemplated actions, have some grasp of motivation, and understand that behavior has multiple causes. If they did not, they would not be able to function adequately in society.[4]

Ever since Piaget first formulated the notion of formal thought, other psychologists have been trying to discover what's behind the transformation of the adolescent mind. Most agree that one important change has to do with an increase in "information-processing capacity." Adolescents can handle information — recognize it, pull it out of memory, compare it with other information — much faster than children. They also have developed more efficient strategies for dealing with information. The net effect is that adolescents' thought becomes more complex and sophisticated because they have more mental energy to focus on the task, just as a personal computer with 512 kilobytes of working memory can "think" rings around a computer with 256 kilobytes.

A second catalyst of change in the adolescent mind is its vast accumulation of knowledge. In many areas where children are "novices," adolescents are "experts." Concepts and problems that children must laboriously work through can be managed by adolescents in an offhand manner. In addition, their knowledge is cross-referenced in a way that a child's is not, so pertinent information that a child might not be able to recall springs quickly to mind.[5]

Their new ability to think about things that don't exist opens another realm of possibility for adolescents: they begin to envision ideals — ideal mates, ideal parents, ideal societies. The ability to imagine the ideal boy or girl opens the way for the adolescent crush. It allows adolescents to attribute beauty, intelligence, understanding, sympathy — all the wonderful qualities — to another, usually unattainable, person. When teenagers visualize ideal parents, their own parents inevitably appear wanting. A mother or father who had always seemed powerful, good, or even perfect now seems unable to walk, talk, dress, or eat properly. Adolescents who once wanted their parents to visit the school, take on a group of cub scouts, or show up at Little League games suddenly begin suffering agonies of embarrassment when caught in their company.

If parents aren't perfect, neither is society. Adolescents can envision an ideal world and want to change the one they're in. They also know that adults have made this world what it is. "Anger arises," says Elkind, "because the adolescent's new idealism is untempered by experience. If one can imagine a world without disease, without war, without hunger, then that kind of world ought to be possible."[6] Adolescents have yet to learn that their ideals cannot be realized immediately, but must be worked toward.

Forming an Identity

Because teenagers can imagine possibilities, they can wonder, "What if I were different?" They can think about who they are and who they might become. New cognitive powers enable them to engage in what Erik Erikson regarded as the primary task of adolescence: forming an identity.

In early adolescence, says Robert Kegan, young people are so driven by a need to establish and maintain relationships with their peers that they cannot conceive of themselves except in the context of how others see them.[7] At this stage, the adolescent feels, "I *am* my relationships." This need for affiliation explains why the friendships of early adolescence are so intense, why adolescents form cliques, and why they are often so cruel to those they see as "different." The self is developing within the context of its relationships, acquiring such qualities as empathy, mutual concern, and self-sacrifice. But the self is one thing in one group and another thing in different social circumstances.

In later adolescence, the self begins to slip out of its envelope of relationships. It becomes something unto itself, consistent from one social situation to the next, "someone you can depend on — and I can depend on," in Nuket Curran's words. Separate from others as well as defined by them, the young person is no longer content with conformity. He or she now feels, "I *have* relationships," and is in possession of what Erik Erikson meant by identity — the confidence that "you know who you are, that you know what you want to be, that you know what you look like to others, and that you will know how to make the right decisions."8

The mature identity includes an image of one's body and a sense of the people to whom one belongs. It includes a knowledge of what it means to be male or female. It is not complete until an occupation has been selected, political beliefs are set, and moral or religious commitments are made. As they go about the process of "rolling all these aspects into one human being," adolescents compare their own thoughts, characteristics, and actions with those of people they admire, love, dislike, or fear. They create "possible selves" — ideas of what they might become, what they would like to become, and what they're afraid of becoming.9 Nuket's possible selves include herself as a good student, as an artist, as someone who's independent and has a good job. These possible selves express her hopes. But she also has fears, which produce possible selves with a bleak future: a poor student, a failed artist, someone unable to support herself, a user of drugs. The importance of possible selves is that they describe how Nuket might change. Without them, she has no motivation to act in ways that will enable her to accomplish her goals.

Some adolescents begin to wrestle with identity by asserting who they are not — by being rebellious. Dramatic changes in clothing and hairstyle, loud music, and sometimes failure in school help them proclaim that they are not like their parents. These adolescents may go on to do what Nuket is doing, trying on possibilities, testing, always testing, and relying on friends for support. Once Nuket's identity becomes clear, she will probably be an independent, self-confident, flexible, and intellectually creative young woman. But Nuket may be well into young adulthood before her identity finally crystallizes and she knows who she is and what she wants to do with her life.

A large minority of adolescents do not take as long as it appears Nuket will. Jason Kennedy may be one of those young people who keep steadily to the course they set in childhood. As he nears adolescence, Jason seems to have already accepted the occupational goals, values, and expectations of his family. He will probably be a dairy farmer, a good Republican, and a faithful member of the church. This smooth passage into a course charted by others is known as an "identity foreclosure," and during much of human history it was the usual pathway to adulthood. In traditional societies, children grow up expecting to assume their parents' occupations and beliefs — few even imagine that another way of life is possible. In fact, a young person in a traditional society who plunges into self-discovery is usually considered strange. If Jason is like other "foreclosed" young men, he will be conforming, respectful of authority, and religious.[10]

Some young people seek an identity and fail to find it. They worry so much about committing themselves to the wrong friend, the wrong sexual partner, the wrong leader, or the wrong career that they wind up making no commitments at all. They remain confused about who they are. Often they seem charming and carefree, but they're usually impulsive, lack a sense of direction, and have trouble relating to other people.[11] But most adolescents eventually develop an identity. Their self-esteem rises steadily across the adolescent years,[12] and when queried, they say they are happy, strong, and self-confident. Best of all, they enjoy life.[13]

Adolescence is the first time in life that we ask the question, "Who am I?" But it won't be the last. We leave this season of life with a capacity that will always be with us — the ability to imagine a self standing in the adult world, a self that's connected to the past, present, and future.

Identity as a Story

The question "Who am I?" is often answered the way Nuket answers it — with a list of characteristics. But it can be answered just as easily with a story. At Loyola University in Chicago, psychologist Dan McAdams believes that the self can be thought of *as* a story, as a personal narrative that first emerges in adolescence. "We all do it a little differently, but it's at this time in our lives that we begin to think about what we do in the present and what we've done in the past and what we may do in the future as all being connected within some grand narrative scheme," says McAdams. "And this narrative scheme — this evolving story — helps us define who we are."[14]

By the time children go to school, their autobiographical memory has been functioning for several years, and they have developed ability to understand and tell stories. But even though they describe discrete events, they spend little time interpreting them. With adolescence comes the ability to see how the episodes in one's life interconnect, to reflect on the significance of overarching patterns, and to think about the origin of beliefs and habits. In adolescence we become able to take stories *from* our life and weave them into the story *of* our life. We become biographers of the self — a self with a beginning, middle, and end.

The first story of the self, says McAdams, is a simple yet heroic myth that David Elkind calls the "personal fable." Elkind found evidence for the personal fable in adolescent diaries, which often appear to be written "in the conviction that the young person's experiences, crushes, frustrations are of universal significance."[15] The personal fable reflects the young adolescent's belief that no one has ever experienced the world the way she or he has. No one has seen what she's seen, done what she's done, loved as she's loved, hurt as she's hurt. No one is destined for the greatness — or the tragedy — that she is. The personal fable is filled with a sense of invulnerability that enables the young person to do things she ordinarily would be afraid of, but also to take risks that can be especially dangerous. And the fable serves a function in identity formation: in the very years in which the self *is* its relationships, the personal fable represents an impulse toward uniqueness, telling the young person how special and unique she is. The first story of the self is full of fantasy, but later versions will become more realistic.

Later versions will also be given a background of belief and value, what McAdams calls an "ideological context." He says, "When you think of a person between the ages of fifteen and nineteen, you're thinking of somebody who is quite preoccupied with coming up with answers to fundamental questions about right and wrong, about relationships among people, about God. At this point in one's life, much of identity work takes the form of getting one's ideology squared away."[16]

The ideological context of one's biography cannot develop earlier in life because children have no concept of "society" or "community." Confined to the here-and-now, they think about social institutions in personal terms, and their views about problems of crime or government tend to be rigidly authoritarian. University of Michigan psychologist Joseph Adelson describes the mind of a twelve-year-old as like the mind of Watergate conspirator G. Gordon Liddy.[17] Over the years, Adelson and his associates have interviewed thousands of children and adolescents, asking them what they thought about society, politics, government, and law. They discovered that no matter how intelligent the child or how extensive his or her political experience, those between the ages of eleven and thirteen had a primitive, highly punitive perspective. Charming, well-scrubbed cherubs casually recommended executions as a good way to stop theft. In the words of a typical twelve-year-old, "If he doesn't improve, I think he ought to be killed. And if that doesn't work, I think we ought to torture him."[18]

Children talk about specific people, specific acts, specific objects. To them, "law" is the police officer or the judge, whose purpose is to punish.

"Government" is the governor or the president, or buildings or highways. "Education" is the teacher. But some time between the age of thirteen and fifteen, a dramatic shift occurs, and adolescents begin to see these issues in a new way. They begin to weigh the competing claims of self and other, the individual and the larger community. By the time they're eighteen, whether they live in the wealthy suburbs or the inner cities, whether their IQ is 95 or 135, adolescents have grasped the purpose of social institutions. They begin to describe laws as making it possible for people to live together. With their new capacity for formal thought, they come to understand the conventions that hold societies together and to appreciate the hopes and ideals they embody. When they consider a political choice, they go beyond its personal consequences to take into account its social consequences, and how it might affect their own values.

Once young people have established a context of belief and value — not only about politics, but also about social, moral, and religious issues — other parts of their story are free to develop. Incidents from the past will be selected and reworked until the tale they tell points toward a particular outcome — the person they have become.[19] As their life changes in the years ahead, so will their reconstruction of the past. When sociologists tracked down more than 300 men and women whose early lives had been so disturbed that they had received treatment at a child-guidance clinic, a curious effect appeared. Those who were still troubled tended to remember their early emotional problems, but those who were now well-adjusted had great difficulty recalling them.[20]

The life story we first write in adolescence and then revise over the years may do more than interpret our past. Jerome Bruner believes that, once we start spinning our story, the version we come up with can affect the kind of person we become.[21] When we encounter a new situation, we often do so with a provisional scenario in hand, its lines dictated by interpretations of our past. We select a course of action that agrees with what's already written in our narrative.

Above all, the life story compiled in adolescence will reveal the self. McAdams calls the key elements in a life story "nuclear episodes." These are the moments that we remember as especially significant — a major decision, a religious conversion, getting fired, having a baby, accidentally meeting someone who changes the course of our lives. Nuclear episodes represent the highs and lows of our lives, as well as the turning points that complicate our story's plot, move it forward, or change its direction.[22] They include our very first memories — those founding myths that often summarize a major life motif.

McAdams has discovered a close link between people's personality and the kind of nuclear episodes they recall. Those for whom power is a dominant motive tend to recall episodes of physical strength or moral courage — times when they displayed some new understanding, influenced others, engaged in vigorous physical activity, or earned a measure of fame or prestige. Those who value intimacy recall episodes that highlight themes of communication, love, friendship, or sympathy. The same connection holds even if nuclear episodes are painful. People concerned with power have "worst" memories of conflict, weakness, failure, humiliation, or the discovery of their own ignorance. For those concerned with intimacy, these "worst" memories usually involve another person — either a misfortune they shared, or a rejection, separation, or disillusionment they suffered.

McAdams has found that the connection between story and personality holds only for accounts of nuclear episodes, not for descriptions of everyday events. Apparently, when we recount the key moments in our life stories, we reveal who we are. When we describe ordinary episodes, we do not.

A story is the way the self makes meaning in response to the biological and social imperatives that drive the life course. Because these imperatives are shared, so are elements in our stories. We can see ourselves in the experiences of others, and they can see themselves in ours. But as life goes on, unexpected events affect "normal" development in ways that make each of our lives, each of our stories, and each of our selves unique.

An Overwhelming Episode

The forces that made Trey Edmondson's adolescence unique were set in motion when he was twelve. His mother, aware that she had only a short time to live, asked her sister, a physician, and her brother-in-law, a minister, to take Trey into their home after her death. The move was quick. Trey's mother died in July; in August, he moved into the home of his aunt and uncle. Used to being an only child, he became the instant big brother of a three-year-old boy and an infant girl. Used to a leisurely life in a suburb of Houston, Texas, he suddenly found himself in the hubbub of crowded Boston.

That was more than five years ago. Today, Trey is nearly eighteen, a handsome black youth counting the days until he graduates from high school. He has a slim, wiry build, sad brown eyes, and a gentle voice.

Trey recalls that his first reaction to his mother's death was numbness. "I knew she was sick, and I knew that she had been in the hospital a while. I didn't know she was going to die. I heard the news, I cried. Later on, gradu-

Trey Edmondson, seven-teen. "I was so young, I wish she could have been around a little longer."

ally and gradually, it hit me. I realized my mother died. But first, I was upset. I was like, 'Why did she have to die?' I was so young, I wish she could have been around a little longer."

Trey had lived alone with his mother since the age of six, when she and his father divorced. His father had moved to Atlanta, Georgia, and had approved the arrangement that found Trey moving to Boston. Most teenagers spend their early adolescent years breaking off in some way from their family, but Trey found himself breaking in with a new one. His aunt Deborah remembers how Trey first reacted. "The anger was there. The tension was there, and the hurt. I can't imagine what it means to have your mother die when you're twelve. I mean, my mother is such an important figure in my life. Someone who always took care of me, whether I was right or wrong — the kind of protection I depended on. So I'm not sure what it all meant for him. We were the people who brought him to Boston, and we were trying to structure his life in a way that perhaps he didn't want. The anger and bitterness came out on occasion. I remember when he and I had a long conversation about what had happened. I said, 'Look, I have no idea why this happened to you. And while it makes you angry and makes you feel bad, this is the situation we're in, and we've just got to figure out how to make it work.'"

At first, school was an issue. Deborah describes Trey's problem as "poor study skills" that developed while his mother was ill. "It took us a couple of years to get him settled and into a pattern of working. Most of that had to do with hiring somebody to meet him in the evenings and go over his homework — just to make sure he did it, more than anything else. I re-member saying one day, 'Trey, I will hire somebody to follow you twenty-four hours a day if I need to, but you are going to go to school. You are going to do your work and you are going to accomplish.' That statement represented my frustration at his resentment about the discipline we imposed, but also the kind of commitment that we were making to him.

"Sometimes the clashes focused on lifestyle and material things. The house in Houston was a suburban house — lots of land around it, community swimming pool a block away, a very idyllic setting. The schools had bands, they had cheerleaders. In Boston, our lifestyle is much more modest by comparison. There was a time when he would say, 'Well, there's nowhere to play here.' Or, 'I can't go anywhere here, I don't know why you all have this junky car.' Our emphasis on schoolwork would sometimes be countered with statements like, 'Well, my mother wasn't that good of a student.' Or, 'My father doesn't care that much about school.' Sometimes he wondered why he wasn't living with his father."

For a long time, Trey wasn't sure he was in the right place. "I was twelve years old, and I didn't really have a choice," he says. "I didn't have any objections, but as the years went on, I kind of wished I'd stayed with my dad. But my uncle said that I had to stay with him until I was eighteen, because that's what my mother wanted. And my dad said the same thing."

Gradually, Trey adjusted to his new world and became part of his Boston family. It helped that his grandmother — his mother's mother — joined the family a year after he did. She represented a tie to Houston, to his mother, and she provided familiar love and security.

Along with adjusting to the loss of his mother, Trey had to assume the responsibilities of being a big brother. That meant putting someone else's needs first — and even after five years, it can be difficult. "I like being a big brother to Mimi and Percy, even though there are times when I just feel like throwing them out of the window. I have to work my schedule around to fit their needs. I like to go out with my friends and sometimes that can be a conflict. Like on a Saturday, if some friends and I are going to a movie and Percy might have to go to someone's birthday party, I have to sacrifice some of the things that I do. Usually Deborah will make it up to me next weekend or something.

"We complain and argue a lot: driving the car, school, parties, phone, chores, everything. When it comes to chores, taking out the trash, sometimes I tell them I'll do it later. But Deborah knows I'm a procrastinator. She knows I like to put stuff off. I'll wait an hour, two hours, a day, a week, before I get it done. We argue about that a lot. I try to change, but I don't think she really sees that. And curfew. I like to stay out late, but I know I have to come in on time. It seems like I argue more with Deborah than with Charles. She's overprotective sometimes. But all my friends have the same problems.

"I wish Deborah and Charles just would try to understand my point of view, not just think of what they're doing for me from a parent's point of view. Think of it from a teenager's point of view. They don't want to let you grow up too fast, but then they want you to grow up and they give you responsibilities. It's that in-between. Right in the middle. I guess that's why so many families have so much confusion between teenagers and parents."

At times, Trey thinks it would all be different if only his mother had lived. But with his new maturity, he realizes that he probably would have had the same conflicts with her. "I wish I could have been with my mother a little longer to see how she would have reacted to some of the situations I'm going through now, as opposed to my aunt and uncle. Sometimes I say to myself, maybe it'd be a lot different. But when I think about it — she was brought up by my grandmother, too, so she might have some of the same sentiments. Still, there are times when I'd like more freedom to be by myself, to be on my own. But then there are times when I have to go to the doctor's, go places or things, that I'm glad that Deborah and Charles are there. I guess everyone needs that mother/father figure till they're really ready to be on their own."

Trey is just about ready to be on his own. He describes himself as "a caring person, a sensitive person who likes to have fun, someone who would help an old lady across the street." He would like to go into business administration or investment — something to do with money. And he can't wait until he graduates and goes off to college. "That's all that's on my mind right now. Sometimes, when I feel upset or something gets me down, I always say to myself, 'Hey, you'll be going off to college soon.' I'm not interested in Harvard. I just don't like Boston and I look forward to leaving it. It's either Howard University or Morehouse College. At first it was Morehouse, 'cause I like Atlanta so much and I'll be with my father more. Then when I got down to Houston last summer, I saw my friends were going to Howard — I mean *all* my friends."

Trey has gradually overcome the loss of his mother and adapted to the change in his life course. A good deal of the credit goes to his aunt, uncle, and grandmother for providing an affectionate, nurturant family situation, one that placed responsibilities on him and set high expectations for him. But as much credit goes to Trey. Perhaps losing his mother forced him to be self-reliant — to depend on his own inner resources. Deborah is aware of the great strides he has made over the years. "We've provided him with a consistency that's been very important. That's probably the ingredient that's gotten us from twelve to nearly eighteen in a pretty intact way. The obnoxious boy at twelve, and the even more obnoxious adolescent at fourteen, fifteen, and sixteen, is certainly less obnoxious now.

"Trey has matured into a very responsible person. He is able to take care of adult tasks in a way that makes me proud of him: caring for the kids, their transportation, his schoolwork, his plans for college. His mother would be proud of him, too. She'd be proud of the schoolwork he's done, his interest in becoming somebody who takes care of himself. Socially, he's a very graceful, very responsible person, and he's got an emotional stability that will carry him a long way.

"He's growing up and he's leaving and he's looking forward to it. Obviously, I feel a little sad but I'm also very excited for him. He's a good person and I think he's gonna do very well. He deserves to have a good life. I hope he's able to cash in on all of that."

Trey's mother still holds a special place in his heart. He has not forgotten her, but he has been able to develop rewarding relationships with his aunt and uncle and their children. Life dealt him a hand he wouldn't have chosen, but he's taken it and used it to grow and develop into an appreciative, rich human being. "I feel that I'm used to her not being with me, but, you know, she keeps coming up in my mind. I really miss the times I could have shared with her. Because I think the times I'm experiencing now are some of the most important times in my life. Teenagers are on their way to adulthood. At times they want to be treated as adults, but then at times they would like to do something that kids would do. It's a big change, and I guess if you can get through your teenage years, a lot of things will be a little easier."

IV

Early Adulthood

10

THE BIOLOGICAL *The Season*

STORY OF *of Fertility*

EARLY ADULTHOOD

"I remember it was around Christmastime and I asked mother, 'Well, Mommy, when's Daddy coming to bring us our presents?' And she looked at me, and I knew that she knew he wasn't coming back."

He didn't come back. May Ling Agosto was only six when her father left her mother and her younger sister to fend for themselves in New York's East Harlem. Now twenty-one, she is a slight, willowy woman with strong yet delicate features — black hair that breaks into soft curls, arching brows, and clear eyes that change from green to brown as the light shifts. She carries with her the legacy of her father's departure, fifteen years of childhood and adolescence trying to take care of the family he left behind. Her voice is deep and mature, with a cadence of both toughness and grace.

May Ling's parents were born in Puerto Rico and came to the United States as children. She was born and raised in Spanish Harlem. "My mother got my name out of a book," she says. "I'm almost positive the name of the book was *The Good Earth*. I like my name. In a way, it's odd. I hate to say this because it's embarrassing, but when I used to give myself a pep talk, I'd say that my mother named me May Ling for a reason. It meant that I was special and that I could accomplish anything I wanted."

Throughout her childhood, May Ling needed whatever strength her name could give her. Her father left when her mother was in her early forties, after the first of her two mastectomies. Her mother struggled to raise

May Ling Agosto, twenty-one. "I was always 'little Mom' at home."

May Ling and her little sister on a sales clerk's salary, but the burden was heavy and she turned to alcohol. That put responsibility for the household squarely on May Ling's shoulders. "I was always 'little Mom' at home. When she came home on Friday with her check, I would always divide up the money for the food and the rent. I started doing that at age eleven, after we moved away from my grandmother who'd been doing it for us. I noticed my mother got frustrated trying to do it. And I wanted to keep peace at home. 'Don't get upset, Mommy, I'll do it.' Anything so she wouldn't come home and drink."

But being little Mom took its toll on May Ling. When she was fourteen, she started using marijuana. "With my mother's drinking and everything, it was difficult for me to study. I got into pot that year — but not too much. Just enough to sleep. I was having difficulty sleeping, so I used to smoke to sleep and then I couldn't get up in the morning. But I'd get to school and I'd pass my work."

At fifteen, May Ling married her childhood sweetheart. She had known Gil since she was ten and he was twelve, when she was the only girl on his softball team. They became engaged when he finished high school and was about to go off to the marines. "I felt I could talk to him, and he was the only one who was willing to listen to me." Once the families were convinced that May Ling wasn't pregnant, they gave permission for the marriage. A few months later, May Ling followed her husband to Camp Johnson in North Carolina. Four days after her arrival, she had her sixteenth birthday. But almost immediately she began to hear how poorly her mother and sister were doing without her.

Then came a shock: her thirty-year-old brother died of a brain hemorrhage. "Three days before, he said to me that if anything ever happened to him, he wanted me to take care of mother."

While she was torn between responsibilities for her mother and her love for her husband, May Ling became pregnant. A month before the baby was due, Gil was sent to Lebanon — just two days after the bombing of the marine barracks there. "We tried to get him out of it, but I found out shortly after he was shipped that he never really tried. We always had that conflict. He said I couldn't always take care of my mother and family, that I was on my own now. I didn't think it was fair that he should make me choose that way. He said, 'You can't save everyone, May.' I told him he was wrong. I had to show my mother that she had something when she felt she had nothing."

Facing childbirth alone, May Ling, now nearly eighteen, went home to New York and moved in with her mother and sister. When her baby boy was born, he was given his father's name, Gilberto. Five months later, big Gil returned from Lebanon, and the family of three went back to North Carolina. But things didn't work out. May Ling left once again for New York, where she moved back in with her mother, her sister, and her sister's newborn baby. It was a household without men, but that wasn't unusual in May Ling's family. Since her great-great-grandmother's time, each generation of children has grown up without a father in residence. "We're really strong, pig-headed women, and we like things done our way," explains May Ling. "I always used to make jokes that we were Amazons because there weren't any men around."

But life without her husband had its own complications. For one thing, there were now five people crowded into the small apartment. "My son slept on a nice, comfortable couch. I slept on the living-room floor, with pillows. Since he was small, he wasn't really aware of what was going on. So I was the one who was upset about it. To him it was a comfortable couch. To me it was a lousy situation."

May Ling applied for public housing and, while waiting for an apartment, enrolled in college. At first, it went well, even though the pressure was as heavy as the expenses. She was going to school, working, taking care of a baby, and trying to keep her mother and younger sister on a steady course. "After a while I couldn't take it anymore. That's when I began experimenting with crack. It wasn't very long before I realized that it was definitely wrong. I sat home a complete month and psyched myself out of it. I told myself, 'Crack is wrong.' I read all types of literature about the harm crack can do to you and what marijuana can do to you. I realized it has to

"This is more than just a little boy. This is my life."

come from yourself. Deep down inside you have to have that flame: 'I don't want to do this. I don't want to be on crack.' My mother thought I was going completely crazy. I would get up in the morning, 'No drugs today, May Ling. You don't need it. Stay away from it. The baby is going to be fine.' Actually, in the mirror — gave myself a pep talk.

"After I stopped smoking crack, I went through a stage of depression. They call it detoxification. I went through paranoia stages. It was terrible. I couldn't sleep. I couldn't eat. Everywhere I went I felt as if I was being stared at. I had a nervous breakdown. Finally, my body and mind said, 'No more. This is it. You need a rest.' So I checked into Mount Sinai Hospital, in the psychiatric ward."

With the pressure off, May Ling's body bounced back. After two weeks, she had gained eight pounds and felt rested. "I looked around me and I felt as if I didn't belong there. There were so many other people there who made my problem look small. I felt like I had a lot of things to get off my chest, but my family didn't show up at any of the meetings. I felt very neglected, very hurt that after I had done so much for my family, no one showed up for me. So I just signed myself out and started life all over again. I knew what had to be done."

May Ling returned to her mother's apartment and made some choices. "I found out I could not handle work, school, and the baby, so I said I'd have to drop one. When I realized that I can't sacrifice the baby and I won't sacrifice my studies, I had to sacrifice my job and get on public assistance, welfare. That hurt me — it hurt me very much. I found it degrading." May Ling finished a year of college but ran out of money for tuition. So she took out a student loan and enrolled in an eight-month course in computer technology. Today, she's working to develop skills in computer maintenance and repair that will lead to a good job and enough money to support herself and her son. She still dreams of going back to college someday, but right now little Gil comes first. He's already three years old. "When you have a child, you have to make a lot of sacrifices. There's a lot of things I'll have to give up for the sake of my son. This is more than just a little boy. This is my life."

While May Ling ponders computer circuits, little Gil goes to day-care. She smiles and laughs softly as she shares her delight in his happiness. "He loves it. He loves it and I love it even more because he loves it. I know that he's being very well taken care of. And he eats properly. And he plays properly. He has proper teachers who are gonna show him while I'm gone. That's important, to find someone who is capable. A place that is capable."

After day-care, big Gil sometimes picks up his son. May Ling and Gil are still friendly. They see each other frequently and once in a while walk hand-in-hand with their boy. "It's important for little Gil. It's important to me that little Gil has life as normal as can be with his mommy and his daddy. I know how it feels to not have a daddy to come home to. It always hurt me, and I don't want him to feel that pain. He'll have both his parents, the way it should be — regardless of whether or not the father and I are together."

Big Gil is working, but he's going to school, too. He and his father help May Ling out with car fare and food money when the welfare checks run out. The Agostos are catching up, preparing themselves for a better future. When asked if the marriage might be mended, May Ling looks into the distance and her eyes soften.

"We've always been good friends and honest with each other. I'm the only one that he can trust and vice versa. I do hope we'll get together again. But not right now. Marriage is hard work, and we don't have time to really work at our marriage and what went wrong with it. As soon as we finish our education, get ourselves together, when we have a bit more time, perhaps then we'll sit down and really find out what's wrong with our relationship. Why can we be friends but not husband and wife? Friends and a marriage relationship are two different things. And we're better at one thing than we are at the other. But we can't settle that just now. There's too much going on. We can't take on the world."

These days things are looking brighter for May Ling. It's been almost a year now since her mother's had a drink. "I preached to her that if you want to stop drinking you can. It has to come from you. They have her on pills that she says make her feel better. She'll spend the whole day shaking if she's not taking them. I think there's gotta be something better for her besides the drugs they're feeding her. But now that she's sober, more or less, I feel my job is accomplished. I'm no longer little Mommy."

And after several years of hounding public-housing authorities for an apartment, May Ling is about to get a one-bedroom unit for herself and little Gil. "I'm very happy I've finally gotten an affordable place to live. I'm gonna leave the bedroom for the baby. I feel every child needs their own space, and so I should give him his room. I'll get Gil's furniture first. I'll make sure his room is what every little boy likes. And it will give me a chance to get some discipline into him. Because in my mother's home, it's difficult to punish. Once in a while I'll say, 'Well, Gil, go to your room. You're being a bad boy, and when you feel like being a better boy, well then you come out and apologize.' But right now, there's no room for him to go to. In my own place, I think it'll be better."

In her own apartment, May Ling will have the space to imagine a future, not just for her son, but for herself. "Well, we all dream about our little house with the white picket fence. So I guess my dreams aren't any different from the next person's. I do want to get off public assistance. That would definitely be a very big step for me. And just pull my own weight and continue my studies.

"It's all been very difficult. Nothing in life is easy, but it can be done. I'm not using drugs. I'm in school. I've got proper day-care. And now I've got my apartment. I think it's very bright. It looks good, very good. It looks excellent. Now it's just up to me."

Biological Adulthood

May Ling Agosto is slowly building an adult life, coming to terms with one season of life as she enters another. With an iron resolve, she's becoming a "grown-up." But in many ways she already was a grown-up as a child — a "little Mommy," she says. Adulthood was a role thrust upon her, one that she occasionally escaped from, one that at times infuriated her with its unfairness. Had life been "fair," May Ling would have been nurtured as a child, not required to provide nurturance. She would have been able to devote her energy to her marriage, to live her own life in North Carolina and not worry about her mother and sister. Yet she took what life gave her, and at critical times she chose to be the adult back home.

Getting married at fifteen was another adult thing to do, and so was having a baby at eighteen. But despite all the adult-ness of her early years, in some ways May Ling doesn't really feel grown up; in some areas, she wants to slow her development down. She does not feel ready to work on an intimate relationship. She and Gil need to complete an education first, she says, and get established in an occupation. They need to get themselves "together" as individuals before they can think about themselves as a couple. Right now, "there's too much going on." May Ling's life raises a question for all of us: when exactly do we become adults?

Each of the developmental clocks has a different answer to that question. Biologically, we become adults when we can reproduce. But socially, adulthood may come five, ten, or even fifteen years later — sooner in the culture May Ling grew up in, later in others. The same is true psychologically. May Ling can imagine a world of possibility, and she can fashion an identity. But the identity she has had, that of "little Mommy," is not the one she wants. She feels there's more to who she is, more parts to fit into the whole. She can see the connection between the past, present, and future in her life, and she can tell a rich, integrated story about her experiences. But the process of separation from her family of origin, which we associate with psychological adulthood, is far from complete. For her, as for any of us, there's no single answer to the question of when we become adults. Assigning an age to the beginning of adulthood is like assigning a date to the beginning of spring. It's nice to have a marker, but it doesn't noticeably alter the weather.

From a biological point of view, adulthood is the season of fertility, the time that demands a response to the newly emerged power to conceive and bear children. It's the "moment of truth" that the Biological Clock has been preparing for from conception on, and that "truth" has as much to do with raising children to reproductive age as it does with bringing them into the world. Biologically, adulthood means that we're at the height of our physical powers, ready to make the investment of energy that children will require. Not everyone will have children, but everyone will have to make some decision about them, some accommodation to what life brings with regard to them.

When May Ling Agosto had her first child at the age of eighteen, she was close to the norm that exists among today's hunter-gatherers. Among the !Kung, for example, first birth occurs typically at nineteen.[1] Whether that norm held true through most of our hunting-and-gathering past is difficult to say, but the pattern of fertility among today's hunter-gatherers raises an interesting question: what is the "normal" reproductive state of a woman's body? The answer may seem new, but in reality it's very old, lost until now in the collective amnesia surrounding our origins. What's "normal" — what the Biological Clock fashioned through evolution — is not constant menstrual cycling interrupted by an occasional pregnancy. Nor, on the other hand, is it a steady succession of pregnancies interrupted by a few menstrual cycles. For nearly all of human history, rather, biological adulthood has meant something else. Physically, what's "normal" for women is a state of lactation — producing milk.

Among today's hunter-gatherers, infants are in almost continuous contact with their mother, sleeping with her at night and carried next to her body during the day. Breast milk is available at all times, so babies eat in a pattern that seems strange to us. During the day, the baby nurses about two or three times each hour, for about six minutes. At night, the baby sleeps with its mother, and her breast is constantly available. Constant feeding is necessary because human milk, designed to grow a large-brained infant, is high in sugar and extremely low in fat. Low-fat food doesn't satisfy for long, and in half an hour, hunter-gatherer infants are hungry again.

This style of nursing, in which the baby controls mealtime, acts as a natural contraceptive. When babies nurse at frequent enough intervals, the mother's bloodstream has such high levels of the hormone prolactin that she neither ovulates nor menstruates.[2] Because hunter-gatherer women nurse their children both day and night, and because they do so for several years, they do not become pregnant again until the youngsters are three or four years old. And so among hunter-gatherer families, children are spaced four to five years apart. Hunter-gatherer women experience menopause in their early forties, so over roughly twenty-five years of fertility, they have no more than five children, two or three of whom survive to adulthood.

This pattern of fertility means that hunter-gatherer women lactate almost continuously, but rarely menstruate. Contemporary women are different. They become fertile earlier than hunter-gatherers and remain fertile longer, experiencing menopause at about fifty. They use artificial contraception to prevent pregnancy. If they have two children, they spend about thirty-five years in menstrual cycling, going through nine times the number of menstrual cycles as hunter-gatherers do.[3] Physically, it's like continually starting a car without ever going for a ride.

From what we can tell, the "normal" state of an adult woman's reproductive organs until about 10,000 years ago was one of quiescence, with the ovaries and uterus more or less dormant. With the spread of agriculture and the transition to settled life, reproductive patterns changed. Infants were weaned earlier, and women started having babies every two years. The biological consequences of today's highly active reproductive system may be more serious than a monthly nuisance. Such a system pours high levels of estrogen into the bloodstream. Estrogen is a known carcinogen, so potent that birth control pills have been reformulated to reduce their estrogen content. It's possible that current high levels of breast and cervical cancer may be the consequences of endless menstrual cycling in a body out of harmony with its evolutionary context.

No one is advocating a return to hunting and gathering, or even claiming that such a way of life is healthier than our own. Today's women, after all, are living longer than any in history. But some laboratories have been so impressed by the anthropological research on our earliest fertility patterns that they have begun work on a different kind of contraceptive — one that mimics the hormonal state of lactation without actually producing milk. With such a contraceptive, women could keep their reproductive systems in the hormonal pattern evolved by our species, in what we're coming to see as the "normal" biological state of their adulthood.

Children: Early, Late, or Never

During the vast era of hunter-gatherer life, the Biological and Social Clocks that signaled the beginning of adulthood were probably in harmony. Teenage women were usually married and enjoying adult status by the time they became fertile. But in contemporary life, the Biological Clock governing fertility has sped up, and the corresponding Social Clock has slowed down. As a result of the discrepancy between the two, we are seeing a new pattern of childbearing. More girls are having children in their early teens, when they become adults biologically, and more women are having children in their early thirties, after they establish themselves socially. Fewer girls and women are having children in the intervening years.[4]

If we look at the typical age of a mother when she *first* gives birth, we find that it has risen significantly. In 1979, only 4 percent of first births were to women age thirty or older; in 1987, 16 percent were.[5] It's extraordinary that in the same society some first births come at fourteen (or even earlier) and others at forty (or even later). The spread of ages is wider than it's ever been, and about as wide as it can get.

Does it make any difference whether women start their families early or late? One way to find out is to ask the parents themselves. Pamela Daniels and Kathy Weingarten, psychologists at Wellesley College, queried a sample of eighty-six couples from diverse socioeconomic backgrounds. They found that most parents who waited to have children were enthusiastic about the postponement; three out of four said they would do it again. But more than half of those who had their children early wished they had waited, if only for a few years.[6]

Delaying the first birth brought many benefits. Because either or both parents had established themselves in their careers, they escaped some of the economic pressures that younger parents felt. Many had bought a home and set aside some money that cushioned them over the rough spots. Having established their careers, women found it fairly easy to juggle the responsibilities of work and family. Those who waited also got more help from their husbands than those who rushed into childbearing. The older men were more involved in child care and helped more around the house than did younger fathers. By contrast, women who had given birth in their late teens or early twenties complained that they had had to mother their husbands as well as their babies. Perhaps the lessened stress and strain among older mothers explains why they seem to enjoy their babies more than younger mothers do, and seem more responsive to their babies' needs.[7]

But babies grow up and parents age. Women who postpone their families until their late thirties face the possibility of serious role overload in their early fifties. They will find themselves coping with adolescent children, the demands of their own jobs, and the frailties of aging parents. When it's time to pay for college tuition, they may feel a heavy financial burden because their earnings have begun to decline. Later, when grandchildren come along, they may not be vigorous enough to enjoy them. And if their children and grandchildren continue the pattern of late first births, the original postponers are not likely to live long enough to see great-grandchildren.

Today's typical family has three living generations, although four generations have become increasingly common. A consistent pattern of timing in childbirth can produce an astonishing succession of generations on the one hand, or make great-grandparenthood virtually impossible on the other. The longest parade of living generations yet discovered was a California family in which every woman was a teen mother. Seven generations were alive at the same time, headed by a great-great-great-great-grandmother of ninety-one.[8] In families with extended lineages, a woman might become a grandmother as early as age twenty-six or twenty-seven. But in families where each woman waits until she's forty to bear her first child, a woman will be eighty before she becomes a grandmother.

University of Massachusetts sociologist Alice Rossi has been studying the implications of postponed birth on the size of today's families. When you ask young women how many children they plan to have, she reports, most say they want two or three. Even those in their early thirties do. Yet if you come back several years later and ask them the same question, they look at you over the head of the toddler on their lap and say, "We're not ready for another child yet" or, "We've decided not to have another one." In the economic realities of a two-career world, the postponement of a family often leads to a one-child family. For many of these women, the first birth is also the last birth.⁹

Many young women who put their personal lives on hold while they carve out a career eventually run up against a shrinking pool of eligible mates. At age thirty-five or so, with their careers well in hand, they discover that most of the men their own age or older are married. Many of the men who are still single may be eligible only because they were never good prospects in the first place. In part it's a problem of numbers, a reflection of a sex ratio that shifts across the life span. In the first half of life there are more males than females, but because more males die, the balance tips in the second half, when females start to outnumber males. The problem is compounded by an unwritten social rule that says women are not supposed to marry men who are younger than themselves.

Once upon a time, that was a prudent precept, because big families were an asset and young women had more child-bearing years stretching before them. In a world of small families, however, the rule no longer makes sense, and some people have realized it. A few women have solved the problem by marrying a man who is five or six years their junior, and this solution will probably become more prevalent in the next decade or so. But for now, the custom against it remains powerful.

As a result, a number of U.S. women will remain childless. How many is impossible to say; the educated guesses of demographers range from a low of one in ten to a high of one in four.¹⁰ Such figures are neither new nor startling. The generation that is now turning eighty lived out their prime childbearing years during the Great Depression of the 1930s, when money was scarce and the future looked bleak. Some delayed marriages and others just couldn't afford to marry at a time when men were expected to support a family by themselves. Many of those who did have children had fewer than they wanted. Among women who were born in 1908, and so were twenty-one when the stock market crash set the stage for the depression, more than one woman in five had no children at all.¹¹

What may be new to the present generation of childless Americans is the number who are childless by choice. Voluntary childlessness is not spread evenly throughout society, but concentrated among young, educated women and men.[12] Instead of fearing that there will be no income to support a child, these couples worry that they cannot manage the demands of children in a two-career family. They believe that the arrival of a baby would force them to give up one income — or at least hobble the woman's rise in her own field. The fear seems to be valid. Childless women in managerial positions earn about 20 percent more than those who have children.[13] And children are becoming more expensive. In 1986, raising a child to the age of eighteen cost about $95,000, and four years at a private college added another $40,000 — figures that are no doubt higher today.[14]

Our distant ancestors, who were few in number and had an entire planet to roam, may have had as many childless women as we. But their infertility was only rarely the result of contraception. It wasn't voluntary. Today, having filled the planet and facing a need to restrain reproduction, we find more choices in the season of fertility, choices that shape both our individual stories and the story of our species.

The Peak Years

Although the twenties and thirties — the years we call early adulthood — are marked by biological fertility, they are not uniformly fertile. The ability to conceive and bear children changes over the course of these decades, and it changes more for a woman than it does for a man.

Teenagers are quite capable of giving birth, but even from a biological point of view the teens are generally not the best years to do so. There are exceptions — Kim Henderson is one — but before sixteen the pelvis is usually immature and may be too small to allow the baby's head to pass safely through. At this age, childbirth is often a complicated, even risky process that ends with a cesarean section and a low-birthweight baby.[15] The ovaries, the uterus, and the eggs themselves seem best adapted to the job of producing a baby while women are in their twenties. About 95 percent of women in their early twenties are fertile; during the late twenties, about 90 percent can conceive. During the early thirties, the picture remains encouraging: 85 percent are fertile. In the late thirties, the vast majority of women — 70 percent — can still conceive if they wish. But once women pass forty, their hopes for healthy children decline sharply: only 37 percent between forty and forty-four are estimated to be fertile, a figure that excludes both those who have been surgically sterilized and those who are currently using contraceptives.[16]

The increase in infertility as women age may be partly the result of ovaries damaged by the monthly eruption of eggs. But most researchers believe that the aging of the uterus is responsible. After the age of thirty, hormone production declines, the uterus starts to dry out, and its tissues stiffen and become less durable. After ten years of this internal process, the uterus may no longer be able to prepare the nourishing lining that a fertilized egg requires. As women move into their late thirties, it takes longer to conceive — perhaps as much as a year. And once the pregnancy begins, the aging uterus may reject the growing fetus. Miscarriages become increasingly common.

Many of those miscarriages result from the quality of a woman's eggs. At birth, a baby girl's tiny ovaries contain all the eggs she will ever produce. By her late thirties, the maturing eggs are nearly forty years old, and an increasing proportion of them have been damaged by radiation, chemicals, or infection.[17]

Sometimes a defective egg has an extra chromosome, which usually means that the fetus will have some kind of structural disorder. If the extra chromosome is the twenty-first one, the baby will have Down syndrome, a disorder that is marked by congenital heart disease and some degree of mental retardation. The chances of this happening rise sharply with age. A twenty-year-old mother has only one chance in 2,000 of producing a child with Down syndrome. At the age of thirty, her chances are one in 1,000. But by the time she reaches forty, the risk is up to one in 100, and in just five more years, her chances are better than one in 50.[18] Women nearing forty are also more likely to develop complications, have difficult deliveries, or die in childbirth than women in their twenties.[19] Yet the hazards of postponed pregnancy are not nearly so formidable as they were only a decade or so ago. Once women in their late thirties or early forties do conceive, the majority have normal pregnancies and deliver healthy babies.

The pressure on men is not nearly so intense. Their prime reproductive years are the twenties *and* the thirties, the entire length of early adulthood. But most men in their early fifties can still father children, and some remain fertile far into old age. Men continually produce new sperm, so at any time the mature sperm are no more than a few weeks old. The quality of a man's sperm seems to increase steadily until he reaches his mid-twenties, and then stabilizes for a decade or so. As he leaves young adulthood and the rate of sexual activity declines, his semen contains more sperm in each ejaculation, but they are less vigorous, and an increasing proportion are defective. Faulty sperm are responsible for as much as 30 percent of all cases of Down syndrome. Some of the damage may come from environmental hazards.

Exposure to lead, alcohol, radiation, drugs, and industrial chemicals at the time sperm are manufactured has been associated with sperm damage and extra chromosomes.[20]

The years in which we peak in a reproductive sense are also the years in which we peak in a general physical sense. Although muscles increase in size all through early adulthood, their strength and tone are at their best during the mid-twenties, which makes the twenties the best decade for athletes and people who perform hard physical labor.

It's no accident that even though healthier people have set ever more impressive athletic records over the years, the *age* at which they set them has not changed. For ninety years, swimmers have been peaking in their teens, while sprinters, jumpers, and tennis players peak in their early twenties. Long-distance runners and baseball players peak later — in their late twenties — perhaps because they don't need the reaction time, explosive strength, and degree of coordination that swimming or sprinting requires. Golfers, for whom aiming, precise control, and arm-hand steadiness are major requirements, peak latest of all — at thirty-one.[21]

Because the Biological Clock is sensitive to how we treat our bodies, we have some control over the heights we reach when we're at our our peak and the decline we experience once we're past it. Those of us who keep active have stronger muscles, lower blood pressure, faster reflexes, and more powerful lungs than those whose lives become sedentary. In other words, some women are healthier at thirty-nine than May Ling Agosto is at twenty-one. But no matter what the state of a woman's health, as her early adulthood comes to a close, so do her choices regarding parenthood.

"Now What?"

At thirty-nine, Christine Osborne is an associate creative director at a major advertising agency in Chicago. She has never married and doesn't know whether she will ever have a child. Christine has large blue eyes and wavy brown hair with an auburn glow. As she tells her story, thin lines of concentration knit her forehead. Her manner displays self-assurance. It becomes clear that she has spent a lot of time thinking about her life and that she has always approached it with intensity.

During her high-school years, Christine focused her energies on winning a scholarship to a good school. "Getting into college and getting a scholarship was what high school was all about. I didn't date. I had activities in my life only so they'd look good on a college application. At a certain point,

I decided that it would probably be better to go to an all-women's school — no distractions and we could keep our nose to the grindstone. When I was applying to college, and even while I was in college, I had no concept of what I was going to do for a career. I got out of Wellesley with a degree in biblical history, literature, and interpretation. Luckily, I got a job as secretary at the Harvard Divinity School."

In her twenties, Christine looked around for an appropriate career. She tried other secretarial jobs and she worked with retarded children. It took a long time to settle on advertising. "I saved up some money and took time off, just to think and read and wait for some duck to drop down from the sky with a sign in its mouth saying what to do next. Went to Europe. Went to Berkeley. Wandered around and finally wound up back in Boston, where I got out the yellow pages and called every advertising agency till I got to M. A little place needed a secretary for the one-man creative department, and I got the job because I could read the man's handwriting."

A book led Christine to make that phone call, a book written by the head of one of Manhattan's successful advertising agencies. "I got into advertising on reading *From Those Wonderful Folks Who Gave You Pearl Harbor,* which is about advertising in the sixties, up and down Madison Avenue. It was a funny book, and peppered throughout it were these astronomical salaries. I mean, I couldn't believe people made that much money — and for having fun and being goofy and playing pranks. Well, the reality seems to be it's not quite so much fun.

"For a long time I thought that copy writing was a forum for me to express my thoughts. Finally, it occurred to me that I have a responsibility to sell a product. But the search for an idea can get very silly. It has to get silly in order for you to live with the pressure. Coming up with ideas is agony. It's the hardest thing in the world. It's stressful. It's exciting. It's infuriating. It's annoying. It pushes just about every button you've got. But eventually it happens, when you're not struggling so much. And coming up with an idea brings those moments of extreme joy."

Christine's talent for coming up with ideas, for writing copy, and for functioning in the pressure-cooker world of advertising soon became apparent. With the same single-minded drive she had used to win a major scholarship and get her degree, she applied herself to getting ahead in advertising. Along the way, she made a lot of job changes, each one propelling her farther up the career ladder.

"I can honestly say that the goal of my professional development has been primarily to make more money. I want to earn good money for work

Christine Osborne, thirty-nine. "I never imagined that I'd be facing this."

well done. I want to live in a certain way, and I certainly want to be generous with what I have. But the major motivation has been moving myself along. I've achieved success — I can afford to live on the twenty-eighth floor of Lakeshore Drive and enjoy the sweeping lake view. I have lots of nice furniture. I have a closet full of clothes. I've provided pretty well for myself, and that's very satisfying.

"I think that it looks as though I may have come a lot further along professionally than in my private life. A lot of people would say — well, I would say — I'm not married, I do not have children. If I *had* married at any point, I would have them. Marriage and children are definitely linked for me. What's happening is that I have not yet found the person I want to marry any more than I've found the job that I want to stay with and be committed to."

Christine's world is wider than a casual observer might think, but she doesn't mention the other part of it unless pressed. She works at a shelter for the homeless run by an organization called the Midwest Immigrant Rights Center. "Working at the shelter is an opportunity for me to serve. The men and women at the shelter didn't even see my face last night. I was hands putting ham and muffins and cake on a plate. But I was there to serve, and it's an honor. It's something I really feel I need to do more of in my life. Serving in some way, because my life is pretty much all about me and it's pretty self-centered. Serving is an opportunity to totally forget myself. But it doesn't make me feel good. It makes me feel like I'm not doing enough. Right now it's a start — doing more work in the community, more work outside of myself and my limited world of concerns."

Some of Christine's friends are single women like herself; others have

"I still think I'm gonna get married and have children. . . . Hasn't happened yet. Now what?"

families and young children. Although she always expected to marry and have children of her own, it hasn't happened yet. "I always thought that marriage and family would happen in due course — in the process of living my life. It would just happen. I never imagined that I'd be facing this. I'm going to be forty this year, and there's only just a little bit more time in which I can have a healthy baby. There's this biological time clock here. It's not comfortable at all, thinking I've got to hurry up and get it done, as though getting married and having children is only a list of things to do. And that's not the way I want to approach this.

"I feel very envious of people who not only have a happy marriage, but are also enjoying their children. What I continue to hear from people who've had children is that you experience a whole different kind of love, and out of that love, joy. Why can't I have that, too? I get warm and runny around babies. I love babies. But I would never consider having a baby on my own."

As Christine approaches forty, she's aware that the marriage market is beginning to work against her. She views her situation with some humor. "I wonder if this has anything to do with my grandmother's dying words to me. She said, 'You're too picky.' If I've been picky, it must mean that I've ruled out a lot of people. I've had some extremely specific notions of who out there in the world would be right for me. Now it begins to occur to me that a lot of the people who *would* have been right for me are married already. Somehow, I didn't meet them. Somehow, I missed them.

"It's not at all easy for me to meet men. And now it seems that fewer men are fitting the picture I had of who I'd be settling down with. I haven't found what I'm looking for. I'm looking for companionship and somebody to share with. Gotta be about the right age. Gotta be fairly intelligent. Preferably a sense of humor. On a date I try to get a sense of what his values are. Right and wrong. And I want to get a sense of whether I can trust this person. And then, probably fairly soon into the evening, within the first half hour, I'm wondering whether he wants to get married." She laughs. "It's always there, but you don't talk about it."

At the moment Christine is not seeing anyone. She had a long, promising relationship in which she and her beau did "talk about it." But then, after considering marriage, they broke up. "I wasn't seeing anyone else. I never see more than one person at a time. I feel as though I wasted a valuable year, but I can't even say that. What I gained apart from a proposal of marriage was invaluable. Maybe it's God's plan whether you hook up with the right person. I used to call it other things. Certainly, I've called it luck. I've called it being in the right place at the right time. But every single thing that happens is somehow for the good. I believe in that very much. Even mistakes. I don't think of them as mistakes. I think of them as choices I've made."

In the evenings, Christine comes home to her apartment and Gary, her cat. Mostly she's content, but now and again, it happens. "I'm sitting in my living room. I've been writing in my journal, Gary's here, there's music playing, and I wish there was somebody to talk to about this. And I look up and I think, 'Boy, that would be very nice.' There's probably some sadness there, but I don't spend a lot of time feeling sad about it.

"I still think I'm gonna get married and have children. Maybe it's that strong sense that gets me through times when I'm feeling sad. Because I always say I don't have it *yet*. I always tack on yet. Hasn't happened yet. Now what?"

11

Two
Families

They sit on the couch in the dim light, exchanging affectionate glances, aglow with the memory of their wedding. On the television screen in the corner of the living room flicker scenes from the ceremony, preserved on videotape: "Anthony, take this ring as a sign of my love and fidelity," Julianne repeats after the priest, "in the name of the Father and of the Son and of the Holy Spirit." They kneel at the altar for communion, she in a white veil and gown, he in a tux. Then the newlyweds turn, face the congregation, and walk down the aisle hand in hand, smiling at well-wishers in the pews. In the back of the church, they turn to each other and kiss.

The memories remain fresh, but a lot has happened in the year since Anthony and Julianne Cugini were married. They have bought a house and had a baby. She has quit work and he has taken a second job. They're now known as "the Cuginis." Anthony and Julianne have created a "traditional" family in an increasingly nontraditional world.

Although they attended the same church all their lives, Anthony and Julianne first met in a bowling alley when she was eighteen and he was twenty-three. It was a Catholic Youth Organization outing, and Julianne had driven to the bowling alley with one of the priests. She liked Anthony's well-groomed looks and his sense of humor. He liked dark-haired Julianne's figure in her tight jeans. Julianne rode home with Anthony that night, and showed up the next day at a soccer game where he was coaching a team of

Anthony Cugini, twenty-eight. "Marriage is forever."

schoolboys. She was amazed at how handsome he was in a pair of shorts and a T-shirt.

"He looked better than I thought he did when I first met him," she recalls. "I was impressed with how physically fit he was and how well he played soccer. He came over to talk to me, and of course I'm trying to keep myself calm while I'm talking to him."

Afterward they went out for ice cream, and soon were dating steadily. It wasn't long before Anthony knew he had found the right woman. "After a month of going out with her, I told her we were gonna get married. Just something seemed right about our relationship. I let her know that, and she was kind of taken aback. It was at that point, really, that I started falling in love with her. It's hard to explain. When you're not together, you think about being together. And when you do something, one of your first impulses is, 'I can't wait to tell Julie. I can't wait to share it with her.' It's something that grows, and I think we're still growing that way."

"We found so much in common," Julie remembers, "our values, our beliefs, the things we like to do. The most important thing was his love and my love of children. It was a nice thought, sharing the rest of my life with him. He knew what he wanted to do, and that felt so solid, so secure. Although I knew I wanted to marry Anthony eventually, I didn't think I was ready for marriage at that point. I knew we had to develop our relationship — and I had to develop myself — for marriage."

It was more than four years before they finally married, four years before pretty, brown-eyed Julie and Anthony, with his heavy eyebrows, sweeping moustache, and dark curly hair, were united in the church that is so important to them. She was twenty-two, he twenty-seven. Anthony speaks for

Julianne, twenty-three. "Something so beautiful, created out of two people's love, how could it be so terrible?"

both of them when he says, "Marriage is forever. Once we got married, I would never even conceive of the possibility that we would ever get divorced. I have this feeling that some people go into marriage with a different attitude: 'Well, if it doesn't work out, we can always change that.' I myself, and I think Julie also, went in with the idea, 'Well, this is it. We're only getting married once in our lives and this is the marriage.'"

Even during the euphoria that surrounded their wedding, children weren't far from their minds. Anna Marie was born just a few weeks before their first wedding anniversary. Julie remembers her feelings. "We were so excited about the fact that we both wanted to have a baby. I had so many people say to me, 'Don't have a baby right away. You'll be tied down. You won't be able to work. You won't get any sleep. You'll be miserable.' My mind never changed or wavered about having a child right away. Something so beautiful, created out of two people's love, how could it be so terrible? And now after having her, I find I was right. The most joyous moment in our marriage was the birth of our child. I never saw such happiness in my husband's eyes as when he looked at Anna Marie for the first time and held her in his arms and then looked at me."

Anthony's joy was mingled with relief that Julie and Anna Marie had come through the ordeal safely. He recalls, "The cord had gone around Anna Marie's neck and every time Julie would have a contraction, it would slow down the heartbeat. And I was getting scared. I remember sitting there praying, and we had to leave the birthing room and go into the delivery room. When I actually held Anna Marie and the doctor said there's no problems with her, that was the greatest moment of my life. During the delivery I suppressed all the emotions I had. I remember going to church the next day, and during mass all those emotions came back. I started crying."

Since Anna Marie's birth, Anthony has become the sole breadwinner in the Cugini family. Julie gave up her job as a secretary to become a full-time mother and homemaker. "We're not old-fashioned," says Anthony, "but we have old-fashioned ideas about raising a family and how relationships should be conducted. We talked a lot before we got married about what type of life we'd like to lead as a married couple. We both felt very strongly that the woman would stay home and take care of the child. I look back on my own childhood, and I can't imagine myself going home from school and not having my mom there to listen to what I did all day. And I feel kinda strong that Anna Marie should have the same thing. And I think Julie feels the same way about that."

Julie does feel the same way. "I always pictured a wife to be the one in the family who made the house pleasant. The one thing that was always important to me was to be there when Anthony came home. You know, to give him a kiss. To have dinner on the table. To be there for him when he needs me. That's the kind of wife I want to be."

Despite their traditional arrangement, Anthony and Julie are more flexible about their roles than their parents were. Anthony often makes breakfast and takes pride in his skill at vacuuming the floors; grocery shopping is always a joint task. With a small baby on the premises, Julie needs his help. But someday, all their children will be in school and Julie will be faced with long days in an empty house. She has thought about that and doesn't rule out working sometime in the future, but she wouldn't consider anything that might interfere with her role as maintainer of the hearth.

"We talked about whether I wanted to go back to work or not. He, of course, said to me, 'That's entirely up to you.' I thought about my decision to stay home with Anna Marie, and I've also thought about being myself, as a person. I think I should see what type of person I can be as a wife and mother right now to my husband and Anna Marie. Then in the future I might work, maybe not taking on a career or a full-time job, but maybe something part time in the home, where I can better myself as a person — and of course contribute more to my marriage and to being a mother."

In order to maintain the traditional relationship they feel is so important, Anthony has had to shift his priorities. "I look back on this year, and I changed jobs, bought a house, and financially that put a burden on me. Now I work a second job, and I had to change my career attitude slightly. I couldn't say, 'Well, my goal is to get a Ph.D. in chemical engineering.' My goal now is to provide security for our family, and if in so doing I could still get a Ph.D., then that's what I would like to do."

Both the Cuginis acknowledge the stresses of their first year. Julie recalls having to adjust to married life. "I'll honestly tell you the first six months of the marriage you're thinking, 'Why did I marry this person?'" Anthony attributes the problem to the multiple pressures of finding and buying a house, and then having to fix it up before they could move in. Julie was pregnant and, pinched by the cost of remodeling, they did all the work themselves. "That was really the biggest strain on our relationship," says Anthony. "It was a tough time for us. A lot of decisions had to be made, and we had to make a lot of compromises, too. It was really a stressful situation."

But Julie and Anthony feel that they have created a good life together, one that meets their expectations. "My dreams aren't farfetched at all," explains Julie. "I want to have the marriage work. That's what we wanted in the beginning, and that's what I still want and that's what we work toward every day. Our marriage is growing now, and we're growing with it, and our love is growing with it. I look at Anthony and can honestly say that I'm very happy with the choice I made."

Anthony is just as pleased with the ways things have turned out. "The really important thing about Julie and about her relationship with me is that right now, we are the family. For the last twenty-eight years of my life, my parents and me were 'our' family. But now Julie and I and Anna Marie are 'our' family. I see something that's making me happy and that'll keep on making me happy. That makes it the best decision I've ever made. I'm as happy as I've ever been in my life."

Youth, Adulthood, and the Social Clock

The Social Clock continues to tick loudly as we enter young adulthood, for society has a great deal at stake in the season of fertility. Its expectations are no longer "age-graded" the way they were in the school years, but they are clear nonetheless. Anthony and Julianne Cugini have responded to the age norms for the twenties: establish an occupation, find a mate, start a family. When researchers at the University of Michigan asked more than 2,000 married women and men what single event made them feel that they were adults, those answers topped the list.[1] Among parents, the birth of the first child was far and away the most important of the three. Among child-less couples, most husbands found their assurance of adulthood in their occupation; wives generally found it in their marriage. Lagging far behind were such milestones as finding a first job, finishing school, or moving out of the family home.

The Cuginis' age at marriage is close to that of other young Americans, who are waiting longer to marry than any generation on record. At twenty-two, Julianne was more than a year younger than the median age for women in 1988, which was 23.6. Anthony was twenty-seven, about a year older than the male median of 25.9. (At the median age, half of all women — or men — are married.) In 1890, when the U.S. government started keeping this statistic, women married at a median age of 22 and men at 25.5. Throughout the first half of the twentieth century, marriage came at a younger and younger age until we bottomed out in 1956, in the middle of the baby boom, at 20.1 for women and 22.5 for men. (This low point for American females, however, was still far above fourteen, the typical age at which a !Kung hunter-gatherer female reaches menarche and marries. But it was close to the norm for !Kung males, who are six to ten years older than females at the time of marriage.)[2] Since 1956, the ages at which we first marry have been slowly edging up, until they now surpass the older records.

These changes in the behavior of young adults reflect changing beliefs about the "right time" to marry. In 1960, 90 percent of adults in the Chicago area were convinced that women should marry before they reached the age of twenty-five. Twenty years later, only 40 percent thought it was a good idea; the rest thought that twenty-five was far too young.[3] Along with society's approval of delayed marriage has come an acceptance of people who never marry at all. During the 1950s, when Americans were marrying young and having large families, nearly half of young adults were suspicious of people who never married; they viewed them as sick, asocial, or selfish. But by the mid-1970s, less than a quarter felt that way.[4] Young women's attitudes showed a similarly striking change; the overwhelming majority now complained that marriage was restrictive.

If marriage is seen as restrictive but relationships remain important, people will start living together without a legal commitment — and that's what an increasing number of young adults are doing. As adult developmentalist Bernice Neugarten sums it up, "Whether you marry nowadays or form a relationship without marriage is not the point, but rather that you find another person with whom you're going to share many of the decisions in your life."[5] Add these cohabiting couples to the couples who marry, and it becomes clear that Americans are pairing off as early as they ever did.[6] Cohabitation has spread among adults of all age and income levels, but it's most popular among young adults — especially those who have dropped out of school. When sociologists at the University of Wisconsin analyzed a recent national survey, they discovered that among adults now in their early thirties, about half of the high-school dropouts and more than a third of the high-school graduates lived together before they were married.[7] About a quarter of college graduates had done so. But the trend is rising at all educational levels, and sociologists predict that cohabitation may soon precede marriage for the majority of Americans. For most people, cohabitation is a temporary state; within a year, 40 percent have either married their partners or gone their separate ways. Only one couple in ten stays together as long as five years without marrying.

Some sociologists maintain that, among educated men and women, the flight from the altar is related to the increasing number of years it takes to develop a work life. For a growing segment of the population, training for careers occupies a good part of their twenties, and the rest is devoted to getting established in a profession. As women like Christine Osborne move into business, medicine, and other traditionally male domains, they follow the male occupational pattern, which means that marriage and children get put on hold.

For many of these people, the ten-year lag between the settings on the Biological and Social Clocks — the lag that gave us the season of adolescence — is getting even longer. It seems that for educated young adults, another stage of life is dawning. The trend was spotted by sociologist Kenneth Keniston back in 1968, when he saw a stage of "youth" (the old name for adolescence) bridging the gap between the end of high school and the beginning of full adult responsibility for self and family.[8] The demand of today's information society for skilled, highly educated workers is the primary force behind the creation of this new period. Its length is largely determined by the requirements of schooling, so that for some — such as Julianne — youth ends in the early twenties, but for others — such as Anthony — it may last until the late twenties. Today, youth is a stage of life confined primarily to the middle class, but that's where childhood and adolescence first took root. Wider recognition of youth will depend on the prosperity and educational demands of society at large.

If youth becomes accepted as a season of life in the twenty-first century the way adolescence did in the twentieth, it would be the second stage to fill the widening no-man's-land between the biological and social markers of adulthood. Twenty-five extra years of life in this century have stretched the lifeline close to its limit. Much of the resulting tension is being felt between childhood and adulthood.

How Families Came to Be

Anthony Cugini ends the story of his first year of marriage with a simple yet profound observation. Before he married, he says, his family was made up of his parents and himself. Now his family consists of his wife, his baby, and himself. This transition from the family of origin to the family of procreation is another sign of his adulthood.

Human children need families. They need a social womb to protect them during their long years of immaturity. But though the need for families is clear — it's rooted in our biological timetable for growth — the origin of families is not. We know little about how families came to be, about the way social and biological evolution worked hand in hand to fashion them.

Not long ago, an extraordinary set of footprints was found in fossilized mud in a region of Tanzania. The area was rich with the remains of *Australopithecus afarensis*, the species of hominids to which the famous "Lucy" skeleton belongs. Lucy's people were distant ancestors of ours, short apelike creatures who seem to have lived into their twenties. The rock in which a few of their footprints were found was between three and a half and four million years old. Remarkably, there was not one set of prints, but two, one larger and one smaller. Some researchers speculate that the larger set was left by an adult and the smaller by a juvenile walking next to the adult.[9] The earliest record we have of a hominid's upright posture may simultaneously be a record of that hominid protecting its young.

When our own species, *Homo sapiens*, came into being millions of years after little *Australopithecus*, our biological schedule for growth already contained time for parents, and even grandparents, to take care of vulnerable children. Somewhere along the line, mothers began to do something extraordinary with children they had weaned from the breast. Instead of leaving them to fend for themselves — the way baboons do, for example — they continued to provide food for them. Fathers, too, were involved in the process. "Males invest in offspring only when the likelihood of a female successfully rearing them is low," notes Jane Lancaster, and that apparently was the case with humans.[10] From the dawn of our species, we've had families — protective adults, male and female, walking next to children and feeding them for at least a decade after weaning.

Anthony, Julianne, and Anna Marie Cugini have created a "nuclear" family, one in which mother, father, children — and no one else — all live together. Human history has seen many kinds of families, but according to researchers who study hunter-gatherers, the nuclear form (or something close to it) may well be the oldest.[11] Despite the enormous difference between hunter-gatherer societies and our own, these two societies share a common feature: families in both are highly mobile. That appears to be why they're stripped down to the bare movable essentials, to the "nucleus" of mother, father, and child.

Mobile as they were, early humans established campsites that they used for several months at a stretch. From them men ventured forth to hunt large game, a risky and unpredictable task that took them far afield, but brought in highly concentrated supplies of food. Women gathered wild fruit, nuts, grains, and roots, a less risky job that could be done near the campsite by a nursing mother, and one that produced large quantities of less concentrated food. This division of labor was uniquely human. In no other species do the sexes exploit different levels of the food chain and share their food with others. Such an arrangement is similar to that of a contemporary couple in which one partner has a steady job that pays a modest income and the other free-lances for higher stakes. Among hunter-gatherers, women had the steady job that provided most of the food. Men roamed more widely for a higher nutritional payoff.

Families seem first to have begun diversifying with the introduction of agriculture, when hunter-gatherers started to grow and harvest their own plant food instead of foraging for it, to keep their own animals in pasture instead of hunting them down. To do so, they had to give up their nomadic way of life and stay in one place. Men still did some hunting, but families began to cluster in small villages near the land they tilled. They began to accumulate possessions they previously had been unable to carry. This transition to a sedentary way of life began about 10,000 years ago and changed the structure of families. Women weaned their babies earlier and were soon producing a child every other year. Families organized themselves in various ways to protect the resources they had accumulated.[12] In some cases, one man married one woman. In others, as among various Islamic groups, he took several wives. In a very few societies, such as the Todas of southern India, several men — often brothers — all married the same woman.[13] Whenever there was a shortage of men to invest in children, women chose single parenthood.[14] There have been many variations on the basic themes of monogamy, polygyny, polyandry, and single parenthood, and families have served many purposes, but their basic intent has remained the same: to provide a womb of protection for our slowly developing young. The roots of the human family may have been etched in Tanzanian mud nearly four million years ago.

In the Wake of the Baby Boom

Families such as the Cuginis, in which the mother stays at home and concentrates on house and family and the father is the sole breadwinner, flourished in the United States after World War II. Those years between 1946 and 1964 were our "baby boom," when Americans seemed intent on rectifying in one generation the continuing decline in birthrate that had been going on for nearly a century. In the middle of the baby boom, the Social Clock pushed the age of marriage to its lowest setting of the century.

The Cuginis were born at the tail end of the boom; Julianne, in fact, is one of its very last babies. The family they are creating as adults is thought of as a "traditional" family, especially by those of us who grew up watching television shows such as "Ozzie and Harriet" and "Father Knows Best." But such families are more the product of a particular generation than they are of a long-standing tradition. And since the days of the baby boom, families have changed enormously.

One dramatic change is the rise in children born outside marriage. In 1986, 23 percent of all babies were born to unmarried women, up from 4 percent in 1950.[15] A happy few are born to single women with good jobs who either want children but have rejected marriage, or else have been pushed by the Biological Clock to the point where they can delay pregnancy no longer. But the vast majority of children born outside of marriage have mothers with less education and fewer financial resources than their married counterparts. This translates into a lack of prenatal care and low birth weights for the babies.[16] One reason for this dismal situation is the unwed mother's age: one out of three are teenagers. Another is her race: among blacks, three out of five babies are born to unmarried mothers; among Hispanics, the figure is one out of three; among whites, it's one out of six.[17] Researchers at the U.S. Census Bureau suggest that the steady increase in births to unmarried women reflects "the opinion of some women that they may be better off in the long run by relying more on the support of their parents and relatives for financial and emotional assistance than by entering a potentially unstable marriage."[18] Whatever the reason, the implications for their offspring are clear: in 1987, 21 percent of children were living below the poverty line, the largest proportion of any age group in the country.[19]

A second change in families stems from women's entry into the world of work. Today, most U.S. marriages have two earners. Among young married women, approximately two-thirds are employed.[20] In 1960, only 19 percent of the mothers of children younger than six were in the labor market. In 1988, 57 percent were.[21] Most mothers work because of financial necessity; seven out of ten say that the family couldn't keep going without their salaries. But an increasing number of young women arrive at young adulthood with broad vocational interests. They may marry and have families, but they never define themselves solely in terms of family roles.

Despite these changes, the American workplace is still geared to the man in a traditional marriage, and children are not considered when hours or benefits are set. Maternal leave has long been offered by every industrialized country in the Western world — except the United States. It was not until 1987 that the U.S. Supreme Court upheld a California law requiring all employers with fifteen or more workers to offer pregnant women four months of unpaid leave and to hold their jobs for them or place them in an equivalent job on their return.[22] Some branches of the federal government already grant employees up to a year of unpaid leave after the birth of a child.[23] Most economists and sociologists agree that some form of maternal leave, probably an unpaid leave of absence, will probably become standard as this century comes to a close. But at present no more than 40 percent of working women have such protection.[24]

Some economists are also betting that, before long, day-care will be as standard a fringe benefit as health insurance is today.[25] At the moment, any kind of day-care for infants is hard to come by. It's also extremely expensive, which explains why so very few working mothers with infants can even consider such arrangements.[26] Decent day-care for preschoolers is somewhat less costly because each caregiver can handle more youngsters, but it's still difficult to find. Parents have worked out a variety of ways to care for their children: couples work different shifts, relatives care for the child, baby-sitters come into the home, or parents use a day-care home.

As 1989 wound down, the United States had no federal standards for child care, but signs of change were in the air. Conservatives and liberals had finally agreed that something should be done for the ten-and-a-half million children, infants, toddlers, and preschoolers whose mothers worked. In California, cities were either opening day-care centers or requiring employers to do so, and Seattle voters agreed to spend five million tax dollars on centers for infants and preschoolers.[27] As the "baby bust" generation follows the baby boom into young adulthood, the shortage of trained workers will force most employers to offer day-care to attract employees. When a family cannot survive without two incomes, society must increase its investment in children.

In the earliest human families, both mothers and fathers worked "outside the home." Mothers didn't stray as far as fathers, and they brought their nursing infants with them. Their other children were often left at the campsite in mixed-age groups supervised by an adult — the original day-care centers. Day-care is a concern of *Homo sapiens* that seems especially new, but in fact is very old. It's become important once again because of the growing number of single-parent and dual-income families.

Divorce and the Movement of Fathers

As the baby boom was ending in the early 1960s, families were changing in yet another way — the most striking way of all. The divorce rate, only about 4 percent at the time of the Civil War, had been increasing throughout the twentieth century and was now starting to accelerate rapidly. It would continue to do so throughout the sixties and seventies, until it leveled off in the 1980s at its present record high. Today, nearly half of all marriages end in divorce. Each year, more than a million children see their parents terminate their marriage.[28]

Some demographers believe the divorce rate is actually higher than 50 percent. The University of Wisconsin's Larry Bumpass and Teresa Castro-Martin predicted in 1989 that 56 percent of recent first marriages would end in divorce.[29] They also believe that this figure seriously underestimates the situation, because the data ignore another 6 percent of couples who permanently separate but never get a legal divorce. Also missing are all the couples who live together and then break up without ever marrying.

Marriages among the young are at greatest risk for divorce, because people in their late teens or early twenties often aren't sure who they are and what they want out of life. They may feel pushed into a legal commitment — about one third of U.S. marriages take place after a child has been conceived or born. Because these very young adults may not have developed the skills to solve their differences, the marriages drift onto the rocks. Four out of every ten divorces occur among couples younger than thirty.

The U.S. divorce rate is the highest in the developed world, but according to Lancaster, it's not far from that in hunter-gatherer societies, where women are free to leave unhappy relationships. Divorce rates are lower in societies where women have no choice. "The most stable marriages in the world," Lancaster points out, "are marriages that are formed on the basis of a patriarchal relationship between the spouses, where divorce means that a woman loses her children and can't support herself. Where women can take the kids and go home and support themselves, you automatically double the divorce rate, because it means that both men and women have to be satisfied for the marriage to be stable."[30] Until recently in the United States, women in unhappy marriages had few options. The salaries they could command in the labor market were so far below those of men that escape was impossible. Although women still earn less than men for comparable jobs, their salaries have climbed far enough to weaken the economic glue that holds many marriages together. That leaves only the psychological glue — sexual bonding and long-term companionship. For many couples, it isn't enough.

When a marriage ends, women's financial burdens increase, while those of their former husbands often become lighter. Andrew Cherlin, a Johns Hopkins University sociologist, has spelled out the situation: "By one estimate, the average divorced woman's standard of living goes down by perhaps 30 percent during the first year after a divorce, while the average standard of living of an ex-husband goes up somewhat — maybe 10 or 15 percent. That's because husbands retain their male earnings, which tend to be higher, while wives either retain their generally low-income jobs or, even worse, have to go back into the job market for the first time after being home taking care of their children for years."[31] The result is often poverty: nearly half of all families headed by women fall beneath the poverty line.

The aftermath of divorce affects an enormous group of children. As of 1988, more than fifteen million of them lived in single-parent homes — one of every four American children. The Census Bureau offers the sobering estimate that six out of every ten children will spend at least some time living with only one parent. In 89 percent of the homes, that parent will be a woman.

Parental partnership may have been a crucial part of our evolutionary success, but when today's marriages break up, the father's investment of energy in the children's care often dwindles or disappears. When fathers maintain contact, they usually act more as pals than parents. They take their children to dinner or the movies, go on trips, or play games, but they rarely become involved in schoolwork or in their children's projects. For the most part, fathers hand over the job of parenting to mothers. They rarely talk to the mothers about the children's activities, schooling, or welfare, and few take part in major decisions concerning their children. Most mothers complain that their ex-husbands take too little responsibility for child-rearing.

These findings come from a large-scale study in which sociologists followed the fate of divorced families.[32] They discovered that within a few years, as many divorced fathers had disappeared as stuck around to become their child's pal. Forty-nine percent of adolescent children whose parents had divorced had not seen their father during the past year. Only one in six had seen him at least once each week. Few fathers made up for their absence with phone calls or letters, and many failed to support their children financially. "Only about half the women in this country who are supposed to receive child-support payments receive the full amount every year," says Cherlin, "and one quarter receive nothing."[33]

Divorced fathers often drift away from their children. Within a few years, the weekly visits become biweekly, then monthly, then sporadic. Fathers lose contact for various reasons. They may find that severing connections is less painful than enduring brief visits with children who are growing emotionally distant. Their ex-wives may make it difficult or impossible for them to visit. Their work may take them to another part of the country, or the mother may move away. Some fathers disappear to escape the burden of child support. No matter what the reason, the crucial investment of paternal energy that allowed our species to flourish is withdrawn.

Sometimes that energy goes into stepchildren. Though remarriage rates are declining, about two-thirds of adults who divorce eventually remarry. The result is a growing number of stepfamilies that the Census Bureau is only starting to catch up with. Child Trends, a private statistics firm, estimates that in 1988 about 11 percent of the nation's children under eighteen were living in a home with a stepparent.[34] About 25 percent of today's children will spend part of their childhood with a stepparent in the house, and in the vast majority of cases, that stepparent will be a man.[35] Because divorced mothers usually maintain custody of their children, fathers tend to do the moving from one family to the next.

Children respond to their parents' marital disruptions in a variety of ways. Few wish for their parents' divorce, and many resent their parents' remarriage. Grief, anger, anxiety, depression, and guilt are common reactions. Many children have behavior problems. Some seem to adapt well in the early stages of change, but suffer ill effects later on. Others are remarkably resilient and actually appear to benefit by coping with the transition.[36] In general, children in single-parent families and stepfamilies are at greater developmental risk than children in intact biological families.[37] But the way a family functions is more important than what form it takes. Research has shown consistently that children are better off in well-functioning single-parent families and stepfamilies than in "traditional" nuclear families that are riddled with conflict.[38]

Stepfamilies are not new to human history. In the seventeenth century, for example, it was common for a young wife or husband to die, and most widows and widowers remarried. A stepchild, in the original meaning of the term, was an orphaned or bereaved child, not a child of divorce. Over the next two centuries, as fewer people were widowed during their prime childbearing years, the number of stepfamilies declined. But in the twentieth century, as divorce rates climbed, so did the number of stepfamilies. They were different, however, from those in the past. Since they followed divorce rather than death, the original parent was not supplanted. Instead, a highly complex family was formed, in which children had an additional parent — or two, if both parents remarried. Sometimes it meant a great deal of adult attention for children; sometimes it meant severe conflicts of loyalty.

The pace of social change in the last three decades has been staggering. "Is young adulthood more difficult than it used to be?" asks Cherlin. "I don't think so. It's probably always been difficult. Is it more varied than it used to be? Sure. What's distinctive about young adulthood today is how new many of these family forms are. Out-of-wedlock pregnancy, living together without marriage, career opportunities for women, large amounts of divorce — these are all developments that on a large scale have come about in just a few decades. It may be that the pace of social change has been too fast for us. But as we enter the 1990s, many of these demographic trends seem to be slowing down. Maybe now we'll have a chance to catch our breath and figure out how we can once again structure a passage through young adulthood that makes sense and that works for us."[39]

Such a passage will work for us only if it works for our children — only if it enables parents to maintain the social womb that protects their offspring. Divorce places a tremendous burden on families. Mothers find it hard to support themselves and their children. Fathers find it hard to stay involved. Both must recover from the shattering of a dream before the family can organize itself in a new way. And both must learn that, although their marriage has ended, their relationship has not.

"It Isn't the End"

"I think I was just trying to get across how desperate the situation was. Finally, one night in the middle of a terrible fight, I left home. I went to my girlfriend's house and stayed there for two weeks. I had made the break and I had no intention of going back. Bill didn't know where I was. Didn't have a phone number to get in touch with me. And I had nothing."

When Donna Radocaj took her two children and left her husband five years ago, she wasn't sure what was happening, or why. She was twenty-six and had been married for five years. They had been a "normal" family, she says, except for the fighting that had been present almost from the beginning. "Bill and I were in love. We couldn't wait to get married. I thought he would provide for the family and I would stay home and bake cookies and make homemade bread." She laughs now at her naïveté, but it has a bitter edge. "It wasn't like that."

How it actually was is something Donna would rather not dwell on. She's a youthful thirty-one, with an appearance that gives lie to the struggle she's been through. She has a pert upturned nose and wears her dark hair in a sleek boyish cut. Her large brown eyes become pensive as she looks back. "Probably two months into the marriage I had thoughts about leaving." But, even with her doubts, she became pregnant. Billy was born two years after the wedding, and Becky a year-and-a-half after that. "I stayed home and Bill became the provider for the family. Neither of us was happy. We considered a divorce, but we chickened out when we started to feel what it would be like to split the family up." They tried a marriage counselor, but to no avail. The fights got worse. When Billy was three and Becky was eighteen months, the break finally came. Donna and the children moved out.

After two weeks in her girlfriend's home, the three of them moved into a small two-room apartment. "I didn't have any furniture," Donna recalls. "Somebody lent me an air mattress, and I slept on the floor for a couple of months. I remember the kids being real sick during that time. It seemed so unreal that my life could go from being so comfortable — you know, it was a normal married life when we weren't fighting — to only having two rooms and no food and no money and no idea of where I was gonna go or what I was gonna do. Not even a way to wash the clothes."

Within a couple of weeks, Bill discovered where Donna and the children were staying. He started sending money, but it wasn't enough — Donna had to move again and get a job as a temporary secretary. She had worked in the past, but now it was different. "When I was single and working, I only had myself to worry about. And when I was married, it was the second income and didn't seem as important. But when I knew that I was the provider now and that these two kids were depending on me, the job seemed so much more important. I had to do my best. I couldn't mess up. I couldn't get fired. I couldn't miss a day of work, anything that might ruin the security of that job for us. So I put a lot of pressure on myself. Even though I was giving a hundred and ten percent, I know I wasn't working at the same potential and capabilities that I had in the past. I couldn't concentrate, and I couldn't handle the hectic atmosphere as easily as I could before. I was really afraid.

"I felt like I was dragging lead weights around. Everything I did as a divorced person I remembered doing as a married person, and it was so different. I remember the first few times I went grocery shopping. I was counting every penny, and all those things I'd walk by, I'd look and I'd remember, 'Oh yeah, Bill used to like that. But, well, we don't need to buy that anymore.' I remember the one time I took the kids to the zoo. It was on the weekend and the weather had just turned nice and I thought, 'Well, we'll go and have a nice day at the zoo.' We were all real happy until we got there and we started walking around, and it just struck me. I looked at all the dads carrying their little kids and the wives standing in line for refreshments. You know, they didn't have all the responsibilities and worries that I had. And it just tore me up seeing all the families. I didn't have that anymore. I cried, and it turned into a miserable day. We ended up leaving.

"I totally lost my identity. I never could understand what that meant before, but now I did. I mean, one day I was Bill's wife. I was married, he was working. We'd been looking to buy a house. His family was such a big part of our lives, and all of a sudden they were gone, for me and for the kids."

Donna didn't understand why she was so confused and depressed until she read a book about loss almost a year after the split. By that time, the divorce was final. "I started to realize that I was actually going through a grieving process, and all of this was normal. No one could go through a divorce or death and not have some kind of emotional upset. If you did, you'd be pretty empty, you know, not really alive. So that helped, and I think it was then that I started to recover.

"I remember one day coming home from work. I walked in the house and I felt like baking brownies. I felt like cleaning. It was the first time in nearly a year that I cared what my place looked like and I felt like doing something creative. From that time I continued to get better. I accepted the fact that this is the way my life's gonna be. And it got easier. We got closer, me and the kids. We became more sensitive to each other. And all those things weren't painful anymore."

During the next year, Donna rearranged her life. She found a cheaper apartment. Bill agreed to increase his support payments. The extra money, combined with food stamps and income from baby-sitting for another toddler, enabled Donna to quit her job and stay home with the children. She has been in her new place for almost three years now.

Donna Radocaj, thirty-one. "I'm giving it everything I got, but sometimes it feels like I'm rowing upstream and still being washed downstream."

"Things really changed after we moved in here," she says. "We all are so much happier. For the first year, honestly, I just took it easy. Then I wasn't content to sit anymore. I've always wanted to go to college. I found out that I could get benefits and financial aid, so I registered for classes and started going to school. And I think going to college has been the best thing I've done for myself. My confidence started to come back. I knew I was headed in the right direction, so I've been going to school ever since."

Donna pays some of her expenses by working three nights a week as a waitress at a local restaurant, even though most of her tips go to pay the baby-sitter. Her goal is to finish school, get a good job, and buy a house in the suburbs where Billy, now seven, and Becky, five, can have pets and plenty of room to play. She knows this is a tall order, and her confidence that she can bring it off is still shaky.

"I feel like it's all on me. You know, nobody's gonna look at Bill and say, 'You didn't raise your kids right.' Or blame him for what they went through. Maybe because I'm the one who walked out and left the marriage, I feel responsible for putting them through all that pain. Other people don't see the turmoil and the tiredness, the fear, the anxiety I feel inside. I don't know if I'll ever recover to the point where I'll be the same person I was before I was married or before I went through a divorce. I'm giving it everything I got, but sometimes it feels like I'm rowing upstream and still being washed downstream. It's just really hard.

"To me, divorce meant that I wouldn't have to put up with the things that I didn't like. I would have the freedom to do what I wanted, see who I wanted, come home when I wanted, spend my money the way I wanted. But divorce isn't what I thought it was gonna be. It's a lot harder. At least

Bill, thirty-one. "The hardest thing was driving away every morning with him screaming."

we're not at each other's throat anymore. The kids don't have to live in that kind of environment. But I'm not as free as I thought I would be. I exchanged one set of problems for a whole new set of problems, and I think the problems I have now are worse than the ones I had before. We've talked about getting remarried, and miserable as my life is sometimes and as hard as it is, and as much as I cry, when it comes to actually giving up all that I've worked for and going back into an unhappy marriage, I haven't been able to bring myself to do that."

For Bill, the worst part of being divorced is separation from the children. In his marriage to Donna, he says, "there was just a gnawing kind of friction." Bill is a trim man in his early thirties, with a rugged face and close-cropped sandy hair. He believes his absence has been harder on his son than on his daughter, who was just one and a half when he and Donna separated. "From what Donna tells me, he took it real hard. He would cry at night and want his daddy. I'm sure he had no idea what was going on. And for a while I had to put him in day-care. The hardest thing was driving away every morning with him screaming."

For a period after the divorce, Billy and Becky spent three days a week with their father. But now that Billy has started school and Bill's days off have changed, they don't spend quite so much time together. Nor does Bill spend much time on discipline. He and Donna agree about the general guidelines, but Bill leaves most of the execution in Donna's hands. He finds that when he disciplines his children, they take it too much to heart, perhaps because he's not with them on a daily basis. Bill has thought a lot about his role as an absent father, and is careful not to become a magical figure who swoops down and takes the children off on grand adventures.

"A lot of parents who don't see their kids try to make up for it by doing something big," he says. "I try to take them places, but I'm also trying to be conscious of doing things with them when we're there, so that the big event of the day was that we did the thing together. I try to make that a conscious effort. We don't always do big things — maybe once or twice a month. The other times we'll go to Grandma's or just stay around the house. As long as I find something for them to do, they're happy. They don't complain about work.

"I've been able to go to Billy's open houses and the parent/teacher conferences. I'm interested in how he's doing in school and want to find out from his teacher. One day I went and talked to his class. He was amazed. You could just see the look on his face. I walked in and he saw me. It just made me feel really good."

Donna has dated a few times, but has not formed any serious relationships. Bill has been seeing other women, but isn't thinking about marrying again. When he brings a friend along on an outing, the children accept her. "The few they've met, it's like somebody else to talk to," he says. "Somebody new to tell stories to, to do stuff with. So I haven't noticed them having any problem. Some women can't handle the kids. That's something I can't compromise on, because they're part of my life. Of course, they're gonna have to get along with each other. If a woman's willing to accept my being divorced and having kids, then you usually don't have a problem with the kids, once they meet."

It hasn't been easy for Donna to think of Bill with other women. "There's been a couple of times when it's really been hard for me to see pictures of him with them. He looked happy, you know?" She can laugh about it now, but in the beginning her reaction surprised her. "It felt like our whole marriage just meant nothing to him if he could find somebody else that quickly and easily and be happy. It still hurts sometimes, but it's not the crippling kind of pain it was in the beginning.

"When we first split up, I was angry and bitter and didn't want to talk to Bill and blamed him for everything. But it would be really hard not to be friendly and have respect for him, after he's kept up his relationship with the kids and always had the child support there on time." She takes a deep breath. "He's a good father. The kids love him, he loves them. It's probably not normal, but I can't imagine ever getting to the point where I don't talk to Bill or where we're not friends. I want him to be happy and have a good life, and I knows he feels the same way about us. You know, divorce isn't the end. It's the end of the marriage, but it's not the end of the relationship."

12

THE PSYCHOLOGICAL *From Dream*

STORY OF EARLY *to Reality*

ADULTHOOD

It's nearly summer in Pittsburgh. On this bright June day, young men and women in caps and gowns file along a grassy aisle on the Carnegie-Mellon campus, their crimson tassels swaying in step. One by one, they accept their diplomas. Among them is Justin Miller, twenty-one, a young man with a dream of the future. With his diploma in hand, he's about to begin transforming that dream into reality.

Back in his apartment, Justin wears jeans and a white shirt, open at the neck. "I'd like to go back to New York to start my career," he says. "I know the city. I grew up there, and it's certainly the place for what I'm doing." Justin has regular features, brown eyes, and brown hair whose curls keep trying to escape from his conventional hairstyle. Most of the time, he wears wire-rimmed glasses. His clothes, like the posters covering the large white walls of his room, are trim, neat, and carefully selected, as befits a young man who intends to make his way in the world. "I studied graphic design, but the field I'm really interested in is advertising. I like to write, and I like to be with people, and I feel that advertising is a good place for that. It's a highly competitive and creative field.

"I always thought I'd end up doing something creative. My father's a designer. His brother's a designer. The aesthetics of taste and style were always part of me when growing up. I just never thought about art and design as something I could study. It was something I could do.

"The best drawing I ever did is hanging on my bedroom wall at home. It's a little line drawing of an owl. I did it when I was about two, and I think it's fabulous. I can't draw like that now; I don't think I ever could again. But I used to draw and sketch and fiddle around — especially in textbooks. In grade school, all the kids used to be jealous, because I'd come in with a report that had a nice cover that was like a little poster with some typography on the bottom. The whole thing was carefully planned. I didn't like research, the writing was okay, but I always looked forward to the end — when I could put the cover on it.

"All the time I was growing up, I was used to the idea that I was the class artist with all the talent and creative abilities that other kids didn't seem to share. Then I went into my first drawing class at Carnegie-Mellon, and we were drawing a nude model. At the end of fifteen, twenty minutes, the teacher asked everybody to hold up their work. I was pretty proud of my piece, and I was shocked that every piece in that room was as good as mine — many of them a lot better. Everybody in that room was 'the little class artist,' and that was the first time I doubted the talent."

During his college career, Justin did not erase all his doubts, but he did take steps to assure himself of his ability. He opens a portfolio and kneels on the floor beside his draftman's table, his glasses pushed up on the top of his head. With obvious satisfaction, he spreads out his work.

"I'm proud of my portfolios. One is my studio portfolio, which encompasses all my better work over the course of four years here. The other is my own little project, my own little campaign. That's more geared toward the profession. My portfolio is a selling tool. It's selling me; it's selling my ability; it's selling my thinking. Fifteen pieces in that portfolio are enough to show somebody how you think, how you solve problems, what you've got to offer a company. I talk with my friends who are studying business, and the only selling tool they can offer a company, besides themselves in an interview, is the résumé. I have a résumé plus the portfolios."

Justin is looking for a job with a company that "puts out good advertising," a company where he feels he can make an immediate contribution. Once his portfolios and his résumé get him hired, he has no intention of burrowing in for the long haul. "I'd like to feel that there's no permanence to the position. I'd like to gain experience and leave soon after. I don't want to get set in a place. I speak with friends who feel that it would be nice to just sit down in one company and spend ten years there, work your way up. But I have no desire to do that. I want to experiment and explore, and hopefully someday open up my own place. By the time I'm thirty, I'd like to be running a business. I'd like to be doing something and gaining some

Justin Miller, twenty-one.
"My biggest fear is that I
won't be successful."

kind of prestige and acknowledgment for whatever type of work I'm doing."

Justin believes strongly in his ideas. Early on in college, his teachers told him he had a "defensive" attitude: in his eyes, he was right and everyone else was wrong. So he devised an "attitude adjustment plan" and consciously worked on himself. He's glad he did, because now he's more likely to stop and reflect. "The tension has made me think a little bit more. The tension of finishing up and getting out of school and seeing my friends worried about finding jobs and myself worried about finding a job, and what's going to happen next year. My biggest fear is that I won't be successful. That's my biggest fear above anything. I can't even define what that means right now — whether it's in material things or not. But success is something that's important to me.

"I've had summer jobs at ad agencies for the past couple of semesters, and they were good jobs. I'm really pleased that I was fortunate to get that kind of experience while I was still in school. It was incredible. I was given responsibility. It was all real: the budget, the clients, the deadlines. And I learned how to work like a professional. When you're in school, you tend not to realize what kind of pressure exists outside, professionally. It was frightening to see, while working, the kind of competitive market that exists in a big city like New York.

"I was worried while I was working there. I know I have talent. I know I'm good at what I do. I just don't know if that's enough. I saw how talented people were taken advantage of, just because the business didn't have a place for them. I learned so fast that it's not your talent and it's not how hard you work that's gonna get you moving into better positions and higher salaries and more power in the organization. Young people who like to work hard are perfect little go-fers for everybody else. They get pushed around. And you can easily get stagnant in some place and just never move anywhere. I saw it happen. And that would be the worst thing that could happen. The worst. The possibility that it could happen frightens me.

"People talk about playing the game in business a lot, and I really believe that a hundred percent. I think it's an incredible game, and I saw it while I was working. A lot of the people I came in contact with had the power and had the positions, but they really weren't worthy of it. I found them asking me my opinions a lot. At first I thought maybe they were trying to include me in, that it was their leadership quality, their way of getting more out of me. Then I slowly realized that some of them just didn't have enough confidence in themselves and their own work. But they had played this game so well that they'd snuck into these positions."

Justin is a savvy young man with an insider's knowledge of his chosen field. He believes that his talents can take him a long way — as long as he remembers his basic philosophy. "Life is a business. When I speak of my little philosophy that life is a business, it's just more of an awareness of the way you're gonna have to live your life today in a business society. I think art for art's sake is gone. When Picasso used to sit and draw, he just drew because he loved to draw. A lot of people today are thinking about how drawing would help them market themselves. My friends have this picture painted for themselves of their own little life and the way they're gonna be successful in their work. A lot of them know that they're gonna have to sell themselves out to a certain degree. Even the painters. They've seen the kind of lifestyle successful painters can have. And they want to have that, too."

There are other things Justin wants as an adult, things you can't get with a game plan or an attitude adjustment plan. "By the time I'm thirty, I'd like to be married. Or at least have somebody serious enough to think that way." But he has found it harder to develop an intimate relationship than to build a portfolio. "It's one thing I really have no control over. And I get to a point where I just don't feel like dealing with it anymore. I'll be miserable when I leave a party because I'll feel like I should have asked someone out, or I didn't talk to this one because we had an argument the other day, and that made it awkward. All these crazy situations turn up. It's so much easier to go to my studio and spend the evening doing some work. At least I'll be happy when I leave because I got something done.

"Sometimes I come home from a great day and I go to my apartment, and there's nobody there. I've got all these terrific things to say and I can't share them with anybody. One of my friends said that all he wants right now is somebody that'll . . . he could put his head down on her lap, and she'll just stroke his head and be there for him. And just talk to him and be close to him.

"I don't want a housewife as a wife. That wouldn't be enough for me. I don't want somebody who'll just sit and say, 'That's terrific, that's great,' just because they don't understand what I'm doing. I want a woman who would fight with me and tell me when I'm wrong and give me trouble once in a while. I need a little bit of knocking in line and putting back into place, because I'm kind of hard to bear sometimes. I'm opinionated, and things go to my head very easily. I think I need a woman who's a professional in her own right. I'd like to work and be there for her as well, and I think that's important."

Justin is certain there are children in his future, but for now he doesn't see just when and where they might fit in. "I'd like to raise a family. My family has been there for me always, and I hope, someday, to be there for mine. I just don't know how that's all gonna work out. With the kind of work I want to do, I don't know if I'll be ready to have a family at thirty. It might be too soon. A family will really tie me down in many respects. It'll make moving the way I want to in work difficult. Because all of a sudden, there's something else I have to think about."

Justin's own family is still an important part of his life. He and his father enjoy going head-to-head. "Sometimes we get into these incredible fights, because we're like two bulls. We're so similar and we see situations and issues the same way. I'm always talking with him about my work, and his favorite comment is, 'How do you know so much? How are you so young and where'd you learn it all?' But we never hold a grudge. Whatever fight we're in always ends quickly." Justin's mother helps him keep his problems in perspective. "I'll call up and say this is what's happening and it's bothering me. And she might say, 'Well, did you ever think of it this way?' It'll be the simplest, most direct thing, but I never thought of it." The separation to come will be hard on all of them.

Justin looks forward to what lies ahead in New York, and to what lies ahead in adulthood, with a mixture of hope and fear. "I still feel very young and inexperienced, especially going into business. Sometimes my head gets a little bit swollen and I don't feel so young and so naive. But then something'll knock me back into place and I'll realize that experience makes a big difference. I just don't know how it's all gonna come out. That's one thing I really can't predict. I can't even try."

Adulthood and the Dream

The diploma in Justin Miller's hand signals the end of his schooling, a continuation of his youth, and the promise of his adulthood. It will take a while for him to achieve the full measure of adult status, but now he can plan for it, worry about it, and be energized by its possibilities. At one and the same time, Justin hopes to be a brilliant success and fears that he won't be. He has a personal timetable to measure his progress: improve his portfolio, get experience in advertising agencies he respects, move from one agency to another, and form his own company — all by the age of thirty — then gain prestige and recognition for what he has accomplished. Other aspects of his adult life are less well envisioned. He pictures a wife who will comfort him, confront him, and above all believe in his talent; but he's not sure whether such a person exists or how to meet her. He wants a family, but cannot imagine starting one for another decade. All these images that Justin has of the future constitute what Yale psychologist Daniel Levinson calls "the dream." The young adult's dream is a later version of the adolescent's personal fable — the work of a constantly evolving self that responds to the predictable and unpredictable events of life by making meaning.

In each season of life, the self makes a different kind of meaning. As the curtain rises on adulthood, says Levinson, we need the sustenance a dream provides. The dream "has the quality of a vision, an imagined possibility that generates excitement and vitality. At the start it is poorly articulated and only tenuously connected to reality, although it may contain concrete images such as winning the Nobel Prize or making the all-star team. It may take a dramatic form as in the myth of the hero: the great artist, business tycoon, athletic or intellectual superstar performing magnificent feats and receiving special honors. It may take mundane forms that are yet inspiring and sustaining: the excellent craftsman, the husband-father in a certain kind of family, the highly respected member of one's community."[1] These examples come from the lives of men, and they stress independent achievement in the world of work. Levinson and his colleagues have found that women's dreams are more likely to include other people: husbands, children, and colleagues.[2] Not everyone has a dream, he says, but everyone faces the task of forming one. Its presence or absence — as well as its nature — plays a powerful role in the process of becoming an adult.

Some of the elements of the personal fable carry over into the dream — the sense of being special, the feeling of invulnerability, the belief in a grand destiny — but by the beginning of young adulthood, they have been tempered. Reality has already tempered Justin Miller's vision of the future. Summer employment, for example, has given him a practical knowledge of the profession he plans to pursue. But parts of his dream exist almost entirely as fantasy, like the ideal woman who will nurture his talent, provide him with children, and still have the energy for a high-powered career of her own. The dream formed at the threshold of adulthood exists on the boundary between illusion and reality. Of necessity, parts of it are fragile and full of contradiction.

In the twenties, the dream plays a number of critical roles. It mobilizes energy to undertake the challenge of the season ahead. It's a vehicle through which our inner timetable for growth — our Psychological Clock — expresses itself. The timeline in Justin's dream bears a resemblance to the one Christine Osborne had in her twenties, but is very different from that of May Ling Agosto and other adults we've met. Each person's dream reveals aspects of the self pressing for immediate expression; it also reveals gaps in the self that need to be filled in later on.

Ironically, the dream's most important role may not involve the future, but the past. Levinson believes that forming a dream enables the young to separate in an emotional sense from their families of origin. Once they do that, once they can say in a meaningful way, "It's my life, not my parents'," they have reached psychological adulthood.

Fifteen-year-old Kim Henderson is an adult in a biological sense, but she is still living with her mother and is dependent on her. May Ling Agosto, six years older than Kim, is in a different place. She hasn't broken her relationship with her mother, but she is redefining it on her own terms. Justin Miller is the same age as May Ling and is in the middle of a similar transition. Moving to New York and beginning to live out his dream will hasten the process of achieving psychological autonomy.

Current research shows that few young people separate in this sense from their parents until they are well into their twenties. The ability to make important choices without parental assistance and to cope with life's demands emerges slowly, as young people become confident of their own values and feel comfortable making decisions about major issues in their lives. Until then, most young men and women are so closely bound to their parents that they find it impossible to develop empathy with their mothers and fathers or see them as people in their own right, with complex roles, problems, and personalities. Researchers at Michigan State University discovered that, during the early twenties, no more than 20 percent of young people have separated enough from their parents to feel competent to make it on their own, while 50 percent harbor serious doubts about their ability to do so.[3] By the late twenties, those figures are reversed. Such findings reflect the emergence of the new stage of youth, a relaxation of society's expectation that young people establish themselves at an early age.

Love

As the dream of adulthood takes form, young people begin brushing in details that usually include love, work, and parenthood. Love is central to the dreams of both women and men. Both want to have a long-lasting, deeply intimate relationship, in which the partners feel free to disclose their deepest thoughts and feelings to each other. Erik Erikson believes that true intimacy is not possible until we have entered young adulthood.[4] That's because only people who have developed a clear sense of their own identity can commit themselves to a relationship that demands sacrifice and compromise. Those without a firm sense of identity may play at love, but their self-image is too fragile to prevent their engulfment by the other. An inability to develop a warm, supportive, mutual relationship may explain why marriages between the very young so often break apart.

In some ways, intimate relationships resemble the first attachments between babies and their parents — the partners feel joy when together and distress when apart. This resemblance has led researchers to speculate that the emotional bonds between marriage partners are as ingrained in our genes as the bond between baby and caregiver.[5] Falling in love often forges an attachment between sexual partners that endures long after sexual desire fades. This bond may have evolved to keep our earliest ancestors together to care for their children during their long years of vulnerability. The strength of such bonds explains why, like Donna and Bill Radocaj, couples who divorce often go through a period of emotional distress.

Shadows of childhood may stretch over the intimate relationships we form as adults. In our first families, we seem to develop a script for intimacy that we use again and again when writing our stories. The script is written when babies become attached to their parents; when babies grow up, they cast their mates or lovers and themselves in the roles they learned at home. Psychologists have found that the way adults describe relationships in their family of origin is connected to the sort of relationship they have with the most important person in their lives.[6] When first attachments are secure and relationships with parents are affectionate and warm, it bodes well for the future. But when those early attachments are insecure, people seem to fall into a vicious cycle of unhappy relationships. Yet it's possible to rewrite the basic script. Deep friendships and loving relationships with caring, considerate people can change our view of what to expect from love. Once the script is revised, the invidious cycle can be broken.

Psychologists have found a common thread running through the relationships of happily married couples.[7] Both partners are deeply committed to the relationship; both believe that it takes hard work to make a good marriage; both are aware that problems are inevitable, but also solvable. And each partner has a solid personal identity and an equally strong identity as a spouse.

When two people form a loving bond and live together under the same roof, their relationship generally follows the same path, whether they are homosexual, heterosexual married couples, or heterosexual cohabiters.[8] The first year is a time of intense passion and high levels of sexual activity, but also a time of learning to live with another person. Habits, chores, and personalities have to be coordinated, and each partner has to compromise a little. The major task is learning to think of oneself as part of an interdependent pair, with each partner's actions having consequences for the other. The second and third years are devoted to exploring the couple's compatibility and making a home. This nesting period may be a time of conflict and stress. Passion has waned, and the couple may clash over how much time to spend together. If they make it through the third year, their marriage may be on a steady course. Each partner feels like an individual as well as part of a couple. Family traditions are falling into place. Most conflicts have been resolved and life tends to run more smoothly.

Much in the process of forming a bond depends on whom we choose as a partner. Pennsylvania State University psychologist Jay Belsky has studied the long-range effects of these choices. "That partnership we establish for better or for worse will have a lot to do with where we go from that point in life forward. If the relationship goes well, it's very likely that we will feel good about ourselves and that there will be benefits, not only to our relationships with our children, but maybe even to the occupational spheres in which we function. If that relationship goes poorly, then all sorts of hazards confront us: coping with a divorce, making a life as a single parent, supporting a family you no longer live with."[9] In other words, the outcome of one component of the dream has a strong effect on the rest of it.

Work

Work is a second major component of the dream in early adulthood, and it may take years for young people to sift through their interests and match them with a specific career. Those who drift instead of exploring possible occupations may reach middle age before they "find themselves" — or they may never get a solid grasp on any line of work.

The choice of an occupation is important because work provides a vital part of identity. Most of us think of ourselves and others in terms of our line of work. When strangers are introduced, they exchange occupations as well as names, and if workers lose a job, their identity and self-esteem are threatened. This intricate entwining of self and job means that much of development during the adult years unfolds within the context of work.

In the early twenties, most young men commit themselves to a vocation, and set about acquiring the skills or credentials they need to forge ahead in their chosen occupation. A good part of these years is spent in on-the-job training for some, and in graduate school for others. It's a time of being in the adult world, but not really being part of it. As novices in their occupations, many are still testing their initial choices, and they tend to be unsure of themselves. Although they may be working hard at establishing themselves in their jobs, most still feel as if they are youths preparing themselves for life.

As Justin Miller creates his occupational dream, he has a great deal going for him. His experiences within his family and at school have left him feeling good about himself and likely to interpret whatever comes his way in a manner that keeps his self-concept high. His family and school background have fostered the skills, habits, and expectations that may help him realize his aspirations. In a large study of career development that took place in Middletown, New York, between 1951 and 1972, the socioeconomic status of a young man's family, his high-school grades, and his self-concept at the close of adolescence were strong predictors of occupational success.[10] These factors, together with an early readiness to make decisions about a career — and then to carry out those decisions — were strongly related to satisfaction with a chosen line of work and career advancement by the mid-twenties.

Many young women spend their early twenties in the same novice position as young men. Then, as they reach their mid-twenties, the majority find their working lives changing abruptly. Just at the time when most young men are moving rapidly up the career ladder, young women often interrupt their occupational lives to bear children. Their temporary absence from the work force, even for a year or two, usually places them on a slower career track and persuades employers that they're not truly serious about their occupations. For women like Christine Osborne who do not marry, careers resemble the male pattern of development — with some exceptions. After interviewing "savvy insiders" and women who have succeeded in climbing the corporate ladder, management specialists discovered that women who reach top management positions have had extra obstacles to overcome. They have had to prove that they are tough enough to handle the job, convince the corporation that they place their occupation before their families, outperform the men around them, and avoid looking like traditional nonprofessional women — while not trying too hard to be "one of the boys."[11] When the *Wall Street Journal* looked at the prospects of corporate women, it concluded that the biggest obstacle of all was the attitude of men: "Men at the top feel uncomfortable with women beside them."[12]

A number of young people enter adulthood with few of Justin's advantages. Yet they often manage to turn an unpromising start into a flourishing future. For one group of young men, the cohort born in 1928-1929, military service was the key. These men were children during the Great Depression of the 1930s, a time of few safeguards against economic hardship and deprivation. Not everyone suffered equally during the depression, but in those families whose incomes were reduced by more than one-third, researchers found that boys often became inadequate, socially inept adolescents who lacked initiative and had no purpose in life.[13] Their adult prospects were dim at best.

Even so, many of these boys succeeded in shaking off the legacy of failure that burdened their adolescence. They joined the service or were drafted, often without graduating from high school, and found themselves in a situation that changed their views of themselves and the world. Their military experiences seemed to strip away their old identities and helped them build new images of themselves in a setting of firm discipline, teamwork, strong leadership, and assertive male models that had been lacking in their childhood. Although military service delayed their occupational timetable, most of these young men took advantage of the G.I. bill and eventually climbed higher in their occupations than young men their age who had no military service. Their marriages also proved to be more stable: nearly three-quarters were still married to the same woman at the close of young adulthood, while less than half of those who did not enter the service had stable marriages.

This litany may sound like a recruiting poster, but for these young men military service offered the sort of moratorium that college gave more fortunate groups in later decades. Their experience illustrates the impact of major historical events on our lives. Events such as war and economic depression can affect our adulthood in profound ways and keep the outcome of our stories a mystery.

Parenthood

For individuals like Anthony and Julianne Cugini, parenthood lies at the heart of early adulthood. But others approach the season in different ways. Some, like Justin Miller, relegate children to the dim and distant future. A few decide not to have children at all. But most young adults want to become mothers and fathers and actually do so. As they embark on parenthood, most have little idea in the beginning how dramatically the experience will change them.[14] Parenthood adds a major responsibility to their lives: the protection and care of a vulnerable human being.

The experience of being a parent so alters people that psychologist David Gutmann of Northwestern University sees it as a key to personality in the adult years.[15] Gutmann believes that parenthood changes women and men in predictable ways that evolved among our ancestors to ensure the survival of their offspring. Plunged into what Gutmann calls the "chronic emergency" of parenting, both partners become willing to surrender many of their personal goals in the interest of the child. Women develop sides of their personality that provide the child with emotional security, and fathers develop characteristics that make them providers and protectors. Such changes require women to suppress their aggressiveness and men to suppress their passive, dependent tendencies.

As Gutmann explains, "After children come, dedicated parents can never completely relax into self-absorption or self-indulgence. From then on, even rest becomes a nurse's sleep, the parent waiting for the child's cry or the alarm in the night. Both men and women respond to the parental emergency by instrumentalizing themselves to meet parental requirements. Thus young fathers become an extension of their hardened, functional tools and weapons. In this service, they tame the extremes of their nature, deploying aggression toward production, curbing passive tendencies, and generally accepting, even with good humor, the responsibilities and sacrifices that come with the productive stance. By the same token, young mothers divest themselves, quite decisively, of the aggressions that could put their vulnerable children at risk."[16]

Perhaps because they are the ones who bear — and usually care for — the children, women find developing all aspects of their dream a difficult task. According to Levinson, many feel faced with an "either/or" choice: either develop an occupational dream and put a family on hold, or else take a significant, but supporting, role in the dream created by a man.[17] Those who take the second path may also be in the labor force, but their jobs will not be so vital to their identity. The identity of young women like Julie Cugini is shaped by intimate relationships, and their self-esteem depends heavily on their husband's achievements.

Not all women feel compelled to choose. Some form a split dream, in which both occupation and family have equal weight.[18] These women's involvement in the family means that it may take them an extra decade or so to settle down in their careers. In fact, some women move into middle age before centering on a particular occupation. Most who succeed in their new work life have two things in common. One is a history of good school experiences. The other is a strong relationship with some person — a schoolmate, a spouse, a teacher, or some other adult who is caring and considerate and whose support enhances the person's feelings of self-worth.[19] Instead of seeing themselves as independent achievers in the world of work, these women see themselves as living out occupational and family lives in a particular kind of community, a community where love and work are intertwined.

"By the Time I'm Thirty"

A time comes when we begin to realize how much of our dream will become real and how much will melt away into the mists of "might have been" — a time when we understand how much of our personal narrative is fiction and how much is autobiography. Levinson believes that reality sets in at about age thirty, when men and women realize they are no longer preparing for life but living out the consequences of their choices. Levinson calls the process of working through this realization the "Age-Thirty Transition."[20] Some men respond by switching careers before it's too late, but those whose first choice has been a good one escape the doubts and self-searching and move into their thirties more committed to their occupations than ever. Most men emerge from the transition feeling that they have come of age, that they are truly adults whose stories have become real.

Whether they have established a career or remained centered on the home, women seem to go through the same transition. For them, age thirty is a time of shifting priorities. Many who have been deeply involved in home and family begin developing personal goals, while some who have been giving their best energies to their careers suddenly become concerned with marriage and the family.[21] Instead of reversing priorities, other women broaden their goals, adding the neglected part of the dream to their picture of the future.

Some researchers have found that the realities of everyday life force many young adults to develop a new way of thinking. Many of them gradually come to see that they are not objective viewers of reality, but interpreters of it. They discover that truth remains elusive; that every situation is full of ambiguities, uncertainties, and contradictions; that workable solutions require them to integrate conflicting information. This adult thinking has been called "postformal thought" to distinguish it from the "formal thought" that emerges in adolescence. The difference between the two shows most clearly when researchers ask adults in their twenties, thirties, and forties to solve the same untidy problems. One situation involves conflicting accounts of a visit to grandparents given by a teenage boy and his parents. Another concerns different versions of a decision about whether to end an unintentional pregnancy, as told by the man and the woman in question. In both instances, the very young adults were not surprised by discrepancies between the two accounts, but they seemed to feel that a neutral party could reach the "truth" of either situation. Adults who were past the age of thirty-five tried to reconcile the differences in the accounts. They separated the facts from the interpretations of the people involved, weighing the needs of each party.[22]

Postformal thought depends on emotional maturity as much as on the sort of intelligence measured by IQ tests. Age is no guarantee that it will develop: many middle-aged adults still think in black-and-white terms. Nor is youth an absolute bar to its development, for some adults in their early twenties can integrate conflicting viewpoints. In most people, the advance is fostered by confronting the developmental tasks of young adulthood.

The gradual emergence of adult thinking may lie behind a second and more realistic attempt to fit the dream to reality, an attempt based on better knowledge of the self and the world. Levinson calls this the "Settling Down" period. It comes after the age-thirty transition, when men (and perhaps women) decide what aspects of their lives are important, commit themselves to their choices, and structure their lives around them. They set about establishing themselves in their work, in their families, and in their communities. This gives their lives the stable structure they need to climb the ladder of occupational and personal success.

The period of settling down represents a second attempt to weave together a satisfying response to the agenda of love, work, and parenthood. Each of us goes about the task on a different schedule and in slightly different ways. When we reach our late thirties, some of us are happy with the place we've found and affirm the path that brought us there. As we remember our past, we organize it in ways that make our present selves, and the present state of our stories, seem inevitable.

Reality at Thirty-Seven

At thirty-seven, the Reverend Charles Stith seems comfortable with the path that has brought him to this point in his life. He is pastor of the 600-member Union United Methodist Chuch in Boston, and the uncle and guardian of Trey Edmondson, the young man who lost his mother at the age of twelve. Charles, whose hair is beginning to recede, wears rimless glasses above a neatly trimmed moustache. His measured words often fall into the cadence of the pulpit.

Charles grew up in an historically black section of St. Louis, Missouri, with his mother and a younger brother. "We probably qualified as poor in material things, but rich in terms of pride and concern for the black community," he says. "My mother and father were divorced when I was very young, and we grew up in the church. As long as we were living at home the standing rule was: you had to go to church. Like most kids, we played hooky a few times, but many of the positive things that happened to me happened as a result of the church."

Charles was a teenager during the civil rights movement, "when the giants of our nation were church people — the Martin Luther King, Juniors, the Andy Youngs, the Jesse Jacksons." These men were powerful role models for young Charles, but his choice to devote his life to the church came later. After starting junior college, he took time out to join a project building churches in the Kenyan countryside. There, he did some dreaming. "Kenya was a rich experience for me, a very fulfilling experience. During the long and beautiful nights, I had a lot of time for reflection. And it was then I made the decision to go into the ministry. I decided that the ministry would be the way in which I would seek fulfillment in my life and attempt to make a contribution to making this world a better place."

Charles returned from Kenya to finish junior college, then went on to Baker University, a Methodist school in predominantly white, rural Kansas. Getting an education there wasn't always easy; money was scarce and racial tensions were high. "It was during the hot'n'heavy days of the movement, and so the relationship between the black and white communities was adversarial. You saw that played out on campuses around the country, and Baker University, as isolated as it was, was really no different. I was president of the Black Student Union, constantly on the point and having to press the case day in and day out," recalls Charles.

"There was a guy there that was a dean of students — I shall never forget this because it confirmed something that's been essential to my ministry — and he had a rightly deserved reputation for being a rather racist character. We had a guest preacher at the school, and there was a point in his service where he asked folks to turn toward the person next to them and look them square in the eyes and say, 'Brother or sister in Jesus Christ, I love you.' And as providence would have it, at that precise moment I was standing next to this dean, and here we were, very awkward and tentative but caught up in the spirit. We turned towards each other and proclaimed our desire to love each other and break through those bonds that caused us to be separate. And the breakthrough was made.

"My last year of school, when finances were really tight, he saw me walking to campus one day. And he said, 'Charles, how you doing?' And I said, 'Well, I'm a little down, dean. I don't know how I'm gonna put my housing package together.' And he said, 'Come and see me in half an hour.' I came back to see him, and when I walked in the office he threw me a set of keys. They were keys to one of the houses that the university owned right off campus. It was a great house. I really appreciated that because, political stuff aside, he was responding out of his sense of humanness."

After graduating from Baker, Charles went to Atlanta to attend the Interdenominational Theological Seminary. Leaving Kansas was like stepping out of a pressure cooker. "I breathed a sigh of relief when I got to Atlanta. It was a predominantly black environment, and I was able to use that experience as seminary ought to be used. It was a time for reflection. I had the opportunity to explore all the parameters of my faith without having to feel defensive, without feeling the need to defend my very humanity."

At twenty-four, Charles began feeling another need. "It was during my last year of seminary. One day it struck me, 'I'm about to leave this place and I need a wife.' That inner clock starts to chime and you know there's something missing in your life. I said a prayer, 'Lord, You know the kind of woman I need in my life, and You know I'm not gonna press and I'm not gonna look under every rock and in every crook and cranny. I want You to put her right there so it is impossible for me to miss her.'"

Apparently, the Lord didn't waste much time. One evening, Charles and his best friend were going to a party when their car's exhaust system blew. "We had to double back to the campus and get the seminary truck that looked like one of these trucks from the Beverly Hillbillies from Hooterville. I mean, we were dressed to the nines and going to this yuppy-buppy party in a rusty, grimy pickup truck. Inside, I asked Deborah to dance and we had a very light but cheery conversation. At the end of the evening, I asked if she would mind my calling on her, and it wasn't two to three weeks before I appreciated that this was a very special person."

Deborah Prothrow was completing her undergraduate studies in mathematics at Spellman College, a small but distinguished college for black women. Not long after she and Charles began to date, they attended a concert that began with jazz, then switched to gospel and spirituals. As a song soared through the auditorium, something happened that altered the course of two lives. "I looked at Deborah, and there was a tear coming out of her eye. I said to myself, 'This woman is really spiritual, and not only is she spiritual but she is a United Methodist!' This was just too good to be true. When I proposed, she wouldn't help me at all. All she would say was, 'Okay, now what are you driving at?' Finally, I spit the words out: 'Will you marry me?'"

At the time, Deborah's thoughts were focused more on becoming a physician than on getting married. But she liked Charles, and something about their meeting seemed "providential" to her. The two of them graduated in June and married in August, just six months after they'd begun to date. As Charles began his career as a minister, Deborah entered Harvard Medical School. Children came somewhat sooner than expected. The first-born was Percy Roderick Michael Stith, now eight. "He's a Sunday child," explains Charles. "I had to miss church that morning to await his birth. One of my friends, another preacher, calls him 'The Reverend.' I was pleased in a fatherly sort of way when he was interviewed by one of the local papers and asked what he wanted to be, and he said, 'A preacher, like my daddy.'"

Charles and Deborah's second child came three years later. "Mary Mildred Butan Stith. Miss Mimi, as we call her, who's now five," says Charles. "Mimi's much more verbal, Percy's much more of the social animal. Percy started singing in the children's choir when he was a little over two years old. That just did not work at all for Mimi. I mean, she could not stay still. She wanted to pull the other kids, she wanted to climb on the altar rail. I mean the whole nine yards. But one of the great things about her

Charles Stith, thirty-seven, and family. "Everybody has a position to play, and if we all play our positions, it'll always be a winning team."

birth was appreciating in another way the beauty and dynamics of human personality. They're brother and sister, but they're different people."

Within two years of Mimi's birth, the Prothrow-Stith household had expanded to six. Twelve-year-old Trey became Charles and Deborah's responsibility when his mother died. Then Deborah's mother joined them. Mildred Prothrow had been alone in Texas, and once she retired from her teaching job, she moved to Boston. "It's been a good experience for the kids to have the opportunity to know their grandmother in an intimate way. They give her a run for her money, but she's a classic doting grandmother. She's been a great addition to our family. It's really helpful to have her there as the anchor. One of the ways we like to talk about our family is as a team. Everybody has a position to play, and if we all play our positions, it'll always be a winnng team. I'd say the past couple of years, she's probably gotten the most valuable player award. She's been a real stabilizing force. Plus, as the kids are not reluctant to say, 'She can cook!' We talk about what it was like eating in the Stith household B.G. and A.G. — Before Grandmother and After Grandmother."

The help that Mildred brought to the family has enabled Deborah and Charles to pursue independent careers. While raising three children, Deborah was able to complete her medical training, begin practicing as a physician, and then become commissioner of public health for the state of Massachusetts. Charles has settled into his ministry and is deeply involved in the Organization for New Equality, a national group dedicated to furthering civil rights and eliminating poverty. "I like pastoring my church. Somebody asked me, 'Don't you see yourself doing something else?' I said, 'Shoot, no!' I mean, now I've finally gotten this thing down right. I know how to do it. Why would I want to leave now?"

Nor would Charles consider leaving his marriage. "One of the things that makes this relationship work is that she gives a lot more than I do. I think she's a lot more tolerant of my idiosyncrasies than I am of hers. Like any relationship, we have those little things. I mean those points when you get pissed off about something. I mean, 'Why does she do that? She knows I don't like it. Why does she respond like that? Doesn't she know the kind of stuff I'm going through? She could be much more sensitive. I really don't have to take this. This is it.' And then you start thinking about all the issues relative to that, and it helps put the things that you're ticked off about into focus. So you get your apologies in order and you go on and live the rest of your life together.

"Like anybody, thoughts of living a life apart have crossed my mind, and I'm sure they've crossed Deborah's mind. If I ever got divorced, I couldn't see myself getting married to anybody else. 'Cause you know, I think in terms of marriage that I probably picked about the best I'm capable of picking, and was picked by about the best capable of picking me. So if this one didn't work out, maybe it would mean that marriage just wasn't for me. But I don't plan on going anywhere any time soon."

Besides, something essential is still alive in Charles and Deborah's marriage. "There are points when you say, after eleven years, 'Is it possible to still really feel this much in love with somebody?' It's kind of weird, because it's the same kind of feelings you had when you were in high school, dancing in the basement with the blue light to Smokey Robinson. Obviously, it's a much more mature relationship, but it's good to know that after a lot of years you can still feel that good about somebody that you're committed to spending the rest of your life with."

There have been rough spots in Charles Stith's adult life, and there have been shocks and disappointments, but his dream remains intact. The dream took shape in Kenya, Kansas, and Atlanta, but its roots go back further, to a wise and compassionate mother. "I can remember her saying again and again, 'You've been blessed with tremendous talent. A talent to talk to people and a capacity to care for people. You've got a responsibility to lead, and if you're gonna lead, you've got to get your own act together.' She instilled in us the insight that money and material things are nice, that we should work to have a better life than the generation before us and do what we can to make life better for the generation to come. But there was something in life that mattered more than material things, and it had to do with the kind of person you are, what you stand for.

"So I look back now, and, at thirty-seven, I'm thankful that I can provide more for my kids materially than my mother was able to provide for my brother and me. But I just pray that I can do half the job that my mother did instilling a sense of virtue in us, a commitment to that biblical reference that you find in Matthew: 'Whatever you've done for the least of these, my brethren, you've done it for me.' And if my children can embrace that and live it as I've tried in all earnestness to live it, then I can say that my job has been well done."

V

Middle Adulthood

13

THE BIOLOGICAL *The*

STORY OF MIDDLE *Midpoint*

ADULTHOOD

"I thought I got better as I got older. I found out that wasn't the case in a real hurry last year. After going twelve years in professional football and twelve years before that in amateur football without ever having surgery performed on me, the last two seasons of my career I went under the knife three times. It happened very quickly and without warning, and I began to ask myself, 'Is this age? Is this what's happening?' Because up until that moment, I'd never realized that I was getting older."

Until recently, thirty-seven-year-old Brian Sipe's life story was that of an athlete. "When I got into professional football, it was always one year at a time, one day at a time. I thought that if football didn't work out, I was just gonna be a student of the world. So here I am, really just a kid again, starting a course of study and hoping I'll be better the second time around." Brian is married and has three children — two daughters and an infant son. Handsome and reflective, he seems comfortable in his chinos and dark plaid shirt — comfortable, too, in the transition he is making.

Brian's life as an athlete began in San Diego, where the sea washes lazily on the sandy shore and the balmy, Southern California air seems to promise perpetual youth. From an early age he felt at home with the lights, the excitement, the roar of the crowd. At eleven, he played baseball on an all-star team that won the Little League World Series. "I remember being so excited, getting my first Little League hat. I was incredibly lucky. I figured

Brian Sipe, thirty-seven.
"Until that moment, I'd
never realized that I was
getting older."

that what every kid wanted to do was to go to Williamsport, Pennsylvania, and win the World Series, and by God, that's what we did. It was every kid's dream. At that point I figured that the world was my oyster and that everything was attainable.

"In reality, I think I was just blessed with an awful lot of athletic ability. I always got to be the kid who was choosing sides, not waiting to be chosen, so I learned about responsibility in that respect. I was also willing to accept discipline, willing to accept being knocked down a notch and know that it's okay, I'll survive it. I won't quit the job, I'll come right back and pick up where I was and go on to someplace better." Brian traces his acceptance of discipline to the strict rules of his childhood, imposed in equal measure by the nuns at his Catholic school and by his father.

Brian played three sports in high school; in his senior year, he was named San Diego's Player of the Year in football. He first attended a junior college, then went on to San Diego State to learn to be a passing quarterback. Brian devoted most of his energies to the gridiron; he felt he was in college to learn about life, not about books. When he found his math major boring, he shifted to telecommunications. During those years at San Diego State, he probably reached his physical prime.

Brian graduated in 1971 and began his professional career in obscurity. A late-round draft pick, he rode the bench for the Cleveland Browns during his early years in the National Football League. But once he got his chance, he became the starting quarterback and earned a reputation for last-minute heroics in the era when the Browns were known as the "Cardiac Kids." "There was no question of whether I was the team leader — either I was the team leader or I wasn't on the team." Back then, Brian's dark brown hair was longer and curlier than it is today. As he recalls those Sunday afternoons, it's clear that football has meant a lot to him.

"The game is just full of incredible highs. There are things that happen between people spontaneously that I don't believe can happen anywhere else except in the arena of sports. It's a psychic link between myself and another person under equal and yet completely different kinds of stress, responding identically to make something happen. Knowing that a linebacker's gonna cross in front of a receiver, and the receiver's gonna sense where that linebacker is and move off him, and I'm gonna throw a ball into a void where I've anticipated the receiver will move, and the ball will be *there* — you can't really explain how it happens. It just happens.

"The thing I find hardest to convey about the completion of a difficult pass is the absolute silence in which it's performed. It all happens without any noise. There's not a bit of noise. And the second that ball is caught, the place explodes. I think that's the way it's supposed to be. That's how this thing works: absolute focused energy. I'm gonna miss that a lot.

"I feel like I've been blessed with an opportunity to know myself in a way that a lot of people don't. Rather than having to constantly deal with externals, I was dealing with internals: fear, courage. These words are too trite. Football gave me the feeling of having somebody chasing me that really wanted to do me harm and using all that God gave me to preserve myself. The sense that I was being hunted and I could elude my hunter and do something his other prey couldn't do always fascinated me. It afforded incredible emotional highs and lows, unlike anything else I've experienced in life. It's an absolute magnification of all of your emotions, and yet right when you think you can't stand it, you have to be your calmest. When it's over with, you're drained. Some of the most euphoric feelings I ever had were after football games. The only important thing was for me to play well. I was just as happy to play well and lose as I was to play well and win. I'm confessing what I would never have confessed as an active player — that it was all right to play well and lose."

And yet, although it meant an end to glamor and adulation, Brian found the closing of his career a relief. "For so long, my time was measured by my career. By football, by what was important to football. I'm anxious to put it behind me, to no longer be known as a football player. I will always be proud of what I did, but don't judge me by what I've done in the past.

"In professional football I was constantly asked, 'What are you gonna do when it's over? What are you gonna do when it's over?' And I used to manufacture answers, because I thought that these people need to know that the quarterback of their football team has something else going. He's not just a dumb jock. In reality, I've always wanted to walk out of football and have the curtain come down and say, 'Okay, here's life. Here's life without football. It's been sports all my life, and here's a new life.' What a great opportunity! How many people have a chance to do that?"

Brian is making the most of his opportunity by becoming a student again and exploring the possibility of a career in architecture. "I find myself sitting at a drafting table, and the hours just fly by, and I can't think of anything I'd rather be doing," he says. This interest has roots in Brian's past. "My father grew up on an Indian reservation and always had a sense of space — of where he was and what was keeping the sun and rain off of him. And I learned that awareness from him. I remember riding in the car once across a very hot desert and looking at a building that he was going to outfit with shutters. I remember being very aware of space — this memory is so vivid — and of how the shutters were gonna affect the warmth and the sunlight in the house. When I was in college, I was always looking for my calling in life and didn't realize that architecture was probably it."

The influence of Brian's mother on what he might now become has been equally strong. "My mother was — and is — a very beautiful woman. She was a fashion model the whole time I was growing up. She had a strong sense of things that flatter the human body, of activity and personality that flatter the human soul. My mother loved to take a chance, and she still does, and I love her for that and my kids love her for that. It drives my wife crazy, 'cause the kids are always on the brink of disaster, but they're always having fun when Grandma's around. She had a lot to do with what I was able to accomplish professionally, and I know that her sense of beauty will have an effect on my future career — if I continue in architecture.

"I keep talking about architecture. At this stage in my life, I'm almost afraid to say, 'Yes, I want to be an architect,' because I almost don't want to peg myself into a hole yet. I like a little uncertainty in my life right now, and I know there's time. Still, I don't like floating around. I don't like getting up in the morning and not being certain what I'm gonna do with my time. I feel a lot of anxiety and stress in my life that I think I inherited from my father. My father died of cancer at the age of sixty, and I'm convinced the cancer was a result of the tremendous amount of stress in his life. He was a very introspective, proud man, but it ended up killing him. I'm still trying to learn from that.

"My wife says I'm a perfectionist. I think that's a source of a lot of the stress I feel. There are so many things I want to do, and true to form for a

*"It's been sports all my
life, and here's a new life.
What a great
opportunity!"*

perfectionist, I delay doing them until I know I can do them exactly right.
Then I feel stress over the fact that those endeavors are never realized.

"I need some regimentation in my life. Football gave me that regimentation. Except for the Sunday mornings when I thought I was gonna puke in
my eggs because of stress, football was a relatively calm time for me, because
I always knew what I was supposed to be doing and where I was supposed to
be. Probably wouldn't have been a bad career serviceman. But, boy, I feel
like I'm armed with some great tools now. I got a good woman by my side,
and I got three great kids, and . . . just nothing's stopping me."

On the Decline

At thirty-seven, Brian Sipe stands in an interesting statistical position.
In the United States today, thirty-seven is the midpoint of life for the typical man — the age at which the years he has lived equal the years he has
left to live. That's three years earlier than the midpoint for the typical
woman, which comes at forty.[1] Even though women reach their physical
prime a few years before men do, men arrive at the halfway mark earlier
because of their shorter lives. The midpoint is also the age at which the
number of men in our population equals the number of women. In the first
half of life, men outnumber women, but in the second half — because of
greater male vulnerability — the uneven balance between the sexes is
reversed.

Because injuries have ended Brian's career as a professional athlete, the
halfway mark brings him to a dramatic change of seasons. He senses that a
curtain has come down on one phase of his life and is about to rise on

another. He is certain about what he has accomplished, knows that he is losing something he will never regain, and is still excited — and apprehensive — about the future. For those of us who are not professional athletes, the biological harbingers of age do not end a season so sharply. They are so small and develop so slowly that they go unnoticed for years. But after a while they accumulate, and one day they make us realize that there are more yesterdays in our lives than tomorrows. We realize we have crossed the midpoint into the season we call middle age.

The Biological Clock does not program a series of events to mark the beginning of middle adulthood, the way puberty announces the onset of adolescence. Our bodies have been aging since their early twenties, but so imperceptibly that it takes decades for any decline to become apparent. Holding a book ever farther from the eyes may keep people from noticing that their lenses are stiffening, but one day, usually during the forties, arms become too short and reading glasses become necessary. Those who already wear glasses find they need bifocals for close work. The heart may work as well as it ever did when people go about their daily affairs, but under the stress of exercise it uses less oxygen, beats more slowly, and pumps less blood through the body.[2] Similar unseen changes have been going on in the lungs, so that no matter how hard they try, forty-year-olds draw less air into their lungs in a single breath than they did at twenty. And they leave more old air in the lungs after each exhalation.[3]

Most of our body's systems follow similar patterns of decline. The changes are magnified in activities that require several organ systems to work together. The individual muscles in Brian Sipe's throwing arm are as strong as they ever were, but when they have to work together in a task, they're probably about 90 percent as efficient as they were when he entered young adulthood.[4] That's the difference between a professional quarterback and a healthy man who can no longer make the team. But data showing progressive change in body functions have to be taken with a grain of caution, because they refer to *average* declines. Hidden in those averages are people with silent, undiagnosed disease, people who smoke and drink to excess, people who eat unwisely, and people who lead sedentary lives. So we don't know how much of the average decline is caused by normal aging, how much by hidden disease, and how much by misuse of the body.

Just a few years ago, physicians believed that our hearts started to become less efficient at about age twenty. With each passing year, the volume of blood pumped each minute declined another 1 percent. That figure had been established by checking hundreds of healthy people at all ages.

But when researchers supervising the Baltimore Longitudinal Study of Aging put their seemingly healthy subjects on a treadmill and tested their hearts under stress, they discovered that many of them weren't so healthy after all. A surprising number showed hidden cardiovascular disease, a condition that cannot be detected by electrocardiograms taken at rest. When those with hidden disease were eliminated from the study, resting heart rates remained unchanged into extreme old age, as did the volume of blood pumped by the heart in each minute.[5]

As we pass through adulthood, the condition of our bodies increasingly reflects the choices we've made over the years. At Temple University, psychologist Diana Woodruff-Pak estimates that factors under our control in middle age can add as many as twenty years to our lives.[6] Diet and exercise play a role, but so does the nature of our personality and the social environment in which we find ourselves.

The foods in the typical American diet can shorten life by upping the chances of hypertension, heart attack, diabetes, and cancer. That's because most of us eat so much saturated fat and so little fiber. Saturated fat, our major source of dietary cholesterol, has been implicated in heart disease, and fiber is associated with reduced risks. Although cholesterol is vital to cell function, too much of it spells trouble. It may even bear some responsibility for the development of cancer of the pancreas, colon, and rectum.[7] Following a prudent, high-fiber diet that derives 70 percent of its calories from grains, beans, fruits, and vegetables (and the rest from animal foods that are low in fat) can lower cholesterol levels by 10 to 15 percent. And with every drop of 1 percent in cholesterol levels, the chances of a heart attack drop from 2 to 4 percent.[8]

One effect of too much saturated fat is a high rate of obese adults.[9] Obesity is dangerous because of the physiological consequences that accompany the unwanted fat: an increase in the body's own production of cholesterol, higher levels of cholesterol in the blood, an increase in blood pressure, the development of heart disease, increased chance of a stroke, and the onset of diabetes. In fact, the typical diabetes of middle age often disappears when people bring their weight back to normal.[10]

Essentially, the kind of diet that seems best for us is one that takes heed of our hunting-and-gathering past. The same is true of levels of exercise. Our Biological Clock evolved in an environment of nearly constant walking, far different from the sedentary conditions most of us experience today. Lack of activity inflicts such damage on the body that many researchers have come to believe that it may be a major cause of physical decline. Most of the deterioration we normally attribute to age can be brought about in healthy young men by simply putting them to bed for three weeks.[11] Driving to work, sitting at a desk, and then relaxing in front of the TV at night may be a prescription for getting old — or dying young. People whose jobs involve physical activity, those who exercise briskly at least three times a week, and those who keep on with their jobs after others retire seem to live a few extra years.

But personality makes a difference, too. Brian Sipe's belief that stress may have played a role in his father's early death is supported by research. It seems that contented, calm, easygoing people tend to live longer than average. So do flexible people and those who avoid risks. Aggressive, hostile, or rigid people, as well as those who delight in taking risks, may pay for their stressful lives with a shorter life span.[12]

The effects of stress are often amplified by social isolation. For years, researchers have known that the death rate climbs among men and women who have recently been widowed or divorced. Men seem especially vulnerable to loss.[13] Now a growing body of evidence indicates that, for all of us, the lack of social relationships exerts as powerful an effect on health as does smoking. At any age, people with few social ties have higher death rates from all causes, even after researchers allow for sex, education, employment status, exercise, cholesterol levels, blood pressure, circulatory and respiratory function, and smoking habits.[14] The death rate climbs steadily as social relationships dwindle, with mortality rates running from two to four times as high among the totally isolated as among those who are married, have extended ties with family and friends, and are active in social groups. The deadly effects of social isolation are as true for rats, mice, and goats as they are for humans, because companionship seems to reduce anxiety and buffers the ravages of stress.[15]

All this research demonstrates that we have some control over the speed at which we age during our middle years. The food we eat, the activities we choose, and the efforts we make to reach out to others may hasten our physical decline — or slow it down dramatically — and exert a profound effect on our next season of life.

Sexual-Reproductive Changes

Among the physical changes that occur in middle adulthood are those that involve the reproductive system and the capacity for sexual pleasure. Individuals such as Brian Sipe who stand at the threshold of this season will find the nature of their sexuality transformed over the next two decades of their life. For men, the changes will occur slowly, gradually, almost imperceptibly. But for women, the transformation is quite different. It includes a dramatic change in what they have come to regard as the normal physical state of their adulthood — the cessation of menstrual cycling.

During their forties, men may notice little change in sexual responsiveness. But in their fifties, a basic biological pattern alters. The pituitary gland, which takes its orders from the brain, changes the way it releases hormones. Instead of sending out regular pulses of hormones, it switches to a steady release, so that the hormones flow through the blood in a continual, slow stream. In response, the concentration of testosterone in the blood no longer rises and falls in a daily rhythm, peaking in the early mornings and ebbing late in the evening. Instead, it remains all day at the same level — roughly that found in young men during the afternoon.[16]

During middle age, almost every phase of a man's sexual response slows down. His mind becomes excited long before his body does, so that it takes longer for the penis to become erect — even when he's in a situation he finds highly arousing. It takes him longer to climax, and he must wait longer before he can become aroused again. But that's not all bad news. Most middle-aged men have better control over ejaculation than they did in their youth, a development that's welcomed not only by the men but by their partners as well.

As men progress into middle age, they become increasingly aware of these changes. A naturally sluggish erection may make a man uneasy and fearful that he will soon be unable to respond at all. When a worried man has sex under the influence of one of the many things that can prevent an erection (anger, fatigue, boredom, anxiety, guilt, or alcohol), he's primed for disappointment. He may interpret an isolated incident as proof that he's over the hill and swear off sex, or become so anxious that future failures are inevitable. He's now a victim of "performance anxiety," a major cause of impotence. Psychologist and sex therapist Bernie Zilbergeld says the problem lies not in the fifty-year-old man's body but in his mind. "Fifty-year-old penises don't feel or act exactly the way twenty-year-old penises do. They can still do their jobs and provide much pleasure to the man and his partner, as long as the fantasy ideal of penises that are hard as steel and always jumping about doesn't get in the way. What needs adjusting in such cases is the standards and expectations, not the penis."[17]

Along with a slowdown in sexual responsiveness comes a diminished ability to father children. Sperm become less lively, which means that they are less likely to swim fast and far enough to encounter an egg before they die. Yet most men remain fertile throughout middle age: almost 70 percent of those in their fifties have live sperm in their semen (as do 48 percent of those in their seventies).[18] In contrast, women experience menopause, an event that brings a discrete close to their capacity to bear children.

The exact cause of menopause remains a mystery. As women travel through their forties, their menstrual cycle lengthens, and their periods become shorter and less predictable. Finally, when women are about fifty, their periods stop altogether. Timing genes may be responsible, or perhaps it's simply a side effect of the body's general aging.

However the process begins, once it gets underway the ovaries seem to become hard of hearing — perhaps because their supply of immature eggs has dropped below a critical point. The "deaf" ovaries begin missing signals from the pituitary gland that tell them it's time to mature and release an egg. So the pituitary gland steps up its hormonal signals, in effect screaming at the ovaries to get busy. Now the woman's hormonal balance has shifted, and the changes of menopause begin. Eventually, the ovaries shut down, stopping not only the release of eggs, but also the production of estrogen. A woman's only source of estrogen becomes the adrenal glands, which manufacture male hormones that the body can convert into estrogen.

Some researchers believe that the process is even more complicated, and that the brain is also involved in the signal mixup.[19] The pituitary gland gets its orders from the brain, and as women age the orders may come in a way that confuses the pituitary. Instead of arriving in pulses every ninety minutes, the hormonal signals come in a slow, steady stream, as they do in older men. This may so bewilder the pituitary that it stops releasing the hormone that tells the ovaries to get busy. The body's organs interact so quickly that no one has been able to figure out whether the brain or the ovaries start the process.

The most common symptoms of menopause are hot flashes and sweating, which afflict about eight out of ten women. Without any warning, a sudden wave of heat rises from their waist to the top of their head. As the hot flash subsides, they may begin to shiver. When the sensation occurs at night, women may wake up sweating heavily. Although these reactions are annoying, they're not painful. One woman who was going through menopause explained how she dealt with it. "At times you do feel terribly warm. I would sit and feel the water on my head, and wonder how red I looked. But I wouldn't worry about it, because it is a natural thing, and why get worried about it? I remember one time, in the kitchen, I had a terrific hot flash . . . I went to look at myself in the mirror. I didn't even look red, so I thought, 'All right . . . the next time I'll just sit there, and who will notice? And if someone notices, I won't even care.'"[20]

Hot flashes have a simple biological explanation. Each time the pituitary notices that estrogen levels are low, it sends out a surge of ovary-stimulating hormones. The pituitary gets so excited that its agitation spreads to a nearby part of the brain that controls body temperature. Fooled into thinking that the body is cold, the brain orders blood vessels to dilate. A rush of blood courses beneath the skin, setting off a wave of heat.[21]

Most women take menopause in stride, with no more than 15 percent developing serious physical problems. Many associated symptoms — headaches, mild depression, feeling tired, irritability, an aching neck, and the like — are probably not directly related to hormonal changes. But many women who are going through menopause seem to attribute every fleeting symptom of mind or body to the "change of life." Psychologists used to do the same thing. They fretted over middle-aged women's tendency to develop "involutional melancholia"— a form of depression that lay in wait for those who couldn't handle the simultaneous impact of a new hormone balance, the loss of youth, and the end of the ability to bear children. Yet studies have found no rise in the rate of depression during the menopausal years.[22] Instead of looking for involutional melancholia, psychologists now see menopause as a transition in a woman's life that causes problems only when other stresses have piled up to the point where they overwhelm her defenses.

Many young women can repeat stories they have heard about menopause ending a woman's femininity, destroying her interest in sex, and sometimes driving her insane. Yet even women who enter menopause with apprehension usually find that its terrors are highly exaggerated. Once the process is complete, women feel better, more confident, and freer than they have for years. Fears that menopause would dampen or destroy their sex lives prove groundless. Estrogen has no effect on a woman's sexual desire, so she feels as sexy as ever. Once women reach their late fifties, they may not lubricate as quickly or as profusely as they once did, but any discomfort can be alleviated with artificial lubricants. Some women discover that they enjoy intercourse more than they ever have before, mainly because they no longer have to worry about becoming pregnant.

An active sex life may even slow aging of the sex organs. Rutgers University researchers have found that regular intercourse — once or twice a week — keeps the vagina pliable and young after menopause.[23] But in women who give up sexual activity, the vagina shrinks and the vaginal opening becomes less elastic.

Many of the changes in the sexual-reproductive system in middle age set the stage for a new "season of eros" — a lengthy period in which conception is no longer possible and in which couples discover a new kind of sexual pleasure. In the United States today, many couples initiate this period through surgical sterilization: vasectomy, tubal ligation, or hysterectomy. More than half of couples between the ages of thirty-five and forty-four have opted for this method of birth control.[24] According to June Reinisch, director of Indiana University's Kinsey Institute, freedom from the fear of pregnancy — and emptying the nest of grown children — makes a difference. "Starting in the early forties," she says, "many couples report that this is the best time of their marriage — the most sensual, the most sexual. They rediscover each other after the children have left, and they find that their sex life is better and more exciting than it was even when they were young people."[25]

This doesn't mean that intercourse becomes more frequent in middle age — studies, in fact, show the reverse — but it does mean that the nature of sexuality changes. "The first language of sexuality is very instinctive and youth-oriented," says psychiatrist Robert Butler of New York's Mount Sinai School of Medicine. "It can be quite exploratory, even explosive, and centered on performance. But with time, there's an accumulation of skill and experience, so that the kind of sexuality that emerges later in life — in the forties, fifties, and sixties — may be oriented more toward nurturing a relationship. We may not be so selfish, simply interested in our own organs, but more sensitive to the partner. We may become concerned with the broader aspect of sensory experience and not only the experience of intercourse itself."[26]

The Mystery of Postreproductive Life

With menopause behind them, women have the potential to live another fifty years, though today the average woman lives another thirty. Some scientists scratch their heads when they contemplate this final stretch of life, the second major period in which reproduction is impossible. If it's difficult to unravel the story of how childhood came to be — and how it came to be so long — it's almost impossible to solve the mystery of postreproductive life.

The reason is that biological events associated with the decline of the body are fundamentally different from those associated with its growth. Events concerned with growth occur before reproduction, when genetic changes can be passed on to descendants and affect the course of evolution. Events concerned with decline occur after reproduction, when the transmission of genetic change is no longer possible. Perhaps evolution shapes late-life events by setting them up early in the life cycle, before the reproduction deadline. Perhaps it shapes them through a few males who live a long time and remain fertile to the end. No one knows for sure. But it's clear that the beginning of life is under far more genetic control than the end. Once we pass the season of fertility, the Biological Clock quiets down.

It's against this background that scientists ask why we live so long once we have produced our young.

Some believe that evolution may not have had the time, the need, or the mechanism to set up a genetic program that would kill us off quickly. For most of human history, predators, accidents, and disease eliminated so many of us that various human families had no chance to outbreed their resources and little chance to outlast their reproductive years. The bones in a thousand-year-old Native American burial mound in northern Ohio, not far from the shores of Lake Erie, contain not a single skeleton as old as sixty. Nearly half the people in this group died before they were fifteen years old, and only about a third survived to the age of thirty.[27] The oldest bones in this ancient graveyard belonged to individuals in their fifties. In hunter-gatherer societies, as in those throughout most of recorded history, relatively few women lived long enough to experience menopause. A thousand years ago, in the societies of medieval Europe, only 25 to 30 percent may have done so.[28]

Thus, it may not have been worth evolution's effort to devise a way to prevent a lengthy postreproductive life. Left on our own, our bodies gradually break down and we begin to dwindle away. Menopause may be a sign of this breakdown, a signal that the system in charge of maintenance and repair can no longer do its job.

But other scientists are not so sure that postmenopausal life is an accident. Once a woman gets past forty, childbirth becomes more hazardous, and a woman who dies in labor leaves not only her baby but her older children without the years of care that human young must have. Unless mothers survive at least a decade past menopause, their children may not live long enough to reproduce. In hindsight, it may have been "wise" for the Biological Clock to end fertility while a woman still had time to raise her youngest to adulthood.

Being around to bring up your own children is only part of the postmenopausal story; being around to help your children's children is also important. Among macaques, having a high-ranking grandmother is as good for a young monkey's fortunes as having a grandfather with a flourishing business is for a human child. The grandmother macaque's social position places her grandchild several rungs above its peers on the dominance ladder. And among langurs, grandmothers will defend a young grandchild against the attacks of a new dominant male even though the infant's own mother will not.[29] Since this sort of assistance may mean the difference between life and death for young monkeys, it helps pass along the grandmothers' genes. If having grandmothers is adaptive for monkeys, it is probably even more adaptive for humans, a species whose young need protection for many more years.

Whether postreproductive life is built into the genetic program of the Biological Clock, or whether it is simply a result of that program running out, our species has turned it into an advantage. "Why do we have elders?" asks David Gutmann. "I think it goes back to this crucial business of human parenting. Our offspring are terribly vulnerable and require a lot of dedicated parenting. And parenting is such a demanding role that it requires a lot of backup."[30]

Gutmann believes that our species has devised two kinds of support for parents. One is an extended system of kin ready to come to the aid of the beleaguered parent. The other is culture — a system of meaning. "Elders are very important in manning these backup systems. In traditional settings, we find the older woman — the grandmother — organizing and administering the extended family. And we find the older men being the guarantors of culture. They are the linkage to myth and to the gods on which the sense of culture is ultimately based. So the typical role of men and women in the postparental years is to serve the parenting enterprise and make it work. We find that as elders drop out of their postparental roles, as we lose the extended family, as we lose the sense of an organized meaning-giving culture, then parenting is at risk and our kids are at risk."[31]

Since the time of hunter-gatherers, grandparents have been the instruments of cultural transmission. In a world without written language, they serve as the memory of the tribe, passing along the "right way" of doing things, from rearing children and healing the sick to making arrows and approaching the gods.[32] Just how important an elder can be is shown by the story of Paralji, an aged Australian aborigine. In 1943, there was a terrible drought in Australia. Across the interior of that land, members of the aboriginal hunter-gatherer tribes were dying of thirst. Old Paralji recalled songs he had learned as a child that described the location of water. Following landmarks contained in the songs, he took his band of twenty people on a trek deep into the desert. After traveling more than 200 miles along trails he had never seen, he came to a series of water holes. The holes still held water, as the songs said they would, and Paralji's band survived until the rains came.[33] When survival depends on culture, the postreproductive years no longer seem so mysterious. It is as critical for elders to have a period of life in which to pass learning on as it is for children to have a special period in which to acquire it.

We will surely come to know more about the involvement of the Biological Clock in the events of later life. But we already have a good idea of what purpose this stage of life serves. It gives us time to tell stories, stories that give meaning to life and sometimes make survival possible. And it gives us time to see a second generation of descendants through their vulnerable years.

What Good Are Grandmothers?

"Two years ago, I remember thinking, 'What am I doing living?' I just felt like a number had been done on me, and I was doing a number on myself. What good was I? I couldn't have any more babies. You know, everybody's gotta look svelte, slim, sharp, sleek, sexy, and I was none of those. I also felt very alone. I kept reaching out for somebody in the family just to talk to me — not to talk *at* me or be patronizing.

"That's one experience I would never want to happen again. I would never want it to happen to anybody. Because being fifty-seven isn't terrible, and not having any more children isn't the worst thing in the world."

Harriet Lyons is an apple-cheeked black woman with a deep hearty laugh and a solid body. She has been many things in her life — a mother of six, a social activist, a single parent on welfare, a domestic, a secretary to an Episcopal priest, a language therapist, and a mental health worker, to name just a few. She has had enough ups and down for several lives, but two years ago she endured one of her bleakest periods. Called on to take care of her grandaughter, Jamillah Johnson, she found that she had nothing to give. She was out of work and had just been evicted from her home. She couldn't take care of herself, much less be a good grandmother.

Harriet grew up in Boston, and she's quick to point out that her grandparents were also raised in that city, so her roots reach deep into northern soil. This is an important point with her, because many people assume that all blacks were born in the South and came north after World War II. Harriet's grandfather Coleman worked for a Boston electric company. "He was a robust, hardy man who was sometimes called the 'black genius of State Street.' Came here from Virginia and settled in the town of Milton, bought up and developed that whole corner where they lived, near the town hall." Harriet's father "had the intelligence and wit of my grandfather, but he was more gentle." Her mother was one of the first black women to graduate from high school, "a city gal with big, pretty eyes, who liked a good time. She was an in-town girl and he was an out-of-town boy. But they met and fell in love and lived together and loved together and fought together and ultimately became very good friends."

When Harriet was only thirteen, her beautiful, wide-eyed mother became crippled with arthritis, and Harriet had to take care of the house, her invalid mother, and her two younger brothers. "It was a rough time. I had to grow up and I had to grow up fast. I knew how to cook and clean, but I had to learn how to make decisions for others. And it became a way of life with me. I had to put my brothers first. I had to put my father first. I got up in the morning and I prepared the breakfast and I walked a couple of miles to school and I came back home and I took care of my mother. She couldn't walk at all. I had to carry her in my arms and take her to the bathroom and do all those things. And I did that for almost a year and a half."

The condition of Harriet's mother became so severe that she was put in a nursing home. Harriet continued to run the household until, about five years later, her mother returned home. "When she came back, we had quite a struggle. My answer to that was to get married, because I felt as though she would be happier if I were not in the house. It was a lousy way to enter marriage, but when you're nineteen you don't think about what's fair, you think about what you can and cannot live with."

So Harriet became Mrs. Philip Jackson; during her twenties and early thirties she had six children. "At that point in my life I had no great ambitions that I really remember. I never wanted to be just a housewife, but I wanted to be a good mother. That was first." Harriet was determined that her children get the best education possible, so she joined other parents and worked out ways to get their children bused to better schools. The struggle absorbed a great deal of her energy, and all the while her marriage was crumbling. "He was a nice man but we were totally incompatible. We didn't look with the same eyes or feel with the same feelings. Half the time he didn't know what I was talking about, and the other half of the time he put me to sleep. It's the truth. Not all marriages are made in heaven, but in all fairness I don't think I always worked that hard at making mine work. My children were the people I wanted to see succeed."

When the marriage broke up, Harriet's father was angry. "He was angry about the divorce, and he was angry about a lot of things. And I was proud, and I thought I was right. So we had a Mexican stand-off for about three years — until my mother finally got tired of the whole thing. She just said,

'This is your daughter and she needs your help. Whether she's right or wrong is unimportant.' And for the first time my father came and spent the night at my house, and we were friends. And then he began to help a lot financially. But being the good person that he was, he never went overboard. My father would help when there was a real emergency, but the bottom line was he wanted you to figure your own way out. And anything he could do to give you the tools, he would do. I loved that old man.

"He was the patriarch. Everybody referred to him as Grampa. He was strict and stern, with a great sense of humor, a tremendous heart, and a poker face. He used to keep those grandchildren in line. He'd say, 'Don't you bounce around here like that, little girl. Sit down in the chair.' And they'd sit. They're very blessed children to have had that kind of man. He was our anchor. He really was. He would disagree with me, but he would tell the children, 'That's your mother, and you wouldn't be where you are if it wasn't for your mother. And don't you ever forget it for one minute.'"

The support her father provided when she needed it as a parent was enormously important to Harriet. A single mother approaching forty, she had to scrape to make a living. "I didn't know how to type. I didn't want to do domestic work, but I wound up doing it. And for three years we lived on welfare. I worked in the evenings, moonlighted. As soon as the children came in from school, I ran over to a little nursing home that wasn't too far from the house. The children would sit down and do their homework, and I could look out from the nursing home and keep an eye on the house."

Eventually Harriet found work as secretary to an Episcopal priest. She began taking courses in business and in writing. At times she worked as many as three jobs. Money was scarce, but the kids never realized how little there was. "Anything that was legal, we did it. All of my children worked. They got part-time jobs after school. My oldest son sold newspapers and shined shoes. Shoveled everybody's walk but ours. At fourteen years of age, everybody automatically got their social security number, and they did better than I in finding jobs."

In her mid-forties, Harriet married for the second time. Her husband was Dr. Ivory Lyons, an economist who taught at a Boston university. Before long, he decided that he wanted to teach at a black college in the South, so Harriet and her younger children moved with him to Columbia, South Carolina. There, Harriet worked first with the Urban League and then as a language therapist in the public schools. But five years later, she was divorced and back in Boston. Although her children were getting tired of her constant moving, that didn't stop her from going to Delaware to take a job with the Mental Health Association. She was in her early fifties.

"I still had my two younger girls with me. All the others, they'd grown up and married or said, 'Mother's crazy. We're tired of her changing her curtains and running up and down the eastern seacoast. We'll just visit her, but we're gonna put down our own roots.' So they did, but the two little girls stuck with me. I call 'em my babies. Great, great people."

When funding for her job was cut, Harriet worked in a variety of church and community programs and even tried catering. But once her youngest child finished school, she returned to Boston and got a job as a school bus monitor. At that point, she took Jamillah into her home. "My little granddaughter came into my life. With all the good things, like everybody else, we all have something in our hearts. My oldest daughter has been addicted to drugs off and on for a number of years. Beautiful girl, so much talent, but I wish she would just know it. Anyway, Jamillah is her daughter."

When the school year ended, so did Harriet's job as bus monitor. She ran out of money and lost her apartment. Her furniture had to go into storage and eventually was lost when Harriet couldn't pay the storage charges. Over the summer, she lived with a daughter in Texas but couldn't stand the blazing heat. "I came back to Boston, and I didn't know what I was gonna do. I had lost everything. By not having a job, I had lost my furniture that was in storage, my pots and pans for forty years. I loved them dearly — great old iron skillets. Kids' albums, little mementos, curls I cut from my oldest son's head, some of my daughters' ribbons they had won in school. I had literally lost everything.

"I felt so miserable. I think part of it was that I could look around and see that I not only couldn't do anything for my children and Jamillah, I couldn't do anything for myself."

That was two years ago, when Harriet was fifty-seven. Then came another of the opportunities that seem to have marked her life. "I was visiting my daughter-in-law, and we were reading the paper. She said, 'We're gonna have to do something about you.' And I said, 'Yeah, but what?' She said, 'Well, for starters you're gonna answer this ad: Fifty-five and over, come see us, we have jobs.' She dialed the number, handed me the phone, and said, 'Speak.' In two weeks I had a job."

Harriet was hired by the Bank of Boston and has been working steadily ever since. "Sometimes I feel as though I've got one foot on a banana peel and the other foot out the door. You know, the pressures get high, but I say, 'So what?' I came here two years ago, I can go somewhere else. The best thing of all is the fear is gone. Just wiped away."

After a life of constant movement, Harriet seems to have come home to

Harriet Lyons, fifty-nine.
"I guess in a lot of ways,
I'm coming to where I
wanted to be in the first
place."

her roots. She's no less spirited than before, and just as headstrong, but she has gained a certain wisdom. Best of all, her job has enabled her to assume the role in the family that her father held a generation before. She has become a strong matriarch and a good grandmother to Jamillah. "A lot of young people don't know it, but parents need them just as much as they need their parents. And it's ironic when you kind of flounder around and your children get angry with you, they don't always see you as being just another human being. We're all imperfect people, you know? That's one of the advantages of getting older. I can look back at my mistakes and not shudder and run away from them but just say, 'Well, I did it. But I won't do it again.'

"I have some goals I want to keep. I might even want to go back in business again. Have to get a little car so Jamillah and I can tootle around town on weekends. But I feel as though I have something to offer. I know I do. My grandchildren call me up now, asking questions, and my opinion means something to them. My children and I are beginning to talk. We have conversations. It's a good feeling. They care about me and I care about them. We've begun to be friends, and that's very important. I guess in a lot of ways, I'm coming to where I wanted to be in the first place.

"I feel good about myself. Got a lot of things I need to polish up on, a lot of edges that need to be kind of fine-tuned down. Still got a lot of loose ends that need to be tied up. Some debts I owe that I will pay back. And not just financial debts. There are some emotional debts I owe. But I know I can do it. That's the best part of all. I know I can do it."

14

THE SOCIAL

STORY OF MIDDLE

ADULTHOOD

The Baby Boom Is Forty

"One of my primary reasons for going back to school was that I knew my children would eventually be leaving the nest. I think in my subconscious I always prepared for that. I wanted to fill the void."

Kathleen Casey Wilkins is forty, at the midpoint of life for women. Like Brian Sipe, she has the feeling that a curtain has come down on the first half of her life, and that the stage is being set for something very different in the second. In a few months, the older of her two daughters will be going away to college, and the younger won't be far behind. But Kathy's nest will be emptier than that of other families whose children have left. This past October, she and her husband separated, and they're in the process of getting a divorce.

Kathy is a youthful-looking forty. Her high-school yearbook describes her as "pretty and peppy," and you can still see the teenager in the adult woman. Kathy watches her diet and keeps in shape with a regimen of aerobics, tennis, and walking. She has noticed physical changes in herself — it's harder to read the fine print, she says, and it takes "ten times more energy" to lose five pounds. She worries about heart disease on both sides of her family. But, she says, "I don't feel middle-aged at all. I think age is relative." In many ways, her experiences are typical of women of her generation. One thing makes her stand out: she was born on January 1, 1946, one second after midnight. She is the first of America's 76 million baby boomers.

Kathy grew up as the middle child in an Irish Catholic family in Philadelphia, and went to Catholic schools. Her fondest memories are of childhood summers on the Jersey shore and dancing with teenage friends on Dick Clark's "American Bandstand." During her high-school years, she "wasn't necessarily the best of students," channeling her energies instead into band, drama, and dating. After graduation, she trained as an X-ray technician at a hospital near her home. "At that time a lot of women were directed into three fields: nursing, teaching, or social work," she recalls. "While I was in training, I met my husband, who was an intern. A month after we were married, he went to Vietnam for a year, and I went back to work. When he returned, we started our family. He chose to go into an orthopedic residency program, and I stayed home and took care of the children."

Married at twenty, Kathy gave birth to two daughters, Beth and Jennifer, by the time she was twenty-five. "My children never had a full-time father because of his profession. He was away from home ninety percent of the time." Through nineteen years of marriage, Kathy and Charlie just "grew apart," she says. "Divorce was a difficult decision for me, because I felt very strongly about commitment. But after nineteen years, I decided that it was just not a workable situation. The separation was a mutual agreement, but no matter who makes the decision, you still come out feeling inadequate. Something went wrong. You failed. And a sadness comes over you."

Kathy had already been preparing for an independent life. When she was twenty-seven, she began taking community college courses and eventually settled on a degree in nutrition and food management. "I started out as a part-time student. Then, when the children were a little older, I went back full time." She received her bachelor's degree in home economics just three years ago, at the age of thirty-seven.

"After I finished my degree, I started to look for a job. That's when I realized that, no matter how good your credentials are, you need actual paid working experience, and the only way to start in any job is from the bottom up. So I took a part-time job as a restaurant hostess — not necessarily for monetary gain, but to get experience so I could work my way up."

Since her separation, Kathy has resolved to further her education and career. "I decided to do something positive that I would enjoy. Something to keep my mind moving, to meet other people. There's no one without problems, and seeing other people going through different stages of suffering would get me out of my own tendency to self-pity. And so I started my MBA at Saint Joseph's University.

Kathleen Casey Wilkins, forty. "I don't think that at twenty I liked myself, but at forty, I do."

"I'm not going to pursue the degree to the point where I'm causing myself as much stress as I did in the undergraduate program. I'm just taking my time with it. I think a lot of the boomers are overachievers and, at this point, have burned themselves out. We fracture ourselves. I really am very aware of that, and I don't want to do that to myself again. When I was in my undergraduate program, I took on too much, with a household and everything else. And that was difficult for me. I don't want to make the same mistake again."

Kathy's older daughter, Beth, has chosen to attend Saint Joseph's, too. The campus in Philadelphia is just half an hour from the Wilkins' home in New Jersey. "When she chose the school, I said to her, 'Would you rather I be in a graduate program elsewhere?' Because I knew this was her domain. And she said, 'Oh, I think I'll like it. I'll rather like seeing you and meeting you for dinner one night a week.' So I said, 'Well, I'd enjoy that too.' I was really happy with that. I feel our relationship will grow and be better than it is now.

"I'm lucky to have two very open, sweet, good children, and I'm not just saying that 'cause every other mother says that about her child. I think they are, and I think they have a good set of values. I worry about this generation because I think the boomer generation has given them so much materially, and I wonder about their discretion and motivation. Maybe it won't hurt in the long run. I think in some instances it has. Because the boomers did all the achieving, and most of them indulged their children.

"In my parents' generation, it was a luxury to go to college. They wanted so much for us, they kept telling us we could do anything we wanted. And I think in essence the boomers have done that." Kathy's father was a machinist, her mother a homemaker. They lived, she says, in a society less materialistic than today's. "A lot of people today are holding down two jobs, some because they have to, others because — I hate to say this — because they want those extras. In our parents' generation, they had one job and one mortgage, and they were comfortable with that."

Kathy sees more anxiety in her own generation. "We had so many major changes. We had civil rights. We had the hippie movement, the feminist movement, assassinations. We had to adapt to change all the time. There were many issues I had difficulty with. Burning draft cards . . . I had a husband in Vietnam, and I didn't want him there any more than anybody else, but we certainly weren't backing the American soldier. So I had difficulty with that. Women's lib . . . I think women's lib was in many ways very positive and helped women in the job force. On the other side, it took women out of the home and in a way was responsible — I'm not going to say totally responsible — for the breakup of the family unit. I wonder if the next generation is going to want stronger relationships, or maybe be more selective about their relationships. Maybe marry later. I think that's good. Because at twenty-five or thirty, you know more what you want. I don't think that was so in our generation, when we got married at twenty and twenty-one."

Kathy has reaped the benefits of what she sees as her generation's ambition. The Wilkins home is paid for, and she and her husband have investments in a New Jersey vacation home and a Florida condominium. Negotiations over alimony and a property settlement have been amicable so far. "I was married to a physician, and physicians make very good incomes. So at this point I don't have to worry about putting a roof over my head and probably won't have to later. But I will have to worry about an incoming salary." Kathy works part-time as a supervisor in charge of a banquet facility, overseeing a staff of nearly twenty waiters and waitresses. "I get a lot of satisfaction and self-achievement from working. I enjoy working with people, helping motivate them, and getting the job done. My field is hotel-restaurant management. My future, I would hope, would be somewhere in middle management. I'm looking for a daytime job, because even though this job is part time, it's nights and weekends, which conflicts with my children's schedule. Right now, they need me to be home, even if they are on their own to a certain extent.

"I don't feel that my age should be detrimental to potential employment. I feel that, at forty, I have more to offer than any twenty-two-year-old going into a major corporation, because I can bring not only an expertise that I went back and studied for, I can bring life experience.

"I think what's more important to me now than my master's degree are the values I've had growing up through the years — values that can never be attained, just strived for. Being a better person, more helpful with other people. Putting things in perspective. Having the time to think of what's really important in life. Certainly, I would like deep and caring relationships. Because I think the only thing we leave in life when we die are the relationships that we had on this earth.

"I value relationships — all kinds of relationships. I value the relationships I have with my girlfriends, but I don't think there's anything better than a good healthy relationship with a spouse. Certainly I would never be afraid to make another commitment, but I don't want to think in terms of that right now. This is a time for me to regroup after the separation and to deal with me. Until I totally deal with me and what I've gone through, it wouldn't be fair to be in another relationship. I'm not afraid of being alone. I'm really kind of enjoying my aloneness — being able to make my own decisions and being totally responsible for me and my two children. I feel like I have Kathleen Casey back again, and I kind of like that feeling.

"If somebody told me twenty years ago I would be what I am today, I'd say, 'Oh, my goodness!' But I'm glad I am who I am today. I don't think that at twenty I liked myself, but at forty, I do."

Middle Age and the Baby Boom

When Kathleen Casey was born shortly after midnight on January 1, 1946, her delivery began the post–World War II flood of births that became a tidal wave, producing a new citizen every seven seconds. By the time the wave ebbed in 1964, the United States had 76 million baby boomers. The boomers were the first generation to grow up to the flickering light of TV, and the first to enter adolescence to the sounds of rock music. They saw the first man walk on the moon, provided the soldiers who fought in Vietnam, and gave us love-ins, happenings, and Woodstock. As they enter each season of life, they change it — simply because there are so many of them.

Kathy is a healthy forty, with a youthful appearance. She is typical of her generation, according to sociologist Gunhild Hagestad of Northwestern University. "Not long ago, the average forty-year-old woman looked like the sixty-year-old woman of today," says Hagestad. "The baby boomers are the first generation who grew up without the ravages of childhood diseases. They had vaccinations and antibiotics. It's going to be interesting to see how they age, because it's possible that some of what we thought were the effects of aging were just the long-term effects of disease in child-hood."[1]

The first members of the baby boom entered early adulthood in the mid-1960s, the last in the mid-'80s. As adolescents and young adults, they bore the brunt of the tremendous changes in family life that occurred in those decades. Baby boomers had fewer children than their parents, squeezed their arrival into fewer years, divorced more quickly, and remarried sooner.[2] The women became working mothers in record numbers; many of the men became absent fathers in the wake of divorce. Adult baby boomers took to living together before marriage and delayed the age at which couples first married and had children. They helped create the separate stage of life called youth.

Many in the later part of the boom had trouble getting started financially because the economy could not absorb their numbers. But those who came along early — especially women like Kathy Wilkins — experienced a different kind of shock. "Those born in the 1940s really have one foot in one era and the other foot in another era," says Hagestad. "And I sometimes wonder if their high divorce rate might, in part, reflect the fact that they have been caught in the crossfires of history. They spent their childhood years with fairly traditional notions about what it meant to be a girl. And then came the sixties, when everything was turned on its head."[3] Like women of a former era, Kathy ended her education with a high-school diploma, married young, and had children in her early twenties. Like contemporary women, she is working and not only returning to school but attending the same university that her daughter will. Women like Kathy, suggests Hagestad, have much more in common with their daughters than they had with their mothers.

Those women are beginning to enter "middle age," a social season of life created in this century. In 1900, the average woman was about fifty-five years old when her last child left home. Chances were good that she was already a widow, but if her husband was still living, they were unlikely to have more than a year or two together before he died.[4] By 1970, a corresponding couple enjoyed thirteen years of the empty nest before one of them died — and the stage of middle age had come into being. The term referred originally to the period between the beginning of the empty nest and the onset of old age.

Yet the boundaries of this season have always been nebulous. Today, it makes little sense to mark its beginning with the departure of children from home. That would work for someone such as Kathy Wilkins, who finished

her childbearing in her early twenties and will probably be in her early forties when her last child moves out. She will have more years of the empty
nest than she had raising children. But when a couple has a child in their
late thirties, the usual season of middle age will be spent in child-rearing
tasks that others struggled with during the season of early adulthood.

Paradoxically, even though women reach the midpoint of their lives later than men, they see themselves as "middle-aged" sooner. Men tend to
agree with them.[5] Perhaps that's because the fading of youth has harsher
social consequences for women than for men. Most of us, whether male or
female, believe that age makes men — but not women — more attractive.[6]

The end point of middle age is as vague as its beginning. Today, most of
us say the season ends at sixty-five, the official age of retirement. But not
everyone retires, either because they haven't been working for pay or
because they want — or need — to keep working. And many people retire
before age sixty-five. Despite the uncertainty of its boundaries, however,
middle adulthood is lasting longer than ever before. In the next century,
we might define it as the third quarter of life, stretching from age fifty to
seventy-five.[7] Right now, however, society seems to be heading in a different direction, creating a stage for the "young-old" to fill the gap between
middle adulthood and our traditional notion of late adulthood.

Few of us march in lockstep in the second half of life. Everyone knows
that a six-year-old ought to be in the first grade of school, but few would
agree on precisely what a forty-six- or fifty-six-year-old ought to be doing.
"Our society is becoming accustomed to the twenty-eight-year-old mayor,
the thirty-year-old college president, the thirty-five-year-old grandmother,
the fifty-year-old retiree, the sixty-five-year-old father of a preschooler, and
the seventy-year-old student, and even the eighty-five-year-old mother caring for a sixty-five-year-old son," observes developmentalist Bernice
Neugarten. We're becoming, she says, an "age-irrelevant" society — at
least in the second half of life, when age norms are less compelling.[8] At that
time the Social Clock follows the lead of the Biological Clock and quiets
down, allowing the Psychological Clock to dominate.

Kathleen Casey Wilkins is part of a youthful, health-conscious generation that may change our definition of when women and men enter and
leave middle adulthood. Already, her Psychological Clock is getting louder.
"I don't feel middle-aged at all," she says. "I think age is relative." Kathy
may be an indication of what to expect from the baby boomers as they cross
the midpoint of their lives.

A Matrilineal Tilt

As baby boomers enter middle adulthood, they may find that the female lineage in their families has become more pronounced. In some ways, an informal matriarchy has always been the rule — not with regard to the inheritance of wealth, but certainly with regard to kinkeeping. Women have traditionally taken care of "business" not only on their side of the family but also on their husbands'. In many societies, their managerial role strengthens in the postreproductive years, when older men turn their attention to the keeping of culture. Harriet Lyons is a good example of the middle-aged woman as matriarch.

For a number of reasons, families today appear to be moving even further in Harriet's direction. Mothers' lines are getting stronger, fathers' weaker. Among adolescents and young adults, this trend has been fed by the increase in births to unmarried women, who form their families without the investment of males. In the later years, it's affected by sheer survival rates. As the gender gap in life expectancy has widened in this century, the ranks of older men have been depleted. That leaves older women to be the links between a family's generations.

But the "matrilineal tilt" is primarily an outgrowth of swollen divorce rates. When families break apart, it's usually the father who moves away and the mother who maintains the home base for the children. In 1960, 8 percent of children in the United States were living with only their mother; by 1988, the figure had grown to 21 percent. The percentage living only with their father increased slightly in the same period, but by 1988 it had reached only 3 percent.[9] The U.S. Census Bureau has estimated that 60 percent of the children born in the last five years will spend some time living with only one parent by the time they are eighteen. That parent will most likely be the mother.[10]

The mother-headed, single-parent family bolsters women's roles as caregiver, provider of emotional support, and family breadwinner. At the same time, men's family roles weaken. If the government steps in to furnish financial support, the man's role as provider is further diminished, if not eliminated. Even if he continues to supply child support, the absent father is not there to share a child's joys and sorrows, provide emotional stability, and encourage academic success. Often, he has formed a bond with a different woman and a different family.

Over the years, these changes in the family will reach up and down the generational chain. If Kathy Wilkins's family is typical, she can expect her daughters to grow closer to her side of the family and more distant from her husband's. During the stress that accompanies divorce, maternal grandparents are usually the ones who step in with emotional support and financial aid — providing "postreproductive backup." In about a third of all separations, the daughter and her children come home to live until the initial turmoil has subsided. In the meantime, many children of divorced parents lose touch with their paternal grandparents, usually because these children gradually lose contact with their father. Sometimes the relationship is disrupted because the mother or father moves away, remarries, or takes a new job that makes contact difficult. But on occasion, the mother simply refuses to let her ex-husband's parents see their grandchildren.

Even in intact families, daughters keep closer ties to their families than sons do. In middle age, daughters are more likely than sons to find themselves in the "life-cycle squeeze" — taking care of children and grandchildren with one hand, and parents and even grandparents with the other. This squeeze has always gripped some people, but long lives are making it ever more common — and changing the source of the pressure. This is the first time in history that the average married couple has had more living parents than children.[11]

Even if they work outside the home, women tend to be caught in the squeeze far more than men. Hagestad, who has been studying relationships across the generations, notes that employed daughters, but not sons, continue to find time to care for aging parents — even those of their husbands.[12] If a parent becomes disabled, the middle-aged woman faces some disagreeable choices: quit her job, hire someone to care for the parent, or place the parent in a nursing home. If a woman has been looking forward to an empty nest, she may find that a parent's (or a grandchild's) needs put a long-anticipated return to school or work on hold.

Even though a family's financial resources generally remain with fathers after a divorce, ties in our society seem to be strengthening along maternal lines. Kathy Wilkins will not experience the poverty of many single mothers, but in a decade or two she may well find herself in the same matriarchal position as they.

A Career of Grandparenting

Whether Kathy experiences a matrilineal tilt in her family will depend in part on whether she becomes a grandparent. If she does, she probably will be a youthful grandmother, because her daughters were born so early in her adult years. It all depends on when Beth and Jennifer have children — if they have them at all.

In 1900, most people became grandparents at about the same age as they do now — in their forties and fifties. But grandparenthood was not the distinct phase of life that it is today. Because births were spread out, many mothers and fathers were still active parents at the time they became grandparents. (It was not at all unusual for children to have aunts and uncles who were a few years older — or even younger — than themselves.) Only since World War II has grandparenthood become a stage in the life cycle separate and apart from parenting. In Kathy's case, it will be quite separate. Her childbearing was compressed into only three years, so she probably will live in the empty nest for some time before a daughter makes her a grandmother.

Because of this century's increase in longevity, most of us will have lengthy "careers" in grandparenting, just as we do in work or marriage. Some of us will spend as much as half our lives in that career. Never before have grandparents and grandchildren been alive together through so many of the seasons of life.

A few women begin their grandparenting careers "too soon." That's what sociologist Linda Burton of Pennsylvania State University discovered when she studied women who became grandmothers at an early age — one as young as twenty-five. The untimely transition of these women was the result of two generations of teenage pregnancy, and it threw their lives out of synchrony. As teenage mothers, they had been forced into adult status before they had a clear sense of who they were or what their life course might be. Then, their life tasks still unsettled, they were pushed into a middle-aged role. At a time when they were trying to develop intimate relationships with men, they were asked to provide care for a baby who wasn't their own. They resented a role that made them seem "old." Among the grandmothers studied by Burton, 83 percent of those under the age of forty rejected their role. But the vast majority of new grandmothers over forty felt that grandparenthood had arrived "on time."[13]

According to sociologist Andrew Cherlin, the career of the "on-time" grandparent normally moves through three phases. The first, and by most accounts the best, begins with the birth of the grandchild, when grandparents establish a close emotional bond with the child. "We asked our grandparents what the favorite age of their grandchildren was," says Cherlin. "The most common answer was the preschool years. The second most common answer was six to twelve."[14] One grandparent called the early years the "fat" part of grandparenting.

When the grandchild reaches adolescence, the relationship moves into its second phase. Most adolescents need to establish independence — from grandparents as well as parents. The bond becomes more distant, as there's less for grandparents to do and as the games, romping, and snuggling cease. Now grandparents' rewards come in indirect forms: pride in their grandchild's accomplishments and the enjoyment of occasional companionship.

In the final phase, which begins when the grandchild becomes an adult, the bond remains warm, but contact generally slackens as grandchildren establish their own families and build careers. By the time grandchildren reach midlife, their grandparents are entering extreme old age. At that point, says Cherlin, they often switch roles, and the grandchild often provides support to elderly grandparents.

Not only has long life brought phases to the grandparental career, but it has also introduced many of us to an entirely new role: great-grandparenting. By the time they are sixty-five, at least four out of every ten Americans are great-grandparents. Their role is different: you're a grandparent, all right, but less so. "Great-grandparents are almost never involved in a hands-on way in their great-grandchildren's lives," says Cherlin. "For one reason, there are too many layers of family between them and the great-grandchildren. For another, most people don't become great-grandparents until they're very old. By that time, many great-grandparents aren't interested in helping out as much as when they were younger. Although they love their great-grandchildren, they usually don't play much of a role beyond that of a valued and loving elderly figure."[15]

When we look to the past, we tend to romanticize relationships between grandparents and their grandchildren. Fifty or a hundred years ago, when a grandparent played a major part in a grandchild's life, it was usually because some calamity had thrown the grandparent into the role of surrogate parent. Perhaps one of the grandchild's parents had died or had a serious illness such as consumption. Or perhaps incomes were so low that the families were forced to share a house. The intense grandparental relationships of song and story were usually the silver lining of some family tragedy.

In the past, grandparents often had plenty to say about how their grandchildren were being raised. But today, says Cherlin, there's a strong "norm of noninterference" that says parenting should be left to parents. "One of the strongest feelings of everybody we talked to was that they had to be careful not to interfere. They had to bite their tongue. They had to hold back. I think the norm of noninterference has gotten stronger because we're all more independent of each other than we used to be. This means that grandparents are trying to balance two very different wishes. One is a desire for autonomy. The other is a desire to have a strong role in the family. And it's not easy to do both."

Today's grandparents are a diverse lot. They range in age from their twenties to their hundreds. Some of their grandchildren are infants; some are close to retirement. A few of us are even grandparents and grandchildren at the same time. But as a group, grandparents are better off physically and financially than they have ever been. And, Cherlin points out, the ratio of grandparents to grandchildren is changing. "If anything, I think grandparents' role in the family may increase in importance, just because elderly people are doing so well economically. At the same time, there are fewer grandchildren for grandparents to spend their time with, which means that the average grandparent has more resources and more time and fewer grandchildren to devote those resources and time to. I don't think we'll see any kind of regular direct economic support. But I think we'll increasingly see grandparents providing funds for big-ticket items like orthodonture, college tuition, or home payments. And I think we'll see grandparents continuing to be important symbols of love and family continuity for their grandchildren."[16]

One Life, One Career?

Kathy Wilkins's career as a grandmother probably will be more orderly than her career as a worker. Already, she's been an X-ray technician, a homemaker, a restaurant hostess, and a supervisor of a banquet facility. She returned to school once to get a bachelor's degree and a second time to begin a master's, and she still has half of her work life ahead of her. Kathy's history is far more typical of today's worker, female or male, than is her physician husband's. Only a small fraction of the labor force — usually professionals, skilled craftpersons, or administrators — experience the career continuity that he has. Today, only rare people, especially in the United States, stay in one job for life.

One demographer has predicted that baby boomers will average about ten different jobs in their lifetime.[17] And while job change is more prevalent among younger workers, between 1965 and 1970 nearly a third of middle-aged U.S. men and women in their forties and fifties changed not just their job, but their occupation — the kind of work they do.[18] That rate of change is almost certainly higher today.

For women, the rate of participation in the labor force has grown steadily in this century. Its pattern has changed as well. At first, the few women who worked did so only once in their lives: before they married and had children. Once they left the labor force to become a wife or mother, they did not return. During World War II, when the demand for workers was great, women entered the labor force in substantial numbers, and many continued to work after the war. These women created a twice-in-a-lifetime pattern of work — once before child-rearing, and once after. This pattern held into the late 1960s, when baby boomers began a profile of nearly continuous employment. During the 1970s and 80s, they returned to work sooner and sooner after each of their children was born.[19]

Many women currently in middle age fall into the twice-in-a-lifetime category. Like Kathy Wilkins, they worked, took time off to raise a family, then re-entered the labor force. Along the way, a number of them returned to school. "Programs of continuing education got their start in the 1960s," says sociologist Alice Rossi. "The students who went in droves to those programs were women in their forties. But with each passing decade, the returning woman is a younger woman because she's been withdrawn from employment for a shorter period of time." Once they begin to work, returning students will surprise employers, says Rossi. "I think employers have to learn a bit more about how much more output they get from someone in their forties or fifties who's newly come to a field, compared with someone who's been in that field for years and years. Someone who comes in fresh could make contributions in ten years equal to what others have made in forty."[20]

Sometimes the income a returning women brings to a household enables a husband suffering from burnout to make a career change of his own. But often middle-aged men are forced to make a change because of factors beyond their control — corporate layoffs, for example. Stephen Lazarus of the University of Chicago Business School has seen their reaction. "A great many of them felt they had a social contract with their corporation," he says. "Simply stated, it was that if they performed well, their employment would continue. Suddenly, they find that contract doesn't exist, and one of the basic premises on which they built their lives turns out to be false." Many in the baby boom, says Lazarus, will find some of their basic premises challenged. In the next decade, their crowded ranks will mean fewer chances for promotion, pressure from younger people behind them, and a reluctance of older people ahead of them to make room. "That forty-year-old is in for a very rude awakening."[21]

Many blue-collar workers have already suffered through that awakening.

With the weakening of unions and the closing of steel, automobile, and other industrial plants across the country, unemployment has become a bitter fact of life for them. Starting in the late 1970s, the United States changed in less than a decade from an economy in which blue-collar workers outnumbered professional, technical, and managerial workers by 30 percent to one in which the work force was almost evenly divided.[22] More than a third of the 250,000 steelworkers who lost their jobs in Pittsburgh are men in middle adulthood, and the best guess is that fewer than half of these older men have found new full-time jobs.[23] It's people like these who suffer the most: workers in their late forties or fifties, with limited training who feel unable to relocate to another community. "They are men who have built strong expectations in almost a linear way," says Hagestad. "You work hard, you build security, and then you rest on your laurels and enjoy the fruits of your labor. And suddenly, one day, all of that is gone. It could happen at any age, but it's devastating in middle age, because it's very hard to rebuild — especially for a man who has little or no formal training."[24]

When we are unexpectedly thrown out of work, we lose more than a job. Because we define ourselves in terms of our work — we *are* what we *do* — we lose our identity and purpose. A counselor who directs a New Jersey program for unemployed workers says that many of the men he sees go through a grieving process, in which they question their self-esteem and wonder if they can ever qualify for another position.[25] Researchers have discovered that, among such men, wife beating and child abuse escalate.[26] Stress isn't the only explanation for the rise in family violence. Unemployed men often find that their status within the family drops, and violence seems in part to be the father's attempt to show that he is still boss, despite his diminished position. But other factors may be just as important.[27] Because he spends more time at home, he has more opportunity to cross swords with other family members. If the kids misbehave while he's around, it's up to him to dispense the discipline. The demands for discipline also increase; because all family members feel the economic pressures, what would once have been a squabble may escalate into a full-scale battle.

The U.S. economy is changing so rapidly — and we're living so long — that it's difficult to find lifetime security, much less lifetime satisfaction, in any single job. Perhaps in our work, as in our lives, we have to think in terms of seasons. Not one career for one life, but several careers, each in its own time, each with its own sense of purpose. From this point of view, nothing can be more damaging than ending one career of employment with no way of beginning the next.

Matt Nort, fifty-two.
"The dream is
gone — probably
forever."

"The Dream Is Gone"

Matt Nort is a fifty-two-year-old unemployed steelworker who knows he has become obsolete. "The dream is gone — probably forever," he says. "And it seems like it tears you apart. It's just disintegrating away. You look alongside the river banks . . . there's all flat ground. There used to be a big scrap pile there where steel and iron used to be melted and used over again, processed. That's all leveled off. Many a time I pass through and just happen to see it. It's hard to visualize it's not there anymore. And even today, I still think of the mill."

Matt has a broad forehead, thinning hair that's slicked down and parted on the side, and the strong, square hands of a working man. He probably weighs more now than he did when he was on the job. He's married, and his two children are still in school.

Life is nothing like Matt expected it to be. He grew up in southside Pittsburgh, the son of a brewery worker and grandson of a steelworker, an altar boy who used to get his hair pulled by the nuns when he wouldn't study. "I was a wiry kid. I was always into the rough sports — baseball, football, hockey. Baseball's what I used to like a lot. Play that day in and day out. I got into mischief and stuff. Got into trouble once, up around 24th Street, around the railroad. They used to have detectives placed there, and one time I set the railroad on fire a bit."

From parochial elementary school, Matt went to a vocational high school, where he did his best work in the machine shop. "I seemed to like to work in the shop more than I did the academic. I'm sorry for it now, but I played hooky a lot. But I always liked to work. Always. I remember in the summertime when I used to pick up various jobs, I worked on a beer truck.

I was making about a buck-and-a-half an hour, which wasn't bad money at that time. I did a lot of shoveling. I'd shovel snow off pavements. At the time they used to have coal stoves, and I used to shovel coal and haul people's ashes and different things like that to make a buck.

"And then one particular day when I was in eleventh grade, I skipped classes and was in town with a couple of my friends. I happened to look at the unemployment office there, and it said you might be eligible for so many weeks of benefits. I went into the office and sure enough I was qualified. But the woman there, she sent me a letter to pick up this job over here at Clark Teaberry gum. When she got me the job, I figured, well, she called my bluff. And I figured I'm gonna take the job, and I'll let on I'm going to school and go to work instead — which I done for a while. Naturally, the principal got wind of it, and they called up home and told my dad about it. So this one day I'm comin' home from work and swingin' my books and stuff, 'cause I used to have a friend who gave them to me. My dad, he says to me, 'How was work?' I was shocked. So then he laid the ball down right there. He says, 'Son, you're choosin' one thing. Either work or go to school.' He says, 'School's your best,' because in my age group a lot of kids, what they would do is take jobs and drop out of school, and then give up the job and be bummin' on the corners. And my dad didn't care for this."

It was a turning point in Matt's life. He chose to drop out of school and continue in the chewing gum factory, where his job was to adjust the machinery so that gum flowed properly and came out the right size. He played some semi-professional baseball at the time and was good enough to get a tryout with the St. Louis Cardinals. At one of his evening ball games, Matt met his wife Gerry. But they couldn't marry right away, because when Matt was just nineteen his fifty-seven-year-old father died of a heart attack, leaving Matt responsible for the support of his mother. The death destroyed one of Matt's boyhood dreams.

"I remember the day he died. I was coming home from work in my car and just made the bend at 24th Street where I lived, and here I seen them carrying my dad out. I knew it was my dad 'cause he was a big man. I was so upset I ran into a pole with my car. I always thought there would be a day when me and him could go across the street and have a beer. I'd buy him my first beer when I hit twenty-one. That's what I always wanted. We lived across the street from this place — it's a friendly tavern — and my dad used to go over, used to always stand on the corner and that. And I always thought, 'Well, maybe I could pal around with him,' but this dream never came true.

"He was a jolly guy, my dad. Always kidding around, you know, to make somebody laugh. He worked all his life for the Duquesne Brewery. During the beer war, he didn't cross the picket line. He stayed out. And some of the scabs, they got the jobs. He was fortunate, he got his job back. But he didn't get his original job — daylight. What he had to do was go to the bottom again, even though he had more time than the scabs. I think a lot of this tore him down, but he kept the worries behind him. He hid it a lot.

"I remember when I was a catcher and had a team, my dad went out and bought me my whole catcher's outfit. I had it for the longest time, and then I gave it to my nephew. My dad was the kind, he could never give me a whippin' because he didn't want to get . . . he used to take a walk and cool off. He'd just take a walk around the block and come stand on the sewer lid where he used to stand always, and he was all right. Whatever problems he had, this is what he done."

About a year after his father died, Matt married the girl he had met while playing ball. He and Gerry eventually became the parents of two daughters, Tammy and Kelly. He worked at the gum factory for about ten years. "Then Philip Morris bought 'em out and went to Richmond, and that job was gone." The year, Matt recalls, was 1964.

It didn't take Matt long to get a job at J and L Steel. One of the general labor gang, his job was to clean out the old open-hearth furnaces. It was hot, dangerous work. Sometimes the furnaces scorched the crew's special wooden shoes until they began to burn. Gradually, Matt moved into other jobs at the mill — pipe fitter, machinist, crane operator, welder, helper at the blast furnace. Whatever the work, Matt relished it. He was happy to be a steelworker; he loved hard, physical labor, loved breaking into a sweat near the mill's coke ovens. "Many a time when I got home, boy, was I sore! But after you take a nice hot shower and relax, you freshen up again."

The 1970s — Matt's late thirties and early forties — were good years. "We were workin' six days them years — steady daylight. And then all of a sudden, it was shut down. I got laid off in December of 'seventy-nine. When we left, they told us, 'Oh, it'll just be a couple weeks, you'll be back.' But it didn't materialize. I was on lay-off for about two or three months, and I coulda stayed 'cause I had coverage and everything. But I went down to the unemployment office one day, and I asked the receptionist, 'Is there any kind of work they got to do?' I know some ways I was dumb for goin' back, but I just wanted to be workin'. When I called my friends up, they says, 'You got all them benefits, why you wanna work?' I just wanted to."

For the next four or five years, Matt worked on and off in the mills. But the day came when they closed their doors for good, and it took him a long time to accept that fact. For the last two years, he has been struggling to support his family with a series of jobs that pay no more than four or five dollars an hour. But most of the time he "lays around" and "gets depressed," he says. "You wake up, you feel broken down, you feel weak. And then sometimes you get a little irritable with the kids, you know, at times."

Matt worries about this, and he has noted a change in the family atmosphere, a change he attributes to the fact that his children no longer see him getting up every day and going off to work. He knows that enforced idleness drags a man down and strains family relations. But his worries are more for the kids than for himself. "I'm to the point now that when I go into town and I buy myself something, I feel guilty that I'm hurting the kids. They're the ones, you know. I'd starve before anything . . . I just want to see them have it.

"I always thought, living in America, we had the dream that you could have a house, car, stuff, and that there. Not extravagant. Something where you could live to your older age and enjoy life without the stress. But they say the American dream went away.

"I remember when I was workin' back in the seventies, gasoline was so high, but I had the money. Now I have to put five dollars in just to get me runnin'. Sometimes I run out of gas on the road, you know, I can't fill the tank up. Like I says, everything's just tore apart. You worked hard all your life, and it's all taken from you. It's just like you take a king or a queen and rip 'em from their throne. What do they got?

"I even had a time I was thinkin' of suicide. I did one time, I did. I told my wife, and she says, 'Ahh, what would that prove?' I figured that's a coward's way. Many a time I was thinking if God would take me in my sleep, but then I figured, 'Hey, I still want to see these kids.' And I want to see them get to the regular age where they can take care of themselves. And I just thought to myself, 'Well, I'm gonna have to bear with it, you know.' And I say a few prayers and things happen."

His wife's paycheck and steadying influence have helped Matt weather his years of unemployment. "She knows things bother me and stuff, so she does a lot of things herself. A lot of times I come home, she has things changed around. She's always kept herself busy, and she tells me to keep myself occupied. Well, I do, but sometimes I'm not as steady 'cause I got things on my mind. I try to repair somethin', I start shakin', and I . . . nerves and tension and whatever. I try to do what I have to do. But, like I said, she's been a big inspiration to me. She keeps the family goin'."

Matt Nort grew up believing that jobs would always be there for every-

Matt's wife, Gerry. "She's been a big inspiration to me. She keeps the family goin'."

one who was willing to work. He believed that if he worked hard, he would build his security and then be able to relax and enjoy the fruits of his labor. Now his belief is gone.

"I hope some of these big congressmen and senators or whatever, they learn from this. I mean, just don't deal with people as numbers. We're human beings. They can send a man up onto the moon and different stuff, they ought to be able to study things more carefully. My dad told me work or go to school, but I was not gonna be a bum on the street. And I chose the hard work in the mill, and now it's gone from me. I hope some of this stuff comes into these leaders' brains and they say, 'Hey, this guy might be right. We're gonna sit down and try to study it carefully.'

"I just hope for the best. That's about all I have is the hope. I figure I'm back where I started out. I'm doing the same thing, but I'm in a lot different circumstances. I have a lot of different bills, and I'm a lot older, where it's hard for me to cope. I'm at the age now, ten more years and I should be out to the pasture. Now in my mellow years, I should be relaxing and having everything. But it just doesn't work that way. It's not that I'm not willing to give it a try — and try and try. Just to have somebody give me the chance — that's all I want. The chance."

15

THE PSYCHOLOGICAL *Time Lived,*

STORY OF MIDDLE *Time Left*

ADULTHOOD

There's a festive mood on the campus of Wheelock College as Daniel Cheever strolls down the street, pausing under a cluster of bright balloons to greet a smiling alumnus. Dan is president of Wheelock, a teacher-training institution in Boston, and he's on his way to a celebration of the college's centennial. He is a member of the establishment and he looks it: clean-cut features, good haircut, light gray suit, buttoned-down shirt, red tie. For him, middle adulthood is a time of fulfillment, a time to reap the personal and professional harvest he sowed and cultivated during the season of early adulthood. At forty-five, Dan seems barely thirty. His hair is dark and curly, and only faint wrinkles at the corners of his eyes betray the passage of time.

One of the day's events is the dedication of a new administration building. Dan's speech is stirring. "The one thing which makes life worth living is to serve a cause," he says, "and the greatest cause that can be served is childhood education. Thirteen million children live in poverty here in America, which is still the wealthiest country in the world. Thirteen million children. I think that's where we at Wheelock come in."

In the summer, Dan, his wife, and their two children spend a lot of time at the family's house on Buzzards Bay. He loves being there. "My uncle Zeke and his wife sold us the land where we built our house. He was my godfather, and I had a very fond and close relationship with him. He called me Danny Boy. He told me that when he was a boy, he loved the cove, too, and used to go there and hunt around and see birds and animals. It was a special place for him, and it always has been for me. I'll always be grateful to both of them for making it possible for us to build our own house here."

The Cheevers have been in this country for a long time. The original Ezekiel Cheever came to the Massachusetts Bay Colony in the 1630s, little more than ten years after the Pilgrims came ashore at Plymouth, a few miles to the south. Ezekiel was a teacher, and through the centuries there have been many teachers in the Cheever family. "We have a very strong sense of family," says Dan. "We know who our ancestors were and what they did, and we have letters and books and portraits that are very much a part of our family life. But you have to realize that they're also insignificant in the present and important only as having partly defined you. You've got to make your own way in the world."

Dan's first memories foretell a theme in his life story — the importance of having a home and his struggle as a young adult to get out from the shadow of his father and become his own person. "One of my earliest memories is of moving from Washington to our new house. I was about three or four. This was right after World War II, and my father was coming back to Cambridge to resume an academic career that had been interrupted by the war. I remember sitting in the back seat of our Chevrolet and waiting and waiting and waiting and asking, 'Is this it? Is this it?' And finally driving down the little street, and the door opening, and my pushing the seat forward to slip out from behind my father's back and stand on the sidewalk and look at our new house."

This moment in Dan's life is linked with a sequence of events that began with the death of his mother from leukemia only a week after his twelfth birthday. "Looking back, I realize that some of my strong feelings about having a home and a place of my own stem from, in quite rapid succession, losing my mother, moving, and being sent away to boarding school. I don't mean I was sent away in the sense that I was unwilling to go. It was what I had always assumed would happen. It was a family tradition."

When Dan completed boarding school and enrolled at Harvard — as his father and grandfather had before him — he didn't know what he wanted to do. But he had always liked kids and enjoyed being with them, so during his junior year he gave teaching a try. He worked as an intern in an experimental school and found that he not only liked teaching but also had skill at getting knowledge across to youngsters. After earning a master's degree at Harvard, he taught in Newton, near Boston — a "superb" school system, says Dan. "So what influenced me?" he asks. "Looking back, more than anything, my father — which I didn't realize at the time. He was and is a teacher. And he is also someone who all his life has been a teaching person. Which most of the time was wonderful — but not always."

In the mid-1960s, Dan served a stint at an extraordinary school in North Carolina — an integrated boarding school that was also a center for curriculum development and teacher training. From there, he went to Philadelphia and then back to Boston so he could finish his doctorate. At the age of thirty, he became superintendent of a suburban school system. He was apprehensive about the task: it was the first time he had ever been his own boss, the first time he was responsible for making sure that an organization met its goals. Something else was frightening him, too, something linked with his thirtieth birthday. "That's when I realized I will die some day. Before, I knew it in the way everybody knows it, but when I turned thirty, I realized it in my gut. That was harder for me than turning forty."

Dan's fears about his administrative skills proved groundless. During his thirties, he successfully supervised first one, then another school system outside Boston. But as he approached forty, he began looking for something else. "It wasn't a time of crisis, but it was a time of some turmoil and stress. I was ready to do something different."

For a while Dan considered a major change. "I had talked with friends who were in other fields about possibly switching careers, and I realized that I wasn't going to walk into a corporate boardroom and be a CEO of a major company. I had a lot of investment and a lot of experience in what I was doing. I had paid my dues in one field, and that's where I'd reap my reward." The reward was the presidency of Wheelock, which he assumed at the age of forty. "I decided to leave the community we'd lived in for eight years and move where the college was located, in Boston. Wheelock fit the ideals that I had and a sense of social purpose, which is a very important part of my life. Public service as somehow working in the community for the common good is a very strong family tradition. It wasn't something we talked about, but it's something my father has done all his life."

Dan feels that he picked up his values from watching his parents and grandparents quietly go about their own lives. His sense of public service has extended itself beyond his leadership at Wheelock. He is director or trustee of half a dozen civic and cultural institutions, and he helped found a children's museum near Boston. Dan also serves others on a more personal basis. For some young people just beginning their careers, he has functioned as mentor, providing guidance, advice, and contacts.

"I have relationships with people who work with me that are similar to

*Abby Cheever, forty-two.
"For me there was no
question — I was going to
go to work."*

the ones I had with influential people in my life when I was younger.
There's a very talented man who was in our admissions office who's just
going on to Princeton as an assistant dean of students. I got a lovely letter
from him as he left that made me realize we have had the same kind of
mentoring relationship that others fulfilled for me. I feel a little strange
having these relationships, because I don't think of myself now as my mentors were when I was this young man's age. But, in fact, it's almost the
same."

As Dan walks along the shore of Buzzards Bay, beside the house where he
hopes to retire one day, the wind ruffles his hair and he looks out to sea.
"I've thought of having myself buried here instead of in Boston or
Cambridge, where our traditional family plot is. It's the place I consider my
home now. And it's a place where I have warm and personal associations.
This little knoll is getting the southwest breeze as it comes up the bay. And
I like the thought of that washing up over my stone for the rest of eternity
or however long it would be. And in these woods are the deer and birds and
wildlife that have all been part of my life here. Even though I don't put a
great deal of stock in where one is buried or belief in an afterlife, this does
seem like a good place to rest."

This cove holds other memories for Dan. Here, in the early 1960s, he
proposed to his wife Abby. He had just graduated from Harvard, and Abby
was ready to begin her junior year at Radcliffe. "We were here on the cape,
and I hadn't really been thinking about asking her to marry me. After dinner, we went for a walk and came through the woods to the cove, which is
a very pretty and private spot. It was dusk, and I felt this strong impulse that
I wanted to act on. Without being too personal about it, we became
engaged. And then walking back in the dark, we almost ran into some deer

Dan, forty-five. "It led to a dramatic shift in our roles."

that were feeding on this path. I remember Abby jumping back, startled, and twisting her ankle badly and having to be helped back to the house. And thinking, 'Here's my companion on my arm.' It was all very romantic."

Soon they married, the first of their group to do so. Dan was a twenty-three-year-old graduate student, and while he worked on his master's degree, Abby, only twenty, finished her undergraduate studies.

Today, Abby is forty-two, a bright, energetic woman with short gray hair that frames a strong New England face. She grew up with the idea that a woman married, raised her children, and took care of her husband. "But running through my whole early childhood was the idea that you got well educated, you worked hard, and you did something with it," she says. "You didn't get educated only to bring up your children and nurture your husband. Something else was going to happen. *When* it was going to happen was not quite clear, but for me there was no question — I was going to go to work."

Abby taught kindergarten until the children came along, first Charles and then Abigail. She stayed home until they both entered school, and then she enrolled in law school. She was thirty-one; Dan, thirty-four. When she finished school and began to practice, a radical change swept through the family. "All of a sudden, Dan wasn't coming home to a wife with a meal on the table. In fact, he was coming home to drop off the babysitter and put a meal on the table for me, because I got home considerably later. So that's probably where he had the hardest adjustment to make. I was going off to something new and exciting, and I liked what I was doing. I still like what I'm doing. For him, maybe he felt he was going backwards."

This change came as Dan was approaching forty and looking for something different himself. "It led to a dramatic shift in our roles," he recalls, "and at times to a fair amount of conflict and stress. We had come from quite traditional families, so for us the change was perhaps larger than it might have been. Well, we worked through all that, and I'd say for the last year the changes have acquired a comfort and a mutual respect that is really quite nice — and which I hadn't expected."

Asked about the continuing stresses of a two-career family, Abby thinks hard for a moment, then describes her guilt at having handed the responsibility for meals over to Dan. "Even to this day, I feel I ought to cook. But Dan is a much better cook than I am. He really doesn't like me in the kitchen, and he doesn't want me fooling around with what he does very, very well. But it's hard, even after ten years, for me to recognize the fact that I don't have that role any longer."

Practicing law has affected Abby Cheever in other ways. She knows she's not the same woman she was when her children were small. "I'm a much more assertive, direct person than I used to be. Part of that is my work world. I have to be. I'm in a competitive profession and a little older than some of the people because I went to law school late. They're good, and I have to be just as good and just as articulate and just as firm. You have to be pretty tough.

"I think some of that has carried over into my relationship with Dan. And even with the kids a little bit. There are just so many hours in the day, and you have to be assertive to play this game. Before I went to work, my life revolved around Danny and the kids. His schedule ran our life — when we took vacations, where we went, what kind of weekends we spent. But that's changed. I have more ideas than I used to about where I might want to spend a vacation, how I want to spend my time. I can't always be free when he's free. I can't be home when he might expect me to be home. That's just reality. Sometimes you have to say, 'I can't be there.' That requires you to be a stronger person."

Dan finds Abby's new strength and independence both interesting and "a little intimidating." But from his point of view, the marriage has worn well. "There's a song called 'My Dear Companion.' And I laugh about it, because that's how I sometimes think of Abby. Not in a saccharin way, but in the notion of companionship, of someone who is dear to you. It's something I feel getting stronger and stronger as we get older and as we go through life experiences like having our own children go off to college and start planning their own careers.

"Our son went off last year and our daughter will in another year. And I think that leaves you with mixed feelings of the freedom you'll have being just a husband and wife again, but at the same time the terror of wondering whether you'll still have the same kinds of interests and common concerns that you did before your children were born.

"I hope for Abby and me that our present relationship continues to grow in the ways it has recently. And that each of us is able to spend a little less time at work so that we're able to spend more time with each other. I hope we're able to camp and travel, go see some of the world which I've never seen. I would like to. And I hope we're both able to be a source of comfort and love and support to our parents in their old age."

A Midlife Crisis?

Dan Cheever is intensely aware of the passage of time in his life and of his place in the succession of generations. "He has a view of what should happen at certain points in his life," says Abby. "There are certain cut-off dates, and you have to take action before those dates or else the opportunities are going to narrow down. I don't think along those lines. I'm much more a person who lives from day to day." Dan's perspective on time may be broader than most, but it illustrates the impact of reaching the halfway mark, of realizing that you have more time lived than you do time left.

Dan was thirty when he became aware "in his gut" that he would eventually die. That may be early, especially in an era when the midpoint of life is getting later and later. But whenever it comes, the awareness of mortality is what psychoanalyst Elliott Jaques believed to be at the heart of what he called the "midlife crisis." Jaques gave this term to a transition he found in the lives of more than 300 artists who lived in different times and places.[1] He published his study of their lives in 1965; in less than a decade, the term he used had become part of our everyday vocabulary. Says psychiatrist Alvin Poussaint of Harvard University, "In my own practice, years ago men didn't come in talking about midlife crises. Now they come in, and they talk about midlife crisis and declining sexual powers and 'Should I change my career?' and 'What is there left for me in life?' Somehow they're making this period into a problem." During the midlife crisis, we supposedly question every aspect of our being and wonder if it's too late to make a change. But is there any substance to the idea that such a crisis is a normal feature of development?

Some research has shown that there is indeed a shifting time perspective in middle age, and that the fear of death is stronger at the midpoint of life than it is at the end.[2] In his in-depth study of forty middle-aged men, psychologist Daniel Levinson found a great deal of turmoil in the transition to middle adulthood. For 80 percent of his subjects, the passage was severe enough to warrant the term "crisis." Levinson concluded that, for the great majority of men, the years between forty and forty-five are a time of disruption. Afraid of dying and convinced that they've let opportunities slip through their fingers, they question their marriage, their jobs, their beliefs, and their values. "Horrified" by what they see and full of recriminations, they grapple with the disparity between what they've done with their lives and what they had dreamed of doing.[3]

In his early forties, a man's dream often becomes a cruel illusion. Those who have been fortunate enough to enact their vision — writing a successful novel, reaching the top of the corporate ladder, having a sound marriage and family — often find that fulfillment does not bring the happiness that was supposed to accompany it. Achieving the dream may have cost too much, and now men must deal with the consequences of that discovery. Those who achieved only part of what they dreamed of must understand that partial success is not a failure. And those who believed that success was inevitable if only they worked hard enough must come to terms with the fact that perseverance does not guarantee results.

Men find their way out of the tumultuous midlife transition, says Levinson, by modifying their dream to bring it closer to reality, and by reducing its power over their lives. This may involve questioning the value of goals that have been reached, looking for alternative (and perhaps more modest) ambitions, or becoming less driven by the need to succeed. By the end of the transition, some men take their reworked dream and continue advancing within the life structure they built in young adulthood. Others abandon their dream, bow their heads, and accept defeat. A few recover a dream they put on hold at the beginning of adulthood. Some of these men break out of the life they have built and make a radical change — they divorce, quit their jobs, or move to another town.

But not everyone agrees that midlife is a time of storm and stress. Researchers at the University of California who have been following several hundred people since they were born in the 1920s found no sign of an upsurge in crises as these men and women entered their forties.[4] In a forty-year study of nearly a hundred Harvard graduates, men's level of depression, divorce, and disenchantment with their occupation remained steady throughout life.[5] And in a national sample of more than 10,000 Americans, there was no increase in emotional upheaval at the midpoint of life.

Instead, levels of insecurity, worry, anxiety, and depression stayed the same from age thirty-five to fifty-five.[6] Apparently, life crises do develop at midlife, but no more often than at other times — and perhaps not as often as in early adulthood. Sociologists have found that young adults show the most signs of turmoil, apparently because they face simultaneous demands — separating from their parents, making their way in the world of work, starting a family — at a time when they're also financially strapped.[7]

Perhaps if researchers had studied women instead of men, the concept of midlife crisis would never have taken hold so quickly. Psychologists who studied 300 women between the ages of thirty-five and fifty-five found that few of them were dealing with the sort of questions that Levinson found to be characteristic of men.[8] Women entering middle age showed no signs of questioning their lives, their goals, or their dreams. Part of their serenity may have resulted from the way they had been socialized. Girls, and especially these members of the pre-boom cohort, escaped the stress on competition and achievement that little boys lived with. But that's not all of the story. These women seemed untouched by men's concerns about mortality. They were worried about having too much time stretching ahead of them, not too little — more concerned about widowhood than their own death. Their sense of well-being spilled over into other areas of their lives. Instead of worrying about declining sexual potency, as middle-aged men tend to do, they reported increasing sexual satisfaction.

In large-scale studies, there appears to be little evidence for a universal midlife crisis. "I do not think more than one person in ten is experiencing a genuine midlife crisis," concludes social psychologist Gilbert Brim, who is coordinating a $10-million study of the middle years. "If they had lived in our times, the midlife-crisis label would have been applied to Paul Gauguin taking off at forty-three to paint in Tahiti, or Albert Schweitzer going to Africa at thirty-eight to build his medical clinic." According to Brim, troubling events usually spread out randomly over a number of years. When they happen to cluster, you have a crisis; when they happen to cluster at forty, you have a midlife crisis.[9]

By the time we reach middle age, there has been a gradual accumulation of "nonnormative" events in our lives — chance encounters, tragic losses, sudden shifts of fortune, changes in the people we are close to. The events that brought Brian Sipe to a major transition were a series of injuries in his mid-thirties. Kathleen Wilkins's life changed at forty, when she and her husband divorced and her older daughter left for college. Dan Cheever was about the same age when his career decisions and the demands of his wife's law practice led to a dramatic shift in their lives. For Matt Nort, change came at fifty, when the doors closed for good on Pittsburgh's steel mills. And Harriet Lyons was close to sixty when her life took a sudden turn with the loss of a job, a move to Boston, and the arrival of a granddaughter. Rarely was it age that brought on a "crisis" for these individuals. More often than not, it was a compounding of life events.

In an earlier era, tragic and unpredictable events were probably much more common than they are today. At the beginning of this century, for example, more than 60 percent of parents in the United States with an average number of children experienced the death of a young child.[10] In Sweden, the prospect was so certain that custom called for a graveyard visit before the marriage ceremony, so couples could select burial sites for some of their future children.[11] But today, the chances that a U.S. family of average size will lose a young child are only about 4 percent, and close to 70 percent of all deaths occur after the age of sixty-five.

"We probably build stronger expectations about what lies ahead than our grandparents did," says sociologist Hagestad. "They were certainly better prepared for death at any age than we are. And I wonder if we aren't going to see a greater diversity in life patterns between those where things go basically on schedule and plans turn out, and those where the dream doesn't come true. That will make it tougher and tougher on those who really have their apple carts toppled, either through untimely death or kids that don't turn out or jobs that don't exist anymore."[12] Adds Poussaint, "Life is not predictable. I don't think we're told enough about that. There are so many events, including global ones like war and famine, that we're all vulnerable to, being the human beings that we are."[13]

In life, it's not age that brings on crises; rather, it's what *happens*. And something else must be kept in mind: some people seem to live from crisis to crisis. Paul Costa and Robert McCrae, psychologists at the National Institute on Aging, have been following adults over the years, assessing the same individuals again and again, and they have discovered that major aspects of personality endure. Whether their subject group consisted of more than 2,000 war veterans or nearly 700 men and women in Baltimore or a national sample of 10,000 people, these researchers found an underlying stability in three basic traits. One was openness. People who were imaginative, independent, and liked variety tended to stay that way, and so did down-to-earth conformers who liked their lives to follow a routine. The second trait was extraversion. People who were sociable, fun-loving, and affectionate retained their expansive, demonstrative nature, as did people who were retiring, sober, and reserved. The third enduring characteristic was neuroticism. Insecure, self-pitying worriers were still anxious after many years, while calm, secure, self-satisfied people still found life serene. These traits existed in various combinations in different individuals, but they tended to remain constant. Age turned out to be a far poorer predictor of personality than did personality tests people had taken up to thirty years earlier. The neurotic individual who had a crisis at midlife was likely to be the kind of person prone to crises throughout life.[14]

From a lifespan perspective, it's easy to see why a crisis in middle adulthood cannot be pegged to a specific age. What brings uniformity to our lives is a shared program of biological growth and the shared expectations of society — the Biological and Social Clocks. But as the influence of these clocks diminishes in the postreproductive years, we are left with the Psychological Clock — the clock that creates diversity. That is why, as the years go by, it's easier to make meaning of a life not by squeezing it into a theory, but by turning it into a story.

Expertise and Creativity

Though Dan Cheever does his best to keep in shape, he has already experienced some of the normal physical losses of middle adulthood. But he can still laugh about them: "As Mae West said, 'I have everything I ever had, only it's six inches lower.' I sometimes feel as though I'm occupying somebody else's body." In our middle years, we can expect a number of losses, even if we can't predict when they will occur. In addition to physical losses, we can expect social losses. It's likely that our parents will die during our middle years, and that a friend — or even a spouse — will suffer a heart attack. As Matt Nort knows so well, events that come out of nowhere can result in the loss of a job, an identity, and even a reason for living.

In the midst of these losses, we have much to gain. In fact, most of us reach the height of our personal and social powers in our middle years. Having been in charge of children, we're now in charge of society. We may not be presidents of a college, but we usually assume other positions of responsibility. We have become members of what Bernice Neugarten calls the "command" generation.[15] On his farm in Butler County, Pennsylvania, Jim Kennedy knows what that means. "If anything's wrong or needs taking care of, or if there's a problem, it's coming on my shoulders," he says. "The decision is made by myself. The bottom line, I'm there."

Dan and Abby Cheever and Jim and Rita Kennedy make their bottom-line decisions from a storehouse of knowledge and experience. They have the kind of practical expertise that Yale psychologist Robert Sternberg believes to be the key to success in adult life.[16] Sternberg has found that business executives who score well on his tests of judgment in everyday situations — knowing how to write effective memos, motivate subordinates, delegate responsibility, and so on — earn higher salaries and receive better performance ratings than those who do not. Their "street smarts" require a certain amount of basic intelligence, but beyond that are not related to IQ. Practical intelligence, says Sternberg, is far more important for managerial success than traditional "school smarts."

When Cornell University's Stephen Ceci and Jeffrey Liker studied middle-aged and older men who regularly attended harness races, they found that some were better than others at handicapping — assigning odds to a horse's chances of winning.[17] The picks of these "experts" were closer to those of paid track handicappers than were those of "nonexperts." But there was no connection between IQ and this particular skill. One man with an IQ of 85 picked the top horse in all ten races. Another, with an IQ of 118, picked the top horse in only three. Ceci and Liker concluded that the challenges of real-world tasks force us to develop a practical expertise that's very different from academic intelligence.

University of Waterloo psychologist Neil Charness agrees; expertise, he says, is limited to specific domains. Within a domain, experts think faster and better than the rest of us. But outside that domain, they are no different. The experienced auto mechanic is baffled by mysterious physical symptoms that seem obvious to a physician, but the physician is just as baffled by a peculiar sound in his automobile engine that the mechanic encounters every day. For several years, Charness has been studying a musical savant who makes it clear just how specific expertise is. Blind since birth, able to use only one side of his body, and with the measured intelligence of a two-year-old, this man has a remarkable ability to recognize and remember music — and even to play it with his one good hand.[18]

Charness has found that expertise is not just *more* knowledge, but knowledge organized in a certain way. If you show a chess position to a grand master and a beginning player, then ask them to reproduce it on a chessboard, the grand master will reproduce all thirty pieces correctly; the novice will place five or six pieces on the right squares. But if you scramble the chess pieces and put them down in a random order, the grand master will do no better than the novice at reproducing the arrangement. What distinguishes experts in any field is their familiarity with meaningful patterns. They see combinations and structures the rest of us don't notice, and they build up a huge repertoire of them — chess is estimated to contain up to 50,000 meaningful chunks.

As they gain command of a repertoire of patterns, experts organize them in a way that permits instant recognition. They develop an intuition that tells them exactly where a situation is heading. Accomplished tennis players know that if they force their opponent into a certain position on the court, the ball is likely to come back at a certain pace and angle. They can anticipate where the ball is going to be. George Zuidema, a professor of surgery at the University of Michigan, has observed something similar. "The expert has a good view of the flow of disease and can make diagnostic connections fairly early," he says, "whereas the novice will say, 'We have this finding, this finding, and this finding' without seeing the whole picture unfold. You have to recognize the early warning signs that may be indicators of a full-blown disease. If you wait for the whole manifestation, you may wait too long."[19]

Familiarity with patterns and the ability to react instinctively frees experts to be on the lookout for the rare pattern — the sudden complication in surgery, the car in front of you spinning out on the expressway, the overlong drought in aboriginal Australia. You have to inhabit a particular domain for a long time for rare patterns to occur, says Charness; that's why it normally takes years to become accomplished at something. Knowing the rare patterns gives experts the flexibility to respond to an emergency. Someone whose body of knowledge isn't organized as efficiently has fewer "Plan B's" to work with.

The time it takes to develop expertise has a bearing on creativity. Novel contributions often build on insights from the past, and it takes years to accumulate those insights. That's why researchers who trace the life course of creativity have found it is relatively low during the first part of adulthood. Masterworks generally come later. "If you look across a variety of domains," says Charness, "from weightlifting and billiards to musical composition and writing plays, most likely your greatest achievement is going to be made in the decade of the thirties. But that varies a bit from discipline to discipline. It's a little earlier for mathematicians and later for historians. In history, you need a greater knowledge base. It takes more time to build that up. In mathematics, you need fewer facts before you can go to work and produce interesting theorems."[20]

Researchers have found that the proportion of masterworks to minor works remains the same across the life span, which means that while creators are producing more masterworks during their peak years, they are also producing more inferior ones. Poets, mathematicians, and theoretical physicists tend to peak early in their careers, while novelists, historians, philosophers, and medical researchers may peak as much as twenty years later. Toward the end of a creative career, output is usually down by about half. Even that pattern is often interrupted by a second, modest peak of productivity during later adulthood.[21]

Creative people tend to resist patterns, cautions Charness, and the peak years of creativity vary not only from one domain to another but from one person to another. "One looks at people like Miguel Cervantes who produced *Don Quixote* in his sixties, or people who become artists and novelists late in life. So I wouldn't rule out all hope that if you haven't won the Nobel prize by the age of thirty, you won't get one."[22]

Reclaimed Powers

Another kind of power becomes available in middle age, a power that Abby Cheever feels when she says, "I'm a much more assertive, direct person than I used to be. I'm in a competitive profession and . . . you have to be pretty tough." Dan feels this power when he talks about the notion of "dear companionship" growing stronger and stronger within him. Both Abby and Dan are discovering potentials in themselves that lay dormant in the first half of life — potentials associated with the opposite sex.

The complementary discovery of these capacities has been recognized by many cultures. According to one Moroccan legend, a boy is born with a hundred evil spirits hovering over his head, and a girl with a hundred angels as her companions. Every year one of the evil spirits jumps from the boy to the girl, and one of the angels flits in the other direction. By the age of fifty, there is no difference between them. If they live to be one hundred, the aged woman ends up surrounded by a hundred devils and the aged man by a hundred angels.[23]

Legends often begin in wise observations about human nature. What Moroccans noticed years ago in the men and women around them, psychoanalyst Carl Jung saw in European adults.[24] Within every man, he proposed, was a feminine, passive element called the anima; and within every woman was a masculine, assertive element called the animus. Jung believed that, during the second half of life, this unexpressed side of the personality asserted itself. Men discovered their tender feelings, and women discovered their sharpness of mind. Unless this happened, personal growth could not occur.

Jung's insight has stood up to scientific investigation. Whether researchers looked at American men and women in Kansas City, at Native American Navajo in the Southwest, at Maya in Central America, or at

Druze in Lebanon, they found the same progression with age.[25] Men lost their consuming interest in their occupations, became less aggressive and more dependent on their wives, and turned toward the pleasures of hearth and home. Women became more assertive, less dependent on their husbands, and tended to become more powerful within the family, if not in the larger community.

Psychologist David Gutmann places these changes in the context of the entire life span.[26] Boys, he says, begin life with a greater biological endowment of aggression than girls — an endowment reinforced by culture. For most of human history, this prepared them for their role as adults: men left the base camp to hunt for food and defended the frontiers of the community. An excess of aggression made them better at what they did. Girls were different. It was their job to nurture — to feed and raise the young. To prepare for their role as mothers, they had to curb aggression, which could prove harmful to their children and deprive them of a sense of basic trust. But once the "chronic emergency" of parenting was over, this sexual division of labor was no longer necessary. Men could reclaim their tender, nurturing side, while women could become stronger and more aggressive. Even today, says Gutmann, should a radical career shift occur during middle age, its direction is usually predictable. A man is likely to leave the life of a business executive to become a social worker or a clergyman, but a woman leaves social work or teaching to attend law school.

Others have suggested that the rebalancing of masculine and feminine elements in personality may be sparked by hormonal changes — the drop in estrogen among postmenopausal women and the flattening out of testosterone levels in middle-aged men.[27] Or perhaps the physical changes of middle age force each sex into a reappraisal. Men can no longer define masculinity as strength, toughness, and power, nor can women define femininity as sexual attractiveness and the bearing and rearing of children. Both sexes have to rethink their gender identity — what it means to be a man or a woman. No one has suggested that either sex "loses" its masculinity or femininity. Instead, both become more flexible. No longer constrained by traditional sex roles, they begin dealing with the world — and with themselves — in ways that combine the features of both sexes. They enter the normal androgyny of later life.[28]

The new male mellowness may be at the heart of men's tendency to become mentors to young adults. As their obsession with power and "making it" fades, men can combine work and friendship. For the first time, they can nurture new talent without feeling threatened by competitive rivalry.

When acting as mentor to a young man, they are less likely to fear that their affection for him might be a sign of incipient homosexuality. And when serving as mentor to a young woman, they are able to help her up the ladder without denying her femininity or exploiting her sexually.[29]

Abby and Dan Cheever are reclaiming the powers of the opposite sex relatively early in their adult lives. But then Abby finished bearing children at twenty-five, and was only thirty-one when she began law school. It's quite possible that the dramatic social changes affecting early adulthood will have similar repercussions down the lifeline of many men and women. Perhaps male and female spirits will be trading places earlier in life, as they did with Abby and Dan. Perhaps, in a generation or two, they will even begin life in closer balance.

The Legacy

All of the positive developments of middle adulthood — the shifting time perspective, the greater sense of command, the reclaiming of other-sexed powers — affect one's thinking about the next generation. Having received a legacy from his father and a whole succession of forebears, Dan Cheever is now thinking about those who will follow him. As a young adult, he had an influence on the next generation with his parenting and teaching. But now the urgency — and the opportunity — is greater. Many in middle age, aware of their own mortality and the time that is left in life, develop a desire to create a legacy for future generations, a legacy that will stake their claim on immortality.

The impulse to create a legacy has been christened "generativity" by Erik Erikson.[30] He coined the term because he found words such as "productivity" and "creativity" too narrow to encompass the myriad ways in which we leave our stamp on the future. Generativity rises out of the human urge to reproduce, but goes far beyond the bearing and rearing of children. In its broadest sense, it's the desire to invest one's energy in forms of life and work that will outlive the self.[31]

Our legacy can be many things. It might be the fruits of our work — a business we have nurtured, books we have written, ideas we have developed, people we have touched. It might be material possessions — property, endowments to colleges, charities, or churches. It might be the children we leave behind — and their children's children. For Dan Cheever, it includes the people he has mentored and the children's museum he helped create. For Jim Kennedy, the legacy is a farmstead and a way of life, the same one he received from his father. "I believe that we've accumulated enough ground and enough experience so that all five of my children can make their own decisions about coming into this busness," he says. His oldest son Jeff has already opted to stay in farming, and the other children are thinking about it. "By the time Jason's down to making choices, I think the die will already be cast — who's going to take over, who's going to do what, and how the farm's gonna be run. And by that time, I'll be saying goodbye."

Often, normal impulses to generativity are amplified by unforeseen events, or by tragedy. The loss of a child spurred one mother to begin full-time work in her church's peace program. "It was Lynn herself who was an inspiration to me," she says. "The heroism with which she lived her life and her need to leave some kind of mark is the stimulus for my doing the kind of work I do." The girl's father gave up his job as a commercial banker to direct a community food bank, which collects surplus food from national companies and distributes it to the unemployed and disadvantaged. "I think she'd like what I'm doing today," he says. "She was a young woman who cared about people." And a mother who lost her son to a drunk driver eventually found meaning by working with Mothers Against Drunk Driving. "Every day I work with victims who have experienced the same thing," she says. "Every day when I help someone, then that's something for Richard. I guess I feel that he's living on in what I can do to help someone else."[32]

A generative outlet has helped these parents recover from loss. Other adults have found that weaknesses in their personality can be turned into strengths precisely because they are put to such use. As an alcoholism therapist said of her fifteen years on binges, "I know what it's like to feel like a worm, to feel alone. To feel helpless, even hopeless, like there isn't a way out. I wouldn't trade that for anything. Now I can help patients see that a lot of negative things in their lives can be turned around to positive." Passing on her experiences has not only been good for her clients; it's been good for her. "It made it more difficult for me to go out and drink on weekends, when I was going to go down and talk to those men about sobriety on Wednesday nights."[33]

Not everyone develops generativity. Those who don't tend to become absorbed in themselves. They may have gained material success, but find life boring and feel that something is missing, even though they're not certain what it is they long for. Neither education nor privilege are connected with generativity, but successfully completing the tasks of life's earlier seasons is. Dartmouth Medical School professor George Vaillant has been studying the course of adult development for decades. Whether he looked at Harvard alumni or men from the inner city, he found that those who were generative by the time they were forty-seven had developed a long-lasting, intimate relationship with another person and a stable career.[34] One man described his progression by saying, "At twenty to thirty, I think I learned how to get along with my wife; and at thirty to forty, I learned how to be a success in my job. At forty to fifty, I worried less about myself and more about the children."

In fact, being a parent seems to spur the development of broad generativity, the sort that goes beyond the nurturing of our own children. Researchers working with Vaillant discovered this by studying a group of young married men who had been unable to have children.[35] Most of those who chose to adopt children showed clear evidence of generativity during middle age, as did the majority of those who eventually had children of their own. But only a few of those who lived a childless life ever developed responsibility for anyone or anything except their wives or their pets. Almost as good a predictor of future generativity was how the men handled their desire for children when they first discovered their infertility. Those who became preoccupied with themselves, showing an absorption in body-building, health foods, and macho sexuality, rarely developed generativity, even if they eventually became fathers. Most remained childless and later divorced. But the majority of those who became involved in youth groups, taught a Sunday School class, or acted as a "big brother" to a neighborhood child clearly became generative. They were also the most likely to adopt a child.

Serving as a parent may cultivate generativity, but childlessness does not necessarily thwart its development. A nun in her fifties — childless by choice — already knows what her life as a communicator has meant to others. "The articles that I write and whose effects I never see, the words I speak on the air that millions of people hear on a Sunday, I don't know where they go, but somewhere in there, there is another touching. . . . I feel very much in touch with a lot of people living and dead who have meant something to me. Our love may not be exchanged in any physical way, but I sense connections. I sense a lot of unexpressed affection, and I know with a certainty that I have mattered."[36]

The Transformation of Loss

Kris Rosenberg is fifty-five, and she, too, knows that she has mattered. Director of student development at La Roche College, on the outskirts of Pittsburgh, she has become a powerful advocate for middle-aged women who are returning to college. But before she could help others, Kris had to transform the losses and failures that had marked her own life. "I was forced to be liberated. I didn't choose it, but in doing it I found something about myself that I'm very glad I found. You lose a certain security and innocence forever, but something else happens that's very great."

Kris's dark hair curls tightly around her face and her sympathetic brown eyes. Her life, she says, has been a mixture of "fun times and agonizing times, wonderful things and good relationships and things that I feel ashamed of or sorry about." So have the lives of most people, but Kris has had more than her share of agony. Crisis seems to have stalked her. Growing up in Alabama, she received lots of love from her extended family, but still believes she was a "totally weird" kid.

"I was a very fearful child. That many bad things didn't happen to me, but I was always very anxious. My dad would take me lots of places and he would say, 'Be friendly! Talk to people!' But I didn't. 'Be brave! Have courage!' Courage was a biggie. I tried very hard although I was very shy."

Kris's family moved several times as she was growing up, first to New Mexico and then to Texas. She became more outgoing in high school, but aside from music and English, academics held little interest for her. "I sang with a band that played for high-school dances, and I sang in a chorus, and I sang in church. That was all I wanted to do." She married when she was only seventeen. "It was assumed when you were a little girl that you'd get married. It was assumed you'd have lots of children. And it was assumed that you'd work only if you absolutely had to."

Kris gave birth to two daughters and then, in her twenties, the first of a series of tragedies struck. She contracted polio. "People say, 'Why me? Why me?' And I always thought, 'Why not me?' Is there anything particular about me that I would be exempt from the tragedies of life? They say, 'Well, you never think bad things could possibly happen to you.' I've never been that way. I always thought bad things could happen to me, and they have. But I don't think I was selected for them."

Polio left Kris with considerable weakness in her right arm and leg. After having two more daughters and moving to Nevada, she gave college a try, but then dropped out. By this time her marriage was failing as well, and she ended up getting a divorce. "That was a really bad time for me. I didn't have any confidence at all. I didn't feel that I was an intelligent person. I felt very unattractive. I was physically clumsy from polio, awkward at everything I tried to do. I thought that I would look silly if I tried to be feminine — that people would say, 'Look at that ugly woman trying to be feminine.' So I did all the wrong things, like no makeup and no jewelry. I didn't have a sense of any of the things about myself that I have now. I look at some of the things

I'm doing now and I'm sort of astounded. And I think how easily I could have never known that I could give anything to anyone or feel successful about anything I did."

One of the people who helped encourage Kris was her younger brother. Shortly after he graduated from the University of Nevada, he helped her register for another try at college. Then he was drafted, sent to Vietnam — and killed.

"He was a kid with a lot of courage and strength, but he was a very sensitive person. As far as I was concerned, it was doomsday from before he left. I never expected to see him again. I'd been brought up as a real patriot, to think that the United States never did anything that wasn't kind and merciful and helpful and generous. I was just beginning to catch on that this country could do something stupid. I talked to him about it before he actually went to Vietnam, but I didn't want him to be divided in his mind if he was going to go. Later, I thought how stupid that was, because other people do influence us and no one ever makes a decision all alone. Then I regretted that I hadn't done something really dramatic to try to keep him.

"That was really a horrible loss for me. I felt that he and I were cut from the same cloth. We were people who could look at each other and laugh about the same things. To this day, the thing I miss most about him is the shared funnies. For a while after he died, something would happen and I'd think, 'Ah, wait till I tell Bobby!'"

Bobby's memory motivated Kris to do well in school. But there were other sources of support — friends in a church and someone who had the patience to teach her to drive. "I had tried to learn a couple of times, but the people who were trying to help me would say, 'You're not coordinated enough to do this.' And I just believed it. I was really scared about it for a long time, and I was embarrassed to be that old going to get my first driver's license. But it was in the desert, and it's a whole lot easier to drive there than it is where it's hilly and icy. And it made me feel really good to be able to do something."

Kris also remarried at this time. Her husband was a scientist who shared her love of the desert and her passion for reading and writing. He had three children and she had four, all between the ages of six and sixteen. "We didn't have them all, all the time, but we had them all in various combinations during that time. We had a little tiny house and a bunch of kids. Harry really wanted me to be in school. He pushed me in the way that I guess some fathers push — not only to go, but to make good grades.

"I was afraid that, at thirty-seven, I would feel old going back to school. On the contrary, I felt much younger in school, even though a lot of people were younger than I was. I enjoyed it a lot. I figured out that I could be an intelligent person and that people could know me and like me. Once I got a taste of it and knew that I could do well, I wanted to do everything well." This time, college worked. Kris earned a bachelor's degree in psychology and went on to get a master's. Then her husband received an offer to come to Pittsburgh. It was a wonderful opportunity for him, and though Kris had begun teaching in Nevada, she encouraged him to take it. She was forty-four when they made the move, and her reaction surprised her.

"I thought I would die! I just felt so transplanted and torn out by the roots. The weather was frightening to me. I was frightened to drive in it. I dreaded and feared to be a stranger. So what did I do but begin to teach? At one time I taught nine college classes in seven locations. I just got in my car every day and learned to drive in bad weather and in places I didn't know. And began to see that I could indeed start over and establish myself.

"Then my husband and I separated. It was his decision to go. I think he left in order to change because he felt there were some things in him that he had never found, and he didn't have much of an identity. Even though he had a doctorate and a good position, he just didn't feel he had much individuality.

"I was terrified and I was furious. I wasn't scared and angry. I was terrified and furious. I felt that my identity had been stripped off me like my skin. I was financially terrified. I knew that any retirement was tied up with him. I didn't have any savings — just jobs I was earning about $16,000 a year on. I went through some awful times, and then I learned to like being alone. I became more self-sufficient. More independent, more able to say, 'Get lost, if that's how you feel,' rather than feeling desperate and that I couldn't make it on my own. I learned to find really rich things in solitude. And I learned to relate to women in ways that were different."

When Kris talks about what she's been through, there's a hesitancy in her voice, as if she's not at all certain that she has seen her last crisis. But she has learned a great deal, and the painful experiences in her past have become the source of her generativity with other women. Kris has gotten stronger since becoming their confidante and advocate in her position at La Roche. Finding the job has meant a lot to her.

"I think when I relate to other women, especially women of mature age who are thinking about going back to school or who are having to do something to change their lives, that we interact so closely, so quickly, and in such a positive way because I can be real to them. I reveal things about myself. I can say, 'I've felt things like that. Let me tell you. Let me tell you when I was so scared. I've been alone. I've been frightened to be alone. I've

Kris Rosenberg, fifty-five. "The ones that are farther along can talk to the ones who aren't so far along."

been a woman who didn't have any way to earn money. I went to school and didn't make it once.' Those things are very effective. It's as though my failures are more important than my successes.

"I've become a repository for all the things that women have gone through. It's like you can see people on a journey. And the ones that are farther along can talk to the ones who aren't so far along. It's almost like I catalyze the situation, but I don't do all the contributing. What we try to do is give women positive experiences and relationships so that they can just see that they can do something."

So strong is Kris's feeling for "her" women that she felt it was something of a betrayal when she and Harry were recently reunited. They had been separated for four-and-a-half years. "We certainly don't have what would be called a typical relationship," says Kris. "We have separate bank accounts, separate telephones, separate rooms — practically a suite. We even have separate newspapers. The *New York Times* comes to the front door and the *Pittsburgh Press* comes to the side door. We have the luxury of having space — both physically and emotionally. We're still different people, we have time for our own things and our own relationships, and that, to me, is good. I don't know what my life's gonna be in a year or two. Harry and I didn't make each other any vows or promises when he moved back in. We have an open thing here. I don't mean an open marriage, but an open relationship where you play the days as they come. I'm comfortable with that, and I think he's comfortable with that, too."

However her relationship with Harry comes out, Kris will always find strength in her solidarity with women. "When I'm in my territory, I feel like I'm really in charge. I know what to do. I know how to do it well. Some days

I'm tired and strung out, and others days I'm excited and say, 'Isn't this fun? Think of it. We get to do this and call it work.' It's taken me all my life to be as comfortable with who I am as I am right now. I think I've gained wisdom about some things and I don't mind expounding it now and then — something I probably wouldn't have done when I was younger.

"I was thinking the other day about the business of a chain only being as strong as its weakest link. And I thought that was stupid, because a lot of us in my group are weak right now. What it should be is: the individual woman is only as strong as the collective woman. It's like a net. You may get a little hole in it here, but it's still a powerful net. And we're all as strong as we are collected together."

VI

Late
Adulthood

16

THE BIOLOGICAL *Twenty-five*

STORY OF LATE *Extra Years*

ADULTHOOD

"The proper way to bone this shoulder pork is first to remove the skin. You work as close as you possibly can to the skin, leaving the meat on the shoulder. If you want to make a pork roast, just roll the meat up in one piece. Or you can cut it up and use it for sausage. Now, you always cut away from you. You don't cut towards you, 'cause you can imagine how sharp these knives are. Just one mistake. . . ."

Harry Crimi knows a lot about meat — and a lot about the meat business. He and his wife Antoinette have been working in the family butcher shop for nearly forty years, and once they started running it themselves, they were farsighted enough to avoid the mistakes that could have meant ruin. "When I got in the business," he recalls, "it was more family oriented. People came down with their whole families and they shopped different. They used to buy half a calf or a whole lamb or a chunk of beef and have it cut up into maybe seven or eight different types of meat. That would last them for two or three weeks. Today, people buy mostly for a day or two, and the cuts are different — maybe a pound of this and a half a pound of that and specific cuts, like for veal scallopini or veal piccante."

The Crimis' shop retains Antoinette's maiden name: Cappuccio. It is located in the Italian Market section of south Philadelphia, an area rich with tradition. "When the shopkeepers first started," Harry explains, "they would go down to Dock Street in the middle of the night — two, three o'clock in the morning — and buy their fruit and vegetables and come up

321

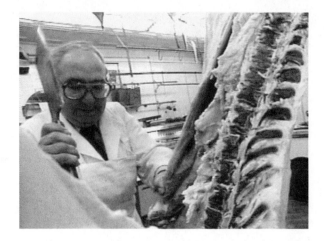

Harry Crimi, sixty-one. "I do more work today than a lot of these young-sters do at thirty or forty."

here and set up in the street, next to the curb. It got to be known as the Curbside Market. Eventually, they bought property and moved in. They'd have a store with a stand in front, and they'd live on top of the store. My in-laws did the same thing. Now the families are going into the third and fourth generations."

The Italian Market has a place on America's political map. "During the election years, all the politicians come. I've had the pleasure of taking President Ford through the Italian Market. Ronald Reagan visited my store here. President Carter, George Bush . . . Harry Truman was down here. We've had as many as six hundred thousand people on the street for the Italian festivals." Moviemakers have also worked the neighborhood: the vivid "meat house" scene from the original *Rocky* was filmed at Cappuccio's market.

The man who has welcomed presidents to his store is a stocky sixty-one years old, with glasses and thinning gray hair. In the shop he usually wears a tie, a butcher's coat, and an apron splattered with old stains. Working seven days a week, he hasn't had the opportunity to think much about the years ahead. "When you're twenty or thirty, you don't imagine being sixty-one." He laughs softly, as if he still can't believe his age. "I wonder where all those years went from being twenty and thirty. My children have grown up so fast. But I don't feel old. I don't even feel sixty-one. I do more work today than a lot of these youngsters do at thirty or forty." But Harry does face some questions. How long will he have his health? And what would hap-pen to the business — the children's legacy — if his health started to fail?

Harry and Antoinette are the third generation to run Cappuccio's meat market. The shop was opened seventy-five years ago by her grandfather,

Antoinette, sixty. "The only worry I have is that I should go before my father."

and Harry was invited to work there when he and Antoinette were married. The two had met on a blind date in his hometown, Atlantic City. "My father-in-law invited me to help him with the business. At the time it was just something I was gonna try. I had no problems, but I had to get used to living in a strange city in a strange environment — and living with the in-laws. Then my father-in-law asked me to stay in the business, because he had no one else in the family helping him. His son was married — a doctor — and his daughter was single. Eventually, we made it a partnership agreement."

Antoinette was a child of the Italian Market — born and bred in the apartment above the shop. "All my life has been spent in this neighborhood," she says. "Grew up here, played here. My friends are from here, right in this neighborhood." At sixty, Antoinette is a slight, energetic woman with dark hair and deep brown eyes. She needs glasses for close work, such as reading or trimming meat. "Harry and I have been very good for one another. He's kind, he's good, and he's considerate. Truth. He's understanding more than anything else, 'cause you have to remember we lived with my family. It's the way we were brought up, and I think I'm a little on the old-fashioned side where a woman is, you know, not to start an argument. She just keeps quiet." For a long time, Antoinette and Harry lived with her parents over the store; their two daughters were born there. After the first of two sons came along, the Crimis moved to their own house. Their first vacation came just two years ago, when one of their boys took over the shop while they went to Florida.

Antoinette finds that turning sixty has brought some surprises. "I thought when I became sixty, life would be easier. But I find it isn't. Because

Domenico Cappuccio, ninety-two (left). "God, when He wantsa me, He can take-a me."

there's more things to do at home. More activities. But I enjoy it. I enjoy cooking. I enjoy taking my father out." Her father, Domenico, the second generation of Cappuccio butchers, is ninety-two. "The only worry I have is that I should go before my father. I wouldn't want anyone to put my father away. My father belongs home. He worked hard all his life. He gave us everything. He deserves the honor and glory of dying at home, like my mother did. My husband could take care of himself. My children can. But I worry about my father. I wouldn't want no one to put him anywhere other than his own home."

Domenico Cappuccio was born in Italy, and its rhythms have never left his speech. He wears a hearing aid attached to his heavy tortoise-shell glasses, but his short, straight hair is mostly black, and his face is almost free of wrinkles. Until he was eighty, he carried a full load in the store. Then his health and his mental powers began to ebb. Today, his grasp on the world is uncertain, but he still gets down to the shop almost every day. He is surrounded by the comfort and protection of his family. "Italy?" he responds when asked. "Oh, I don' remember. Been here a long time. Since I took the business, I never move. Just a long time." He throws his arms wide and says, "God, when He wantsa me, He can take-a me."

All the Crimi generations are close. Harry and Antoinette's four children have their own keys to their parents' house; they come and go as they please. One daughter still lives with them while her husband finishes medical school, and one son lives above the butcher shop. Harry and Antoinette are satisfied with the way they have raised their children; they say they have never had to worry about drugs or trouble with the law. Harry attributes this success to their strong family bonds and the active role the

Catholic religion has played in their lives. Antoinette thinks it's something she learned from her mother. "My mother used to say, 'You get more out of sugar than you do out of vinegar.' So they'll bend. They'll come around if you talk to them. But you have to do it in a diplomatic way. You have to go with them real nice — calm, cool, and collected. 'Cause if they start gettin' angry with you, they won't tell you anything."

Each afternoon at two, Antoinette picks up her grandson at school and brings him to the butcher shop. At the age of six, he is already helping out, learning how to make hamburger patties. Antoinette freely admits that it's different from having her own children around. "I spoil my grandchild more than my own. My children always say that. He asks me for everything, and I buy him everything he wants. I know it's spoiling him. But that's a grandmother's love. What else can you do?"

Harry also takes great enjoyment in the boy. "When you raise your own children and you're in business, you don't have time to cater to them. Even though I don't have time, I go out of my way for my grandchildren. Whereas with my own children, I either didn't have the time or I didn't make it."

When Harry and Antoinette think about the future of the family business, the talk always comes back to their sons. One is a pharmacist, the other a photographer. Both grew up in the butcher shop. "Both of my boys are meat cutters," says Harry. "They know the business one hundred percent. They know how to buy, how to sell, how to cut. If they ever have hard times, they'll always have a trade to fall back on. I told my boys, I says, 'Look, you have your own profession, fine. You know the meat-cutting business, fine. If you ever want to fall back on it, you know it.' I've given my children options. But I'll be honest with you. Being in a professional field is fine, but when you work for somebody else, even though you're a professional, there's no guarantee how long you're gonna be there."

So far, neither of the Crimi sons has chosen to enter the business, but both keep the possibility alive. For the present, things will continue as they always have. Harry Crimi, who can't think of himself as old, has no plans to stop working. He says he enjoys being a butcher and cannot conceive of retiring completely — even if one of his sons took over the shop. "If I ever got to the point where I didn't enjoy it, I think I'd just turn the keys in." He chuckles at the absurdity of the thought. "I don't want to work as hard, but I would never retire a hundred percent. I feel that when you retire, then you just open yourself into a lazy life. I think this is why a lot of people — not only men, but women too, eh? — die prematurely or become a burden on other people. I wouldn't want that. I wouldn't want to be put in an old-age home. I want to keep moving as I've moved all my life — at a slower pace, but independent.

"There's a certain thing in being in business for yourself. You know nobody's gonna chase you out. You know what you're gonna do that week. You know what you're gonna do that day. When I open the door, it's another day's work. For thirty-nine years, opening the door, setting up your store, putting the signs on, greeting your customers. Having my health, being able to do that, I feel fine."

The Watch and the Water

Harry and Antoinette Crimi have passed their sixtieth birthdays, and by that definition have entered the season of late adulthood. But sixty is a milestone that is becoming insignificant for a growing number of people. Considering the Crimis' health and vigor — and their desire to remain active and productive — they're no different from someone in middle adulthood. In fact, they still see themselves as middle aged.

The Crimis at sixty provide the background for the major biological story of late adulthood: the period of more than twenty-five years that has been added to our lives since the beginning of this century. But because the basic settings of the Biological Clock have not changed, it's necessary to consider what this increase does and does not mean. It *doesn't* mean that sixty-year-olds, on the average, can expect another twenty-five years of life. Nor does it mean that they will live twenty-five years longer than their counterparts in the past. In fact, sixty-year-olds have gained only five years of life expectancy in this century. In 1900, they could look forward to celebrating their seventy-fifth birthday; today, they can anticipate seeing their eightieth.

What this century's change in life expectancy *does* mean is that the typical *newborn* will live a quarter of a century longer than in 1900 — twenty-eight years, to be exact. It means that unprecedented numbers of people are reaching their sixtieth birthday. It means that more people are attaining more of their genetic potential for long life. At the age of sixty, most of us, like the Crimis, have the ability to "keep going."

As long as we have our health, we may discover that late adulthood is more like an extension of middle age than the beginning of old age. Nearly 70 percent of older adults say that their health is excellent, very good, or good. Because they have built up a resistance to various bacteria and viruses, they suffer from fewer acute illnesses — short-term bouts with a cold or the flu — than they did when they were younger. However, they're likely to have some chronic disorder that seems to worsen with time — a condition such as arthritis, hypertension, heart disease, or diabetes.[1] But even when afflicted with chronic disease, most older adults can care for themselves. Only about 3 percent of adults in their late sixties need help with their personal care, and even among those past the age of eighty-five, less than 20 percent need assistance for the basic requirements of living.

Still, it's hard to make generalizations about a season of life that includes sixty-year-olds such as Harry and Antoinette and ninety-year-olds such as Domenico. In no other season of life is the range of physical responses at any given age so varied.[2] As people pass through late adulthood, differences in sight, taste, hearing, lung capacity, strength, reaction time, sexual response, vulnerability to disease, and the integrity of organ systems continually widen. It seems that there is no biological reason to grow *old* in any particular way, though there are plenty of reasons to grow *up* in a particular way. Once we have reproduced, we no longer walk the biological "straight and narrow." Instead, our bodies show the effects of the different conditions they have experienced.

This diversity, as well as this century's increase in length of life, has forced scientists who study the biology of aging to look at the later years in a new way. What, they ask, is truly intrinsic to the process of aging? Let's consider that question in another way. Suppose you put your watch in a pitcher of water. If it malfunctioned, would you say the problem was with the watch or the water? Are the physical changes of late adulthood built into the Biological Clock or do they come from some external source — from hidden disease or even from something in the environment?

We know, for example, that as people get older, brain tissue seems to contract, the brain weighs less, and space opens up within the skull. Brain scans confirm this shrinkage, which seems to begin in middle adulthood and accelerate thereafter. But many of these scans come from hospital patients or studies that include older adults with chronic disease. When brain scans are limited to healthy older adults who've been carefully screened for disease, the shrinkage is so slight as to be insignificant.[3]

We know, too, that hidden disease is a prime cause of the cardiovascular system becoming less efficient with age. Disease — in the form of fatty deposits in arteries and veins — may also explain why a man's sexual response slows down as he gets older. "We're recognizing that some of these changes may eventually be treatable or preventable," says psychiatrist

Robert Butler. "The more we learn about certain medications — or even surgery to recreate blood supply — the more we'll have to rewrite the books about the impact of 'aging' on sexuality."[4]

Not only disease affects the Biological Clock; environmental factors have a strong influence as well. Everyone "knows" that shortness of breath after exertion is an inevitable companion of age. No matter how hard they try, sixty-year-olds can draw in only about two-thirds of the oxygen they could in their youth. But we're learning that much of that loss may come from smoking, air pollution, or frequent respiratory infections. Former athletes aren't nearly as short of breath as the average adult, and — even more striking — some portion of the average adult's loss can be reversed. Regular exercise increases the amount of oxygen that an older person can breathe in and expel.[5]

Factors other than disease and pollutants in the physical environment can also affect the Biological Clock. The water surrounding the watch is partly social in nature. It was once an established scientific "fact" that levels of the male hormone testosterone declined with age. But the studies establishing that "fact" were all performed on older men who were institutionalized and segregated from women. When later studies were made of men living at home or in nursing homes that housed both sexes, the decline disappeared. Today we know that testosterone levels normally remain constant with age, although their daily rhythm alters. And we know that social context makes a big difference: no matter what a man's age, his testosterone level usually rises after sexual activity — or even when he's in the presence of a sexually attractive partner.[6]

"Think of the implications," says Richard Adelman, a biologist who heads the University of Michigan's Institute of Gerontology. "Several decades ago, some well-intentioned nursing-home administrator made the perfectly reasonable policy decision that men and women should not be housed together in their institution. As a consequence of that decision, a biological change was provoked which for decades has been interpreted as an example of the biology of aging. And it's simply an artifact."[7]

So many of the "normal" changes of age turn out to be the ravages of disease or the effects of the environment that it's becoming difficult to say what is intrinsic to the Biological Clock. A slowing down of reactions is one possibility. As we grow old, it takes us longer to unwrap a stick of gum, zip up a jacket, tie our shoes, or program a microwave oven. Some psychologists explain this slowdown as sluggish transmission in the nervous system. It takes longer, they say, for sights, sounds, tastes, and touches to reach the brain and for the brain's instructions to travel back down to the muscles. Other psychologists contend that it also takes more time for the brain to figure out what to do with sensory information once it is received. This slowdown seems so general that it probably is an essential feature of aging.

But at least one study suggests that we should reserve judgement even in this case. In a test of reaction time, researchers matched a group of highly active older women against college students. These women, who had been on a vigorous program of physical activity for ten years, reacted as quickly as the younger students.[8]

Many older people get along well without giving much thought to their slower reaction time, because they have been able to adapt to it and compensate for it. Typists are a good example. Based on laboratory studies of motor response, we would predict that older adults could not hope to type as fast as twenty-five-year-olds. Yet they do, even though their reaction time is much slower. Older typists retain their speed by looking farther ahead in the material they're copying than younger typists do. If the material to be copied is masked so that they cannot see ahead, older typists' speed immediately drops, but the younger typists are as fast as ever.[9] Speed, grace, and precision need not decline in later life. As older musicians have shown — Vladimir Horowitz, Artur Rubinstein, Wanda Landowska, Pablo Casal — continued exercise of a skill and the ability to compensate can fend off the effects of age.

A Season of the Senses

Whether it's a matter of aging or disease — the watch or the water — the nature of our sensory experience changes as we get older. Many older adults find they are restricted by impairments in vision and hearing. But at the same time, they take new pleasure in what they *can* see, hear, taste, and touch. For those fortunate enough to enjoy good health, says David Gutmann, late adulthood is a "season of the senses."

One national survey found that 90 percent of Americans over age sixty-five had some visual impairment, and that only 10 percent could see well without glasses.[10] And there are problems that glasses cannot solve. Most older adults find that when looking ahead, they don't see as far to each side as they once did. When the light level suddenly changes, it takes their eyes longer to adjust. Glare bothers them. They need more light to see objects clearly, and even with adequate light, they don't see as well as they once did. Together, glare and fuzzier vision may obscure many of the cues that disclose the distance of objects, making it more difficult to judge depth.

Driving poses additional problems. Although older people are involved in more crashes per million miles than drivers between the ages of twenty-five and sixty-five (but fewer than drivers younger than twenty-five), their accidents are less likely to involve fatal injuries. Older drivers often compensate for their slowed reaction time and dimming vision by driving defensively. They avoid rush hours, stay off freeways, drive more slowly, and anticipate light changes or sudden moves by other drivers. Many also avoid driving at night, to escape a special problem. As drivers go from lighted intersections to dark stretches of highway, or as they face the lights of oncoming cars, their eyes switch back and forth from receptors that function in dim light to those that function in bright light. For many older drivers, this switch takes so long that they find themselves experiencing brief periods of blindness, a situation that can be both frightening and dangerous.[11]

Changes in hearing are nearly as common as changes in vision. The slow, progressive loss of hearing that begins in midlife — and even earlier in hunters, rock-music fans, and industrial workers — may not become troublesome for decades. But by age eighty, three out of every four people have noticeable hearing problems.[12] Severe hearing loss is more common among men, but it can disrupt the lives of either sex. At parties, older people find themselves unable to follow a voice against normal background noise. Some stop listening and grow silent. Others guess at the content of a conversation and risk the embarrassment of making a foolish statement. But many compensate by watching people's faces and bodies, picking up cues from their tone of voice, expressions, lip movements, and gestures.[13]

If our senses become less acute with age, in many ways they become more important. Gerontologists have observed that later life is frequently a time for greater enjoyment of all the senses. Freed from overriding concerns with achievement, possession, and power, older adults relish the smell and taste of morning coffee, the sound of a river rushing over rocks, the sight of the setting sun or a rainbow after a storm. Overall skin pleasure becomes more important in sexual encounters. "You see older people delighting in the things they can feel and hear," says Gutmann. "The eyes are no longer recruited to the purpose of advancing a career or getting through the tangled pathways of society. They can be receptors of pleasure. And older people spend a lot of time, if they can manage it, going around to beautiful places. They take up painting. They take up bird-watching. They start to use their eyes as instruments of enjoyment."[14]

In studies of several cultures, Gutmann has found that the pleasures of food become more important in the thinking of older men. They dwell on memories of how they were first nourished in life. "As they recast their lives, they often think about the foods that were available to them as kids, given to them by their mothers. And they often turn back in later life to the kinds of foods they first enjoyed as kids, and they first received from a loving mother."[15]

Old age is a time when the senses respond more slowly and with less precision. Yet some people turn that very loss into a gain. As one seventy-year-old woman said of sexuality, "It's not so much how powerful the orgasm is or how many orgasms you have. It's just touching and being together and loving." And as an eighty-two-year-old woman said of driving, "I will generally choose the back roads to drive on rather than expressways just because it's prettier. It's nicer." She added something that's often true of the season of the senses. "I don't have to be concerned about traffic now. I can enjoy what's going by."[16]

Sleep: The Mysterious Third

It's astounding to think that, if we lived to be a hundred, roughly thirty-three of our years would be spent sound asleep. Sleep occupies about a third of our time — more than any other activity — yet we probably know the least about that part of our existence. We aren't even certain why we sleep. Some scientists believe that humans — and other animals — evolved to sleep whenever they were safe and not in need of carrying out some activity that promoted survival. Sleeping at night was a means of keeping out of harm's way. Our early ancestors who persisted in prowling about in the dark either fell over a cliff or were eaten by a leopard lurking in a tree. Those who slept survived to pass on their genes. But other scientists say the purpose of sleep is simply to restore our physical and mental powers.

Whatever its purpose, the pattern of sleep changes over the course of a life. When we enter the world, we sleep about sixteen hours a day, usually in four-hour cycles. Slowly, we shift to a day/night cycle, getting our longest sleep at night and napping during the day. By age two, our need for sleep has dropped to about twelve hours a day. It keeps on declining until adolescence, when most of us keep the adult schedule of eight hours a night.[17]

The differences among us are as pronounced in sleep as in any other aspect of life. Though most of us sleep between seven and nine hours each night, some sleep ten or more hours and others seem to need only a couple of hours. Our sleep differs in other ways, too. Some of us are "larks," who function best when we go to bed early and rise with the dawn. Others are "owls," who find mornings a trial, grow more alert as the day progresses, and aren't ready for bed until long after midnight. Whether we are larks or owls depends on the way the Biological Clock manages our daily temperature cycle. Everyone's body temperature varies about a degree and a half during the day. A lark's temperature peaks during the morning hours; an owl's, during the evening.[18]

About half of a newborn's sixteen hours of slumber is spent in a kind of sleep known as REM (which stands for "rapid eye movement"). During REM sleep, our eyes move rapidly back and forth beneath the closed lids. This is an odd kind of sleep, because our heart, lungs, and brain behave much like those of a waking person, yet we are slow to respond to touch or sound, and our muscles are limp and unable to move. Most of our dreams take place during REM sleep — dreams that have some sort of story line, not just fleeting images. The limpness of our muscles apparently keeps us from acting out our dreams. Since newborns have few memories to draw on during sleep, their dreams probably consist of a random light-and-sound show.

Fifty percent of a newborn's sleep involves REM, but only 20 percent of a five-year-old's does. From that age on, the proportion of sleep devoted to REM remains steady until extreme old age, when some decline appears.[19] As we age, the quality of sleep also changes. Older adults spend less time in very deep sleep than they did in their youth, and most wake at least once in the night. At least a third complain about waking often and sleeping poorly. Most of them make up for lost sleep with daytime naps, so that they sleep as long as they ever did, but don't feel as refreshed. When researchers recorded the sleep of adults between the ages of sixty-five and ninety-five in their own homes, the average adult slept eight hours and eighteen minutes.[20] Yet many of these adults complained of not getting enough sleep. This belief led many to use sleeping pills — which usually aggravate the problem.

Some research indicates that many complaints about lost sleep could be eliminated if older adults spent less time in bed. When adults spent no more than six hours in bed each night and avoided naps, they slept like young people.[21] It seems to be another case of the watch and the water. Changes in the pattern of sleep may have as much to do with the way in which we live our lives as with the shifting rhythms of the Biological Clock.

Why We Die

When Florence Knapp died on January 11, 1988, the life of America's oldest living person came to an end. Florence's immediate family spans the history of the republic: her grandfather was born in 1792, shortly after the constitution made us one unified nation. When Abiram Knapp came into the world, George Washington was president; when he left it, he had seen the Civil War and the presidency of Abraham Lincoln. He lived until 1876, when Florence was three years old. At Florence's birth, the president was Ulysses S. Grant and the pace of the world was still slow. There were railroads and telegraphs, but no automobiles or radios. When she died at the age of 114, television, transcontinental jets, atomic energy, and computers were part of our daily lives.

Florence never married; in her era, women who had careers rarely had families. She graduated from college in 1894 and spent forty-two years as an elementary school teacher. She was a lifelong feminist; she could recall parading down Philadelphia's Broad Street in 1919, dressed all in white and carrying a placard that demanded "Votes for Women." In 1920, when Florence was forty-seven, women finally won the right to vote in all the states.

Florence spent her entire life on the family farm in Pennsylvania, in the midst of her extended family. Long past her hundredth birthday, she was climbing stairs, weeding the garden, and living an active family life. Although she was a fragile, tiny woman, she survived three bouts of pneumonia and a broken hip. Some time after her hundred and tenth birthday, her health at last failed, and she moved into a nursing home.[22]

One hundred and fourteen years is pushing what many scientists see as life's upper limit. Biologically, we are designed to live perhaps 115 years — but surely no more than 120. Only one of us has yet made that date. The year before Florence died, Shigechijo Izumi of Japan died at the age of 120.

From time to time, we hear of considerably older people, such as a man named Charlie Smith, who convinced the Social Security Administration that he was 137, or yogurt-eating Russians who routinely reach 130 or so. But none of these claims has stood up to investigation. When researchers checked up on Charlie Smith, they found he had died at a comparatively young 104 — making him a good bit older than the yogurt eaters in remote Russian villages. If the records of those villagers are examined, people who claim to be well into their second century generally turn out to be about ninety-five.

Still, each year more of us live on into our eighties and nineties, and some of us join the ranks of centenarians. But even the Florence Knapps of the world run up against that 115- or 120-year barrier. Why should we have evolved to die once we reach that limit? That's one of the most complex

Florence Knapp in her twenties. The photo was taken in Atlantic City in the 1890s. Courtesy of Mrs. Ruth Oberholtzer

biological puzzles that has ever been posed, and even preliminary answers still lie far in the future.

Apparently, no single gene prescribes the hour of our death — no fatal bullet in a biological time capsule. Yet each cell in our body seems to have its own genetic timing mechanism. Microbiologist Leonard Hayflick of the San Francisco campus of the University of California established that when he discovered a built-in life span for human cells.[23] More than twenty years ago, Hayflick grew fetal cells in the laboratory and found that the cells died after reproducing about fifty times. Cells from adults doubled only twenty times before they stopped dividing. When cells from different species were grown in the lab, the longer the animal's natural life span, the more often the cells divided before dying. This "programmed death" within cells, known as the Hayflick limit, has convinced some biologists that the genetic program does indeed run to the end of life — but they can't decide

Florence on her 113th birthday. Courtesy of Mrs. Ruth Oberholtzer

whether it's a matter of inactive genes being turned on or active genes being turned off.

While struggling with this complexity, researchers have proposed various theories of aging. One theory suggests that we grow old because our bodies lose the ability to repair damage to the genetic library — the DNA — in our cells. Environmental pollutants, radiation, even the basic process of metabolism continually damage our DNA. But because each of our cells has a built-in repair crew, we fix the damage almost as fast as it occurs. The key word is "almost." As cells become more susceptible to damage and less competent at repair, the proportion of damaged DNA gradually increases.[24] Because neurons and muscle cells cannot reproduce themselves, they eventually become so damaged that they stop functioning.

Other researchers believe that changes in the immune system may be responsible for aging. As we get older, the workings of the immune system falter. Researchers know that, with time, the system becomes weak and can mount only feeble efforts to fight off foreign invaders. Many also suspect that it loses its ability to distinguish between friend and enemy, so it attacks normal body cells and makes no effort to destroy renegade cancer cells.

Another contending theory is the "free-radical" explanation of aging. During metabolism, cells produce chemical compounds with an extra electron, usually oxygen. These compounds, known as "free radicals," are unstable; on the slightest provocation, they bond to other molecules. All this bonding is bad for our health: it harms the membranes of body cells, damages chromosomes, and unites free radicals with unsaturated fats to form a compound that eventually makes body tissues so rigid that vital systems cannot function normally. As this damage builds up within our cells and tissues, we begin to age.

Maybe more than one of these theories of aging is correct, and maybe none of them are. Adelman finds all the current proposals unsatisfactory. "There are more theories of aging than there are investigators in the field of biological gerontology," he says. "In my opinion, most of those theories are not worth the paper they've been printed on. They're based on the problems of old age rather than on the developmental sequence of events that makes an organism more susceptible to damage or disease with the passage of time."[25] Perhaps the key to longevity, says Adelman, is genetic resistance to the chronic disorders that we once thought were intrinsic to the process of aging.

The contribution of genes to longevity shows clearly in Florence Knapp's robust old age. All four of her grandparents lived past seventy, three of them lived into their eighties, and one grandmother reached the age of ninety-five. Nor is Florence the first centenarian in her family; an aunt and one of her sisters both lived to be 107. The example of the Knapp family is echoed in longevity studies. When researchers followed the remaining years of all twins older than sixty who lived in New York State, they discovered that the life spans of identical twins (with identical genes) were closer than those of fraternal twins (who shared only some of their genes).[26]

Some scientists have begun to toy with the possibility that our maximum life span may someday break the 120-year barrier. At the UCLA Medical School, pathologist Roy Walford has been trying to figure out a way to extend the life span using the information we already possess.[27] His program draws on findings from research with rats, mice, and other mammals. For some time, researchers have known that by radically restricting a rat's diet — giving it highly nutritious food but not much of it — they could nearly double the animal's life span. When rats got only half their normal calories, they lived more than four years instead of the normal three.

For nearly a decade, Walford has been using himself as a test subject in a diet-restricting program for humans. His first step was to eliminate virtually all sugar, honey, alcohol, and nonessential fats from his diet. He consumes so few calories that he cannot get all the essential nutrients unless he takes a wide variety of minerals and vitamins. His daily diet is low in fats (15 percent) and high in protein (25 percent), and it ranges from 1,500 to 1,800 calories per day — most of them from vegetables, grain, legumes, and fruit. Years of following this diet have brought Walford's weight down below the normal range for his height and build. He is willing to forgo the pleasures of the table because he believes that following his rigorous plan will keep him alive for at least 120 years — perhaps longer. If everyone ate that way, he says, we would all celebrate our seventy-fifth birthdays looking like today's fifty-year-olds.

As biologists acquire the ability to modify DNA, some wonder if timing genes in the Biological Clock can be changed so that people might live even longer than Walford hopes to. "We can now make tobacco plants light up in the dark the same way a firefly lights up," says Adelman. "Although we're at a very rudimentary stage in this technology, the day will come when certain physiological functions that are lost today will not be lost. Certain diseases that affect us today will not affect us. As we understand the genetics of our system, as we become sufficiently civilized to control our environment, there is no limit, in my opinion, to the quality or quantity of life that we can anticipate."[28]

Yet few older adults *want* to live beyond the present limit of life. "No doubt it is hard to die," wrote Jean-Jacques Rousseau in the eighteenth century, "but it is sweet to think that we shall not live forever. . . . If we had the offer of immortality here below, who would accept the sorrowful gift?"[29] Researchers have confirmed Rousseau's sentiments; in one large study, nearly seven out of ten older adults said they had no interest at all in reaching their 150th birthday.[30] Even those who have escaped poor health and poverty are not impressed by the idea. Among the affluent residents of a retirement community, only about two in ten were willing to live until they were 100 — and then only if they could continue to be active.[31] Life was of less concern to them than the freedom to be productive.

Still Free at Ninety

"I have fun, yes, I have fun. I hope it continues. I have the philosophy that if you don't like a thing, change it. If you can't change it, put up

Minna Citron, now ninety, as a young woman. "Well, I can't change that I'm old now, so I must put up with it."

with it. Well, I can't change that I'm old now, so I must put up with it."

After nine decades of life, age is beginning to restrict the exuberance of Minna Citron, an artist who lives by herself in a New York apartment. "I find the city rather difficult," she says. "It's difficult to get around. I used to ride in the subways, but I don't do that anymore — largely because there are a lot of stairs to climb. I don't have enough money to take taxis everywhere, so I'm limiting my activities mostly to this neighborhood. I don't go uptown as much. And, like Winston Churchill, I like a nap. If I can take my shoes off and lie flat, that sets me up so I think I have two days in one.

"I tire easily, you see. I can't work a full day, which I used to. It takes too long to set up oil paintings and wait till they dry and all that sort of thing. So for the most part I work on collages. I'll have something lying over there on the table, and I'll come in and I'll look at it. It'll draw me, you see? So it's easier to work on collages."

Minna's world is getting smaller, but there's a freedom in her spirit, a freedom she has cultivated through all of her ninety years. "What could I not live without?" she asks. "Well, I think Jack Daniels. I don't overdo it, but I must say that he and I get along very well once or twice a day." Minna tells her story with flair and humor — and a strong voice. She is a slim woman who loves to dress stylishly for most any occasion. Her face bears deep wrinkles, but she doesn't hesitate to apply color. Today, with her hair swept back and tied on top of her head, she is wearing blue eye shadow to match her earrings.

Minna's life began in New York just before the turn of the century. Her father ran a talcum powder company. "My mother and father had four sons. And my mother felt terrible, 'cause she always wanted a daughter — she wanted a doll. So they kept trying. I finally came along, and I was the only daughter. They made a great fuss about me. My mother was beautiful, and I was always content to be near her. I loved to listen to her because her taffeta petticoat rippled when she walked. That petticoat had a ruffle on it and a rhythm that I loved, and it also had my mother in it, and I loved her."

Minna's love for art goes back to her earliest childhood, when she played with her brother in the attic, making glorious designs from colored paper and beads. "Color to me was a born thing, like Joe Louis used to say. In kindergarten we made costumes out of colored paper, and I enjoyed it very much." Although school held little fascination for Minna, she did well in her classes, graduating from high school when she was only sixteen. Shortly afterward, she married. "I guess I was in love with love, you know. And there were lots of boys around that I was attracted to. They loved to come to my mother's house because she was very friendly and beautiful, and she welcomed them. We had a houseful of them all the time. I was always surrounded by boys.

"I married this young man that I went around with. We were kids. I was sixteen and he was eighteen, and we had good times together. He was a very good dancer, and we were very athletic — both of us. He was a good playmate. But when you get married and you're having children, a playmate isn't exactly what you need. You need a thoughtful person to be a good father to your children and to recognize that you're becoming a different kind of person. He made a success of his business, and my son and grandson are in it now. But that was all, you see? He used to say, 'I never know where to put my hat when I come in 'cause you've moved the piano.' He meant, 'Why can't you just stay put? Do nothing.' He didn't realize that if people want to develop, they have to change.

"What he wanted and what he's still interested in today is a woman to do his bidding. And since I had a mind of my own, I wasn't doing anybody's bidding. That would make him mad. He had a terrible temper, and after losing it, he would say, 'Well, now, come into my bed.' Getting in bed with a man who has just had a temper tantrum and called you all kinds of names isn't the way to start a sexual relationship.

"We had the two children and I thought, 'That's it! That's all I want. They're wonderful. Now, what am I gonna do with the rest of my life?' I didn't like being a kept woman, so I thought maybe I should do something that I could earn a living at. So I went to the New York School of Applied Design for Women, and I came out with some honors. Then I realized I didn't know how to draw a figure, so I went to the Art Students League. I signed up with Kenneth Hayes Miller, and he said, 'Do what you feel like doing.'"

What Minna felt like doing was finding herself. Intrigued by Freud's writings, she began to see a psychoanalyst. "He said to me, 'How is your sexual relationship with your husband? Do you have orgasms?' I had never heard the word before. This was back in the thirties. I thought yes sounded better than no, so I said yes." Minna laughs, but her psychoanalysis was important to her. It enabled her, she says, to cut the "silver cord" connecting her to her mother. And it was through analysis that she got the nerve to start going out on her own.

At first, she went to Miller's weekly gathering for art students. "I used to feel like a chicken whose brood wasn't following her anymore, see? Here I was, disconnected from my mother, my husband, and my children." The sense of freedom was exhilarating. "Every Wednesday I used to go to this little tea party on 14th Street. There were some very interesting people there, and as I sat on the bus I used to feel, 'I'm free!' I used to stay out for dinner, and of course my husband was very suspicious — the fact that I was staying out without him, you know? By this time, I realized my marriage was on the rocks, but I was marking time until after my psychoanalysis to decide what to do. Takes courage to be a woman without any money and leave a man who is very comfortable and get out into the world. Well, I suppose courage is not lacking in me. It's difficult, but you do it. So I up and left."

Minna's departure started a custody battle, one that she was determined to win. "I fought very hard to keep my two sons. A friend was in divorce at the same time, and she said, 'Look. Stop fighting. Give your sons over to your husband. I gave my son over to my husband and I'm going to Europe.' Well, I don't think her son turned out very well, and I do think my sons have. I fought for them. I always think you have to fight for what you want."

After the divorce, Minna's life revolved around her two boys and her art. Her paintings in the turbulent 1930s had a representational, socially conscious sweep. But later, the advent of such American abstract painters as Jackson Pollock had a freeing influence on Minna. Once her children left the nest, she was off to Paris, where she stayed for nearly half a year, painting, painting, painting.

"I just did what I felt like doing. Once you learn what makes you tick, you're freer to change, you see? As I changed, naturally my work changed. For instance, my early work had a gravitational pull. People stood on the ground or stood up. If you don't have that compulsion any more, you're freer. At the time, Kenneth Hayes Miller warned me, 'Minna, if your work changes, you'll lose your following.' Well, I said, 'I'm gonna do what I wanna do.' And I think that's been the thing that has made me very happy in life. If you're not free to do what you feel you should be doing, it's just as though you were handcuffed or chained. If somebody or something is holding you back, maybe you have to pay a price to break the connection, but why not pay it if it's something that's important to you?

"I think art is a wonderful therapy. It's like a good physic. You know, it's a psychological physic. It gets rid of a lot of tensions and a lot of difficulties." She motions at a painting leaning against the wall. "I can't tell you how I did it. I just go ahead and work. A friend used to ask, 'How did you do this?' That's very much like saying to a person, 'Tell me what you do in a sexual relationship.' You don't write a story about he did this and I did that. You just do — just do and take the consequences.

"A lot of my friends have sold better than I have because they've repeated themselves. Once I needed a gallery very badly, and I showed a lot of things — twelve works, all different. The dealer wasn't interested unless I could paint twelve things all alike, so Mrs. Jones could buy a painting like Mrs. Smith's. But I didn't get to be an artist because I expected to make a killing."

Freedom echoes through Minna's words — freedom, independence, and responsibility for her own decisions. That philosophy has permeated her life and her work, and is still evident even as her physical world becomes more confined. "Well, there used to be more men courting me," she jokes, "but they don't court me at ninety." Minna feels close to her grandchildren, who are scattered around the country — one in Atlanta, another in Denver. She holds on to her old connections, at times visiting her ex-husband and ex-daughters-in-law. Each morning she gets up early, exercises, has breakfast, and is off to her studio. After lunch, she goes home and takes her nap, then gets up and writes letters or goes out to the movies.

"When you get to be my age, you don't think so much about the future. You think more of the past, see? And if you're talking about dying, well, that's something people have to think about any time. Some people die younger, some people die older. I don't want to live to be terribly, terribly old. And when I die, that's that. I'm not interested in what happens after. One of my daughter-in-laws said, 'Minna, when you die, could we have a good Episcopalian ceremony?' I said, 'I don't care what you do with me after I die, but give my parts to people that need them, and don't let anybody say I did this or I believed that, since I didn't.'

"What happens right here and now, that's good enough for me. I just

"I'm a satisfied customer. . . . I love people and I love my friends. And I like new friends — like you."

want to go on enjoying life if I can — working and being free and staying well. I'm a satisfied customer. I have fun. I hope it continues. I feel as though I'm curator to a career. I've done work which I'm proud of, and it's a lot to take care of, I want to say that. And I'd just like to go on. I love people and I love my friends. And I like new friends — like you."

17

THE SOCIAL STORY *Pioneers*

OF LATE ADULTHOOD *of Aging*

"I don't know where the word 'retiring' came from, but the only thing it means to me is I'm retiring from the paid work force. That's all it means, because I have no intention of 'retiring.'"

Vivian Russell has put forty years of her life into paid employment. With the help of her husband Tom, she has also raised three children. Both the Russells have just retired, she from her job as a drug-abuse counselor, he from a supervisory position with the U.S. Postal Service. Soon, they will be moving into a smaller home in suburban Detroit. They plan to enjoy the rewards of hard work in seasons past, but they do not plan to sit still.

Vivian looks much younger than her sixty years. She is a black woman with light skin, reddish hair, a smooth, unlined face, and a ready smile. "Chronologically, I'm an old woman. But physically, I don't feel old," she says. "Mentally, I don't feel old. I try to be an example of growing old gracefully. I mean, I don't want to go and sit in a chair and pick my teeth. I want to look as nice as I can. I want to be as energetic as I can. I want to live as long as I can take care of my basic needs. When I get to the point where I can't, I hope my fairy godmother just ships me aloft.

"Work was important to me over the years. It gave me a sense of responsibility. It gave me a sense of pride. It gave me a better understanding of life and a better understanding of people. But it had gotten to the point where it wasn't fulfilling any longer. It was just a matter of pay day. And I don't like working like that. It's been a long journey, but I have no regrets — none. Because had it not been for those past forty years, I wouldn't have the future forty years that I'm gonna have."

From the very beginning of her life, hard work was part of Vivian's existence. It had to be for a girl who was one of nine children in a poor family in Arkansas. Her first memories are of the depression. "My mother did not want to take her kids and an unskilled husband on welfare. Her foresight was to sell the urban property they had and buy two acres of land in rural North Little Rock. My oldest brother and my father built a four-room house. My mother sewed and my father got a janitor job in a business building. We had everything we needed because we raised everything. We had pigs and chickens and you-name-it. Fruit trees, all kinds of vegetables. In the fall, my oldest sisters and my mother, they canned, canned, canned, canned. We were very poor, but in my mind I guess we weren't, because everybody around us was on plantations. We were the only ones who had our own property."

Vivian is convinced that her early poverty gave her the ability to make something out of nothing. "The best thing I got from the experience of my humble background was to be able to improvise, to set priorities. My mother worked very hard. She sewed and did all the things that mothers do for kids and then she would go out to work — leave at six o'clock in the morning. My father worked as a janitor and he'd come home and work on the little farm. I guess it instilled in me a sense of pride. You don't just sit around and wait for somebody to take care of your needs. You set about taking care of them yourself."

When Vivian was sixteen, her family moved from Arkansas to Detroit. World War II was raging, and she went to work in a defense plant. "I dropped out of school and worked in the plant, changing my birth certificate to make me old enough. And then the war ended, so I went back and finished high school. What really made me decide to do something different was doing day work. One time, this young lady was sitting there at a piano, playing 'Clair de Lune,' and I'm doing her kitchen floors. And her husband came in and complimented her on her gorgeous clean house. I said to myself, 'Hey, this won't work. This is *not* gonna work!' And at that point I decided I have to do something more than graduate from high school. So I went to night school and learned to type."

In 1946, when Vivian was nineteen, she met Tom at a ballroom dance. "She was a doll," he recalls, "a real pretty girl. And I had lotsa problems with her, because she was tall and I was short. She tol' everybody I was a little too short for her, you know. But when I blew in her ear, I became six feet tall.

"It was just somethin' about her that she was different, completely different. She was ambitious. I'd never tell her this, but I would never be a success today if it wasn't for Vivian. The skills were there, but I had to have somebody kinda hone those skills and push me in the right direction. And that's what she done."

At sixty-four, Tom has close-cropped gray hair and a narrow mustache. His deep, warm voice is marked by the rhythms of his native Georgia. He spent his first eighteen years in Atlanta before his family, like Vivian's, moved north to Detroit in search of wartime jobs in the factories. "I'm from a poor sharecropping family," he says. "My father was just an ordinary laborer, and my childhood was a kind of childhood that you would get from a black in the South back in the late thirties. It was a cold, segregated South — black/white washrooms and public facilities. That's our history, you know, and I'm a product of that environment. So it was a struggle, a struggle all the way. Lord, it was tough!

"My escape from that environment was the army. It might be naïve to say this, but I think the army was one of the best things that happened to the black man in the forties, because it gave him a chance with the G.I. bill and everything. It gave him a chance to go to college and to do some of the things that ordinary humans had been able to do. It gave him a chance to go overseas and to kinda get out of that niche he was in."

During the war, Tom served in North Africa and Italy. When it ended, he was able to take some courses at the University of Florence before he was shipped back to the states. He was still in his military uniform when he met Vivian at that ballroom dance. Before long, they married — in secret — in a Detroit courthouse and moved into a one-room apartment. Five years later, the first of three daughters was born.

Tom is convinced that his comfortable life today would not have been possible without sacrifice, perseverance, and Vivian's encouragement — the sort of push that he calls "bootin' me in the behind." He says, "My wife is my best friend. Always was. She's the greatest soundin' board for me. And she's a mistress, every way. She's a partner — all those things rolled into one. We struggled together and we sacrificed, and I think that's what made us so real close. We had lotsa hard climbs. My first priority was to accumulate some money. So we lived in one room for seven years, and I just can't think of anyone else who would live in one room for seven years and save every nickel and dime like that.

Vivian Russell, sixty. "It's gonna be interesting."

"We put our money in the bank. And my wife made all her own clothes, and she did her own hair, and that was bona fide. There's a lotsa sacrificin' and there's a whole lotsa things you have to do without to maintain that goal. But when we bought our first home, we was the youngest couple in the subdivision."

Tom started working for the post office in 1954, when he was thirty-one. Whenever he and Vivian had the chance, they took courses at local colleges. Sometimes they worked more than one job. "I consider myself a success," says Tom, "because of the humble background I came from to where I am now. And it just didn't happen. I didn't hit a lottery. I didn't get a million-dollar sweepstake. I was a hardworkin', honest guy that saved his money and had priorities.

"I have no more mountains to climb. I've achieved what I wanted to achieve. Now it's time to do some of the things that give you a kinda personal satisfaction, you know? Motivate the people I come in touch with. Playin' golf is good, but golf only satisfies the person that's doin' it. You don't achieve nothin' by playin' golf. I want to do something where it will be a benefit to a person that's less fortunate than I am."

These days, Tom spends a lot of time working on the house that he and Vivian will soon move into. The two of them are active in a grandparents' rights organization, and they're helping one of their daughters, a divorced single parent, care for her son. But Tom also finds time to participate in a ministry that brings a message of Christian love and guidance to inmates of a federal prison. He takes pride in his work. "Bringin' Christ to the guys in the prison is an achievement. It gives them a sense of confidence and a sense of Christianity and love for your fellow man. A prisoner needs some-

Tom, sixty-four. "I wanna go out in a blaze of glory."

one to come in there and tell him that he's loved and someone cares for him, and you can change your ways, and you got a second chance at life. And I think that's what we do. We come in and we give them a new sense of direction, a new sense of ways to go. If we get only one out of ten, that's one more than we had before.

"It gives me a good warm inner feeling. And that's the kinda thing you can't buy, the kinda feeling that I need more than anything else. It makes me feel that I'm really doing somethin' worthwhile. I wanna go out in a blaze of glory. I want people to say, 'Oh, he was a hell of a guy. He helped people.' That's one of the greatest things that people can say when you die — that you was the kinda guy that would help."

Vivian's small gold earrings glitter as she tilts her head, reflecting on her past and wondering at the fact that she is now in late adulthood. She shares Tom's outlook. "I feel like I've been successful. For me, success is having my children grow to adulthood without any disasters and seeing them choose what they want to do with their lives. I've accomplished that." She did it while working. When their three girls were small, Vivian spent nine years as a licensed practical nurse, working the midnight shift so she could be at home during the day. Now, she looks forward to setting her own hours and gardening on the acre of land at their new home. She also wonders what it will be like to spend so much time with Tom. "It's gonna be interesting," she says, smiling, "because he doesn't really know me. He thinks he does, but he has some surprises in store."

Vivian has already found meaningful volunteer work, spending a good deal of her time at a local hospice, where she gives nursing care to dying patients. This service allows her to use some of the skills she developed as a nurse so many years ago. "I'll have patients who are completely helpless. I have a sense of how they feel if I turn them over and I give them a backrub to stimulate the circulation, make the sheets cool and dry, and then turn them in a different position. I feel how they feel. And I think that it's important for everybody to feel that someone cares. That's an emotion that I don't think we ever outgrow.

"I need to feel useful. I need to feel that I'm doing something constructive. I'm not one to sit and waste time. And there are so many needs, you see? I could very well join a bridge club, but I feel that this is what God wants me to do. And I'm happy to be able to do it. You don't just be on earth to take up space. It's important to make some kind of contribution."

The Squaring of the Triangle

In many ways, Vivian and Tom Russell represent what's new in the social story of late adulthood. Having reached their sixties in good health, they are entering a newly created stage of life called "retirement." Like the majority of elderly people today, they have benefited from Social Security and pension plans, and they are in sound financial condition.

The number of Americans reaching their sixties, seventies, eighties, and nineties is unprecedented. And there are societies — Japan, Sweden, and Canada — where life expectancy is even greater than in our own. Older adults today are truly pioneers of aging. They are enabling us to learn more about the final season of the Biological Clock, to test the upper limits of intellectual potential. For the first time in history, a substantial portion of a society — not just a few rare individuals — is taking advantage of the "wisdom" in the Biological Clock's plan for a lengthy postreproductive life.

Already these pioneers are changing the very shape of our population. In 1900, only one out of every twenty-five men and women in the United States had reached the age of sixty-five. Today, one out of nine is that old, and by 2030, one out of five will be. Among this group, the fastest growing segment is adults over eighty-five. At the turn of the century, only one American in 500 had reached that age. Today, about one in a hundred is eighty-five or older, and by 2030, nearly one in thirty-five will be. To see how dramatically our society is changing, we can stack its various age groups as if they were blocks. In 1900, the U.S. population made a perfect triangle, with the blocks regularly decreasing in size with age. By the year 2030, when the baby-boom generation hits late adulthood, the group of young people under the age of eighteen and adults past the age of sixty-five will be virtually identical in size. The population triangle will have become a square, with no single age group dominating society. The median age of our population will be forty-one, compared with only twenty-three in 1900.

Today, the Social Clock says that the official time to retire is sixty-five, an arbitrary date that coincides with the Western world's first specific retirement age, which was set in 1889 by Otto von Bismarck, the first chancellor of the German Empire. Legend says that Bismarck picked that age as a way of removing political rivals older than himself. In 1935, when the Social Security system was established in the United States, we settled on the same age, but it could just as easily have been sixty or seventy.

With each passing decade, Americans start their work lives later and end them sooner. Because we also live longer, the proportion of adult life spent working has been shrinking rapidly. As late as 1950, every other man past

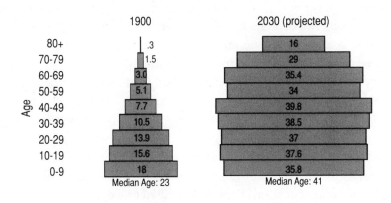

The United States population (in millions), 1900 and 2030.

the age of sixty-five was still employed; today, fewer than one in seven are still at work. As more pensions based on years of service instead of age become available, men are stopping work in their late fifties or early sixties. Some retire early because of poor health, but for those who are healthy and have adequate funds, retirement begins a life of leisure. Although their income has dropped by half, more than 80 percent of older Americans say that they have enough money to live on. In 1987, only 12 percent of those sixty-five and older lived in poverty, down from 35 percent in 1959.[1] In addition to Social Security and pensions, savings and "in-kind" income (tax benefits, health services, food stamps, reduced transportation fares, discounts, and the like) have given older adults a freedom unknown to previous generations.

Not everyone retires. A few keep working because they cannot afford to quit, but the majority of those who stay with full-time jobs are either professionals or people such as the Crimis who own small businesses. Their occupations bring them personal as well as financial rewards, and they tend to have control over the conditions and hours of work. More elderly people would probably work into their later years if they had such control. When researchers at the Ethel Percy Andrus Gerontology Center in Los Angeles surveyed employees of two large companies, they discovered that the majority of their senior workers would forgo their planned retirements if the company would allow them to work part time and still get a portion of their pensions.[2]

Perhaps the reluctance of older workers to completely sever their ties with the labor force explains the recruiting success of fast-food chains offering "rehirement, not retirement." At close to minimum wage, the appeal of such work is unlikely to be monetary. One sixty-nine-year-old who responded to McDonald's recruitment program says simply that he loves his job. He enjoys watching people come and go, and he has decided that the exercise he gets mopping, sweeping, and carrying out the trash is good for him.[3] Not long ago, *Modern Maturity*, the official magazine of the American Association of Retired Persons, asked its readers about work in the later years. Only 32 percent of those who had started second work careers said that their primary reason was money, and 19 percent said they had entered new occupations because they *liked* to work.[4]

Like Vivian and Tom Russell, some retirees become active volunteers. In Walnut Creek, California, older adults who belong to Senior Tutors for Youth in Detention travel across the bay to San Francisco, where each volunteer spends several hours a week with a boy or girl who has been confined by the Juvenile Court. They work on school assignments with the youngster, play games, carry out craft activities, or simply talk. The group's goal is to encourage in the children a sense of self-worth and hopes for a better life.[5] Many older people find niches on their own. At seventy-five, Lorena Casey spends fifty hours each week answering the hot line at a Kansas City house for battered women; at seventy-seven, George Sable, a retired engineer, spends one day each week designing and adapting equipment for the disabled at a rehabilitation center in Minneapolis.[6]

Leaving your occupation means giving up the role of worker and, for most people, making do with less income. Yet — as long as they keep their health — most retired adults seem as satisfied with life as are workers of the same age. Eight out of ten say that retirement has brought them the benefits they expected, and seven of those eight say that, given another chance, they would retire at the same age.[7] Whether the golden years bring contentment has a good deal to do with the retiree's occupational level as well. Those who retire from middle- or high-status jobs enjoy their retirement years much more than workers who leave low-status jobs. It's not just the difference in retirement income or the fact that low-status workers are more likely to have health problems — it's also a matter of social isolation. Working-class women and men are less likely than those in the middle class to be involved in the community or to have friends who aren't connected with their former jobs. Many such people find that their only social contacts are with their family.[8]

Three out of ten retired workers are dissatisfied with the timing of their retirement, and two out of those three are just plain discontented. Some discontented retirees have poor health or severely inadequate incomes, but others have found hidden thorns lurking in retirement's bouquet of roses. Having lost the identity that comes from working, they lack a sense of purpose. In a society where you *are* what you *do*, adjustment can be difficult if there's nothing you're particularly interested in doing.

Most older Americans "retire in place"; they live in the same houses they have always occupied, in the midst of the community where they have strong social ties. A hundred years ago, when only a handful of people lived into old age, most were dependent on others. Seven out of ten older couples, and nine out of ten unmarried adults past the age of sixty-five, lived with someone else, usually a child, brother, or sister, but sometimes a niece or nephew. Those who had no relatives lived in the "old folks' home" or the "poorhouse" — the specter that haunted those who outlived their health and savings. But today, the vast majority of older Americans have the independence of their own homes — whether a house, an apartment, or a furnished room.

Many retirees find psychological benefits in staying in the home they own and in which they raised their children. Besides the boost in self-esteem that owning a home provides to those who have lost their occupational status, the home provides a familiar setting in which older people can move about confidently.[9] Pervaded by memories, the house may reflect the person's life and be filled with meaning, or even be seen as part of the self.[10]

There are many jokes about the annoyance of having a retired husband around the house all day, and for women who have been homemakers all their lives, there seems to be a grain of truth in such stories. In one study, 78 percent of the wives polled said that their husbands' retirement had decreased their own freedom, brought them too much togetherness, and created too many demands on their time.[11] Among older wives, the happiest were those who had retired from their own jobs while their husbands kept on working, and the least happy were those who were still going off to a job every day while their husbands stayed at home.[12]

Until recently, no one paid much attention to the condition of retired women, primarily because so few spent their lives in the labor force. In most cases, their economic situation is worse than that of male coworkers. Lower wages across their working lives have left most women with only two-thirds the retirement benefits of most retired men.[13]

When Chancellor Bismarck decided that sixty-five was the age to withdraw from work, he could not have imagined that the proportion of retired — and unproductive — adults would become so large. If we applied his rule of thumb and set a retirement age that would provide about the same number of leisure years as he anticipated in the nineteenth century, people today would work until they were at least eighty years old. Fifty years after the introduction of Social Security, an enormous leisure class has developed in the United States. Its members are generally well off and in good health. Their productivity will be needed in the years ahead.

Already, ideas such as phased retirement, contract work, and part-time work are being introduced to tap the resources of this class. And the first steps have been taken to reset the Social Clock. In the year 2009, today's forty-seven-year-olds will have to be sixty-six years old to qualify for full Social Security benefits, and in 2027, today's thirty-year-olds will have to be sixty-seven. By that time, our population will have completed its transition from a triangle to a square.

The Social Climate of Late Adulthood

As seasons shift and people move into and through late adulthood, their social situation changes dramatically. As more and more relationships are broken by death, those that remain — or are created — become critically important.

Like Vivian and Tom Russell, older couples consistently tell researchers that their marriages are happy — very happy. Only couples in the first year of marriage are as delighted with their union as are the old. One reason older couples say they are so satisfied may be that the alternative seems so bleak. The prospect of being alone during later adulthood may make marriage — any marriage — look good. Another reason may be people's reluctance to admit that they have invested fifty years of their lives in a joyless union. Or, the rise in happiness may come about because most truly unhappy marriages have ended in the courts.

The first glance at marriages over time was taken at the University of California's Institute of Human Development in Berkeley, where researchers have been following a group of adults since their first children were born in 1929.[14] In this study, most of the marriages that persisted past the half-century mark either had been satisfying throughout, or had shown a dip in middle adulthood and renewed satisfaction later on. None of the marriages that lasted fifty years or more had started out unhappy and gotten better with age, and none had begun happy and steadily gotten worse. The key to lasting marriage seems to be commitment to the relationship and acceptance of the partner.

When they leave middle adulthood, three-fourths of women are married, but by age seventy-five, less than a quarter are.[15] Widowhood has become a role that women must expect to endure for at least a decade. Few widows remarry. Some don't want to, but even if they would like to find a husband, the odds are against them. There simply aren't enough partners to go around. The biological shortage of eligible men in late adulthood becomes magnified by the male tendency to marry younger women. While less than a quarter of women aged seventy-five and over are married, nearly three-quarters of men are.[16]

Eight out of ten widows live by themselves. Most adapt to their solitary life; once they have finished mourning their loss, some even find their independence liberating. But the quality of their lives may depend on whether their need for companionship is filled. Throughout life, women rely more on their friends for intimacy than do men. In old age, they are more likely than men to use a friend as a confidante, and more likely to involve that friendship in all areas of their lives. If their need for companionship is not met, women who are widows may find their loneliness overwhelming.

Older parents are more likely to find a confidante among their grown daughters than among their sons.[17] Perhaps the bond with daughters is stronger because they visit, call, or write their aging parents more often than sons do. What parents tell researchers confirms the old saying, "A son is a son till he takes a wife, a daughter's a daughter the rest of her life." The solidity of the bond with daughters reflects the matrilineal tilt in U.S. society. Ties across the generations are different in China, where the son remains close to aging parents; when a Chinese daughter marries, she joins her husband's family and often loses contact with her own parents.

Although good family relationships are strong predictors of morale and life satisfaction among the elderly,[18] older adults often say that friends provide more important and satisfying companionship than children do. Researchers at the University of Illinois and the University of Waterloo recently have shed light on this apparent contradiction.[19] They asked older men and women to wear electronic pagers as they went about their daily activities. Each time the pager beeped, the adults filled out a short report, describing what they were doing, whom they were with, and how they felt. The reports showed that when they were with their friends, older adults were happier, more alert, and more sociable than when they were with their children. They were going to church or theaters, pursuing hobbies or sports, or having lively conversations — about their games, religious activities, or opinions. But when they were with their children, they spent a lot of time doing housework, eating, or watching TV, and their conversations focused on weather, transportation, home maintenance, and finances.

It may be the voluntary nature of friendship that makes it so important in late adulthood. We cannot choose who is in our family, but we can choose our friends. Friends usually understand us, because they often have similar problems. They tend to be sympathetic at times when children might be impatient. Older people are also concerned that they not be a burden on anyone; they want to help others as much as others help them, and it's easier to establish a reciprocal relationship with peers than it is with children.

Sometimes these peers are our brothers and sisters. As we get older, we tend to renew bonds with siblings that may have lapsed during early or middle adulthood. This phenomenon is stronger among siblings who have never married, but brothers and sisters with intact marriages also find that psychological ties to siblings become stronger in late adulthood. Even the very old who have let friends drift away stay in contact with their siblings.[20] Perhaps older people feel comfortable with their brothers and sisters because they have so much in common. They share a genetic heritage, cultural surroundings, early experiences, and the memory of their parents.[21] As relationships come to an end in the final season of life, it's comforting to renew those that came first.

Being Old-Old

Most of the pioneers who are swelling the ranks of the elderly today are what Bernice Neugarten calls the "young-old." They function well and have no health problems that limit their daily activities. They live comfortably and are actively engaged in their families and communities. "They act very much like middle-aged people, except they're retired or their work patterns have changed markedly," says Neugarten.[22] People in late adulthood who are frail, sickly, and unable to care for themselves she calls "old-old."

It's the young-old who are new to the seasons of life. A separate stage has emerged between middle adulthood and old age, a period when one is retired from work but far from incapacitated. And even though all of us worry about becoming frail and dependent, most never will. The odds are that death will come to us suddenly or after a short illness — before a prolonged period of being old-old.[23]

Neugarten estimates that about 80 percent of those over sixty-five are young-old, and 20 percent, old-old. By age eighty-five, nearly 45 percent might still be considered young-old. Their health is good and they need no assistance in preparing meals, shopping, managing money, or doing heavy housework. The rest are old-old: the 25 percent who find their activities somewhat limited, and the 30 percent who need substantial help.[24] At eighty-six, writer and critic Malcolm Cowley complained that he no longer could depend on his reflexes. He had to learn new ways to get out of bed, stand up, sit down, walk, and dress. "For a man of uncertain balance, the big problem is pulling on his pants. It is something that can't be done in the middle of a room without danger of falling. . . . The safe procedure is to stand next to a wall, or better still in the angle formed by a wall and a bureau, so you can steady yourself with an elbow while standing on one foot. Be content if you don't put both of your own legs into one leg of the pants.

"I avoid basement stairs, which are always perilous. For other stairs, I grasp the railing firmly, take one step up or down, then pause to survey what is ahead. I take the other steps more quickly, but I count them as I go. Remembering the number of steps is an interesting game and it can prevent stumbling in the darkness."[25]

When health deteriorates too far, old-old age may mean life in a nursing home. Arthritis, accidents, or emphysema may make some of us unable to function without the help of others; the memory failure of Alzheimer's disease may make it unwise to live alone. The statistics tell the story: only 1 percent of adults between sixty-five and seventy-four live in nursing homes, and only 6 percent of those between seventy-five and eighty-four do, but the proportion rises to 22 percent among adults who are eighty-five or older.[26] Residents of nursing homes tend to be women who are single, widowed, childless, or with only one living child. Eighty percent are on Medicaid, which means that they fall below the poverty level. Nursing care is so expensive that even middle-class adults, who thought they had sufficient resources to live comfortably during their final years, quickly exhaust their life savings. When that happens, they turn to Medicaid, a step into the welfare system that many take with great reluctance.

For every disabled person who lives in a nursing home, at least two others live with their families.[27] Families tend to rally around their aging members and keep them home as long as possible, which means that a lack of relatives plays an important role in the decision to enter a nursing home.[28] Many older adults who enter nursing homes don't need the kind of care provided there; they simply have no one to do the small tasks that would keep them independent. And so a decision made earlier in life to have many children, or few, or none at all may have unforeseen consequences. Adults who are entering the ranks of the old-old today were parents during the Great Depression, when the birth rate was low and families were relatively small; many of them have no one to handle the routine chores that would enable them to stay at home. The next generation of the old-old, parents of three or four baby boomers, may have enough assistance to stay independent longer.

Too often, admission to a nursing home is followed by physical decline, psychological deterioration, and death. Researchers suspect that the reason can be found in the radical and sudden life changes that mark the strange new institutional world, where rules, regulations, and arbitrary schedules take precedence over personal inclinations. Residents lose control of the conduct of daily life, and that may have serious biological consequences.

Psychologist Judith Rodin of Yale University believes that having such control keeps us healthy, because it reduces the destructive effects of stress and even alters our physiology.[29] If we feel we can prevent stress or limit its severity, it no longer bothers us as much. So when we feel in control, even though stress may be heavy, our blood pressure and heart rate decrease, the chances of developing stomach ulcers decline, and a drop occurs in the factors that promote the formation of fatty deposits in the arteries. Rodin has also discovered that, when older people feel helpless and unable to deal with stressful events, their bloodstream contains fewer cells that help the body's immune system attack foreign substances and more of the cells that suppress the immune system's defenses.

The old-old present a special problem for society. On the one hand, they need a great deal of support and often have no one to champion their plight. On the other, they raise the excruciating question of the extremes to which we should go in prolonging human life. Great as their challenge is, however, it is no greater than that of the young-old.

The Young-Old: Retirees or Elders?

In recent decades, we have witnessed a gradual but striking redefinition of both ends of the life cycle. Psychologists who once viewed infants as passive and unresponsive now see them as active and competent. The same is true of the elderly: once assumed to be useless, they are now considered to be full of "reserve" potential. These redefinitions can be understood in light of health changes in this century. More babies survive infancy, so we can afford to believe in their abilities and invest in them from the very beginning of their lives. And more adults survive to their later years, demonstrating a capacity that was characteristic of only a few in the past.

For the first time in history, older people are exploring the boundaries of life after reproduction in huge numbers. No longer are the pioneers of aging a few select individuals; they are now coming in waves — healthy, vigorous young-olds who want more than a life of leisure, and whose society needs more from them. "We've got a group of people with an enormous productive potential, walled off by a kind of enforced obsolescence," says psychiatrist Carl Eisdorfer of the University of Miami Medical School. "It's a ticking time bomb." Eisdorfer believes that we have to start thinking about new roles for later life. "Millions of older men and women could be trained as teachers' aides, particularly in the lower grades. There are a lot of older native-language speakers who could be incorporated into our school system. We could pay the expenses of people to be foster grandparents to retarded or disabled kids in institutions. Even old people who have a physical disability may not be handicapped for certain functions — sitting at a computer terminal, for example. We need to find ways of reinvesting old people in a future society."[30] The ways we select will have to accommodate the desire of retired people to retain their flexibility, and to rest and enjoy the "season of the senses."

Neugarten sees in the young-old a special opportunity — the possibility of resurrecting the ancient concept of "elder." She says, "It's a role that's unique to old age and one that occurred in traditional societies. It consists of the ability to develop a perspective that goes beyond oneself and one's family. The elder draws on long experience and sees what's good for the whole community, and acts in ways that forward that good. Now that we have so many older persons who are capable of acting in that role, we need to put effort into creating the twentieth-century version of the elder."[31]

Throughout history, older men and women have been seen as repositories of wisdom and useful members of society. They have been responsible for setting the cultural tone, for seeing the place of their people in the world and the place of their world in the universe. They have maintained the foundation on which the family is built. Because of their presence, parents could bring the next generation safely into adulthood.

To become an elder in the traditional sense, one must transcend self-interest and take a broader view of life — something that cannot be done when you still have "mountains to climb" and are actively running society. Elders must be able to step back and see the condition of their world, and they must have the generativity to leave it in better shape than they found it. With the political power that comes with wealth and numbers, older adults in the late twentieth century are in a position to do just that.

Reinstating the old as elders might do more than enable society to cope with the growing proportion of old people; it might mean the difference between retaining our humanity and losing it. "We do not have elders because we have a human gift and modern capacity for keeping the weak alive," says David Gutmann. "Instead, we are human because we have elders."[32] The role of elders in the care and transmission of culture has had much to do with the success of *Homo sapiens* as a species. When the pioneers of aging swell our ranks in the twenty-first century, much of our well-being will depend on whether they assume this time-honored position.

A Broader Vision

"I've always enjoyed doing things in the mountains — hiking or, more recently, active cliff-climbing. When climbing a route of any difficulty at all, it's absolutely necessary to become entirely absorbed in what you're doing. You look for a crack that you can put your hand in. You have to think about whether the foothold over there will leave you in balance or not. Otherwise you can get trapped in a difficult situation. And if you don't remember where you put your hand or feet a few minutes before, then it's very difficult to climb down.

"The more difficult the climb, the more absorbing it is. The climbs I really remember are the ones I had to work on. Maybe a particular section where it took two or three tries before I found the right combination of moves that got me up easily — and, preferably, elegantly. It's a wonderful

Lyman Spitzer, seventy-four. "It's a wonderful exhilaration to get to the top . . . and be so grateful that it's still possible for me to do that sort of thing."

exhilaration to get to the top and sit down and perhaps have lunch and look out over the landscape and be so grateful that it's still possible for me to do that sort of thing."

For seventy-four-year-old Lyman Spitzer, the intellectual challenge of a climb is nearly as great as the exhilaration of getting to the top. Although he has always loved the mountains, he began to climb the sheer face of cliffs only in his mid-fifties. Tall and trim, he appears to be in excellent condition, though he has noticed some changes over the years. "I'm sure that age has had some effect on my climbing ability. I could do more arduous routes ten years ago than I can now. I no longer do ice climbing. That was lots of fun while it lasted, but it finally took more strength than I felt I could develop. The fact that I'm able to continue rock climbing I attribute to two factors. One is just luck. I don't have any of the disabilities that some people have at my age. The second factor is that I make an effort to keep in reasonably good physical shape. I go swimming every day for about half an hour and I bicycle around. Without some regular exercise, I don't think I could continue climbing. But I see no reason why I can't go on climbing for some years yet."

Lyman, an astrophysicist, has been a faculty member at Princeton University for forty years — retired for the last five. "One of the advantages of the academic life is that retirement is much less of a perturbation than it is for people in the business world, who have to change their way of life when they retire — which must be very difficult for somebody in his later years. Retirement for me has meant rather minimal changes. I don't teach any more, which I miss in a way, but that was a small part of my activity. I've done what I was going to do that's of any importance. And it creates a certain feeling of relaxation, I must say, not to feel that I have to push myself. I can take time off to enjoy certain things. I still enjoy science, but I don't have the ambition to write the most brilliant paper ever written."

Lyman has a warm voice and an exuberance in his eyes that can be seen even through his black-rimmed glasses. Born in Toledo, Ohio, in 1914, he went off to prep school as an avid science-fiction enthusiast. "I read science-fiction magazines and books and was always interested in space travel, travel to other planets. I remember becoming fascinated with the thought of connecting cities in the world by underground tubes. You could shoot cars through them in vacuums, accelerating and then decelerating them electromagnetically. You could get from New York to San Francisco in eight or nine minutes. I was going to have the tubes integrated with the internal transit system of each city, so you could get into a little car on the sixty-fourth floor in New York somewhere, dial a number, go down an elevator shaft and then through a tube to San Francisco and on up another elevator to the thirteenth floor of a building. I told my parents about it and they became seriously worried! I suppose a light came into my eyes when I talked about it." Lyman laughs at the recollection. "They thought I was getting a little batty. Maybe they were right!"

His days in prep school were critical to Lyman's future. "I was exposed for the first time to some books on astronomy, and they painted an utterly fascinating picture of the structure of the universe as a whole. It was with a feeling of awe and wonderment and admiration that I read those books. There was a keen desire on my part to share in some of the excitement of studying those problems. And there was a physics class I took where I found that I had this ability to take isolated problems and visualize what happened in a way that made it possible to comprehend the subject without having to remember a lot of details. That was really a fun process for me."

Lyman went on to earn a doctorate in physics and astronomy at Princeton, and married just before the outbreak of World War II. During the war, he studied the characteristics of underwater sound and played a leading role in the development of sonar. Then, in 1946 — more than forty years ago — another light came into his eyes. "During the war, it became evident from what the Germans were doing with V-2 rockets that the techniques for launching big rockets were being rapidly developed. This laid open the possibility that man could send objects into space to orbit around the earth or go to other planets. And since I was interested in astronomy, I began to think what it might mean to astronomy if one could send a telescope into space."

Lyman published his ideas in a brief paper. To some of his colleagues, they seemed about as feasible as a vacuum tube connecting New York and San Francisco. "They thought I was a little odd and impractical and perhaps too enthusiastic. I gave a talk at an astronomical society about how one would build a space telescope, what the components would be and how one would solve certain problems, and one man came up to me afterward and said, 'Well, I admire your courage,' and went away. Some of my friends remarked at one point that I was a visionary. I think all of us have visions — goals that we set for ourselves, pictures of what we might try to achieve, or what mankind might hope to achieve. My visions just happened to be in a particular direction that coincided with what the nation was about to develop, which was the space program."

Placing a huge telescope in space became Lyman's major goal for four decades, and — almost single-handed — he convinced astronomers, politicians, and budget cutters that the telescope was not only possible but of prime importance. Lyman's vision became the driving force behind the Hubble space telescope, which was launched by NASA in 1990. The instrument does more than magnify objects at great distances. Because it takes light so long to cross the vastness of space, the telescope enables us to see events as they occurred billions of years ago. We may be able to look back — almost — to the very beginning of time.

"The lights in very distant galaxies have taken as much as seven or eight billion years to reach us," explains Lyman. "So when we look out in distance, we're also looking backwards in time, and the further out we can look, the younger the universe was when those photons left on their long pathway through space to our telescope. On the ground, the atmosphere gets in the way. This wonderful life-giving ocean of air makes images shimmer and stars twinkle. That's very romantic, but it messes up pictures taken on the ground. Out in space, stars do not twinkle, and we can obtain sharp pictures. I'm sure the space telescope will not answer all of our questions, but it will certainly get us closer to the goal of answering the big ones: How did the universe start? What is its fate?"

Most nonscientists imagine that such questions motivate astronomers on a day-to-day basis — or that they choose their profession because they're enthralled by the sight of the star-filled heavens. But stargazing never fascinated Lyman. "My reactions to seeing the sky and galaxies through a telescope have been perhaps different from those of many of my colleagues. I'm not so stirred by looking at the sky at night as I am by thinking. It's inner contemplation that brings out the sense of wonderment and the desire to understand, the push to do something.

"I have the knack of being able to visualize physical processes and work out their consequences. My children used to ask me, 'What are you doing today, daddy dear?' and I'd say, 'I'm trying to figure out what I would do if I were an electron.' That was a partially facetious answer, but it's partially true. Once you can visualize what the principles of physics are, that's all you need to remember. The details of any problem can always be worked out. You don't need to remember formulae — you can always derive them if you have a picture for what happened."

Lyman Spitzer has been called the "father-spirit" of the Hubble space telescope. His work will help us see the universe in a new way. And at seventy-four, his life will help us see old age in a new way. "I think the human animal is made in such a way that it's difficult for too long a period to get satisfaction from what one *has* done," he says. "I think one needs more than that. At least I do. I don't spend much time contemplating my past. I enjoy each week for what it has to offer and I enjoy my work.

"I believe that change is easier, obviously, when one is young. But I don't think it's impossible by any means as one gets older. I've been thinking of ways in which I might change some aspect of my professional activity. My office at the moment is the only one in the astronomy building that doesn't have a computer console on the desk. I let graduate students do the computing for me. But maybe it's time to change. Maybe I should take time out and learn computing. My children have been encouraging me to take up some musical instrument, which I may do. I used to play the piano and still do occasionally, but not very well."

His family has always been important to Lyman. He and his wife Doreen, who heads the American School in Greece, have been together for forty-eight years, exploring the paths around their lakeside home as well as more rigorous trails — a quest that once took them to the top of the Matterhorn. "I enjoy my work, but I got the most satisfaction from my family life. The luckiest thing I ever did was to get married. Doreen was fun to be with, amusing and witty, and it was only after our marriage that I discovered how nice she really was. I think my wife and I have been fortunate that we're so well suited to each other. We didn't have any long period of adjustment when we were first married. We got along fine, and we still do.

"A few months ago, we had a series of hiking trips with each of our four children and their families. We hiked in Vermont on the long trail — different sections with each of the families — and we watched these small tots going along, climbing up little cliffs along waterfalls. It was a rewarding experience, both for us and I think for the families. It's really true what they say — it's a great pleasure having grandchildren one can enjoy and for whom one has very little responsibility."

"*Long after we know all that we need to know about the universe, we may still be trying to understand the nature of life and the long-range fate of humanity.*"

In his lifetime, Lyman has seen parallels between the development of a star and the development of a person. "There are certain similarities: the early phase of formation which lasts for some time, the period when the end is approaching. The main difference between the evolution of a star and the evolution of a person is that we have some hopes of understanding as simple a thing as a star. Life is much more complicated than the physical processes that astronomers study. I can well imagine that long after we know all that we need to know about the universe, we may still be trying to understand the nature of life and the long-range fate of humanity."

18

THE PSYCHOLOGICAL *How the*

STORY OF LATE *Story Ends*

ADULTHOOD

"We were married for over fifty years. I can only look back on it with the fondest . . . Well, the love for my husband just grew. As a girl, I never thought, you know, that this would happen to me. In my wildest dreams, I never thought that the two of us would ever get together. But we did, and it made my life.

"When I look back, I have only the most beautiful innermost thoughts, because our life was good. We understood each other. We went through whatever we had to go through together. Oh, we had our little tiffs, but they weren't anything that spoiled our marriage. We went through a lot with the children, but we weathered it. And we weathered it to such an extent that the children remained with us, that they understood us. And there's nothing, nothing that I can think of in our marriage that would have made it any more wonderful for me."

At eighty-six, Miriam Cheifetz is sustained by the memory of her husband. His name was Samuel, but she always called him "Cheif" — short for "Cheifetz." He has been deceased now for seventeen years, and Miriam feels a void that will never be filled, that she doesn't *want* filled. "You lose part of your life," she says, "and when you lose that, there's nothing else that can replace it. This is part of you, and you want to keep it. I have to live with what I have — my memories, the good things in my life."

Miriam wears glasses and her gray hair is neatly curled. Time has carved deep grooves in her face. She has lived long enough to understand the whole story of a marriage — and to realize that hers was far more satisfying

Miriam Cheifetz, eighty-six. "I have to live with what I have — my memories, the good things in my life."

than her parents'. "In the first place, my mother was ten years older than my father. They were married in Russia. He was a student, and she was illiterate. She couldn't read. She couldn't write. When she married him, she was a widow with three children. She had a little store, and she took care of that store with the help of her children. My father studied all day long. He wasn't a worker. In Russia in those years, they would pair together a woman who didn't have a big dowry with a Talmudic student who didn't expect too much. When I was born, my mother still had her store, and she would leave me at home with one of my sisters. My father didn't bring in any money, so my mother was the breadwinner of the family."

Miriam remembers almost nothing of her life in Russia. She was still a little girl when the family emigrated to America — first her father and stepbrother, then her mother, her two stepsisters, and herself. "I grew up on the west side of Chicago. We lived on the third floor of a walk-up over a saloon, which made it easy to get a pail of beer for supper. When we first came here from Russia, my father had to get a job in a factory, but in those years you had to work on Saturday. He was not a real Orthodox Jew, but he was a religious Jew. He wore a large beard, and to him working on Saturday was something that you couldn't do. For six months he did not work and we almost starved. Then he decided that's no way to go. So he went back to work, and, of course, over the years that beard got smaller and smaller until just a little beard remained."

Her father adjusted, learning on his own to read and write English. But her mother never became literate, and that was only one of many differences between her parents. "I don't remember having real intimate feelings with my mother. She was not a woman who would tell you about these things. Talk to her was superfluous. She was interested in the meaty things of life, and she would have wanted that my father should be a little bit more practical. Unfortunately, that never happened. It just didn't. My father was not that kind of a guy.

"I became aware of this difference between the two of them. I felt a deep sympathy for my mother, and yet I could understand my father one hundred percent. So there was always this feeling with me as I grew older. I realized that when I wanted to marry someone, it would have to be a person that would think as I do, that would want the things that I want. Because I was ambivalent a lot. I understood my mother, and I understood and was swayed — more — towards my father."

How Miriam met her husband is a "long story," as she puts it. "He was about eight or nine years older than I was. His background was very much like my father's. The only difference was that he came from a rich family in the Ukraine, whereas my father was poor. My husband was a very learned scholar. When he came over here, he went from door to door on the west side to recruit children for a Yiddish secular school. I went to that school and he was my teacher. I used to have Hebrew lessons with him once a week. That meant that we met on a one-to-one basis, and that became very important to me. But I never in my wildest dreams thought that this was the man I was going to marry.

"Well, it happened that he fell in love with me. In the beginning, there was never any feeling on my part that matched the feelings he had towards me. I just looked at him as a person who understood me and to whom I could go with whatever was troubling me. He was somebody I looked up to, that I had a great deal of respect for. It was more of an intellectual feeling, if I can put it that way. I think he played it very wisely. He kept a diary. It was written in Yiddish, and it was all about me. All about me. I still have it."

Miriam and her former teacher were married and had two children, first a son, and then a girl seven years later. For a while they lived in South Bend, Indiana, where Cheif tried his hand at the grocery business. Then they moved back to Chicago, and he began to sell insurance. When her daughter was five, Miriam went back to work. She and Chief became active in various political groups. As she talks about their time together, specific ages and dates fade in importance. What matters instead is the changing shape of their relationship and the character of the man who meant so much. If the beginning of their life together stands out in her mind, so does the end. There came a time when problems with his heart changed the way they lived.

"He really couldn't do too much. We had an apartment, and I worked and he would do all of the shopping and cooking. We had someone in who did the cleaning. Weekends, he would teach in the Yiddish secular school. Those years were a bit difficult, but it didn't change our feelings or our behavior. I never, never had a feeling that I was going to outlive him, even when he became ill later on with cancer."

The cancer was discovered in a routine physical examination. "God, how can I talk about something like that? It was discovered as a spot on the lung by the doctor we had for many years. It was so foreign, but it was there, and it had to be dealt with.

"He became ill, but before he passed away, we still made a trip. We went to Europe. We visited Israel. We visited the Soviet Union. How he made the trip I'll never know, because it must have taken every bit of strength that he had. I wanted to cut it short and go back. But he wouldn't listen to it because he knew that our whole lives . . . I had to go through with it, and it was not a good trip."

When Cheif died, Miriam's life changed forever. "You feel the loss every day. Every minute. There's so many things, from the time you open your eyes in the morning. He would always get up first, and I would always beg for five minutes more. And the good soul that he was, he would say okay with a smile on his face. Now those are the things that may sound petty, but they're not petty when you live together with a person. And when you get up in the morning and he's not there, it takes a long while to get accustomed to it.

"I went through some very difficult times. There were hours when I sat and cried, and I was happy that I could cry. Even with all of the people that I knew through work and through my activities . . . that didn't help. People cannot help you. These are things that no one but yourself can go through. You have to live with it. And you have to find a way for yourself. The thing that saved me was the fact that I worked, and that I was working in a situation where I had support and where my work was pleasant. That was a great help. Without that, I don't think I could have made it."

But Miriam never adjusted to her years of living alone. "I went through a period of deep depression. I would go into the supermarket and I would stand there. I wouldn't know what to buy. I couldn't manage the shopping, the carrying of packages. Physically, it drained me. I talked to the children and I said, 'This I cannot do.' And my son said, 'Well, Mom, I think we have to seek some help.' So I went through a period with a psychiatrist who helped me a great deal. I was doing very well, but then I got congestive heart failure. I had to go to the hospital to take care of the situation."

About five years ago, Miriam left the hospital. She tried living by herself in a new apartment, but once again loneliness began to overwhelm her. She wouldn't consider living with her children, nor did she like the idea of a nursing home. Eventually, her daughter found a group living arrangement close to where she herself lived. Miriam moved in about a year ago and lives there today with ten other widows and one widower. She has her own room and as much independence — and help — as she wants.

Despite her heart condition, Miriam tries to take long walks each day. Occasionally, she shops or goes to the library. She understands that being a widow is not unusual and tries to be philosophical about it. "Many women go through this. Unfortunately, we're in a period of our lives when the men die earlier than the women. Women are left alone. Many women do not want to live with their children. Their children have different lives, different interests, and all it would mean is that they'd become a burden. This is the hurdle that women have to deal with. And each one deals with it in her own way."

It helps that Miriam has found a friend and confidante in her new home. "When Trudy was ill, I did all I could for her. If I'm not well, she's there on the button. I like to be with her. There are times when it's a bit difficult, but it doesn't bother me that much. We get along well. We understand each other. There's nothing hidden. If there's something that I want to say to her, I'll say it, and she'll do the same to me. It depends how you feel. Some days you don't want to do that. Some days you do. But it's there, and that's the important part."

It helps, too, that Miriam can visit frequently with her family. "Those are highlights in my life. Really highlights. I have two children. I have grandchildren, and I have five great-grandchildren. I love them for who they are. It isn't that I'm the 'bubby' or the grandmother. It's that I'm one with them, which is very important to me. I love the little ones very much. And then to watch them grow, to see them develop, to listen to their stories. I feel very, very good about it, and it adds to my life."

At one of those family get-togethers, Miriam's daughter brought out a little diary that Miriam had started when she was on the brink of adolescence. As the family gathered round, Miriam read from the diary, sharing parts of her story with her children, grandchildren, and great-grandchildren — how she combed her hair, what she did at parties, and how much she enjoyed playing Wink, Post Office, and Spin the Bottle. It was a happy evening, filled with laughter and love. Afterward, Miriam reflected on it. "We just had one wonderful time with that little diary. It was written in pencil and every page had a different topic on it. And some of the things

"A child, I was a child! And they found it very interesting. They found it funny!"

that I recorded there were absolutely fantastic. Things that I thought about, things that happened to me, things that I lived through, little intimate things that never should have been recorded. There were things there that were so personal that I never would have been able to tell them, I'm sure. And who could? A child, I was a child! And they found it very interesting. They found it funny!

"It brought out things that they were able to relate to in their own process of growth — particularly my older great-grandson, the one who's going to be twelve. He's a wise little boy, and I enjoyed being able to share it with him. It helped to bridge the time from my own youth to some of the things they had already lived through. There was a connection that they could understand.

"I never accepted the death of my husband. That is something that is very difficult for me to contend with to this day — and it's already seventeen years. But there's a thread that goes through your whole life, and when you see some of that in your own children, you feel that your life was not in vain. You feel that you lived a good life. You feel that you did what you possibly could under the circumstances, and there's a good feeling of knowing that your children have learned from what you have gone through, what your life has meant."

Preserving the Self

When asked whether she thinks old people are all alike, Miriam Cheifetz answers with the fierceness of a crusader. "Incorrect! Absolutely incorrect! All old people are *not* alike. They never could be because they're part and parcel of what their whole lives have been." One of the sources of diversity in the season of late adulthood, as Miriam observes, is the unique accumulation of events that have entered each life — events such as the death of a spouse. Another is the quieting of the Biological and Social Clocks. A third source — probably the most important in terms of day-to-day living — is the great variation in the health of older adults. In late adulthood, what matters is not how far we are from the beginning of our lives, but how close we are to the end.

Until the end is in sight, psychological development in late adulthood continues the themes of middle age. There are, of course, some changes: we leave positions of command in society, and if our health is good we discover a new freedom in retirement. But most young-olds experience what fifty-year-olds do: gradual physical decline, over which they have some degree of control; the exchange of masculine and feminine "spirits"; a career of grandparenting that may lead to great-grandparenting; the need to establish a legacy through some form of generativity.

In fact, most young-olds still see themselves as middle-aged — a tribute to the power of the Psychological Clock. "Chronologically, I'm an old woman," says Vivian Russell at sixty. "But physically, I don't feel old. Mentally, I don't feel old." Nor does Harry Crimi pay much attention to the year on his birth certificate; it's how he feels that counts. "I don't even feel sixty-one," he says. "I do more work today than a lot of these youngsters at thirty or forty." Whether they are sixty or seventy-five, the young-old tend to keep a youthful self-concept and ignore signals from others that say they should slow down or "act their age." If someone offers them a seat on a bus, they believe it's because they look tired or have a lot of packages to carry — not because they're old. Years after they have retired, most old people still think of themselves in terms of their former roles: as plumbers, lawyers, teachers, or carpenters. And those who keep working past sixty-five feel even younger than those who have retired.[1]

A seventy-four-year-old with a youthful self-concept once asked, "Who has time to get old? I've a wife and child who need me."[2] And at eighty-three, retired journalist Bruce Bliven wrote, "A year ago, when I was only eighty-two, I wrote somebody that 'I don't feel like an old man, I feel like a young man who has something the matter with him.' I have now found out what it is: it is the approach of middle age, and I don't care for it."[3]

This perpetual "middle-aged self" helps explain why most young-olds remain active and interested in society, family, and friends. Research has shown that a youthful self-concept is generally coupled with physical and mental health Apparently, if we have our health, we feel young, no matter what our age. A youthful self-concept is also found in those who see some purpose in life — and believe that they have control over their own.[4] Some have suggested that feeling younger than our years is one way of denying death. But studies do not support this idea. Fear of death appears to be greater in middle adulthood than in late adulthood, and when entering the final season of life, those who are least fearful feel the youngest.[5]

For a number of years, Miriam Cheifetz has felt far from young — even far from middle-aged. Her psychological challenge has been that of someone — of whatever age — who faces the end of life. "You don't want to think of what else is ahead of you," she says, "because there's nothing much that's left. Most of it has been taken up. Most of it has been gone through. And what you have left now is to stand on your own two feet and to function — not to lose what counts." Miriam's challenge is to preserve her self and to arrive at a sense of integrity.

Since the death of her husband, Miriam has had difficulty maintaining her identity. So much of it was bound up with who he was. Her enduring attachment to Cheif is not that unusual, according to Camille Wortman, a psychologist at the University of Michigan who studies the process of grief. "A majority of widows will turn to their lost spouse for advice. They will try to understand how he would have wanted them to react, will have imaginary conversations with him, will frequently think through how he would have dealt with a certain problem. These are all kinds of attachment, and they're all perfectly normal."[6]

Often, friends of those who lose a loved one expect them to be "over it" in a year or two. But Wortman has found that this expectation is not only unrealistic, but hurtful — at least when a death is sudden. One of her studies focused on people who had lost a spouse or child four to seven years earlier in a motor-vehicle accident. Wortman found that they were still having considerable difficulties. "The vast majority had been unable to make any sense out of what happened. They had painful memories that they were unable to shut out. Ninety-eight percent had thoughts on a daily basis about their loved one." Even those that recovered, she says, "did not come back to normal in the sense of being like they were before the loss. They were very different people, with what I would consider permanent changes."[7]

When such changes come in late adulthood, the reality of death becomes personal and immediate. The middle-aged self evolves into something else — but not necessarily an "old" self. Even with her physical limitations, Miriam Cheifetz resists defining herself as "old." She is angered by the way other residents of her home drag old age around with them. "So very often I feel like saying, 'Okay, so you're old! So what? You're alive. You have a head. You can think. You can do things — whatever you want to do." Her reactions are typical of the older Americans studied by Sharon Kaufman, an anthropologist at the University of California, San Francisco. The people she interviewed thought of themselves as ageless. "Old people know who they are and what matters to them now," writes Kaufman. "As they talk about these subjects, they may, in passing, describe themselves as 'feeling old' in one context and 'feeling young' or 'not old' in another, . . . [but they] do not perceive meaning in aging itself; rather, they perceive meaning in being themselves in old age."[8]

Near the end of life, the challenge for the self that first emerged in infancy is to exchange a picture of "me" as middle-aged for a picture of "me" as ageless. "I'm a person," insists Miriam. "I'm not an old person, because there are many things about me that are not old — besides my years and the difficulties I have physically. Whatever I am, it has nothing to do with age." As physical losses mount, the elderly need to marshal whatever energy they have to preserve their ageless self, to say, until the last breath of life, "It's still the same me" — still the same self that was there in the beginning.[9]

Forgetting — and Wisdom

The loss of memory is a special concern in late adulthood. Older adults may forget names, misplace the car keys, lose their glasses. So, of course, may adults of any age, but in later life an unspoken dread often lurks behind normal lapses in memory. A sixty-eight-year-old woman relates, "One night when I was trying to find something that ordinarily was on the top shelf of the front hall closet, I came back and I started to cry. And when I started to cry, I said to my husband, 'Well, I have something terrible I've got to tell you. Your wife is coming down with Alzheimer's.'"[10] Alzheimer's disease is so frightening because it takes its victims on a slow slide into senility. Instead of forgetting where they put their glasses, they forget that they ever wore them. Instead of forgetting the name of a new acquaintance, they forget the names of their own children. Eventually, thought disintegrates and language disappears. The self can no longer say, "It's still the same me."

At Pennsylvania State University, psychologist Warner Schaie has spent more than thirty years studying the way aging affects the mind. He stresses that Alzheimer's disease is not part of later life for most people.

"Alzheimer's disease is exactly what the term implies," he says. "It's a disease. It's not a condition of normal aging. If you live until your late seventies, the chances are nineteen out of twenty that you will *not* be affected by Alzheimer's or some similar condition. If you live past the age of eighty-five, your chances of escaping are four out of five."[11]

Even so, many older people worry when they forget to turn off the oven. Aware of such concerns, Schaie offers a way to put the worries to rest. "The best way to know whether you have Alzheimer's disease is to undertake some new mental challenge. Take up square dancing; see if you can figure out how to run a personal computer; try to outguess the contestants on TV game shows. If you can handle any of these things, even if not quite as fast as you might have ten or twenty years ago, you don't have Alzheimer's disease."[12]

Schaie has been following a large group of older adults for fourteen years, periodically testing their ability to remember, think, and solve problems. He has found that few people show much change from their fifties to their sixties. But sometime during their seventies, the mental powers of most — but not all — begin to slip. "Keep in mind," he explains, "that there are vast individual differences, but at seventy-five or so there's a kind of watershed in the sense that people's bodies don't function that well anymore. As a consequence, they restrict their environment and restrict their exposure to new and interesting things. So then we begin to see a quickening of the pace of mental decline."[13]

In their eighties, none of Schaie's subjects were as mentally sharp as they once had been. Yet the vast majority were competent, and the decline was usually slight. Some eighty-five-year-old professionals who had slipped from their earlier peak were still more alert and knowledgeable than the average twenty-five-year-old.

Schaie believes that much of the mental decline he has found is unnecessary. "The popular belief is that there comes a point when your mind goes down the tube," he says. "That's nothing more than a myth, but it can be a self-fulfilling prophecy. Just as you can let your body go to pot by sitting in an easy chair until you can no longer get out of it, so you can let your mind go to pot by failing to exercise it. If you stop making decisions, at some point you no longer *can* make decisions." Once people leave the world of work, Schaie believes, they stop using many of the intellectual skills that were needed for their jobs. Unless they take up a second career or some kind of volunteer work — or make an effort to learn new skills — their mental powers may begin to decline early.

But even decline, says Schaie, can be reversed — as long as we remain in good health. In a surprising study, he and Sherry Willis showed that just five hours of training were enough to offset the loss of certain mental skills.[14] More than 100 older adults whose powers had begun to slip completed their program. Some were as young as sixty-four; others, as old as ninety-five; all were screened by physicians and those with physical or mental disabilities were excluded. For some of the participants, the training consisted of instruction in reason: drawing general rules from examples. For others, the training involved instruction in spatial orientation: learning how to rotate objects mentally and predict their subsequent appearances. Both skills are important aspects of intelligence tests. After they completed the brief course, four out of every ten participants were as sharp on the tested skill as they had been fourteen years earlier. Another two out of ten improved, although they did not return to their earlier peaks. Those who showed improvement were as likely to be in their nineties as in their sixties.

Schaie's training program apparently taps mental reserves that most older people don't know they possess. Another 100 adults in his program, whose ages ranged from sixty-four to eighty-five, had shown no decline over the previous fourteen years. About half of them also responded to the five-hour training course with marked improvement. In Berlin, at the Max Planck Institute for Human Development and Education, psychologists Paul Baltes and Reinhold Kliegl have found even more remarkable mental reserves among select women and men.[15] They have trained adults between the ages of sixty-seven and seventy-eight to match the performance of professional memory experts in remembering long strings of numbers or words. The feat requires intensive training, but seems within the grasp of many older people, who apparently have such large reserve capacities that they can learn to exceed their youthful proficiency.

One sixty-nine-year-old woman in the Berlin study has no trouble remembering a string of 120 digits, as long as they are presented slowly, one every eight seconds. She does it by attaching the digits — in groups of three — to the last three digits on a list of historical dates she has committed to memory. Then she matches the incident connected with each date (Columbus' discovery of America, the end of World War II, the French Revolution) with some landmark on the streets of Berlin. To recall the numbers, she takes a mental stroll past the landmarks and calls off each digit triplet in turn. These memory wizards are somewhat above average in intelligence, but neither brilliant nor blessed with an exceptional memory. They have simply tapped their unused reserves.

Apparently, we can retain — or regain — our mental powers as long as we keep our health and stay mentally active. Ask the three mathematicians who spent an afternoon in 1960 discussing technical mathematics with British philosopher Bertrand Russell. It had been nearly thirty years since Russell had done any work in mathematical logic, but he had no trouble keeping up with the younger men. "It was not merely that his brain was beautifully clear for somebody of eighty-seven," said one. "It was beautifully clear for anybody at any age."[16] Or ask the history department at New York University, where Frederick Bloch earned his doctorate in 1983 at the age of eighty-one, writing a dissertation on the common soldier in the Victorian British army. Fresh from his studies, Bloch planned to write a few books and do a little teaching.[17]

Training programs for the elderly can help them recover some of the intellectual abilities they possessed earlier in life. But late adulthood offers more than the possibility of recovery. Some researchers speculate that this season has a special gift — something we commonly call "wisdom."

Because wisdom involves subjective value judgments, it tends to elude attempts to study it. Even defining wisdom is a problem. It bears a resemblance to the practical intelligence possessed by people who are successful at managing life's problems. It involves the familiarity with patterns and the flexibility that mark the person with expertise. And it's related to "postformal thought": the wise know that they are merely interpreters of reality, not objective viewers of it. They have come to accept that life is messy and full of contradictions.

Although wisdom presumes these kinds of knowledge, it goes beyond them. According to Marion Perlmutter, a lifespan psychologist at the University of Michigan, it includes a global concern — not just the recognition of repeated patterns in specific domains, but the appreciation of the pattern in life itself.[18] Wise adults may not have more factual knowledge than younger people, and perhaps not even as much, but they understand the significance of what they know. They are sensitive to what is important in life and what isn't. And they can integrate the emotional side of their being with the intellectual. "There's some things you can't get out of books, you can't get out of computers, you can't get out of anything," says sixty-four-year-old Tom Russell. "They have to come out of the human soul, out of the human mind and heart." The combination of mind and heart is one of the ingredients of wisdom.

Perlmutter has found that young people are pretty well convinced they will get wiser with age, but older people aren't so sure that they have attained wisdom. Perhaps, she says, wisdom involves knowing what you don't know, and knowing what is unknowable. Lyman Spitzer knows that a space telescope will raise more questions than it answers, and he knows that human life is far more complicated than the physical processes he studies as an astronomer. That's a kind of wisdom. So is the appreciation of mystery in one man who was asked the most important thing he knows. "I know there is a spiritual force in the universe which is inexplicable to me," he answered. "I can't explain it. I can't define it. I can't describe it. I have to assume it's there whether I can see it or not. Otherwise, I'm completely thrown. I couldn't understand what the hell is going on."[19]

In some individuals, wisdom encompasses a belief in a world beyond the self. They relinquish the "I" as the vantage point from which valuing and knowing are done. This move beyond individualistic concerns to universal issues helps account for the long-range perspective taken by the wise, and for their deep understanding of philosophical and religious issues.

Wisdom can flourish alongside the typical cognitive declines of old age, because these declines have little effect on judgment. The slowing down of reactions that comes with aging may even open the door to wisdom. So may some forgetting. The experience of Shereshevskii, a Russian journalist who would have won the gold medal for memory in an intellectual Olympics, is convincing proof that remembering every detail of our lives can be disastrous.[20] Shereshevskii, who came to the attention of psychologists in the 1920s, could memorize a list of fifty words within three minutes. Fifteen years later, he could recall that list perfectly, forwards or backwards. Everything he learned stuck firmly — and that was the problem. Over the years, the information piled up until, as he went about his daily business, his memories kept flooding into awareness. The slightest cue evoked so many memories from his cluttered store of knowledge that he couldn't follow a simple conversation. At last he could not hold a job, because the continual cascade of memories kept him thoroughly confused. Shereshevskii could do only one thing: travel from town to town across the Soviet Union, demonstrating his peculiar talent.

Much of the wisdom of old age is knowing the forest from the trees — being able to see the shape of things rather than their specific parts. If we remembered all the trees in our life, as Shereshevskii did, we would never see the forest. Miriam Cheifetz has forgotten many of the details of her life, but she remembers the founding events that took place in the beginning and all the turning points that came thereafter. It may be embarrassing for her to stumble over a name, and it may be frustrating to misplace her keys, but it would be far worse if she forgot the story of her life. Her memory protects what is most important to her, what gives her life meaning. If she lost her story, she would lose her self.

Integrity: Was It a Good Story?

Older people spend a good deal of time reflecting on their past. If they made meaning as young adults by fashioning dreams, now they make meaning by shaping memories. They may tell stories to family members, recounting their first day at school to a great-grandchild or reminding a middle-aged son about the day of his birth. Reminiscing can be pleasant, and so can the sharing of awakened memories. But according to psychiatrist Robert Butler, something more serious is going on — something that's part of the psychology of the end of life. As we survey old relationships, old conflicts come to the fore, and a final chance arises to put our house in order. Butler calls this process the "life review."

"One may have been fragmented for a long, long time about a variety of competing thoughts, guilts, and conflicts," he explains. "With successful resolution of these, one may have a sense of integrity that one's never had before. And that doesn't necessarily mean something grand in the sense of a great memoir that's produced, or a work of art. It may be pure survival in which someone can feel very proud, very whole, to realize that they've brought their life to a fruitful culmination."[21]

According to Erik Erikson, the integrity Butler is speaking of comes from seeing how the story of your life is turning out — then changing what can be changed and accepting the rest.[22] Those who gain integrity emerge with a deepened wisdom about life. Having come to terms with death, they find meaning in their own life and believe, as Miriam Cheifetz does, that they did the best they could under the circumstances. Even though they remain saddened over particular incidents in their lives, they show none of the despair that characterizes those who yearn for another chance. People with integrity affirm that their story was a good story, with continuity from beginning to end — and true to the person who was its author. "There's a thread that goes through your whole life," says Miriam, "and when you see some of that in your own children, you feel that your life was not in vain. . . . There's a good feeling of knowing that your children have learned from what you have gone through, what your life has meant."

Signs of integrity can be seen in the "late style" of visual artists such as Rembrandt, Titian, and Monet, according to Rudolph Arnheim, professor emeritus at the University of Michigan and a pioneer in the psychology of art.[23] Arnheim has found that older artists develop a detached contemplation that changes their approach to their craft. In their work, they transcend outward appearances and search out underlying essentials. The result is a world view in which similarities outweigh differences and in which the power of a common destiny pervades the figures on the canvas — even the torturer and the victim in Titian's "The Crowning with Thorns," for example. The late style affects composition, the use of light, and the internal dynamics of a painting. Not all older artists achieve this world view, but when they do, their works celebrate life in a manner that exceeds all their earlier accomplishments.

Psychologist Dean Keith Simonton of the University of California, Davis, discovered a kind of late style in the work of more than 150 composers of classical music.[24] He called it the "swan-song phenomenon." As these composers got closer to death, they produced works that had a special character. Most were brief and had a relatively simple melodic structure. They were not as original as earlier compositions, but they were judged to be more profound, and they eventually became more popular. Many had a calming effect. Simonton sees swan songs as expressions of resignation and even contentment in the face of death, and he finds no traces of despair. Perhaps, he says, as creative artists realize that their careers are coming to a close, they reshape their works-in-progress to produce a final testament.

A sense of integrity at the close of life may depend more on the resolution of guilt and conflict than on the achievement of youthful dreams. Rutgers University psychologist Daniel Ogilvie has found that how close older adults come to their idealized self-image has far less influence on satisfaction with life than does the distance they create from parts of themselves they abhor — from fears, shameful impulses, memories of embarrassing events, guilts, and regrets.[25] The story of Miriam's marriage illustrates what Ogilvie means. By distancing herself from the bad things in her life — inevitable problems with children, the pain of the last trip with her husband — she has created an island of only "the most beautful innermost thoughts." She retreats to that island as often as she can, drawing nourishment from it. "There's nothing, nothing that I can think of in our marriage that would have made it any more wonderful for me," she says. Miriam has taken the best part of her story and made it into myth.

The integrity in Miriam's story already has a power for her children, grandchildren, and great-grandchildren. They relish her written remembrances of playing Wink, Spin the Bottle, and Post Office the way the Kennedy clan relishes accounts of being born and growing up in Butler County.

These families will tell their stories when they gather for births and deaths, and during the transitions from one season of life to the next. The stories will entertain them, guide them, warn them, nourish them with meaning — and provide a template against which each member develops his or her own biography. It's family stories that greet us when we're born, and family stories that we grow up on. And when we die, we can leave our family no greater legacy than the story of our life — the story of our dramatic journey from birth to death.

The Soul of a Tree

Sometimes the journey through life takes us around the world and ends in something simple — as simple as a tree. At eighty-two, George Nakashima of Bucks County, Pennsylvania, has carved his integrity out of the tradition of wood. His work is known internationally — furniture with butterfly joints and undulating edges that preserve the character of the original timber, furniture with holes and cracks turned to artistic advantage, furniture in which the soul of the wood comes through. "I'm interested in furniture because I think it's the closest relationship to wood that most people have. Each piece of wood that I have I use to its utmost utility and utmost beauty," he says. The wood may become the back of a sofa, a captain's chair, a desk, or a boardroom table. Special trees have special destinies. Once, says George, "I came across this great tree that I felt could have no other end but to be made into a symbol of peace." It is now the altar at the Cathedral of St. John the Divine in New York City.

George's hair is thinning and his mustache is gray. He has a round, well-preserved face and his posture is slightly hunched. He presents an air of peace and detachment — a serenity that comes from knowing his place in a tradition far older than himself. "It's sort of in your genes, this love of wood. I remember as a kid I used to chop quite a bit of wood because we burned wood for heat in our house in Seattle. When I would run into a very fine piece of wood, even though it was firewood, I'd put it aside to find a use for it later. This feeling toward wood is something that developed as I grew."

George's grandfather was a samurai warrior, and his father was "something of an adventurer," a man who emigrated to the United States and became a labor contractor for western railroads. George's mother came to this country as his father's "picture bride." They settled in Spokane, where George was born in 1905.

*George Nakashima,
eighty-two. "One arrives
at simplicity."*

By the time George was fifteen, he was working summers on the railroad, laying ties and carrying rails in the wilds of the Pacific Northwest. "Have you ever heard of a gandy dancer? It's a kind of dancing movement that you do with a shovel to get the gravel underneath the ties. I made the handsome sum of twenty-seven cents an hour, as I remember. Which at that time wasn't bad. And I was able to save enough to more or less put myself through college."

During those summers, George's love of the forest grew. "On weekends I used to hike in the mountains, and very often fish for my food and stay overnight under a ledge or a tree. I used to hike rather long distances, crossing the foothills of Mount Olympus and seeing the glacier there. It was very hard going, and if you ever got your foot or leg caught in a rock, well, you'd probably be a goner. Nobody would ever find you. But the thrill of crossing a pass and looking down at deer grazing all over the place! Magnificent olympic elk — sometimes you'd scare them, and they'd rear up on their legs. They must have been at least ten feet tall. I guess they weren't that tall, but they seemed awfully tall to me."

In college, George studied forestry for two years, then switched to architecture. He did graduate work at the Massachusetts Institute of Technology, began to practice his profession, and then, in 1933, went to Paris to see "what was going on." He was twenty-eight and searching for something.

"Everybody was poor. Nobody had any money. And it was a wonderful, creative life. But gradually I felt that was not the answer. There'd be times when I would turn a corner in the crooked streets of Paris, and I'd have an overwhelming feeling of death. So I felt that I had to go on, to seek something else. I went to Japan, the land of my ancestors, and I spent five years there, working as an architect. I learned the traditions and appreciation of Japanese art and architecture.

"I remember designing some houses and becoming so interested in the construction that I would spend half a day just watching the men work. There would be people who were more skilled than others. When someone would get a piece of work done, with the joints fitted perfectly and the proportions just right, he'd put it someplace where it could be seen. And everybody would gather around and praise him for his work. There was that sort of attitude. There wasn't any jealousy. It was just an appreciation of fine work.

"In 1936, I had an opportunity to do a design for the main building for the ashram of Sri Aurobindo in south India. I went there and I soon made friends and I became a follower of Sri Aurobindo. I became very much attached to his teachings, which are very simple and very profound. There's a type of life there that had a beauty and creativity that really didn't exist anyplace else in the world. And in my building I was given almost a free hand. I think everything I recommended was accepted.

"Well, I almost stayed for good, but I finally decided that I really should relate to the world. So I came out of India. At several points I almost didn't make it. Japan and China were at war, and I had to go through China to get back to Japan. I finally got to Shanghai, where I got on almost the last Japanese refugee ship out of Shanghai into Nagasaki, and made it back to Japan."

Once in Tokyo, George returned to architecture. In December 1939, he met his future wife at a party — Marion, a Japanese-American woman from Seattle who had spent the previous year in Australia and was teaching English in Tokyo. After dating for a few months, George asked her to marry him. He was thirty-five.

When the Nakashimas came back to the United States in 1940, modern architecture was in a period of exciting experimentation. "A friend and I decided to take a survey trip up and down the West Coast to see what was really being done. We saw this house by Frank Lloyd Wright under construction. I was used to the finest type of craftsmanship in Japan, and I was appalled by the crudity of the framework. The bones of the structure were just banged together with nails. There was hardly any exposition of the wood. And then the whole thing was covered up by what's called 'finished carpentry.' And it was actually a kind of stage set. I thought, if this was architecture as practiced by one of the greatest architects in this country, I'd better start all over again.

"So I gave up my profession and got into the construction of little things with wood. That's how I got into furniture work. A priest let me use the basement of a church-owned building in Seattle. He let me use it free of charge and even helped me buy my first piece of machinery. But it was a hard beginning."

Things got even harder. Within weeks, the United States and Japan were at war. Although they had been born in America, George, Marion, and their six-week-old daughter were sent to a Japanese internment camp. "Right after Pearl Harbor, it was clear that something was going to happen," George recalls, "and there wasn't anything much we could do. It happened very swiftly. We were given, I think, about two weeks' notice that we should get out of our homes and just take what we could carry and gather at a certain point.

"We were put into these camps in the desert of Idaho. It was a very rough life. It gets thirty degrees below zero there. I think I had shoes, but sometimes I would wear wooden clogs even in mid-winter. It was much more difficult for my wife. She was very much concerned about whether she could feed our daughter properly.

"But we made the best use of our time. I found a very fine Japanese carpenter trained in the traditional manner. And he and I pooled our forces. I did the designing and became his apprentice as far as carpentry went. I learned a great deal from him. He would sometimes decide that the teeth in the saw weren't quite right. So he would remove all the teeth and then file them back in again. And then there were so many facets of fine woodworking that aren't even thought of in Western carpentry. For instance, you can spend a whole day dressing down a wood post. You take a bit and put it in a plane and get it adjusted perfectly and then you start from one end of the timber and go to the other. You come out with a perfect shaving. It has no skips, no thickness and thinness. You get a finish that shines like a mirror, just from the planing. It never requires any sanding to smooth it off. And then if you take this one stroke, you have to take your plane bit out and sharpen it again. And this is done for the whole post."

The Nakashimas left the internment camp the only way they could — under the sponsorship of an American. A Czech-American architect whom George had worked for in Tokyo offered him farm work in Pennsylvania. In 1944, the Nakashimas came to Bucks County, where they still live today. "I enjoyed the area. I enjoyed the people. At that time, it was a series of sleepy little towns and farms and very beautiful stone houses that the early Quakers built. The stone houses are a marvel. They've been here for 200 years, some of them. Sometimes the walls are gone, but the stonework is as true as the day it was made."

George worked as a farm hand for a year and gradually got back into woodworking. At forty, his inner searching was done, and though he would continue to travel the world, he always came back to Bucks County — to his wife, to his daughter and son, and to the tradition of wood.

Now, forty years later, the end of his life is in sight. "Mentally, I'm not quite sure I am where I was before. But my aspirations and hopes are virtually the same. I have absolutely no interest in sitting on a beach or sitting in a rocking chair. I'm more interested in life than I am in death. I feel that I have things to do in this world that are necessary. Essentially, I'm interested in creating beauty. I'm still buying a lot of lumber, which I will probably never use. But I hope that my son and my daughter might use it. In a nice way, they're both interested in continuing on our work. Which is rather unusual in our society, because most young people like to get as far away from their parents as possible. If we can pass on our traditions and our skills and our knowledge to our children, I think the whole thing would be very much worthwhile.

"My son and daughter see things from quite a different angle than I do. But that's their prerogative — to tie the tradition together with their own lives. You can only reach a certain depth of influence with other people, and I don't think there's any use in trying to do more. I have no intentions of doing that, even to my own family. If they understand me and accept my beliefs, well, I think that's fine. But I don't think I should press it.

"There's an ultimate truth that's very important, and if one searches for it, one arrives at simplicity. And to search for this truth, one has to seek inwardly. There are no complications. There's no dogma. There are no rules. There's no necessity for great intelligence. Actually, intelligence is overrated anyway. In the Hindu concept, intellectual consciousness is one of the lowest forms. From it, one develops a very high form of consciousness of the spirit. It's something that can be developed by anyone.

"Good things flow inwardly, in an integrated way, so that you find the nicest things in simplicity, in directness. I have a one-man war against modern art, for instance. It's the predominance of a personal ego that bothers me. My ideal is that a craftsman should be unknown rather than known. He doesn't have to throw his ego around. This goes back to other civilizations. For instance, in the Sung Dynasty in China, the craftsman never signed his pieces. I think that's indicative of a healthy civilization. Everything that they produced was worthy, artful, beautiful. In the thirteenth

"With a tree, you can read its whole history — if you have the eyes to see."

century, many of the northern European cathedrals were anonymous; there was no architect. They just evolved. I would venture to say that every little guy, say, in the town of Chartres, contributed to that cathedral — perhaps did one of the gargoyles or put up a stone. It's a wonderful, inspired piece of work. And that's what we need today. And I think that's why I got into the sort of work I'm doing. I wanted to come as close to the spirit of Chartres as I could.

"Until a few years ago, I completely disregarded getting old. But I'm afraid that there are certain things happening in my body that I can't deny anymore. I'm certainly curtailed physically. It was only four, maybe five years ago that I climbed a mountain in Japan, but I don't think I could climb it anymore. We were looking for the great cedar. Did I ever tell you?

"There's a great cedar in Japan, which they say is around seven thousand years of age. I think it's considerably older than the bristlecone pine, which for quite a while was considered the oldest inhabitant on earth. I've always been interested in this cedar, for ever since I was in Japan, I've heard about it. But only recently did I have the chance to go there.

"We arranged this safari — friends of mine and myself. The lower part one could do in an automobile. And then we went on a little logging cart to the base of the mountain. From there it was all on foot — pretty much a half-day climb. And I was determined to see this tree. Every once in a while the younger fellows asked me if I wanted to continue. And I'd say, 'Yes, we go on!' Parts of the mountain were almost vertical. We couldn't even climb up the rocks — we had to go on ladders. But we finally made it. And it was a great sight, to see a spectacle like that. And actually going up to it and touching it was something else again."

Back in Bucks County, Pennsylvania, a huge oak stands near George's home. It's not nearly as old as the great cedar in Japan, but it's equally majestic. George has touched it often. "I feel that trees have a soul. In my work, I have to find the living spirit in a tree, explore it, and develop it. With a tree, you can read its whole history — if you have the eyes to see. You can tell when there was a great drought. You can tell where there was an injury that was healed over. You can tell when there's great happiness in a tree — a joy that expresses itself in its grains and its bark and its fibers. Trees have their problems, too. They have their bad moments. They have joy and they have sorrow, just like human beings. Some trees have character and others end up in something that's almost futile.

"The great oak down below, I think, is a tree that has tremendous character. How it's going to end up is a little hard to say. It will die, eventually. And one of our jobs is to take these great living things that have died or will die and give them, well, a second life. If I can bring the nature and the spirit of a tree back, the tree lives again. It's the continuity of life that sparks from one thing to another. It's a great, great feeling to be a part of that — to be a part of nature and to be a part of life itself."

Notes

Notes for Prologue

1. Weiss, K. M. 1984. On the number of members of the genus Homo who have ever lived, and some evolutionary implications. *Human Biology, 56,* 637-649.

2. Wish, H. 1950. *Society and Thought in Early America.* New York: Longmans, Green.

Notes for Chapter 1

1. Hyde, J. S. 1982. *Understanding Human Sexuality.* 2nd ed. New York: McGraw-Hill.

2. Marx, J. L. April 3, 1987. Probing gene action during development. *Science, 236,* 29-31.

3. Details of prenatal development come from: Nilsson, L., A. Ingelman-Sundberg, and C. Wirsen. 1966. *A Child Is Born.* New York: Dell.

   Hooker, D. 1952. *The Prenatal Origins of Behavior.* Lawrence, Kansas: University of Kansas Press.

4. Gould, S. J. March 19, 1984. Triumph of a naturalist. *New York Review of Books,* 3-6.

5. Gould, S. J. Interview, *Seasons of Life.*

6. Miyamoto, M. M., J. L. Slightom, and M. Goodman. 1987. Phylogenetic relations of humans and African apes from DNA sequences in the ψη-globin region. *Science, 238,* 369-373.

7. Walford, R. L. 1983. *Maximum Life Span.* New York: Norton.

8. Bogin, B. 1988. *Patterns of Human Growth.* New York: Cambridge University Press.

9. Bogin, B. 1990. The evolution of human childhood. *BioScience, 40*, 16-25.

10. Gould, K. G., M. Flint, and C. E. Graham. 1981. Chimpanzee reproductive senescence: A possible model for the evolution of the menopause. *Maturitas, 3*, 157-166.

11. Lovejoy, C. O. 1981. The origin of man. *Science, 211*, 341-350.

12. Reinisch, J. M. 1983. Hormonal influences on sexual development and behavior. In M. F. Schwartz, A. S. Moraczewski, and J. A. Monteleone (eds.), *Sex and Gender: A Theological and Scientific Inquiry*. St. Louis: The Pope John Center.

13. Gualtieri, T., and R. E. Hicks. 1985. An immunoreactive theory of selective male affliction. *The Behavioral and Brain Sciences, 8*, 427-441.

14. Holden, C. 1987. Why do women live longer than men? *Science, 238*, 158-160.

15. Nowakowski, R. S. 1987. Basic concepts of CNS development. *Child Development, 58*, 568-595.

16. Rakic, P. 1988. Specification of cerebral cortical areas. *Science, 241*, 170-181.

17. Goldman-Rakic, P. S., A. Isseroff, M. L. Schwartz, and N. M. Bugbee. 1983. The neurobiology of cognitive development. In M. M. Haith and J. J. Campos (eds.), *Infancy and Developmental Psychobiology*. Vol. 2: *Handbook of Child Psychology*. 4th ed. New York: Wiley.

18. Schultz, A. H. 1969. *The Life of Primates*. New York: Universe.

19. Gould, S. J. 1977. *Ontogeny and Phylogeny*. Cambridge, Mass.: Harvard University Press.

Gould, S. J. Interview, *Seasons of Life*.

20. Lancaster, J. B. 1988. Women in biosocial perspective. Essay prepared for the Project on Gender and the Curriculum sponsored by the American Anthropological Association. Unpublished manuscript.

21. Bogin, *Patterns of Human Growth*.

Notes for Chapter 2

1. Neugarten, B. L. Interview, *Seasons of Life*.

2. Kaye, K. 1982. *The Mental and Social Life of Babies*. Chicago: University of Chicago Press.

3. Ibid.

4. Papoušek, H., and M. Papoušek. 1984. Learning and cognition in the everyday life of human infants. *Advances in the Study of Behavior*. Vol. 14. Orlando, Fla.: Academic Press.

5. Ibid.

6. LeVine, R. A. 1980. Adulthood among the Gusii of Kenya. In N. J. Smelser and E. H. Erikson (eds.), *Themes of Work and Love in Adulthood*. Cambridge, Mass.: Harvard University Press.

7. van den Berghe, P. 1983. Age differentiation in human societies. In J. Sokolovsky (ed.), *Growing Old in Different Societies*. Belmont, Calif.: Wadsworth.

8. Linton, R. 1936. *The Study of Man*. New York: Appleton-Century-Crofts.

9. Rosenmayr, L. 1985. Changing values and positions of aging in western culture. In J. E. Birren and K. W. Schaie (eds.), *Handbook of the Psychology of Aging*. 2nd ed. New York: Van Nostrand Reinhold.

10. Lerner, M. 1980. When, why, and where people die. In E. S. Shneidman (ed.), *Death: Current Perspectives*. 2nd ed. Palo Alto, Calif.: Mayfield.

11. Weiss. On the number of members of the genus Homo who have ever lived.

12. Laslett, P. 1985. Societal development and aging. In R. H. Binstock and E. Shanas (eds.), *Handbook of Aging and the Social Sciences*. 2nd ed. New York: Van Nostrand Reinhold. (For British and American colonies figures.)

Siegel, J. S., and C. M. Taeuber. 1986. Demographic perspectives on the long-lived society. *Daedalus, 115,* 77-117.

13. Neugarten, B. L. Interview, *Seasons of Life*.

14. Borstelmann, L. J. 1983. Children before psychology. In W. Kessen (ed.), *History, Theory, and Methods*. Vol. 1: *Handbook of Child Psychology*. 4th ed. New York: Wiley.

15. Greenleaf, B. K. 1979. *Children Through the Ages: A History of Childhood*. New York: Barnes & Noble.

16. Hareven, T. K. 1978. The last stage: Historical adulthood and old age. In E. H. Erikson (ed.), *Adulthood*. New York: Norton.

17. Lutz, C., and R. A. LeVine. 1983. Culture and intelligence in infancy: An ethnopsychological view. In M. Lewis (ed.), *Origins of Intelligence*. 2nd ed. New York: Plenum Press.

18. Harkness, S., and C. M. Super. 1983. The cultural construction of child development. *Ethos, 11,* 221-231.

19. *Le grand proprietaire de toutes choses, tres utile et profitable pour tenir le corps in sante*. de Glanville, B., compilers, translated by Jean Corbichon, 1556. In P. Aries, 1962. *Centuries of Childhood*. New York: Random House.

20. deMause, L. 1975. The evolution of childhood. In L. deMause (ed.), *The History of Childhood*. New York: Harper & Row.

21. Boswell, J. 1989. *The Kindness of Strangers*. New York: Pantheon.

22. Stone, L. February 27, 1989. Dead end kids. *The New Republic,* 31-34.

23. French, V. 1977. History of the child's influence: Ancient Mediterranean civilization. In R. Q. Bell and L. V. Harper (eds.), *Child Effects on Adults*. Hillsdale, N.J.: Lawrence Erlbaum Associates.

24. DeCasper, A. J., and W. P. Fifer. 1980. Of human bonding: Infants prefer their mothers. *Science, 208,* 1174-1176.

25. Cernoch, J. M., and R. H. Porter. 1985. Recognition of maternal axiliary odors by infants. *Child Development, 54,* 1593-1598.

26. Kalnins, I. V., and J. S. Bruner. 1973. The coordination of visual observation and instrumental behavior in early infancy. *Perception, 2,* 307-314.

27. DeCasper, A. J., and M. J. Spence. 1986. Prenatal maternal speech influences newborns' perception of speech sounds. *Infant Behavior and Development, 9,* 133-150.

28. Field, T. M. 1987. Interaction and attachment in normal and atypical infants. *Journal of Consulting and Clinical Psychology, 55,* 853-859.

29. Lamb, M. E. Interview, *Seasons of Life*.

30. Klaus, M. H., and J. H. Kennell. 1976. *Maternal-Infant Bonding* . St. Louis: Mosby.

31. Goldberg, S. 1983. Parent-to-infant bonding: Another look. *Child Development, 54,* 1355-1382.

Lamb, M. E. 1982. Early contact and mother-infant bonding: One decade later. *Pediatrics, 70*, 763-768.

Myer, B. J. 1987. Mother-infant bonding: The status of this critical-period hypothesis. In M. H. Bornstein (ed.), *Sensitive Periods in Development: Interdisciplinary Perspectives*. Hillsdale, N.J.: Lawrence Erlbaum Associates.

Palkovitz, R. 1985. Fathers' birth attendance, early contact, and extended contact with their newborns: A critical review. *Child Development, 56*, 392-406.

32. Lamb, M. E. Interview, *Seasons of Life*.

33. Singer, L. M., D. M. Brodzinsky, D. Ramsay, M. Stein, and E. Waters. 1985. Mother-infant attachment in adoptive families. *Child Development, 56*, 1543-1551.

Notes for Chapter 3

1. Mahler, M., F. Pine, and A. Bergman. 1975. *The Psychological Birth of the Human Infant*. New York: Basic Books.

2. Kegan, R. 1982. *The Evolving Self*. Cambridge, Mass.: Harvard University Press.

3. Linde, E. V., B. A. Morrongiello, and C. K. Rovee-Collier. 1985. Determinants of retention in 8-week-old infants. *Developmental Psychology, 21*, 602-613.

4. Lewis, M., and J. Brooks-Gunn. 1979. *Social Cognition and the Acquisition of Self*. New York: Plenum.

5. Piaget, J., and B. Inhelder. 1969. *The Psychology of the Child*. New York: Basic Books.

6. Goldman-Rakic, P. S. 1987. Development of cortical circuitry and cognitive function. *Child Development, 58*, 602-622.

7. Ibid.

8. Scarr, S. 1983. An evolutionary perspective on infant intelligence. In M. Lewis (ed.), *Origins of Intelligence*. 2nd ed. New York: Plenum Press.

9. Sroufe, L. A. 1979. Socioemotional development. In J. Osofsky (ed.), *The Handbook of Infant Development*. New York: Wiley.

10. Gallup, G. G. 1970. Chimpanzees: Self-recognition. *Science, 167*, 86-87.

11. Lewis and Brooks-Gunn, *Social Cognition*.

12. Lewis, M., J. Brooks-Gunn, and J. Jaskir. 1985. Individual differences in self-recognition as a function of the mother-infant attachment relationship. *Developmental Psychology, 21*, 1181-1187.

13. Reinert, G. 1979. Prolegomena to a history of life-span developmental psychology. In P. B. Baltes and O. G. Brim, Jr. (eds.), *Life-Span Development and Behavior*. Vol. 2. New York: Academic Press.

Bühler, C. 1968. The developmental structure of goal setting in group and individual studies. In C. Bühler and F. Massarik (eds.), *The Course of Human Life*. New York: Springer.

14. Erikson, E. H. 1963. *Childhood and Society*. 2nd ed. New York: Norton.

Erikson, E. H., and E. Hall. 1987. The father of the identity crisis. In E. Hall, *Growing and Changing*. New York: Random House.

15. Levinson, D. J. 1986. A conception of adult development. *American Psychologist, 41*, 3-13.

16. Ibid.

17. Elder, G. H., Jr. 1974. *Children of the Great Depression*. Chicago: University of Chicago Press.

18. Lamb, M. E. Interview, *Seasons of Life*.

19. Bowlby, J. 1969. *Attachment and Loss*. Vol. 1: *Attachment*. New York: Basic Books.

20. Kagan, J. January 1978. The baby's elastic mind. *Human Nature*, 1, 66-73.

Goleman, D. March 13, 1984. Traumatic beginnings: Most children seem able to recover. *New York Times*, C1-2.

21. Kagan, J. 1984. The Nature of the Child. New York: Basic Books. (Citing C. Rathbun, L. DiVirgilio, and S. Waldfogel, 1958. A restitutive process in children following radical separation from family and culture. *American Journal of Orthopsychiatry*, 28, 408-15.)

22. Clark, E. A., and J. Hanisee. 1982. Intellectual and adoptive performance of Asian children in adoptive American settings. *Developmental Psychology*, 18, 595-599.

Winick, M., K. K. Meyer, and R. C. Harris. 1975. Malnutrition and environmental enrichment by early adoption. *Science*, 190, 1173-1175.

23. Goldsmith, H. H., A. H. Buss, R. Plomin, M. K. Rothbart, A. Thomas, S. Chess, R. A. Hinde, and R. B. McCall. 1987. Roundtable: What is temperament? Four approaches. *Child Development*, 58, 505-529.

24. Thomas, A., S. Chess, and H. Birch. 1977. The origins of personality. *Scientific American*, 223, 102-109.

25. Kagan, J., and E. Hall. 1987. The fearful child's hidden talents. In E. Hall, *Growing and Changing*. New York: Random House.

26. Arens, N. C. May 1987. Nature meets nurture: The behavior balancing act. *Human Development Research at Penn State*, 2, 25-27.

27. Plomin, R., N. L. Pedersen, G. E. McClearn, J. R. Nesselroade, and C. S. Bergeman. 1988. EAS temperaments during the last half of the life span: Twins reared apart and twins reared together. *Psychology and Aging*, 3, 43-50.

28. Chess, S., and A. Thomas. 1987. *Know Your Child*. New York: Basic Books.

29. White, S. Interview, *Seasons of Life*.

Notes for Chapter 4

1. Bogin, *Patterns of Human Growth*.

2. Whiting, B. B., and J. W. M. Whiting. 1975. *Children of Six Cultures*. Cambridge, Mass.: Harvard University Press.

3. Bogin, *Patterns of Human Growth*.

4. Gould, S. J. Interview, *Seasons of Life*.

5. Bogin, B. 1990. The evolution of human childhood.

6. Lancaster, J. B., and C. S. Lancaster. 1987. The watershed: Changes in parental-investment and family formation strategies in the course of human evolution. In J. Lancaster, J. Altmann, A. Rossi, and L. Sherrod (eds.), *Parenting Across the Lifespan: Biosocial Dimensions*. New York: Aldine de Gruyter.

7. Lancaster, J. B. In press. Parental investment and the evolution of the juvenile phase of the human life course. In A. Brooks (ed.), *The Origins of Humanness*. Washington, D.C.: Smithsonian Institution Press.

8. Chomsky, N. 1975. *Reflections on Language*. New York: Pantheon.

9. Oller, D. K., and R. E. Eilers. April 1988. The role of audition in infant babbling. *Child Development, 59,* 441-449.

10. deVilliers, J. G., and P. A. deVilliers. 1978. *Early Language*. Cambridge, Mass.: Harvard University Press.

11. Curtiss, S. R. 1977. *Genie*. New York: Academic Press.

12. Anderson, J. R. 1983. *The Architecture of Cognition*. Cambridge, Mass.: Harvard University Press.

Moerk, E. L. 1989. The LAD was a lady and the tasks were ill-defined. *Developmental Review, 9,* 21-57.

13. Bruner, J. S. 1983. *Child's Talk: Learning to Use Language*. New York: Norton.

14. Maratsos, M. P. 1983. Some current issues in the study of the acquisition of grammar. In J. H. Flavell and E. M. Markman (eds.), *Cognitive Development*. Vol. 3: *Handbook of Child Psychology*. 4th ed. New York: Wiley.

15. Greenough, W. T., J. E. Black, and C. S. Wallace. 1987. Experience and brain development. *Child Development, 58,* 539-559.

16. LeVay, S., T. N. Wiesel, and D. H. Hubel. 1980. The development of ocular dominance columns in normal and visually deprived monkeys. *Journal of Comparative Neurology, 191,* 1-51.

17. Bertenthal, B. I., and J. J. Campos. 1987. New directions in the study of early experience. *Child Development, 58,* 560-567.

18. Goldman-Rakic, Development of cortical circuitry.

19. Witelson, S. F. 1987. Neurobiological aspects of language in children. *Child Development, 58,* 653-688.

20. Gottfried, A. W., and K. Bathurst. 1983. Hand preference across time is related to intelligence in young girls, not boys. *Science, 221,* 1074-1076.

21. Thatcher, R. W., R. A. Walker, and S. Giudice. 1987. Human cerebral hemispheres develop at different rates and ages. *Science, 236,* 1110-1113.

22. Bruner, J. S. 1970. The growth and structure of skill. In K. J. Connelly (ed.), *Motor Skills in Infancy*. New York: Academic Press.

Notes for Chapter 5

1. White, S. Interview, *Seasons of Life*.

2. Ibid.

3. Harkness and Super, The cultural construction of child development.

4. Whiting and Whiting, *Children of Six Cultures*.

5. Greenleaf, *Children Through the Ages*.

6. Borstelmann, Children before psychology.

7. Lewisboro History Book Committee. 1981. *A History of the Town of Lewisboro, Westchester County, New York*. South Salem, N.Y.: Lewisboro History Book Committee.

8. Furnas, J. C. 1969. *The Americans: A Social History of the United States, 1587-1914*. New York: G. P. Putnam's Sons.

9. Morris, R. B. (ed.). 1953. *Encyclopedia of American History*. New York: Harper.

10. White, S. H., and D. B. Pillemer. 1979. Childhood amnesia and the development of a socially accessible memory system. In J. F. Kihlstrom and D. B. Pillemer

(eds.), *Functional Disorders of Memory*. Hillsdale, N.J.: Lawrence Erlbaum Associates.

     Goldman-Rakic, Isseroff, and Bugbee, The neurobiology of cognitive development.

11. Thomas, R. M. 1979. *Comparing Theories of Child Development*. Belmont, Calif.: Wadsworth.

12. Kagan, J., R. B. Kearsley, and P. R. Zelazo. 1978. *Infancy: Its Place in Human Development*. Cambridge, Mass.: Harvard University Press. (Citing unpublished paper by Lawrence Stone.)

13. Locke, John. 1963/1964. *Some Thoughts on Education*. New York: Barron's Education Series.

14. Rousseau, J.-J. 1969; orig. pub. 1762. *Émile*. New York: Dutton.

15. Kessen, W. 1979. The American child and other cultural inventions. *American Psychologist, 34*, 815-820.

16. Borstelmann, Children before psychology.

17. Elkind, D. Interview, *Seasons of Life*.

     Elkind, D. 1981. *The Hurried Child: Growing Up Too Fast Too Soon*. Reading, Mass.: Addison-Wesley.

18. Remley, A. October 1988. From obedience to independence. *Psychology Today*, 56-59.

19. Richman, H. A., and M. W. Stagner. Winter 1986. Children in an aging society: Treasured resource or forgotten minority? *Daedalus, 115*, 171-190.

20. Child Trends, Inc. 1989. *U.S. Children and Their Families: Current Conditions and Recent Trends*. Washington, D.C.: U.S. Government Printing Office.

21. Hess, R. D., and S. D. Holloway. 1984. Family and school as educational institutions. In R. D. Parke (ed.), *Review of Child Development Research*. Vol. 7. Chicago: University of Chicago Press.

22. Ibid.

23. White, S. Interview, *Seasons of Life*.

24. Siegler, R. S. 1986. *Children's Thinking*. Englewood Cliffs, N.J.: Prentice-Hall.

25. Seligmann, J. January 12, 1987. Memorizing vs. thinking. *Newsweek*, 60-61.

26. Collins, G. February 1, 1984. Does early teaching of infants have merit? *New York Times*, C1+. (Kagan's comments also come from this article.)

27. Trotter, R. J. December 1987. Project Day-Care. *Psychology Today, 21*, 32-38.

28. Asher, S. Interview, *Seasons of Life*.

29. Ibid.

30. Ibid.

Notes for Chapter 6

1. Carraher, T. N., D. W. Carraher, and A. D. Schliemann. 1985. Mathematics in the streets and in schools. *British Journal of Developmental Psychology, 3*, 21-29.

2. Bruner, J. S. 1972. Nature and uses of immaturity. *American Psychologist, 27*, 687-708.

3. Siegler, *Children's Thinking*.

4. DeVries, R. 1969. Constancy of generic identity in the years three to six. *Monographs of the Society for Research in Child Development, 34*, Serial No. 127.

5. Harter, S. 1983. Developmental perspectives on the self-system. In E. M.

Hetherington (ed.), Socialization, personality, and social development. Vol. 4: *Handbook of Child Psychology*. 4th ed. New York: Wiley.

6. Harter, S. 1983. Developmental perspectives.

Carroll, J. J., and M. S. Steward. 1984. The role of cognitive development in children's understandings of their own feelings. *Child Development, 55,* 1486-1492.

7. Money, J., and A. A. Ehrhardt. 1972. *Man & Woman; Boy & Girl.* Baltimore: Johns Hopkins University Press.

8. Bem, S. L. 1983. Gender schema theory and its implications for child development. *Signs, 8,* 598-616.

9. Fagot, B. I., and M. D. Leinbach. 1989. The young child's gender schema: Environmental input, internal organization. *Child Development, 60,* 663-672.

10. Maccoby, E. E. 1988. Gender as a social category. *Developmental Psychology, 24,* 755-765.

11. Gibson, J. Interview, *Seasons of Life*.

12. Bem, S. L. 1989. Genital knowledge and gender constancy in preschool children. *Child Development, 60,* 649-662.

13. Bem, Gender schema theory.

14. Huston, A. C. 1985. The development of sex-typing. *Developmental Review, 5,* 1-17.

15. Proust, M. 1934. *Remembrance of Things Past.* New York: Random House.

16. Nelson, K., and J. Hudson. 1988. Scripts and memory: Functional relationships in development. In F. E. Weinert and M. Perlmutter (eds.), *Memory Development: Universal Changes and Individual Differences.* Hillsdale, N.J.: Lawrence Erlbaum Associates.

17. Nelson, K., and J. Gruendel. 1981. Generalized event representation: Basic building blocks of cognitive development. In M. E. Lamb and A. L. Brown (eds.), *Advances in Developmental Psychology.* Vol. 1. Hillsdale, N.J.: Lawrence Erlbaum Associates.

18. Barclay, C. R. 1986. Schematization of autobiographical memory. In D. C. Rubin (ed.), *Autobiographical Memory.* New York: Cambridge University Press.

19. Nelson, K. 1986. Preface. In K. Nelson (ed.), *Event Knowledge: Structure and Function in Development.* Hillsdale, N.J.: Lawrence Erlbaum Associates.

20. Doyle, C. 1989. Young children as authors: The creative process in first stories. Paper presented at annual meeting of American Psychological Association. New Orleans.

21. Smith, N. Interview, *Seasons of Life*.

22. DeAngelis, T. October 1989. Kids have inner sense of how to weave a tale. *APA Monitor,* 30-41.

23. Waldvogel, S. 1948. The frequency and affective character of childhood memories. *Psychological Monographs, 62,* Whole No. 291.

24. Wetzler, S. E., and J. A. Sweeney. 1986. Childhood amnesia: An empirical demonstration. In D. C. Rubin, *Autobiographical Memory.* New York: Cambridge University Press.

25. Nigro, G., and U. Neisser. 1983. Point of view in personal memories. *Cognitive Psychology, 15,* 467-482.

Kotre, K. 1990. The external observer in autobiographical memories. Unpublished master's thesis. University of Michigan.

26. Adler, A. 1931. *What Life Should Mean to You*. Boston: Little, Brown.

27. Interview, *Seasons of Life*.

28. Ibid.

Notes for Chapter 7

1. Bogin, *Patterns of Human Growth*.

2. Beitins, I. Interview, *Seasons of Life*.

3. Brooks-Gunn, J., and M. P. Warren. 1988. The psychological significance of secondary sexual characteristics in nine-to-eleven-year-old girls. *Child Development*, 59, 1061-1069.

4. Katchadourian, H. A., and D. T. Lunde. 1980. *Fundamentals of Human Sexuality*. 3rd ed. New York: Holt, Rinehart and Winston.

5. Johnston, F. E. 1974. Control of age at menarche. *Human Biology*, 46, 159-171.

6. Roche, A. F. 1979. Secular trends in stature, weight, and maturation. In A. F. Roche (ed.), Secular trends in human growth, maturation, and development. *Monographs of the Society for Research in Child Development*, Serial No. 179.

7. Frisch, R. 1978. Population, food intake, and fertility. *Science*, 199, 22-30.

8. Lancaster, J. B. Interview, *Seasons of Life*.

9. Winikoff, B. 1978. Changing public diet. *Human Nature*, 1, 60-65.

10. Brooks-Gunn, J., M. P. Warren, and L. Homek. 1983. The development of eating problems in adolescent dance students: The contribution of maturational status, weight, and body image. Paper presented at the Biennial Meeting of the Society for Research in Child Development, Detroit.

11. Garn, S. M. 1980. Continuities and changes in maturational timing. In O. G. Brim, Jr., and J. Kagan (eds.), *Constancy and Change in Human Development*. Cambridge, Mass.: Harvard University Press.

12. Lancaster, J. B. 1986. Human adolescence and reproduction: An evolutionary perspective. In J. B. Lancaster and B. A. Hamburg (eds.), *School-Age Pregnancy and Parenthood: Biosocial Dimensions*. New York: Aldine.

Lancaster, J. B. Interview, *Seasons of Life*.

13. Bogin, B. Interview, *Seasons of Life*.

14. Richardson, D. W., and R. V. Short. 1978. Time of onset of sperm production in boys. *Journal of Biosocial Science Suppl.*, 5, 15-26.

15. Bogin, B. Interview, *Seasons of Life*.

16. Gutmann, D. 1987. *Reclaimed Powers*. New York: Basic Books.

17. Petersen, A. C. September 1987. Those gangly years. *Psychology Today*, 21, 28-34.

18. Magnusson, D., H. Stattin, and V. L. Allen. 1985. Biological maturation and social development. *Journal of Youth and Adolescence*, 14, 267-284.

19. Livson, N., and H. Peskin. 1980. Perspectives on adolescence from longitudinal research. In J. Adelson (ed.), *Handbook of Adolescent Psychology*. New York: Wiley.

Steinberg, L. 1985. *Adolescence*. New York: Knopf.

20. Ibid.

21. Ibid.

22. Steinberg, L. Interview, *Seasons of Life*.

23. Livson and Peskin, Perspectives on adolescence.

Steinberg, *Adolescence*.

24. Offer, D., E. Ostrov, and K. I. Howard. 1981. *The Adolescent: A Psychological Self-Portrait*. New York: Basic Books.

25. Petersen, A. C., and B. Taylor. 1980. The biological approach to adolescence: Biological change and psychological adaptation. In J. Adelson (ed.), *Handbook of Adolescent Psychology*. New York: Wiley.

26. Steinberg, L. Interview, *Seasons of Life*.

Notes for Chapter 8

1. Simmons, R., D. Blyth, E. Van Cleave, and D. Bush. 1979. Entry into early adolescence: The impact of school structure, puberty, and early dating on self-esteem. *American Sociological Review*, 44, 948-967.

   Simmons, R. G., R. Burgeson, S. Carlton-Ford, and D. A. Blyth. 1987. The impact of cumulative change in early adolescence. *Child Development*, 58, 1220-1234.

2. Petersen, A. C. Interview, *Seasons of Life*.

3. Simmons, et al., Impact of cumulative change.

4. Karsh, E. January 3, 1987. A teen-ager is a ton of worry. *New York Times*, 23.

5. Elkind, D. Interview, *Seasons of Life*.

6. Jessor, R. Interview, *Seasons of Life*.

7. Child Trends, Inc., *U.S. Children and Their Families*.

8. Bolton, F. G., Jr. 1980. *The Pregnant Adolescent*. Beverly Hills, Calif.: Sage.
   Furstenberg, F. F., Jr. 1976. *Unplanned Parenthood*. New York: Free Press.
   Moore, K. A. Summer 1985. Teenage pregnancy. *New Perspectives*, 11-15.

9. Kantrowitz, B. February 16,1987. Kids and contraceptives. *Newsweek*, 54-65.

10. Kovach, J. A., and N. W. Glickman. 1986. Levels and psychosocial correlates of adolescent drug use. *Journal of Youth and Adolescence*, 15, 61-78.

11. Hoffman, L., S. Paris, E. Hall, and R. Schell. 1988. *Developmental Psychology Today*. 5th ed. New York: Random House.

12. Dornbusch, S. M., J. M. Carlsmith, S. J. Bushwall, P. L. Ritter, H. Leiderman, A. H. Hastorf, and R. T. Gross. 1985. Single parents, extended households, and the control of adolescents. *Child Development*, 56, 326-341.

13. Hoffman, et al., *Developmental Psychology Today*.

14. Steinberg, *Adolescence*.

15. Elder, G. H., Jr. 1980. Adolescence in historical perspective. In J. Adelson (ed.), *Handbook of Adolescent Psychology*. New York: Wiley.

16. Hall, G. S. 1904. *Adolescence*. New York: Appleton-Century-Crofts.

17. Petersen, A. C. Interview, *Seasons of Life*.

18. Steinberg, L. Interview, *Seasons of Life*.

19. Ibid.

20. Steinberg, L. 1987. Bound to bicker. *Psychology Today*, 21, 36-39.

21. Steinberg, L. Interview, *Seasons of Life*.

22. Offer, Ostrov, and Howard, *The Adolescent*.
    Richardson, R. A., N. L. Galambos, J. E. Schulenberg, and A. C. Petersen. 1985. Young adolescents' perceptions of the family environment. *Journal of Early Adolescence*, 4, 131-154.

23. Steinberg, L. 1981. Transformations in family relationships at puberty. *Developmental Psychology*, 17, 833-840.

24. Csikszentmihalyi, M., and R. Larson. 1984. *Being Adolescent*. New York: Basic Books.

25. Crockett, L., M. Losoff, and A. C. Petersen. 1984. Perceptions of the peer group and friendships in early adolescence. *Journal of Early Adolescence, 4*, 155-181.

26. Buhrmester, D., and W. Furman. 1987. The development of companionship and intimacy. *Child Development, 58*, 1101-1113.

27. Crockett, Losoff, and Petersen, Perceptions of the peer group and friendships.

28. Buhrmester and Furman, Development of companionship.

29. Steinberg, *Adolescence*.

30. Gavin, L. A., and W. Furman. 1989. Age differences in adolescents' perceptions of their peer groups. *Developmental Psychology, 25*, 827-834.

31. Dunphy, D. C. 1963. The social structure of the urban adolescent peer group. *Sociometry, 26*, 230-246.

32. Offer, Ostrov, and Howard, *The Adolescent*.

33. Hoffman et al., *Developmental Psychology Today*.

34. Elkind, D. Interview, *Seasons of Life*.

35. Brown, B. B., D. R. Clasen, and S. A. Eicher. 1986. Perceptions of peer pressure, peer conformity dispositions, and self-reported behavior among adolescents. *Developmental Psychology, 22*, 521-530.

36. Ibid.

37. Steinberg, L., and S. B. Silverberg. 1986. The vicissitudes of autonomy in early adolescence. *Child Development, 57*, 841-851.

Notes for Chapter 9

1. Elkind, D. Interview, *Seasons of Life*.

2. Osherson, D. N., and E. M. Markman. 1975. Language and the ability to evaluate contradictions and tautologies. *Cognition, 3*, 213-226.

3. Braine, M. D. S., and B. Rumain. 1981. Development of the comprehension of "or": Evidence for a sequence of competencies. *Journal of Experimental Child Psychology, 31*, 46-70.

4. Hoffman, et al., *Developmental Psychology Today*.

5. Flavell, J. 1985. *Cognitive Development*. 2nd ed. Englewood Cliffs, N.J.: Prentice-Hall.

6. Elkind, D. Interview, *Seasons of Life*.

7. Kegan, R. 1982. *The Evolving Self*. Cambridge, Mass.: Harvard University Press.

8. Erikson, E. 1980. *Identity and the Life Cycle*. New York: Norton.

9. Markus, H., and P. Nurius. 1986. Possible selves. *American Psychologist, 41*, 954-969.

10. Marcia, J. E. 1980. Identity in adolescence. In J. Adelson (ed.), *Handbook of Adolescent Psychology*. New York: Wiley.

11. Hoffman et al., *Developmental Psychology Today*.

12. McCarthy, J., and D. Hoge. 1982. Analysis of age effects in longitudinal studies of adolescent self-esteem. *Developmental Psychology, 18*, 372-379.

O'Malley, P., and J. Bachman. 1983. Self-esteem: Change and stability between ages 13 and 23. *Developmental Psychology, 19*, 257-268.

Savin-Williams, R., and D. Demo. 1984. Developmental change and stability in adolescent self-concept. *Developmental Psychology, 20*, 1100-1110.

13. Offer, Ostrov, and Howard, *The Adolescent*.

14. McAdams, D. P. Interview, *Seasons of Life*.

15. Elkind, D. 1981. *Children and Adolescents: Interpretive Essays on Jean Piaget*. 3rd ed. New York: Oxford University Press.

16. McAdams, D. P. Interview, *Seasons of Life*.

17. Adelson, J., and E. Hall. 1987. Children and other political naifs. In E. Hall, *Growing and Changing*. New York: Random House.

18. Ibid.

19. Spence, D. P. 1982. *Narrative Truth and Historical Truth*. New York: Norton.

20. Robins, L. 1985. Early home environment and retrospective recall: A test for concordance between siblings with and without psychiatric disorders. *American Journal of Orthopsychiatry, 55*, 27-41.

21. Bruner, J. S. Spring 1987. Life as narrative. *Social Research, 54*, 11-32.

22. McAdams, D. P. 1987. A life-story model of identity. In R. Hogan and W. Jones (eds.), *Perspectives in Personality*. Vol. 2. Greenwich, Conn.: JAI Press.

Notes for Chapter 10

1. Short, R. V. 1976. The evolution of human reproduction. *Proceedings of the Royal Society, B195*, 3-24.

2. Konner, M., and C. Worthman. 1980. Nursing frequency, gonadal function, and birth spacing among !Kung hunter-gatherers. *Science, 207*, 788-791.

3. Lancaster, J. B. Interview, *Seasons of Life*.

4. Child Trends, Inc., *U.S. Children and Their Families*.

5. Brody, J. July 20, 1989. Number of first-time mothers over 30 on the rise. *Ann Arbor News*, D3.

6. Daniels, P., and K. Weingarten. 1982. *Sooner or Later: The Timing of Parenthood in Adult Lives*. New York: Norton.

7. Ragozin, A. S., R. R. Basham, K. A. Crnic, M. T. Greenberg, and N. M. Robinson. 1982. Effects of maternal age on parenting role. *Developmental Psychology, 18*, 627-634.

8. Burton, L. M., and V. L. Bengtson. 1985. Black grandmothers: Issues of timing and continuity of roles. In V. L. Bengtson and J. F. Robertson (eds.), *Grandparenthood*. Beverly Hills, Calif.: Sage.

9. Rossi, A. S. Interview, *Seasons of Life*.

10. Rossi, A. S. 1986. Sex and gender in an aging society. *Daedalus, 115*, 1, 141-169.

11. Jones, L. Y. 1980. *Great Expectations: America and the Baby Boom Generation*. New York: Coward, McCann & Geoghegan.

12. Hoffman, L. W. 1982. Social change and its effects on parents and children: Limitations to knowledge. In P. Berman and E. Ramey (eds.), *Women: A Developmental Perspective*. Washington, D.C.: U.S. Government Printing Office.

13. *Newsweek*. Sept. 1, 1986. Three's a crowd, 68.

14. Ibid.

15. McCluskey, K. A., J. Killarney, and D. R. Pappini. 1983. Adolescent pregnancy and parenthood. In E. J. Callahan and K. A. McCluskey (eds.), *Life-Span Developmental Psychology: Nonnormative Events*. New York: Academic Press.

16. Menken, J., J. Trussell, and U. Larsen. 1986. Age and infertility. *Science, 233,* 1389-1394.

17. Harman, S. M., and G. B. Talbert. 1985. Reproductive aging. In C. E. Finch and E. L. Schneider (eds.), *Handbook of the Biology of Aging.* 2nd ed. New York: Van Nostrand Reinhold.

18. Omenn, G. S. 1983. Medical genetics, genetic counseling, and behavior genetics. In J. L. Fuller and E. C. Simmel (eds.), *Behavior Genetics.* Hillsdale, N.J.: Lawrence Erlbaum Associates.

19. Vider, E. 1986. Late motherhood. In H. E. Fitzgerald and M. G. Walraven (eds.), *Human Development 86/87.* Guilford, Conn.: Dushkin.

20. Schwartz, D. et al. April 1983. Semen characteristics as a function of age in 833 fertile men. *Fertility and Sterility,* 530-535.

Harman and Talbert, Reproductive aging. In Finch and Schneider.

Gunderson, V., and G. P. Sackett. 1982. Paternal effects on reproductive outcome and developmental risk. In M. E. Lamb and A. L. Brown (eds.), *Advances in Developmental Psychology.* Vol. 2. Hillsdale, N.J.: Lawrence Erlbaum Associates.

21. Schulz, R., and C. Curnow. 1988. Peak performance and age among superathletes: Track and field, swimming, baseball, tennis, and golf. *Journal of Gerontology, 43,* 113-120.

Notes for Chapter 11

1. Hoffman, L. W., and J. D. Manis. 1979. The value of children in the United States: A new approach to the study of fertility. *Journal of Marriage and the Family, 41,* 589.

2. Short, R. V. 1976. The evolution of human reproduction. *Proceedings of the Royal Society, B195,* 3-24.

3. Hagestad, G. O., and B. L. Neugarten. 1985. Age and the life course. In R. H. Binstock and E. Shanas (eds.), *Handbook of Aging and the Social Sciences.* 2nd ed. New York: Van Nostrand Reinhold.

4. Rossi, Sex and gender in an aging society.

5. Neugarten, B. L. Interview, *Seasons of Life.*

6. *Wall Street Journal.* June 14, 1988. Soon, most people may have 'lived in sin,' 37.

7. Barringer, F. June 9, 1989. Doubt on 'trial marriage' raised by divorce rates. *New York Times,* A1, A28.

8. Keniston, K. 1968. *Young Radicals: Notes on Committed Youth.* New York: Harcourt Brace Jovanovich.

9. Konner, M. 1982. *The Tangled Wing.* New York: Holt, Rinehart and Winston.

10. Lancaster, J. B. Interview, *Seasons of Life.*

11. DeVore, I. Interview, *Seasons of Life.*

12. Lancaster, Women in biosocial perspective.

13. Hunter, D. E., and P. Whitten. 1976. *Encyclopedia of Anthropology.* New York: Harper & Row.

14. Lancaster, J. B. In press. Evolutionary perspectives on single parenthood. In R. B. Bell (ed.), *Sociobiology and the Social Sciences.* Lubbock: Texas Tech University Press.

15. Ventura, S. J. April 1985. Recent trends and variations in births to unmarried women. Paper presented at biennial meeting of the Society for Research in Child Development. Toronto.

16. Ibid.

17. Child Trends, Inc., *U.S. Children and Their Families*.

18. Berke, R. L. June 22, 1989. Late childbirth is found on rise. *New York Times*, A16.

19. Child Trends, Inc., *U.S. Children and Their Families*.

20. U.S. Bureau of the Census. 1986. *Statistical Abstract of the United States*. Washington, D.C.: U.S. Government Printing Office.

21. Child Trends, Inc., *U.S. Children and Their Families*.

22. Wilentz, A. January 26, 1987. Garland's bouquet. *Time*, 14-15.

23. Noble, K. B. May 1, 1988. Child care: The federal role grows in the 80s. *New York Times*, E4.

24. Wallis, C. June 22, 1987. The child-care dilemma. *Time*, 54-60.

25. Bloom, D., Harvard economist, quoted in C. Wallis, June 22, 1987, The child-care dilemma. *Time*, 54-60.

26. Klein, R. P. 1985. Caregiving arrangements by employed women with children under 1 year of age. *Developmental Psychology*, 21, 403-406.

27. Bishop, K. May 1, 1988. On the West Coast, it's a local matter. *New York Times*, E4.

28. Child Trends, Inc., 1989. *U.S. Children and Their Families*.

29. Bumpass, L., and T. Castro-Martin. 1989. Recent trends in marital disruption. *Demography*, 26, 37-51.

30. Lancaster, J. B. Interview, *Seasons of Life*.

31. Cherlin, A. J. Interview, *Seasons of Life*.

32. Furstenberg, F. F., Jr., and C. W. Nord. 1985. Parenting apart: Patterns of child-rearing after marital disruption. *Journal of Marriage and the Family*, 47, 893-904.

33. Cherlin, A. J. Interview, *Seasons of Life*.

34. Child Trends, Inc., *U.S. Children and Their Families*.

35. Zill, N. 1988. Behavior, achievement, and health problems among children in stepfamilies. In E. M. Hetherington and J. D. Aratesh (eds.), *Impact of Divorce, Single Parenting, and Step-parenting on Children*. Hillsdale, N.J.: Lawrence Erlbaum Associates.

36. Hetherington, E. M., M. Stanley-Hagan, and E. R. Anderson. 1989. Marital transitions: A child's perspective. *American Psychologist*, 44, 303-312.

37. Zill, N., Behavior, achievement, and health problems.

38. Hetherington, Stanley-Hagan, and Anderson, Marital transitions.

39. Cherlin, A. J. Interview, *Seasons of Life*.

Notes for Chapter 12

1. Levinson, D. J., C. N. Darrow, E. B. Klein, M. H. Levinson, and B. McKee. 1978. *The Seasons of a Man's Life*. New York: Knopf.

2. Roberts, P., and P. M. Newton. 1987. Levinsonian studies of women's adult development. *Psychology and Aging*, 2, 154-163.

3. Frank, S. J., C. B. Avery, and M. S. Laman. 1988. Young adults' perceptions of their relationships with their parents: Individual differences in connectedness, competence, and emotional autonomy. *Developmental Psychology*, 24, 729-737.

4. Erikson, *Identity and the Life Cycle*.

5. Weiss, R. S. 1982. Attachment in adult life. In C. M. Parkes and J. Stevenson-Hinde (eds.), *The Place of Attachment in Human Behavior*. New York: Basic Books.

6. Hazen, C., and P. Shaver. 1987. Romantic love conceptualized as an attachment process. *Journal of Personality and Social Psychology*, 52, 511-524.

7. Laurence, L. T. 1982. *Couple Constancy: Conversations with Today's Happily Married People*. Ann Arbor: University of Michigan Research Press.

8. Kurdek, L. A., and J. P. Schmitt. 1986. Early development of relationship quality in heterosexual married, heterosexual cohabiting, gay, and lesbian couples. *Developmental Psychology*, 22, 305-309.

9. Belsky, J. Interview, *Seasons of Life*.

10. Super, D. E. 1985. Coming of age in Middletown: Careers in the making. *American Psychologist*, 40, 405-414.

11. Morrison, A. M., R. P. White, and E. van Velsor. August 1987. Executive woman: Substance plus style. *Psychology Today*, 18-26.

12. *Wall Street Journal*. March 24, 1986. The glass ceiling. lD.

13. Elder, G. H., Jr. 1986. Military times and turning points in men's lives. *Developmental Psychology*, 22, 233-245.

14. Alpert, J. L., and M. S. Richardson. 1980. Parenting. In L. W. Poon (ed.), *Aging in the 1980s*. Washington, D.C.: American Psychological Association.

15. Gutmann, *Reclaimed Powers*.

16. Ibid.

17. Brown, P. L. September 14, 1987. Studying seasons of a woman's life. *New York Times*, 23.

18. Roberts and Newton, Levinsonian studies.

19. Belsky, J., and E. Pensky. In press. Developmental history, personality, and family relationships: Toward an emergent family system. In R. Hinde and J. Stevenson-Hinde (eds.), *Towards Understanding Families*. London: Cambridge University Press.

20. Levinson et al., *Seasons of a Man's Life*.

21. Roberts and Newton, Levinsonian studies.

22. Blanchard-Fields, F. 1986. Reasoning on social dilemmas varying in emotional saliency: An adult developmental perspective. *Psychology and Aging*, 1, 325-333.

Notes for Chapter 13

1. U.S. Bureau of Statistics, *Statistical Abstract*.

2. Lakatta, E. G. 1985. Heart and circulation. In C. E. Finch and E. L. Schneider (eds.), *Handbook of the Biology of Aging*. 2nd ed. New York: Van Nostrand Reinhold.

3. Spence, A. P. 1989. *Biology of Human Aging*. Englewood Cliffs, N.J.: Prentice-Hall.

4. Weg, R. B. 1983. Changing physiology of aging: Normal and pathological. In D. S. Woodruff and J. E. Birren (eds.), *Aging: Scientific Perspectives and Social Issues*. 2nd ed. Monterey, Calif.: Brooks/Cole.

5. Lakatta, Heart and circulation.

6. Woodruff-Pak, D. Interview, *Seasons of Life*.

   Woodruff-Pak, D. 1977. *Can You Live to Be One Hundred?* New York: Chatham Square Press.

7. Schaefer, W. R., R. Kim, R. Sterne, J. Thorner, S.-H. Kim, and J. Rine. 1989.

Genetic and pharmacological suppression on oncogenic mutations in RAS genes of yeast and humans. *Science, 245,* 379-385.

8. Brody, J. E. November 30, 1989. Personal health. *New York Times,* B27.

9. National Center for Health Statistics. 1985. *Health: United States, 1985.* Washington, D.C.: U.S. Department of Health and Human Services.

10. Bierman, E. L. 1985. Arteriosclerosis and aging. In C. E. Finch and E. L. Schneider (eds.), *Handbook of the Biology of Aging.* 2nd ed. New York: Van Nostrand Reinhold.

Kannel, W. B. 1985. Hypertension and aging. In C. E. Finch and E. L. Schneider (eds.), *Handbook of the Biology of Aging.* 2nd ed. New York: Van Nostrand Reinhold.

11. deVries, H. A. 1983. Physiology of exercise and aging. In D. S. Woodruff and J. E. Birren (eds.), *Aging: Scientific Perspectives and Social Issues.* 2nd ed. Monterey, Calif.: Brooks/Cole.

12. Woodruff-Pak, D. Interview, *Seasons of Life.*

13. Brody, J. E. December 13, 1983. Divorce's stress exacts long-term toll. *New York Times,* C1+.

Perlmutter M., and Hall, E. 1985. *Adult Development and Aging.* New York: Wiley.

14. House, J. S., K. R. Landis, and D. Umberson. 1988. Social relationships and health. *Science, 241,* 540-545.

15. Cassel, J. 1976. *American Journal of Epidemiology, 104,* 107. Cited in J. S. House, K. R. Landis, and D. Umberson, 1988, Social relationships and health. *Science, 241,* 540-545.

16. Harman and Talbert, Reproductive aging.

17. Zilbergeld, B. 1978. *Male Sexuality.* Boston: Little, Brown.

18. Harman and Talbert, Reproductive aging.

19. Ibid.

20. Neugarten, B. L., V. Wood, R. J. Kraines, and B. Loomis. 1968. Women's attitudes toward the menopause. In B. Neugarten (ed.), *Middle Age and Aging.* Chicago: University of Chicago Press.

21. Harman and Talbert, Reproductive aging.

22. Skodol, A. E., and R. L. Spitzer. 1983. Depression in the elderly: Clinical criteria. In L. D. Breslau and M. R. Haug (eds.), *Depression and Aging: Causes, Care, and Consequences.* New York: Springer.

23. Leiblum, S., G. Bachmann, E. Kemmann, D. Colburn, and L. Swartzman. 1983. Vaginal atrophy in the postmenopausal woman: The importance of sexual activity and hormones. *Journal of the American Medical Association, 249,* 2195-2198.

24. U.S. Bureau of the Census, *Statistical Abstract.*

25. Reinisch, J. M. Interview, *Seasons of Life.*

26. Butler, R. N. Interview, *Seasons of Life.*

27. Bogin, *Patterns of Human Growth.*

28. Kirkwood, T. B. L. 1985. Comparative and evolutionary aspects of longevity. In C. E. Finch and E. L. Schneider (eds.), *Handbook of the Biology of Aging.* 2nd ed. New York: Van Nostrand Reinhold.

29. Hrdy, S. B. 1981. Nepotist and altruist: The behavior of old females among macaques and langur monkeys. In P. T. Amoss and S. Harrell (eds.), *Other Ways of Growing Old.* Stanford: Stanford University Press.

30. Gutmann, D. Interview, *Seasons of Life*.

31. Ibid.

32. Goody, J. 1976. Aging in nonindustrial societies. In R. H. Binstock and E. Shanas (eds.), *Handbook of Aging and the Social Sciences*. New York: Van Nostrand Reinhold.

33. Birdsell, J. B. 1979. Ecological influences on Australian aboriginal social organization. In I. S. Bernstein and E. O. Smith (eds.), *Primate Ecology and Human Origins*. New York: Garland.

Notes for Chapter 14

1. Hagestad, G. O. Interview, *Seasons of Life*.

2. Spanier, G. B., P. A. Roos, and J. Shockey. 1985. *Journal of Marriage and the Family*, 47, 993-1003.

3. Hagestad G. O. Interview, *Seasons of Life*.

4. Glick, P. C. 1977. Updating the life cycle of the family. *Journal of Marriage and the Family*, 39, 5-13.

5. Hagestad and Neugarten, Age and the life course.

6. Nowak, C. A. 1977. Does youthfulness equal attractiveness? In L. E. Troll, J. Israel, and K. Israel (eds.), *Looking Ahead*. Englewood Cliffs, N.J.: Prentice-Hall.

7. Pifer, A., and D. L. Bronte. Winter 1986. Introduction: Squaring the pyramid, *Daedalus*, 115, 1-11.

8. Neugarten, B. L. 1979. Time, age, and the life cycle. *American Journal of Psychiatry*, 136, 887-893.

9. Child Trends, Inc., *U.S. Children and Their Families*.

10. *Ann Arbor News*. January 21, 1988. 1 child in 4 lives in single-parent household, C1, C5.

11. Preston, S. H. December 1984. Children and the elderly in the U.S. *Scientific American*, 44-49.

12. Hagestad, G. O. 1985. The aging society and family life. *Daedalus*, 115, 119-139.

13. Burton and Bengtson, Black grandmothers.

14. Cherlin, A. J. Interview, *Seasons of Life*.

15. Ibid.

16. Ibid.

17. Russell, C. 1986. *100 Predictions for the Baby Boom*. New York: Plenum.

18. Treiman, D. J. 1985. The work histories of women and men: What we know and what we need to find out. In A. S. Rossi (ed.), *Gender and the Life Course*. New York: Aldine.

19. Ibid.

20. Rossi, A. S. Interview, *Seasons of Life*.

21. Lazarus, S. Interview, *Seasons of Life*.

22. Ehrenhatl, S. M. August 15, 1986. Economic scene: Work force shifts in 80s. *New York Times*, D2.

23. Greenhouse, S. October 13, 1986. Surge in prematurely jobless. *New York Times*, D1+.

24. Hagestad, G. O. Interview, *Seasons of Life*.

25. Lueck, T. C. August 5, 1986. After Manville: Middle-aged and jobless. *New York Times*, B1+.

26. Parke, R. D., and C. W. Collmer. 1975. Child abuse. In E. M. Hetherington (ed.), *Review of Child Development Research*. Vol. 5. Chicago: University of Chicago Press.

27. Hoffman, L. W. 1986. Work, family, and the children. In M. S. Pallak and R. O. Perloff (eds.), *Psychology and Work*. Washington, D.C.: American Psychological Association.

Notes for Chapter 15

1. Jaques, E. 1965. Death and the mid-life crisis. *International Journal of Psychoanalysis, 46*, 502-514.

2. Neugarten, B. L. 1968. The awareness of middle age. In B. L. Neugarten (ed.), *Middle Age and Aging*. Chicago: University of Chicago Press.

Bengston, V. L., J. B. Cuellar, and P. K. Ragan. 1977. Stratum contrasts and similarities in attitudes toward death. *Journal of Gerontology, 32*, 76-88.

3. Levinson, et al., *Seasons of a Man's Life*.

4. Eichorn, D. H., J. A. Clausen, N. Haan, M. P. Honzik, and P. H. Mussen (eds.). 1981. *Present and Past in Middle Life*. New York: Academic Press.

5. Vailliant, G. E. 1977. *Adaptation to Life*. Boston: Little, Brown.

6. Costa, P. T., Jr., R. R. McCrae, A. B. Zonderman, H. E. Barbano, B. Lebowitz, and D. M. Larson. 1986. Cross-sectional studies of personality in a national sample: 2. Stability in neuroticism, extraversion, and openness. *Psychology and Aging, 1*, 144-149.

7. Pearlin, L., and J. S. Johnson. 1977. Marital status, life strains, and depression. *American Sociological Review, 42*, 704-715.

8. Baruch, G., R. Barnett, and C. Rivers. 1982. *Lifeprints: New Patterns of Love and Work for Today's Women*. New York: McGraw-Hill.

9. Teltsch, K. December 12, 1989. 'Midlife crisis' is investigated by one who doubts it's there. *New York Times*, C3.

10. Hagestad, G. O. 1986. The aging society as a context for family life. *Daedalus, 115*, 119-139.

11. Kastenbaum, R. 1985. Dying and death: A life-span approach. In J. E. Birren and K. W. Schaie (eds.), *Handbook of the Psychology of Aging*. 2nd ed. New York: Van Nostrand Reinhold.

12. Hagestad, G. O. Interview, *Seasons of Life*.

13. Poussaint, A. Interview, *Seasons of Life*.

14. McCrae, R. R., and P. T. Costa, Jr. 1984. *Emerging Lives, Enduring Dispositions: Personality in Adulthood*. Boston: Little, Brown.

Costa, et al., Cross-sectional studies of personality.

15. Neugarten, Time, age, and the life cycle.

16. Sternberg, R. J., and R. K. Wagner (eds.). 1987. *Practical Intelligence: Origins of Competence in the Everyday World*. New York: Cambridge University Press.

17. Ceci, S. J., and J. K. Liker. 1986. A day at the races. *Journal of Experimental Psychology: General, 115*, 255-266.

18. Charness, N. Interview, *Seasons of Life*.

19. Zuidema, G. Interview, *Seasons of Life*.

20. Charness, N. Interview, *Seasons of Life*.

21. Simonton, D. K. In press. Does creativity decline in the later years? Definition, data, and theory. In M. Perlmutter (ed.), *Late-Life Potential*. Washington, D.C.: Gerontological Society of America.

Simonton, D. K. 1988. Age and outstanding achievement: What do we know after a century of research? *Psychological Bulletin*, 104, 251-267.

22. Charness, N. Interview, *Seasons of Life*.

23. Westermarck, E. 1926. *Ritual and Belief in Morocco*. 2 vols. London: Kegan Paul.

24. Jung, C. J. 1933. *Modern Man in Search of a Soul*. New York: Harcourt, Brace.

25. Gutmann, *Reclaimed Powers*.

26. Ibid.

Gutmann, D. Interview, *Seasons of Life*.

27. Livson, F. B. 1983. Gender identity: A life-span view of sex-role development. In R. B. Weg (ed.), *Sexuality in the Later Years*. New York: Academic Press.

28. Ibid.

29. Levinson et al., *Seasons of a Man's Life*.

30. Erikson, E. H. 1980. On the generational cycle: An address. *International Journal of Psycho-Analysis*, 61, 213-223 .

31. Kotre, J. 1984. *Outliving the Self*. Baltimore, Md.: Johns Hopkins University Press.

32. Interviews, *Seasons of Life*.

33. Kotre, *Outliving the Self*.

34. Vaillant, G. E., and E. Milofsky. 1980. Natural history of male psychological health: IX. Empirical evidence for Erikson's model of the life cycle. *American Journal of Psychiatry*, 137, 1348-1359.

35. Snarey, J., L. Son, V. S. Kuehne, S. Hauser, and G. Vaillant. 1987. The role of parenting in men's psychosocial development: A longitudinal study of early adulthood infertility and midlife generativity. *Developmental Psychology*, 23, 593-603 .

36. Kotre, *Outliving the Self*.

Notes for Chapter 16

1. U.S. Senate Special Committee on Aging. 1987/88. *Aging America: Trends and Projections*. Washington, D.C.: U.S. Government Printing Office.

2. Weg, R. B. 1983. Changing physiology of aging: Normal and pathological. In D. S. Woodruff and J. E. Birren (eds.), *Aging: Scientific Perspectives and Social Issues*. 2nd ed. Monterey, Calif.: Brooks/Cole.

3. Duara, R., E. D. London, S. I. Rapoport. 1985. Changes in structure and energy metabolism of the aging brain. In C. E. Finch and E. L. Schneider (eds.), *Handbook of the Biology of Aging*. 2nd ed. New York: Van Nostrand Reinhold.

4. Butler, R. N. Interview, *Seasons of Life*.

5. Goldberg, A. P., and J. M. Hagberg. 1990. Physical exercise in the elderly. In E. L. Schneider and J. W. Rowe (eds.), *Handbook of the Biology of Aging*. 3rd ed. San Diego: Academic Press.

6. Adelman, R. C. 1989. Myths and realities of biological aging. In D. S. Carlson

(ed.), *Monograph 22, Craniofacial Growth Series*. Ann Arbor, Mich.: University of Michigan Center for Human Growth and Development.

Rosen, R., and E. Hall. 1984. *Sexuality*. New York: Random House.

7. Adelman, R. C. Interview, *Seasons of Life*.

8. Rikli, R., and S. Busch. 1986. Motor performance of women as a function of age and physical activity level. *Journal of Gerontology, 41*, 645-649.

9. Salthouse, T. A. 1984. Effects of age and skill in typing. *Journal of Experimental Psychology: General, 113*, 345-371.

10. U.S. Bureau of the Census, *Statistical Abstract*.

11. Perlmutter and Hall, *Adult Development and Aging*.

12. Olsho, L. W., S. W. Harkins, and M. L. Lenhardt. 1985. Aging and the auditory system. In J. E. Birren and K. W. Schaie (eds.), *Handbook of the Psychology of Aging*. 2nd ed. New York: Van Nostrand Reinhold.

13. Thomas, P. D., W. C. Hunt, P. J. Garry, R. B. Hood, J. M. Goodwin, and J. S. Goodwin. 1983. Hearing acuity in a healthy elderly population: Effects on emotional, cognitive, and social status. *Journal of Gerontology, 38*, 321-325.

14. Gutmann, D. Interview, *Seasons of Life*.

15. Ibid.

Gutmann, *Reclaimed Powers*.

16. Interviews, *Seasons of Life*.

17. Dement, W., G. Richardson, P. Prinz, M. Carskadon, D. Kripke, and C. Czeisler. 1985. Changes of sleep and wakefulness with age. In C. E. Finch and E. L. Schneider (eds.), *Handbook of the Biology of Aging*. 2nd ed. New York: Van Nostrand Reinhold.

18. Bootzin, R. R., G. H. Bower, J. Crocker, and E. Hall. In press. *Psychology Today: An Introduction*. 7th ed. New York: McGraw-Hill.

19. Dement et al., Changes of sleep.

20. Ancoli-Israel, S., D. F. Kripke, W. Mason, and O. J. Kaplan. 1985. Sleep apnea and period movements in an aging sample. *Journal of Gerontology, 40*, 419-425.

21. Carskadon, M. A. 1982. Sleep fragmentation, sleep loss, and sleep need in the elderly. *Gerontologist, 22*, 187.

22. Woodruff-Pak, D. S. Interview, *Seasons of Life*.

23. Hayflick, L. 1977. The cellular basis for biological aging. In C. E. Finch and L. Hayflick (eds.), *Handbook of the Biology of Aging*. 1st ed. New York: Van Nostrand Reinhold.

24. Tice, R. R., and R. B. Setlow. 1985. DNA repair and replication in aging organisms and cells. In C. E. Finch and E. L. Schneider (eds.), *Handbook of the Biology of Aging*. 2nd ed. New York: Van Nostrand Reinhold.

25. Adelman, R. C. Interview, *Seasons of Life*.

26. Falek, A., F. J. Kallmann, I. Lorge, and L. F. Jarvik. 1960. Longevity and intellectual variation in a senescent twin population. *Journal of Gerontology, 15*, 305-309.

27. Walford, *Maximum Life Span*.

Walford, R. L. 1986. *The 120-Year Diet*. New York: Simon & Schuster.

Weindruch, R., and R. L. Walford. 1988. *The Retardation of Aging and Disease by Dietary Restriction*. Springfield, Ill.: Charles C. Thomas.

28. Adelman, R. C. Interview, *Seasons of Life*.

29. Rousseau, *Émile*.

30. Back, K. W., and K. J. Gergen. 1966. Personal orientation and morale of the

aged. In I. H. Simpson and J. C. McKinney (eds.), *Social Aspects of Aging*. Durham, N.C.: Duke University Press.

31. Marshall, V. W. 1980. *Last Chapters: A Sociology of Aging and Dying*. Monterey, Calif.: Brooks/Cole.

Notes for Chapter 17

1. Child Trends, Inc., *U.S. Children and Their Families*.

2. Robinson, P. K., S. Coberly, and C. E. Paul. 1985. Work and retirement. In R. H. Binstock and E. Shanas (eds.), *Handbook of Aging and the Social Sciences*. 2nd ed. New York: Van Nostrand Reinhold.

3. Bird, C. December/January 1988/89. The jobs you do! *Modern Maturity, 31*, 40-46.

4. Ibid.

5. *Modern Maturity*. June/July 1986. Troubled kids get help building hope, 86-87.

6. *Newsweek*. July 10, 1989. Healing an old wound, 49; A design for the good life, 51.

7. Parnes, H. 1981. *Work and Retirement*. Cambridge, Mass.: MIT Press.

8. Ward, R. A. 1984. *The Aging Experience*. New York: Harper & Row.

9. Lawton, M. P. 1985. Housing and living environments of older people. In R. H. Binstock and E. Shanas (eds.), *Handbook of Aging and the Social Sciences*. 2nd ed. New York: Van Nostrand Reinhold.

10. Rubinstein, R. L. 1989. The home environment of older persons: A description of the psychosocial processes linking person to place. *Journal of Gerontology: Social Sciences, 44*, S45-53.

11. Keating, N., and P. Cole. 1980. What do I do with him 24 hours a day? *Gerontologist, 20*, 84-89.

12. Lee, G. R., and C. L. Shehan. 1989. Retirement and marital satisfaction. *Journal of Gerontology: Social Sciences, 44*, S226-230.

13. O'Rand, A. M. 1990. Stratification and the life course. In R. H. Binstock and L. Y. George (eds.), *Handbook of Aging and the Social Sciences*. 3rd ed. San Diego: Academic Press.

14. Weishaus, S., and D. Field. 1988. A half century of marriage: Continuity or change? *Journal of Marriage and the Family, 50*, 763-774.

15. U.S. Bureau of the Census, *Statistical Abstract*.

16. Ibid.

17. Aldous, J., E. Klaus, and D. W. Klein. 1985. The understanding heart. *Child Development, 56*, 303-316.

18. Burrus-Bammel, L. L., and G. Bammel. 1985. Leisure and recreation. In J. E. Birren and K. W. Schaie (eds.), *Handbook of the Psychology of Aging*. 2nd ed. New York: Van Nostrand Reinhold.

19. Larson, R., R. Mannel, and J. Zuzanek. 1986. Daily well-being of older adults with friends and family. *Psychology and Aging, 1*, 117-126.

20. Field, D., and M. Minkler. 1988. Continuity and change in social support between young-old and old-old or very-old age. *Journal of Gerontology: Psychological Sciences, 43*, P100-106.

21. Cicirelli, V. G. 1982. Sibling influence throughout the life span. In M. E. Lamb

and B. Sutton-Smith (eds.), *Sibling Relationships: Their Nature and Significance Across the Life Span*. Hillsdale, N.J.: Lawrence Erlbaum Associates.

22. Neugarten, B. L. Interview, *Seasons of Life*.

23. Ibid.

24. Neugarten, B. L., and D. A. Neugarten. 1986. Age in the aging society. *Daedalus*, 115, no. 1, 31-50.

25. Cowley, M. 1985. Being old old. *New York Times Magazine*, 58.

26. U.S. Senate Select Committee on Aging. 1987/88. *Aging America: Trends and Projections*. Washington, D.C.: U.S. Government Printing Office.

27. Siegel, J. S., and C. M. Taeuber. Winter 1986. Demographic perspectives on the long-lived society. *Daedalus*, 115, 77-117.

28. U.S. Senate Select Committee on Aging, *Aging America*.

29. Rodin, J. 1986. Aging and health. *Science*, 233, 1271-1276.

30. Eisdorfer, C. Interview, *Seasons of Life*.

31. Neugarten, B. L. Interview, *Seasons of Life*.

32. Gutmann, D. Interview, *Seasons of Life*.

Notes for Chapter 18

1. Barak, B., and B. Stern. 1986. Subjective age correlates: A research note. *Gerontologist*, 26, 571-578.

2. Baum, S. K., and R. L. Boxley. 1983. Age identification in the elderly. *Gerontologist*, 23, 532-537.

3. Cowley, M. 1980. *The View from 80*. New York: Viking Press.

4. Baum and Boxley, Age identification in the elderly.

5. Montepare, J. M., and M. E. Lachman. 1989. 'You're only as old as you feel': Self-perceptions of age, fears of aging, and life satisfaction from adolescence to old age. *Psychology and Aging*, 4, 73-78.

6. Wortman, C. Interview, *Seasons of Life*.

7. Ibid.

8. Kaufman, S. 1986. *The Ageless Self*. Madison: University of Wisconsin Press.

9. Tobin, S. 1988. Preservation of the self in old age. *Social Casework*, 69, 9, 550-555.

10. Interviews, *Seasons of Life*.

11. Schaie, K. W. Interview, *Seasons of Life*.

12. Ibid.

13. Ibid.

14. Schaie, K. W., and S. L. Willis. 1986. Can decline in adult intellectual functioning be reversed? *Developmental Psychology*, 22, 223-232.

15. Kliegl, R., and P. B. Baltes. 1987. Theory-guided analysis of mechanisms of development and aging through testing-the-limits and research on expertise. In C. Schooler and K. W. Schaie (eds.), *Cognitive Functioning and Social Structure over the Life Course*. New York: Ablex.

16. Clark, R. W. 1975. *The Life of Bertrand Russell*. New York: Knopf.

17. Johnston, L., and S. H. Anderson. June 9, 1983. New York day by day: A sense of history. *New York Times*.

18. Perlmutter, M. Interview, *Seasons of Life*.

19. Spitzer, L. Interview, *Seasons of Life*.

20. Luria, A. R. 1968. *The Mind of a Mnemonist*. New York: Basic Books.

21. Butler, R. N. Interview, *Seasons of Life*.

22. Erikson, E. H. 1982. *The Life Cycle Completed*. New York: Norton.

23. Arnheim, R. 1986. *New Essays on the Psychology of Art*. Berkeley, Calif.: University of California Press.

24. Simonton, D. K. 1989. The swan-song phenomenon: Last-works effects for 172 classical composers. *Psychology and Aging, 4*, 42-27.

25. Ogilvie, D. 1987. The undesired self: A neglected variable in personality research. *Journal of Personality and Social Psychology, 52*, 379-385.

Index

Brim, Gilbert (psychologist), 303
Brooks-Gunn, Jeanne (psychologist), 67
Bruner, Jerome (psychologist), 90, 97,
    121, 188
Buhler, Charlotte (psychologist), 68–69, 72
bulimia, 153–154
Bumpass, Larry (demographer), 226
Burton, Linda (sociologist), 285
Butler, Robert (psychiatrist), 268, 327, 377

cancer, 205, 263
cardiovascular disease, 263
cardiovascular system, 327
career. *See* work
Castro-Martin, Teresa (demographer), 226
Ceci, Stephen (psychologist), 306
cell
    division, 25, 34
    substance, 27
    types, 27, 34, 96
cesarean section, 208
change of life. *See* menopause
Charness, Neil (psychologist), 306–308
Cherlin, Andrew (sociologist), 227, 228,
    285, 286
Chess, Stella (psychologist), 75, 77
childbearing. *See also* pregnancy
    late, 206, 207, 209
    patterns, 206
child care
    by other children, 86
    in other cultures, 102
    for working parents, 225–226
childhood
    brain development, 90–97
    described, 81–84, 99–101, 116–119
        133–137
    fears, 114
    gender identity, 124–127
    hormones, sex, 29
    intellectual development, 119–124
    legal status, 102
    length, cause for, 85, 88
    as life stage, 49, 68
    memory in, 128–133
    in other cultures, 102, 104
    psychosexual theory, 69
    rejection, 113–114
    responsibilities, 85, 102, 105
    self-concept, 123, 127
    shyness, 113
    Social Clock in, 99–115
child labor laws, 49, 52, 104
childlessness
    causes, 207

and generativity, 312
voluntary, 208
children
    abuse of, 54, 58, 289
    aggression, 126
    authoritarian views, 188
    and divorce, 227–228
    emotional problems, 113
    and grandparents, 270, 284
    historical view, 105–109
    mortality, 47–48
    parental treatment, 41, 49, 86,
        88, 104–109
    population ratio, 109
    and poverty, 107, 224
    in primitive cultures, 44–46
    of unwed mothers, 224
chimpanzee. *See* primates
cholesterol, 263
Chomsky, Noam (linguist), 88
chromosomes, 24, 26
    and aging, 336
    and death rate, 33
    extra, 209, 210
    sex determinant, 31, 33
circumcision, 45, 166
Clock, Biological. *See* Biological
    Clock
Clock, Social. *See* Social Clock
Clock, Psychological. *See* Psychological
    Clock
cognition
    in adolescence, 86, 131, 163,
        182–185
    decline, 376
cohabitation, 220–221, 229
communication, 40, 42
conception
    age ratio, 208
    beginning of life, 46
    middle age, 267–268
    in older women, 209
    sex determinant, 31
    time required, 209
conflict, 69–70, 168–170
contraception
    middle age, 268
    natural, 204
    pills, 205
    tubal ligation, 268
    use, 55, 56, 163, 208
    vasectomy, 268
cortex, 34–35, 65, 94
Costa, Paul (psychologist), 304
Cowley, Malcolm (writer), 355

Nelson, Katherine (psychologist), 128–129
neoteny, 59, 87
nervous system
   adult, 328
   development, 33–34
   glial cells, 34, 35
   neurons, 33–35
   in primates, 34
   synapses, 34–36, 65, 92–94
nesting period, 243
Neugarten, Bernice (developmentalist), 40
      49, 53, 220, 282, 305, 354–355, 357
neuroticism, 305
nonnormative events, 303
norm of noninterference, 286
norms
   age, 40, 44, 101, 203, 219
   social, 39
nuclear episodes, 188–189
nuclear family, 222–223
nursing homes, 355–356

obesity, 263
object permanence, 65
occupation. See work
Offer, Daniel (psychiatrist), 153
Ogilvie, Daniel (psychologist), 378
old age. See adulthood, late
old-old, life stage, 355–357
oral stage, 69
Osherson, Daniel (psychologist), 183
ovaries
   in adolescence, 32, 145
   in adulthood, 204, 208, 266–267
   tumors, 147
ovulation, 32, 146

parental
   aging, 284
   conflict with adolescents, 168–170
   influence on gender identity, 125
   protective function, 222, 223
   relationship with infant, 41, 42,
      43, 57–61
   support systems, 270
   treatment of children, 41, 49, 86,
      88, 106–109
parenthood, single
   described, 157–161, 197–202, 223
   increase, 283
   percentage of families, 227, 283
parenting. See also postparental period
   in early adulthood, 246–247
   empty nest, 281–282
   and menopause, 269

and puberty, 168–170
peers
   in adolescence, 164, 171–172, 185
   in childhood, 113–114
   importance, 162, 170–172
   at retirement, 353
penis, 265
Perlmutter, Marion (psychologist), 375
permissiveness, 108
personality
   in adolescence, 163
   in adulthood, 304–305, 308
   androgyny, 308–309
   biological determinants, 75, 76
   definition, 75
   differences, 75, 81
   effect on life span, 263–264
   and parenthood, 246
Petersen, Anne (psychologist), 162, 168
phallic stage, 69
Piaget, Jean (psychologist), 65, 121, 122,
      126, 131–132, 183, 184
pituitary gland, 32, 145, 265–267
placenta, 25
play
   animal, 86
   biological influence, 125
   in infancy, 43
   learning from, 120, 121
   parent-child, 43
   sex separation, 125
pleasure principle, 108
Plomin, Robert (geneticist), 76
Plutarch, 55
polyandry, 223
polygyny, 223
postformal thought, 248, 375
postmenopausal period, 269, 271–275
postparental period, 270–271
Poussaint, Alvin (psychiatrist), 301, 304
poverty
   causes, 164
   childhood, 107, 224
   and divorce, 227
   effect on adolescence, 164
   in retirement, 349, 356
   statistics, 295
pregnancy
   in adolescence, 163, 164
   age distribution, 205
   complications, 209
   described, 3–8, 157–161
   increase, 223
   out of wedlock, 229
   patterns, 205